RAFFAELE MATTIOLI LECTURES

In honour of the memory of Raffaele Mattioli, who was for many years its manager and chairman, Banca Commerciale Italiana has established the Mattioli Fund as a testimony to the continuing survival and influence of his deep interest in economics, the humanities and sciences.

As its first enterprise the Fund has established a series of annual lectures on the history of economic thought, to be called the Raffaele Mattioli Lectures.

In view of the long association between the Università Commerciale Luigi Bocconi and Raffaele Mattioli, who was an active scholar, adviser and member of the governing body of the University, it was decided that the lectures in honour of his memory should be delivered at the University, which together with Banca Commerciale Italiana has undertaken the task of organising them.

Distinguished academics of all nationalities, researchers and others concerned with economic problems will be invited to take part in this enterprise, in the hope of linking pure historical research with a debate on economic theory and practical policy.

In creating a memorial to the cultural legacy left by Raffaele Mattioli, it is hoped above all that these lectures and the debates to which they give rise will prove a fruitful inspiration and starting point for the development of a tradition of research and academic studies like that already long established in other countries, and that this tradition will flourish thanks to the lasting partnership between the Università Commerciale Luigi Bocconi and Banca Commerciale Italiana.

SOME BRITISH EMPIRICISTS IN THE SOCIAL SCIENCES 1650-1900

RAFFAELE MATTIOLI FOUNDATION

Richard Stone

SOME BRITISH EMPIRICISTS IN THE SOCIAL SCIENCES 1650–1900

CAMBRIDGE UNIVERSITY PRESS
Cambridge, New York, Melbourne, Madrid, Cape Town, Singapore,
São Paulo, Delhi, Dubai, Tokyo

Cambridge University Press
The Edinburgh Building, Cambridge CB2 8RU, UK

Published in the United States of America by Cambridge University Press, New York

www.cambridge.org
Information on this title: www.cambridge.org/9780521128452

Edited by Angelo Marcello Cardani and Giovanna Stone

First published 1997
This digitally printed version 2009

A catalogue record for this publication is available from the British Library

ISBN 978-0-521-57145-6 Hardback
ISBN 978-0-521-12845-2 Paperback

Additional resources for this publication at www.cambridge.org/9780521128452

CONTENTS

LIST OF TABLES

LIST OF DIAGRAMS

LIST OF ILLUSTRATIONS

The following illustrations are available as a download from www.cambridge.org/9780521128452

FOREWORD

My husband's belief in the importance of the quantitative side of economics went back to his undergraduate days. Theories, he thought, must be as far as possible tested against numerical data to be considered acceptable. This is why he devoted most of his professional life to econometrics and economic statistics. He also believed that the workings of an economic system cannot be properly understood in isolation from their demographic and social context, and here too he put his belief into practice.

He was very interested in the history of his subject, and he welcomed the invitation to deliver the Mattioli Lectures and expand them into a book as an opportunity to express publicly, so to speak, his admiration and respect for those of his British predecessors whose contributions he considered the most significant. There were heroes from other countries in his Pantheon, such as Vauban and Quetelet to mention only two, and he would have liked to write a parallel book on them, but time did not allow it.

When he died in December 1991 he had almost finished writing the present volume, in fact the first nine chapters were already in proof. The last three were unfinished, but fortunately he had carried them far enough for me to think I could complete them. I had followed his work closely and knew his intentions. The more technical parts, including all the tables, were done and all I had to add were some of the missing links. I hope the joins will not be too apparent.

There are a number of friends I would like to thank for their invaluable help first to my husband and then to myself: Roger Schofield and Peter Laslett for their kindness in supplying important material connected with Gregory King and Patrick Colquhon; Manfredi Lamanna, John Shaw, Paul Lunde and Pier Luigi Porta for their patience in tracing some of the more recondite bibliographical references; Christine Hudson, Lesley Pepper and Asha Patel for producing a succession of impeccable typescripts, particulary Asha, who typed the last three chapters with infinite care as a labour of love; Phyllis Deane, who kindly read what I had done and gave it her reassuring imprimatur; and

Luigi Pasinetti, who gave me great encouragement and support at the Italian end of things.

I also wish to thank all those who have helped me in my search for the portraits of the principal protagonists. In some cases this search has involved several people and much painstaking detective work on their part. The fact that I was unknown to them and that most of the research had to be carried out by correspondence makes their cooperation all the more deserving of gratitude. I shall list them in the order in which the portraits appear in the book. For the portrait of Petty I have to thank Mr. K. K. Yung, Registrar of the National Portrait Gallery, London. For that of King, Mr. R. C. Yorke, Archivist of the College of Arms. For that of Fleetwood, Miss Melanie Barber, Archivist of Lambeth Palace Library, the Rev. M. J. Higgins, Dean of Ely, and Dr. Thomas Cocke. For that of Young, Mr. Peter Philby and Sir John Ruggles-Brise, the original owner of the portrait. For that of Colquhoun. Miss Anne Escott of The Mitchell Library, Glasgow, Mrs. Margaret Marshall of the Glasgow Chamber of Commerce, Professor Andrew S. Skinner, Vice-Principal of Glasgow University, and Mrs. Alison Webster of the Department of Political Economy in that University, all of whom tried hard to trace the lost painting from which the engraving reproduced here was taken. For that of Halley, Miss Joan Sanderson, Librarian of the Institute of Astronomy, Cambridge. For that of Farr, Miss Patricia Broad of the Office of Population and Census Surveys, Miss Sandra Cumming, Information Officer of the Royal Society, and Miss Joanne Harris of the National Portrait Gallery. For that of Florence Nightingale, Sir Ralph Verney. And for that of Booth, again Mr. K. K. Young. All efforts have failed to produce portraits of Davenant, Graunt and Eden, who are therefore represented by the title pages of their books.

Giovanna Stone

Cambridge, 1997

PROLOGUE

It is for me a great pleasure as well as a great honour to be here today and I want first of all to express my thanks to the President of the Banca Commerciale and to the Rector of this University for inviting me. I would also like to thank Dr. Crippa for his thoughtfulness in easing a task which in my present state of health seemed at first rather daunting.

Not only is this invitation an honour, it has also given me the impulse I needed to come back to Italy, from which I had been absent for too long. My wife is Italian and for many years we spent our summer vacation with her father in his country house in Romagna. Then things changed and that pleasant habit came to an end. Our last trip to Italy was eight years ago and I thought, pessimistically, that my travelling days were over. You can imagine therefore what a pleasure it is for me to return to a country with which I have such close links.

It was delightful to be invited and delightful to feel that I could accept. But I am not an economic theorist, and when it came to choosing a theme for my lectures I was somewhat perplexed. Finally I thought I had better talk on a subject of which my head was rather full when Dr. Crippa came to see me, namely the foundations of empirical social science in England. For this purpose I have chosen the lives and work of twelve people whom for one reason or another I find particularly sympathetic. There are many other writers I could have mentioned, and it would also have been interesting to compare the English contribution with similar quantitative work in Italy, France and elsewhere. But my plate is overloaded as it is.

The eleven men and one woman who are the chief protagonists of my story came from all walks in life and had very different careers, but they had one thing in common: none of them had any formal training in the fields to which they contributed so much. Few of them went to university, and those who did studied subjects, such as medicine, astronomy and divinity, which had nothing to do either with economics or with demography. As far as their contributions to these two disciplines are concerned, they are all twelve outstanding examples of the English amateur tradition.

Today I shall concentrate on economics, beginning with the political arithmeticians of the seventeenth century, Petty, Davenant and King, who between them laid the foundations of the subject; and going on to Fleetwood's index numbers, Young's production accounts and Colquhoun's balances of income and output. Tomorrow I shall turn to demography and what I have loosely called social studies: John Graunt, another seventeenth century character, who can be called the founder of quantitative demography; Halley and the first life table; Farr and vital statistics; Eden and the study of poverty; Florence Nightingale and the reform of the hospital service; and finally Booth and his monumental survey of the London poor.

In the time at my disposal I cannot do full justice to my twelve characters, but I hope to do so when I expand these lectures for publication. Gregory King, indeed, will appear twice on the scene: once in his own right as the first great economic statistician, and the second time with Graunt, of whom he was the ablest follower. Here and there I may also introduce some minor actors who have played a smaller but still significant part on a stage which was not so crowded with stars that their more modest talents should pass unnoticed.

RICHARD STONE

Richard Stone

SOME BRITISH EMPIRICISTS IN THE SOCIAL SCIENCES 1650–1900

The *Raffaele Mattioli Lectures* were delivered by
Richard Stone at the Università Commerciale Luigi Bocconi
in Milano, from 20th to 21st October 1986.

FIRST LECTURE
THE POLITICAL ARITHMETICIANS

William Petty (1623-1687)
Charles Davenant (1656-1714)
Gregory King (1648-1712)

William Petty, Professor of Anatomy at Oxford

CHAPTER 1

William Petty and the Birth of National Accounting

1. Brief Life

William Petty, the originator of national accounting, was one of the most remarkable products of the English seventeenth century, an age of great intellectual vigour, scientific curiosity and inventiveness. In Petty these qualities were reinforced by exceptional versatility, a brilliant wit, great practical acumen and unbounded energy. His mind was like a geyser, constantly spouting ideas which he pursued with irrepressible enthusiasm, and he managed from modest beginnings to carve out for himself an amazing career: professor of anatomy at Oxford while still in his twenties, reader in music at Gresham College, London, Physician-General to Cromwell's army in Ireland, land surveyor, cartographer, naval engineer, adviser both to the Cromwell government and, after the Restoration, to Charles II and James II, friend of the foremost scientists of his time, joint initiator of the Royal Society and, what is most interesting to us economists, founder of 'political arithmetick'. Not suprisingly, he got going early in life. The story of his boyhood and early manhood reads like a picaresque novel and is worth recounting in some detail.

Petty was born at Romsey in Hampshire on 26 May 1623, the son of Antony Petty, a cloth maker and dyer. His mother's surname is not known but her first name was Francesca: could she have been Italian, one wonders. William went to the local school, where he acquired some mathematics, a competent smattering of Latin and the rudiments of Greek. His chief amusement as a child was 'to look on the artificers, *e.g.* smiths, the watch-makers, carpenters, joiners etc.; and at twelve years old he could have worked at any of these trades'. He had a satirical turn of mind and a talent for drawing caricatures which earned him in his town the reputation of 'a perfect cheiromantes'.

Around the age of twelve or thirteen, his imagination fired by tales of adventure, he thought he would try his fortune by embarking as cabin boy on a ship that plied between England and France. He had managed to save a few shillings, one of them a gift from an aunt when he embarked. When he reached France he invested this small capital in a few 'pitiful brass things with colour'd glass in them instead of diamonds and rubies' and on his first return home sold them to the young fellows of his town 'whom he knew had sweet-hearts'. He also brought back a present for his good aunt, 'a bracelet bought in France for 4d but judged to be worth 16d'. After ten months at sea he broke his leg while on board ship and his mates, who did not like a cabin boy who knew more about the art of navigation than they did and probably laughed at them for their ignorance, took him ashore and left him to fend for himself in a small inn near Caen. The locals looked after him and he recovered.

Disenchanted with a sailor's life, he decided to give up the sea, stay on in Caen and resume his studies. To this end, with characteristic directness, he offered himself as a pupil to the Jesuit Fathers of Caen. As he tells us,

> 'I made verses to the Jesuits, expressing my desire to return to the muses, and how I had been drawn from them by reading legends of our contryman, Cap^{n} Drake, in these words:
>
> Rostra ratis Dracis nimis admiratus, abivi
> Nauta scholam fugiens, et dulcia carmina sprevi.'

The Jesuit Fathers took him in, allaying his religious scruples by promising to do nothing to upset his faith except pray for his conversion.

It was not in Petty's nature to subsist on charity. After his recovery he had had to pay one *écu* to 'la Grand Jane, ye farrier's wife' for setting his leg, 10 *sous* to the apothecary who doctored him and 8 *sous* for a pair of crutches. With what money he had left, supplemented by 'the remainder of two cakes of beeswax', he set up in trade, buying and selling improbably heterogeneous articles such as playing cards, white starch, 'hayre hats', tobacco pipes and shreds of parchment 'wherewith to size paper'. He also gave lessons. As '*le petit matelot Anglois qui parle Latin et Grec*' he had excited much curiosity and one imagines much goodwill in the neighbourhood. One gentleman asked him to teach him English, another navigation, which he did in Latin. Thus he earned enough money to support himself and pursue his studies.

By the time he left Caen, aged about fifteen, he had 'obtained the Latin, Greek and French tongues, the whole body of arithmetic, the practical geometry and astronomy conducing to navigation and dialling' and had also managed to save £4. With these qualifications he came back to England and entered the King's Navy, in which he served until 1643. In that year, 'when the civil war betwixt the King and Parliament grew hot', he returned to the Continent with the intention of resuming his studies.

This time he went to Holland. By now he had saved £60 and this enabled him not only to support himself but also to take charge of his brother Anthony, who apparently accompanied him. William spent two years in Holland, matriculating as a student of medicine at Leyden on his twenty-first birthday, studying 'vigorously' at Leyden, Utrecht and Amsterdam and making friends with everybody who was anybody in Dutch academic circles. At the end of 1645 he went to Paris to continue his medical studies at the School of Anatomy there, armed with letters of introduction to Thomas Hobbes. Hobbes had left England for political reasons and was at the time engaged in writing his *Leviathan*. He took the young man under his wing and introduced him to some of the most influential political exiles there, such as the Marquis of Newcastle, and, more importantly, to his friend the mathematician Marin Mersenne, at whose house the cream of the philosophical, literary and scientific world of Paris used to meet. With his zest for life and eagerness to learn, Petty must have enjoyed himself immensely in Paris, in spite of the fact that his finances were at times at a very low ebb: there was one week, as he told Aubrey, when he had to survive on two pennyworths of nuts. Somehow or other he managed to straighten out his financial affairs and in 1646 returned to Romsey, as he tells us, 'bringing back my brother Anthony, whom I had bred, with about ten pounds more than I had carried out of England'.

His father had recently died and Petty took on the management of the family business, improving it by a number of mechanical devices of his own invention. But he could not be expected to settle down as a clothier in a small town. He got to know some of the leading philosophers and scientists in London and was 'admitted to several clubs of the virtuosi', in particular the London Philosophical Society, nicknamed 'the Invisible Club', whose membership included Samuel Hartlib, Robert Boyle, John Wallis and John Wilkins, all future founders of the Royal Society. Another friend was John Graunt, with whom he was later to collaborate on the *Observations upon the Bills of Mortality* and who was then an influential City merchant with a good standing in the Parliamentary party.

In London Petty resumed his medical studies and at the same time tried to exploit commercially his mechanical ability. In 1647 he invented an instrument which would enable two copies of any writing to be made simultaneously and was granted a patent upon it for seventeen years. The device was not a success and, as Hull suggests, it may have been this experience which later prompted the remarks about 'the poor inventor', whose brains are picked by others and who gets no thanks, in chapter XI of the *Treatise on Taxes*.

Petty announced his invention in a pamphlet on education which he wrote in 1647 and in which he advocated the institution of schools where children would be taught manual trades as well as reading and writing 'since few children have need of reading before they know or can be acquainted with the things they read of; or of writing, before their thoughts are worth recording, or they are able to put them in any form'. This pamphlet he dedicated to Hartlib, who was well known as a patron of scientists and scholars, and Hartlib sent it on to Boyle with a letter of introduction which shows why Petty was always so readily admitted to the friendship of eminent men:

'I have put into your hands the design of the history of trade; the author is one Petty, twenty-four years of age, a perfect Frenchman, and a good linguist in other vulgar languages, besides Latin and Greek; a most rare and exacting anatomist and excelling in all mathematical and mechanical learning; of a sweet natural disposition and moral comportment. As for solid judgement and industry, altogether masculine.'[1]

Boyle, who was later to become famous as a chemist, was then only twenty but was already one of the central figures of the Invisible Club. The two young men got on well together and remained friends for life.

Political events now gave a new twist to Petty's career. In 1646 Oxford had surrendered to the Parliamentary army and shortly afterwards the university was reorganised. In 1648 Wilkins was appointed Warden of Wadham College and the Philosophical Society apparently followed him *en masse*, including Petty who was now bent on getting a degree. Their ranks swelled by some of the local talent, including Christopher Wren, the future architect of St. Paul's who was then an undergraduate at Wadham, they continued their meetings either at Wilkins' house or at Petty's lodgings, which being at an apothecary's were convenient for inspecting drugs.

In 1649 Petty took the degree of doctor of physic. He was made a fellow of Brasenose College and deputy to the Professor of Anatomy, and succeeded to the professorship at the beginning of 1650. At about the same time he became Vice-Principal of his college and, through the good offices of his friend Graunt, Reader in Music at Gresham College, London. This college had been founded in the reign of Elizabeth by the financier Thomas Gresham and was administered by the City corporation.

A strange event occurred at the end of 1650. A certain Anne Green was hanged at Oxford for the murder of her illegitimate child. She seemed to take a long time in dying but was eventually certified dead. The body was put in a coffin and taken to the dissecting room. At this point Petty and his colleague Dr. Thomas Willis appeared on the scene and, recognising signs of

1. Lord Edmond Fitzmaurice, *The Life of Sir William Petty*. London, 1895, p. 12.

life, attempted successfully to revive the supposed corpse. She lived, it is said, to marry and become the mother of other children. This episode added considerably to Petty's reputation.

In April 1651 the university granted Petty two years' leave with an allowance of £30 a year. It is not sure what he did in the following months but it is supposed that his intention was to travel. However, the position changed completely at the end of the year, when he was appointed Physician-General to the Parliamentary army in Ireland and to the commander in chief, General Ireton. A fact which may have some bearing on this appointment is that Oliver Cromwell had recently been elected Chancellor of Oxford University. However that may be, Petty's new post carried a salary of £1 per diem and he was allowed to take private patients, which brought in an additional £400 a year, as he tells us himself in his will.

Petty arrived in Ireland in 1652 and put his practical talents to good use in reorganising the army medical services, but the war was over. There was, however, another problem. The Commonwealth had decided to 'resettle' Ireland, that is expropriate the Irish landowners who had resisted Cromwell and divide the forfeited estates among the government's numerous creditors; in particular the soldiers, who were owed large arrears of pay, and the 'adventurers' who had financed the equipment of the army. In order to carry out this plan it was necessary to survey the country and map out the forfeited estates. This task was in the hands of Benjamin Worsley, the Surveyor-General. Petty considered Worsley a charlatan and his methods inefficient and proposed an alternative scheme of action.

After some false starts and a good deal of acrimony Petty's scheme was accepted at the end of 1654: he was to survey, measure and map all the forfeited lands, together with all Crown and ecclesiastical lands, within a period of thirteen months from a date eventually agreed on as 1 February 1655, at a rate of payment of a little over £7 per 1000 acres of fruitful profitable land and £3 for Church and Crown lands. Petty employed a workforce of about a thousand, which he organised on the principle of the division of labour. Many of those engaged in making the measurements were soldiers, which was just as well, as the terrain was extremely rough and the measurers were frequently attacked by bands of Irish. There were some delays in carrying out this huge undertaking but the work was completed by the autumn of 1656. This first survey, which came to be known as the 'Down Survey', was principally concerned with lands to be allotted to the army. At the end of 1656 another survey was started in respect of forfeited lands in counties where the adventurers had a joint claim with the army. This work was again carried out speedily and finished about the autumn of 1658.

Concurrently with the surveys Petty agreed, as a separate undertaking, to map the whole of Ireland. For this he was to receive a separate salary but he was never fully paid and the work was not finished until 1673, largely at his own expense. The map was printed at Amsterdam and according to Evelyn was the most exact map of its kind that had yet appeared.

As soon as the surveys were completed there was a scramble of beneficiaries to obtain their land 'and much complaining and disputation about the allotments'. Petty was deeply involved in the settlement of these disputes and it was fortunate for him that he had the firm support of Oliver Cromwell's son Henry, the Lord Deputy, who had made him his private secretary and appointed him an Additional Clerk to the Council at a salary of £400.

By now Petty was a rich man and a big landowner: he had been paid largely in land for his services and had added to his possessions by buying more land as the opportunity arose. But he had also made many enemies. Although a friend of the Cromwell family he was a man of moderation both in political and in religious matters. Oliver Cromwell held that 'the State, in choosing men to serve it, takes no notice of their opinions. If they be willing faithfully to serve it, that satisfies'. But not everyone agreed with this view. In the confusion that followed the death of Oliver in September 1658, Petty fell foul of the fanatics in the army and in particular of a certain Sir Hierome Sankey, an officer who had turned anabaptist and was one of the leaders of the extremist anti-Cromwell faction. Richard Cromwell succeeded his father as Protector and a new parliament was summoned in which Ireland was represented by a number of newly elected members, Petty and Sankey among them. Sankey lost no time: in March 1659 he impeached Petty for bribery and malappropriation of funds. He did not have the sympathy of the House, however, and did not succeed in making good his charges. Petty defended himself successfully and the day after his speech, on 22 April 1659, Parliament was dissolved.

Both England and Ireland were now in a state of turmoil. Richard and Henry Cromwell were divested of authority, the extremists triumphant, and Petty, dismissed from all his posts, decided to await events in London. During his years of service in Ireland he had remained in touch with his learned friends, especially Boyle, who was Irish and lived on his family estate there and whom he had helped with some anatomical experiments. His interest in science was as keen as ever. On his return to London he found that the group of scientists and philosophers who had moved to Oxford ten years earlier were now back and holding their meetings at Gresham College. Petty resumed his place among them and read them a number of papers, notably one in 1659 on 'the philosophy of shipping', written in collaboration with Wren, and one in 1660 on the history of shipbuilding. At the end of 1660 the group agreed to form themselves into 'a college for the promoting of physico-mathematical learning'. They drew up a list of persons 'willing and fit to join', fixed a subscription rate and elected officers. Wilkins was chairman, Lord Brounker was president and Petty, though not one of the officers, sometimes deputised for him.

The political climate was propitious to scientists. The country, tired of factious quarrels that seemed to lead nowhere, had welcomed the monarchy back, and Charles II was proving an easy-going and not vindictive monarch, with a taste for natural philosophy and for the company of clever men. Two subjects he was especially interested in were medical chemistry and the art of navigation. Almost immediately after his accession he gave Petty an audience at which, brushing aside Petty's apologies for his Cromwellian connection, he proceeded to question him closely on 'the philosophy of shipping, loadstones, guns, etc., feathering of arrows, vegetation of plants, the history of trades, etc., about all of which', Petty wrote to his cousin John, 'I discoursed *intrepide* and I hope not contemptibly. . . . Since I began this letter the Marquis of Ormonde met me and told me he had express orders to bring me to the King, saying that the King's head and mine lay directly one way'. The king's brother, the future James II, then Duke of York and Lord High Admiral, was 'a most navarchal prince' and also took a liking to Petty. The two brothers looked with favour on the activities of the Gresham College group; it was not for nothing, after all, that during his exile in France Charles had been a pupil of Hobbes. And so in July 1662 the college for the promotion of physico-mathematical learning was granted a royal charter and became the Royal Society. Petty, as one of the original members, received a knighthood.

In November 1662 Petty addressed two communications to the Society concerning a 'double-bottomed vessel', that is a ship with two distinct keels clamped together with huge timbers, rather like a catamaran. A committee was appointed consisting of the members of the Royal Society in Ireland. The prototype, built in Ireland, was about thirty tons in burden, had good accommodation for thirty men and carried ten guns weighing five tons. After some teething troubles the *Experiment*, as it came to be called, outsailed three other ships and won a flag offered by the committee. It also succeeded in outsailing the Dublin-Holyhead packet boat: on the return journey they started from Holyhead together; the *Experiment* arrived first at five o'clock at night and the packet not till eight the next morning. A second ship was built and sailed to England to interest the king. At the end of 1664 a third was launched in the king's presence and the fortunes of the invention seemed assured. But in the following year the ship perished, along with many others of orthodox design, in a great storm. Petty continued to have faith in his invention but we hear of no more double-bottomed ships being built.

In 1661 Petty had again been elected a member of parliament for Ireland and thereafter he spent long periods there, attending to business both public and private. One of the first concerns of the new government had been to review the land situation in Ireland, and in 1662 an Act of Settlement was passed which is a good example of Charles II's liberal attitude: apart from a few prominent republicans who were dispossessed, most of the beneficiaries of the Cromwellian settlement were to be either confirmed in their ownership or compensated elsewhere if the lands they had been allotted were returned to their original owners. As can be imagined, the Act pleased nobody. The executive commission set up to administer it came under strong pressure from the original landowners, both protestant and catholic, and the provisions of the Act were eventually considerably modified to meet their protests. Petty was a member of this commission and exerted himself successfully to save from total confiscation the property of his old friend Henry Cromwell, a mark of loyalty which earned him the approbation of the king.

Petty was specifically named in the Acts as one of the beneficiaries who were to retain their possession. He had become attached to Ireland and had great ideas for promoting its economic development. His estates were mainly in County Kerry, a wild and apparently unprofitable district, and he set about putting them to productive use. It was poor land for agriculture but rich in forests, with mountains that could be quarried and a coastline abounding in natural harbours. He established there an industrial colony with iron and copper works, importing the ore from England and using his own timber for fuel, and encouraged the sea fisheries. The local population was too unskilled and perhaps too hostile to be trusted and the colony was manned by English protestants.

Petty gave much thought and care to its organisation and administration and the enterprise prospered, but in the teeth of bitter opposition. For the rest of his life he was involved in constant litigation, parrying the attacks of old enemies and of new ones who had arisen with the change in political circumstances. His liberal turn of mind and non-denominational form of christianity suited neither catholics nor protestants. Also, he could not resist making a good joke, and his jokes rankled. One of his turns was climbing on a chair and imitating various kinds of preachers, speaking 'now like a grave orthodox [anglican] divine; then falling into the presbyterian way; then to fanatical, to quaker, to monk, to friar, to popish priest'. Once, pressed to show his talent by the Duke of Ormonde, he got carried away and launched into a satirical imitation of 'some princes and governors', at which point the Duke 'became very uneasy', not knowing whether to laugh or be angry. At last Petty turned the subject and got off his stool 'but my lord would not have him preach any more'. No wonder his adversaries were bitter and sometimes even violent. But Petty was irreducible. Somebody once challenged him to a duel. As the challengee Petty had the right to choose the place and the weapon. Being very shortsighted he chose a dark cellar and a carpenter's axe. Everyone laughed and the duel came to nothing. Another time a certain Colonel Vernon assaulted him in the street and ran the ferrule of his cane into his left eye; Petty drew his sword and the colonel decamped. In the course of one of his innumerable law suits his adversaries charged him with using in his defence words libellous of the Lord Chancellor. He was found guilty and sentenced to a short prison term. He consoled himself in prison by translating the 104th Psalm into Latin verse.

If Petty had many enemies he also had many friends. He continued to enjoy the royal favour and was twice offered a peerage which he twice refused, saying the first time, 'I had rather be a copper farthing of intrinsic value, than a brass half-crown how gaudily soever it be stamped and gilded'. More significantly, he retained to the end of his life the admiration, respect and affection of his intellectual associates. Whenever he was in London he attended the meetings of the Royal Society and several of his papers were published in the Society's *Philosophical Transactions*. In Dublin he played an active part in the Philosophical Society of Ireland and the Dublin College of Physicians, both of which were largely his creation. Apart from his scientific contributions, his wit and conversational powers made him always welcome. The three great diarists of the period, Aubrey, Pepys and Evelyn, have left us lively impressions of his personality. Here is Aubrey:

'He is a proper handsome man, measured six foot high, good head of brown hair, moderately turning up. His eyes are a kind of goosegray, but very short sighted, and, as to aspect, beautiful, and promise sweetness of nature, and they do not deceive, for he is a marvellous good-hearted person. Eyebrows thick, dark, and straight (horizontal).

He is a person of an admirable inventive head, and practical parts. He hath told me that he hath read but little, that is to say, not since 25 aetat., and is of Mr Hobbes' mind, that had he read much, as some men have, he had not known so much as he does, nor should have made such discoveries and improvements . . .

To be short, he is a person of so great worth and learning, and has such a prodigious working wit, that he is both fit for, and an honour to, the highest preferment.'[1]

Here is Pepys:

'To the coffee-house, where I sat with Sir G. Ascue and Sir William Petty, who in discourse is, methinks, one of the most rational men that I ever heard speak with a tongue, having all his notions the most distinct and clear.'[2]

And here is Evelyn:

'There is not a better Latin poet living, when he gives himself that diversion; nor is his excellence less in council and prudent matters of state; but he is so exceeding nice in sifting and examining all possible contingencies, that he adventures at nothing which is not demonstration . . . If I were a prince, I should make him my second counsellor at least . . . Having never known such a genius, I cannot but mention those particulars amongst a multitude of other which I could produce.'[3]

One of the happiest events in Petty's life was his marriage in 1667 to Elizabeth Fenton, widow of Sir Maurice Fenton and daughter to Sir Hardress Waller, a distinguished Parliamentary officer who had materially assisted Petty at the time of the Down survey. Aubrey describes her as 'a very beautiful and ingenious lady, brown, with glorious eyes'. 'She was an extraordinary wit as well as a beauty,' says Evelyn. Her tastes were on

1. John Aubrey, *Brief Lives*. Penguin, 1972.
2. Samuel Pepys, *Diary*. London, 1893, vol. iv, pp. 23-4.
3. John Evelyn, *Diary*. London, 1906, vol. ii, pp. 307-8.

the grand scale, whereas Petty's were simple. To quote Evelyn again:

'When I, who have known him in mean circumstances, have been in his splendid palace, he would himself be in admiration how he had arrived at it . . . but his elegant lady could endure nothing mean, or that was not magnificent. He was very negligent himself, and rather so of his own person, and of a philosophic temper. "What a to-do is here," would he say; "I can lie in straw with as much satisfaction".'[1]

From the correspondence between husband and wife it was clearly an extremely harmonious union. They had three surviving children, two sons who died without issue and a daughter, Anne, through whom the strain continued. The fifth Marquis of Lansdowne (1845-1927), who edited some of Petty's unpublished papers and his correspondence with Robert Southwell, and Lord Edmond Fitzmaurice (1846-1935), who wrote his life, were both direct descendants of his.

Petty died in London on 16 December 1687. His last year was darkened by the fate that overtook his industrial estate in County Kerry. The political situation, never really settled since the end of the Civil War, had worsened under the reign of James II, whose strong leaning towards catholicism was much resented by a preponderantly protestant England. In Ireland the catholics were again up in arms. In 1687, while Petty was lying ill in London, his estate was attacked by a band of Irish and though most of the colonists managed to escape by sea to England the house in which they defended themselves was set on fire and destroyed, and all his improvements laid to waste. Petty heard of the attack on the colony. We must hope he did not live to hear of its total ruin.

Further details of Petty's life can be found in Fitzmaurice[2] and Hull.[3]

1. *Ibid.*

2. LORD EDMOND FITZMAURICE, *The Life of Sir William Petty*. London, 1895. ID., 'Sir William Petty'. *The Dictionary of National Biography*, vol. xv, pp. 999-1005.

3. C. H. HULL (ed.), *The Economic Writings of Sir William Petty*. Cambridge University Press, 1899.

2. An Essay on Public Finance

Throughout his life Petty was an inveterate writer, beginning at the age of fourteen, when he was a student at Caen, with 'A Course of Practicall Geometry and Dialling'. His writings range from Latin poetry through medicine, chemistry, mechanical and naval engineering, education, religion and politics to demography and of course economics. His works on economic subjects began shortly after the Restoration and continued until the end of his life. They are extremely lively and, given their content which he himself often refers to as 'a dry discourse', very amusing. They are cogently argued and to the point, showing that he was well aware of practical considerations and social justice and not concerned solely with abstract principles. They reflect his Baconian attitude to the understanding of the world we live in: first study the facts, the natural history of our subject, and on that basis form inductive generalisations outside the scope of our immediate experience.

I shall begin my account of Petty's economic writings with his first work in the field, *A Treatise of Taxes and Contributions*, published in 1662.[1] Despite some inconsistencies and exaggerations the *Treatise* is a solid and well constructed book. It starts with an enumeration of the public charges that must be met by the State, each of which Petty examines to see whether a saving could be effected or whether the expenditure should be increased. He then gives a number of reasons for complaint even by those who accept the necessity of taxation. Finally he goes through the different forms of tax and discusses their good and bad points. He gallops at full tilt through his arguments, raising showers of digressions some of which show him to have ideas far ahead of his time.

He considers public charges under six heads: (i) foreign war and civil strife; (ii) the 'Governours', namely the king, the ministers and the civil service; (iii) the Church; (iv) education; (v) care of the poor; and (vi) measures to alleviate unemployment.

As regards war, he agrees with Vegetius that being prepared

1. Reprinted in C. H. Hull (ed.), *op. cit.*

for it is the cheapest way of preventing attack. But he deplores offensive war and the illusions that support it, such as that greatness lies more in the extent of territory than in the number, art and industry of the people; and that it is cheaper to take land by force from a neighbour than to buy it 'from the Americans'. Civil strife, he contends, has two main causes: religious differences, which would be better dealt with by imposing 'tolerable pecuniary mulcts' on the heterodox than by the bloody methods current in his time; and the unbalanced distribution of wealth whereby 'luxury is allowed while others starve'.

As regards the 'Governours', he thinks that the most exalted of them 'must be kept in such a degree of splendour as private endeavours and callings seldom reach to'. At the same time many antiquated and superfluous offices could be abolished and the fees for the work of those that remain could be reduced to what the work they do requires.

As regards the Church, his proposals, though wrapped up in suitably tentative language, are fairly revolutionary. In the first place he thinks that great economies could be effected by reducing the number of parishes, which had not changed since the Reformation: half the number would be sufficient for the 'pastorage of men's souls', with a consequent reduction at all levels of the Church hierarchy. In the second place, parsons should be made more dependent on the free contributions of their flocks instead of being supported by compulsory tithes. He counters the argument that the alienation of tithes is sacrilege by a characteristic sally: suppose the money were used to defend the Church of God from the Turk or the Pope, would it be sacrilege? In the third place, since, as Graunt says, there are more males than females in the population, it would be no bad thing if the clergy returned to celibacy, for then the parson could live as well with half his benefice.

As regards education, he considers school charges money well spent, since 'school work, reading, writing and arithmetic, is useful to every man', but 'whether Divinity etc. ought to be made a private trade is questionable'; and he goes on at great length about the wastage of resources in the universities. The main subjects taught at university were divinity, law and medicine.

Concerning the first, we have already been told that there were more clergy, and by implication more divinity students, than were necessary. Concerning the second, the need for lawyers could be greatly reduced by establishing two institutions: registers of lands, conveyances and mortgages; and loan and credit banks in which not only money but also every kind of durable good could be deposited. Concerning the third, it would be possible to estimate the number of sick people from the Bills of Mortality and thus calculate the number of doctors and hence medical students needed, as also the number of surgeons, apothecaries and nurses. If this were done, in all probability there would turn out to be far too many of them and it would be possible to 'cut off and extinguish the infinite swarm of vain pretenders to, and abusers of that God-like Faculty'.

He then launches into a few calculations. Suppose there are 13,000 men bred in the universities at the present time and that these could be reduced to 6,000. Suppose that one in forty of the 13,000 dies each year, then less than 350 need graduate annually, and if each spends five years as an undergraduate, then 1,800 students would be enough for those who mean to make their livelihood by learning. Here he makes an unexpected suggestion: assuming there are in England 40,000 parish children and foundlings, 'it were probable that one in twenty of them might be of excellent wit and towardness; what if our professors of art were in this manner selected and educated'?

Having thus indicated some savings under his first four headings of public charges, he comes to the last two, on each of which he would like more to be spent. The first of these he calls care of the poor, which he deals with under several headings: homes for the aged, blind, lame and so on, hospitals for chronic, acute and contagious diseases; and homes for orphans and foundlings. The second is the provision of employment for indigent people other than the 'lazy and thievish' who are restrained by the law.

His ideas about the type of employment suitable for the deserving workless are interesting. He thinks that road and bridge building, river clearing, tree planting and various mining and metal-working activities would be the most useful: 'first, as works wanting in this nation; secondly, as works of much labour, and little art; and thirdly, as introductive of new trades into England, to supply that of cloth, which we have almost totally lost'. He asks the question, who shall pay those engaged in public works. He answers, everybody, and supports this by a rather fanciful numerical example purporting to show that 900 men can produce all that is needful for 1000. In this example there is very little food and clothing and a great deal of 'magnificence', but in principle we can agree that his proposal is better than forcing the unemployed to beg or steal or emigrate. 'Now,' he concludes,

'as to the work of these supernumeraries, let it be without expence of foreign commodities, and then 'tis no matter if it be employed to build a useless pyramid upon Salisbury Plain, bring the stones at Stonehenge to Tower-Hill, or the like; for at worst this would keep their minds to discipline and obedience, and their bodies to a patience of more profitable labours when need shall require it.'

Compare this with Keynes' contention in the *General Theory*, that rather than have unemployment it would be better for the community if the Treasury were to fill old bottles with banknotes, bury them in coal mines filled in with town rubbish and leave the public to dig them up again for a suitable fee.[1] Though Keynes often cites Petty he does not mention him in this connection.

In the third chapter Petty considers various objections to taxes. He assumes that a tax system is fair if taxes are proportional either to the capital (material and human) of individuals or to their income or to their expenditure. What angers men most is being taxed above their neighbours; there could really be no complaint if taxes were 'proportionable', for in this case every man would remain equally rich relative to his neighbour. And the riches of the sovereign and the people would differ only a little while, until the spending of the tax returned it to the people.

Though an interesting recognition of the circular flow of

1. John Maynard Keynes, *The General Theory of Employment, Interest and Money*. London, 1936, bk III, ch. 10, p. 129.

income and expenditure this is going too far, and Petty himself gives as a better reason for not grumbling that the people are not in a position to determine how far what they might have spent on consumption must in fact be spent on defence and public order. In other words it is for the sovereign, not the taxpayer, to decide what State expenditure is needed.

Some complain that taxes are spent on 'entertainments, magnificent shews, triumphal arches etc'. But this does no harm since the money goes back to the tradesmen who work on such things, and 'the Prince hath no more pleasure in these shews and entertainments than 100,000 others of his meanest subjects have, who, for all their grumbling, we see to travel many miles to be spectators of these mistaken and distasted vanities'.

Some say that the sovereign asks for more than he needs. But he never would do this if he could be sure of payment in due time; for it would be folly to take money out of the subjects' hands, where it would be usefully employed, in order to hoard it in his coffers where it would be no use even to himself. Incidentally, it seems somewhat hard that all taxes should be paid in money since the king has need of commodities, for instance to victual ships; and gold and silver coins are less than one per cent of the national capital.

Another reason for understandable vexation is ignorance of the number, trade and wealth of the people, which causes needless confusion: better statistics would avoid a great deal of trouble. Obscurities about the right of imposing particular taxes may lead to 'ugly reluctancies in the people', as demonstrated by the ship-money case which had so exacerbated the country's hostility to Charles I. Also, a better informed public might understand that under-population leads to the need for high taxes because the overhead costs of government do not greatly increase with numbers.

Petty concludes this chapter by saying that if taxes are spent on domestic commodities they do little harm to the whole body of the people; quite the reverse, in fact, since they tend to transfer riches from the landed and lazy to the skilled and industrious. Finally, if all the money raised in taxes were thrown into the sea, then in a State which knew how to prevent beggary and thievery the result would be that every man must work proportionately harder, to the extent that foreign trade be improvable, or retrench his consumption, if it be not. But if the State is not well-policied, the want of employment will give rise to rapines and frauds which will result in punishments to the State as well as to the offenders.

In the rest of the book Petty discusses the advantages and disadvantages of different types of tax and other methods of raising money for the State, such as debasing the coinage and selling patent rights. He distinguishes between taxes on what people put into production (income taxes) and what they take out of it (expenditure taxes) and makes it fairly clear that his first choice is a tax on consumers' expenditure, an opinion in which he follows the views of his mentor Hobbes.

Petty starts his discussion with four basic types of tax: land taxes; taxes on housing; import and export duties; and poll money, or capitation tax.

Beginning with land taxes, he first considers cutting out a certain portion of land whose rent is equal to the sum to be raised and giving this to the sovereign as Crown lands. Alternatively, an appropriate part of the rent might be paid to the sovereign as 'quit rent'. In a newly settled country like Ireland the second arrangement would be better, provided the cost of collection were not much greater than under the first. But in a country like England, where different financial commitments have already been contracted, the results would be rather chancy. There follows an example which traces the effects of a new tax in an established system if everyone reacts as he might be expected to.

Take two landlords, A and B, each of whom owns land worth £20 a year. Along comes a tax of 20 per cent. A has let his land on a long lease and so must pay £4 in tax for the duration of the lease, retaining only £16 for himself; but B is not tied to a long lease and Petty assumes that he can now let his land for £25 a year, so that after paying £5 in tax he retains his original £20. To meet the increase in rent, B's tenant farmers will increase their prices, whereupon A's tenants will do the same. Thus B and his tenants will break even; A's tenants will be gainers; and the losers will be A, who will suffer a cut in his income, and consumers in general, who will have to pay higher prices for their provisions.

A tax based on the rent of housing has further complications because a house may contain a workplace as well as dwelling space; and the former, though smaller and less expensive to build, may yet be more valuable than the latter. Also, any such tax is partly a tax on production and partly a tax on consumption.

Petty is not much in favour of duties on foreign trade or of prohibitions on imports and exports. As regards export duties he is prepared to make an exception where excessive profits can be made by exporting: 'Suppose', he says, 'tin might be made in Cornwall for fourpence the pound, and that the same would yield twelve pence at the nearest port in France, . . . this extraordinary profit ought to be esteemed a mine royal or trésor trouvé and the sovereign ought to have his share in it'. But he must not take so much as to make Cornish tin uncompetitive. Also, care must be taken not to encourage smuggling. This applies also to import duties, which might be set high on all superfluities 'tending to luxury and sin' but not to the point where it is better to 'smuckle' than to pay. High duties should not be laid on intermediate products. In general, since the costs of collection are heavy it might be a good idea for every ship that goes in or out to pay a tonnage of, he suggests, 4 per cent in place of customs duties.

As to poll money, it is easy to collect but of late this tax has become 'wonderfully confused'. Some rich, single persons are taxed at the lowest rate and, with the collusion of the assessors, some bankrupts pay at a high rate, thus making the world think them rich men. Apart from such abuses, taxing each head alike would be very unfair: not only are incomes unequal, but those with most children would pay most. It would be better 'if the heads were distinguished by titles of mere honour, without any kind of office or faculty; as Dukes, Marquesses, . . . and Gentlemen if they write themselves so,' since for the most part men are rich in proportion to their title.

The following chapters deal with lotteries, 'benevolence' (an occasional offering solicited by the sovereign as a mark of good will), penalties and fines, monopolies and offices, tithes, and several smaller ways of levying money which excite Petty's deepest contempt: 'When the people are weary of any one sort of tax, presently some Projector propounds another, and gets himself audience, by affirming he can propound a way how all the public charge may be borne without the way that is'. There have been suggestions for taxing total wealth, estates real and personal, offices, faculties and even imaginary estates, 'about which way' he says, 'may be so much fraud, collusion, oppression, and trouble . . . that I have not patience to speak more against it; daring rather conclude without more ado, in the words of our Comick, to be naught, yea exceeding naught, very abominable and not good'. Above all, he is against debasing the coinage and concludes by saying that 'raising or embasing of money is a very pitiful and unequal way of taxing the people; and 'tis a sign that the State sinketh, which catches hold on such weeds as are accompanied with the dishonour of impressing a Prince's effigies to justify adulterate commodities, and the breach of public faith, such as is the calling a thing what it really is not'.

This brings us to the last chapter, which treats of excise, or expenditure tax. 'It is generally allowed by all,' he says, 'that men should contribute to the public charge but according to the share and interest they have in the public peace; that is, according to their estates or riches'; and these can best be estimated from a person's expenditure, since 'a man is actually and truly rich according to what he eateth, drinketh, weareth, or any other way really and actually enjoyeth'. So 'the first thing to be done is, to compute what the total of the expence of this Nation is by particular men upon themselves, and then what part thereof is necessary for the public'. He continues:

'The very perfect idea of making a levy upon consumption is to rate every particular necessary, just when it is ripe for consumption; that is to say, not to rate corn until it be bread, nor wool until it be cloth, or rather until it be a very garment; so as the value of the wool, clothing and tailoring, even to the thread and needles, might be comprehended. But this being perhaps too laborious to be performed, we ought to enumerate a catalogue of commodities both native [natural] and artificial [manufactured], such whereof accounts may be most easily taken . . . being withall such, as are to be as near consumption as possible. And then we are to compute what further labour or charge is to be bestowed on each of them before consumption, that so an allowance may be given accordingly.'

There is some difficulty about imported goods and goods for export but the conclusion seems to be that the former should be charged but not the latter. The charge on imports would be in place of customs duty, which Petty speaks of at this point as 'unseasonable and preposterous, the same being a payment before consumption'.

Petty uses the term 'accumulative excise' for his consumption tax. Small items, he thinks, may be accumulated upon the excise of the main item but this idea must not be carried too far, as by those who suggest that beer should be the only excisable commodity on the assumption that a man's expenditure on beer is in proportion to all his other expenditure; this is absurd and unfair and would result in poor artisans paying far more than their share, partly because they drink relatively much strong beer and partly because they accumulate relatively little other consumption on it. If one wants to choose a single item as representative of a man's expenditure, the best of the accumulative excises in Petty's opinion is hearth money, that is a tax based on the number of chimneys in a house.

He concludes the book by giving a number of reasons for favouring excise, among them that 'by this way an excellent account may be taken of the wealth, growth, trade and strength of the Nation at all times'. This was his great idea and a few years later he gave it concrete form in one of his most important works, *Verbum Sapienti*.

3. The Accounts of the Nation

Verbum Sapienti, written probably in 1665,[1] is the first example of Petty's political arithmetic, although when he wrote it he had not yet coined the term. His purpose in writing it was to consider how

1. First published with *The Political Anatomy of Ireland*, London, 1691; reprinted in C. H. Hull (ed.), *op. cit.*

best to spread the tax burden consequent upon the war with Holland which had begun in that year. The work, however, was not published until 1691, after Petty's death, possibly because his criticism of the tax system and its abuses was too outspoken or possibly because he himself was not satisfied with it.

The introduction relates to the 'unequal' levying of taxes and to the rise that may be expected if the war continues, and concludes with the words:

'. . . But if the public charge were laid proportionably, no man need pay above 1/10 of his whole effects, even in the case the tax should rise to £250,000 per mensem, which God forbid.

That is to say, according to the present way, some pay four times as much more as they ought, or needed; which disproportion is the true and proper grievance of taxes . . . Whereas by mere method and proportion, the same may be corrected as aforesaid; and withal, just accounts might be kept of the people, with the respective increases and decreases of them, their wealth, and foreign trade.'

In the first chapter Petty starts in on his calculations. He begins with the population of England and Wales, which he puts at about 6 million inhabitants. He next estimates their annual expenditure per head on food, housing, clothes and 'all other necessaries' at £6.13s.4d a year, or about 4½d a day (in decimal terms approximately £6.67 and £0.02), making for the whole population £40 million a year. Surprisingly, since he later explicitly mentions 'superlucration' or saving, he does not think of including it among the outlays.

He sees that income should be equal to expenditure, and so tries to match his £40 million by calculating the income generated by the various factors of production. In the *Treatise of Taxes* he had subscribed to the view that 'labour is the father and active principle of wealth, as lands are the mother'. Here he adds to them the capital embodied in such assets as buildings and merchandise.

He begins with land. He estimates its extent at 24 million acres and the average annual rent at 6s.8d an acre, giving a total income of £8 million. At the same time he calculates the capital value of land by applying 18 years purchase to the rent, thus obtaining £144 million.

He next considers 'other personal estates' which he divides into five categories: housing, shipping, cattle, coined money, and stocks of merchandise and durable goods. He starts his calculations with housing. He estimates that: (i) the City of London contains 28,000 houses at an average annual rent of £15 each or £420,000 in total, which at 12 years purchase gives a capital value of £5.04 million; (ii) outside the City but within the area covered by the London Bills of Mortality there are a quarter more houses but they probably add up to the same value, that is another £5.04 million; (iii) the number of houses in all the other cities and market towns is probably double the number of those in all London but worth no more, that is £10.08 million; and (iv) the houses outside the cities and towns are more in number than those within (London excepted) but of no greater value, that is another £10.08 million. Thus the total capital value of housing is £30.24 million.

His estimates of the remaining four categories are less circumstantial. Shipping he puts at about 500,000 tons, which 'including their ordinary apparell' he values at £6 a ton, giving a total value of £3 million. Cattle he defines as consisting of horses, oxen, sheep, swine, deer, and fisheries, parks and warrens; these he puts at 1/4 the value of land, that is at a capital value of £36 million. The coined gold and silver of the Kingdom, he says, is scarce worth £6 million. Finally there are the 'wares, merchandizes, and utensils of plate, and furniture', to which he attributes a capital value of £31 million though he considers this the most uncertain part of his estimate, which might be criticised as being perhaps too high.

To sum up: the value of land is £144 million, which at 18 years purchase is equivalent to an annual income of £8 million; and the value of other personal estates is, in round numbers, £30+3+36+6+31=106 million, which at 15 years purchase (since these items yield on average more than land) is equivalent to an annual income of £7 million.

'Now,' he says, 'if the annual proceed of the stock or wealth of the Nation yields but 15 million, and the expence be 40, then the labour of the people must furnish the other 25; which may be done, if but half of them, viz 3 millions earned but £8.6s.8d per annum.' This, he calculates, is equivalent to 7d per working day.

He obtains the 7d a day from a rectangular distribution of the workforce, each sixth earning 2d, 4d, . . . 12d a day in a working year of 287 days. He capitalises the £25 million at a little less than 17 years' purchase to yield a capital value of £417 million, remarking that 'although the individuum of mankind be reckoned at about 8 years purchase; the species of them is worth as many as land, being in its nature as perpetual, for aught we know'. If the capital value is related to the whole population we obtain £69 a head, and if it is related to the workforce we obtain £138 a head.

In the foregoing passages I have considerably simplified Petty's somewhat involved reasoning but I have tried to preserve enough of it to show how he reaches his estimates of the national capital, income and expenditure. His final results can be presented in a modern format as in tables 1.1 and 1.2 below.

Table 1.1

THE CAPITAL AND INCOME OF ENGLAND AND WALES *c.* 1665

	Quantity (million)	Capital value (£ million)	Income (£ million)
Land (acres)	24	144	8
Other personal estates	. .	106	7
Labour (people)	3	417	25
Total		667	40

Source: William Petty, *Verbum Sapienti* (ed. Hull, vol. 1) pp. 111-12.

Table 1.2

THE NATIONAL INCOME AND EXPENDITURE OF ENGLAND AND WALES *c.* 1665

(£ million)

Income at factor cost		Expense at market prices	
Land	8	Food, housing, clothes and all other necessaries	40
Other personal estates	7		
The labour of the people	25		
Total	40	Total	40

Source: William Petty, *Verbum Sapienti* (ed. Hull, vol. 1) pp. 111-12.

On the basis of these figures Petty proceeds to explain his system of fair taxation. His principle is simple: taxes should be assessed as a uniform proportion of capital. As a demonstration he calculates what it would take to raise £1 million. Taking as a point of departure the capital values given in table 1.1, he shows that if a flat rate of 1.5 per mille were applied to each type of capital, land would contribute £216,000, other personal estates £159,000, and human capital, 'the people', £625,000.

He then considers how this would impinge on the various types of income. Allowing for the costs of collection, he envisages for land a tax of about 2.8 per cent on rents; for housing, a chimney tax varying with the district but averaging about 1.8 per cent on rents, and for other assets a straight capital levy of about 1.6 per mille. As to the sum to be raised from 'the people', he suggests that this should take the form of a poll tax of 6d a head and an excise averaging 19d a head, equivalent to 1.2 per cent of their annual expenditure on consumption.

Any requirements in excess of £1 million can be met by simply multiplying the rate on capital by a common factor. The highest requirement he contemplates is £3 million, to which must be added the revenue to be expected from crown lands, customs duties, the post office and other minor sources, which he reckons to come to £300,000 a year and to remain constant. He purports to prove that £3,300,000 would amply cover all military and civil charges and that the current money supply would be sufficient to meet the increased tax bill without prejudice to trade. He then contrasts his tax system with the existing one and concludes, typically, with a plea for a policy of industrial expansion and full employment as the surest way to national prosperity.

Compared with his *Treatise* of 1662, Petty's disquisition on taxes in *Verbum Sapienti* is weak and contradictory. At first sight his central principle appears fair and straightforward, but had it been applied one wonders how fair and straightforward 'the people' would have found it. It assumes a correct valuation of capital, almost impossible to achieve, especially where human capital is concerned, and its impact on income is far from 'equal'.

What makes *Verbum Sapienti* a landmark in economic history is not its doubtful tax proposals but the estimates of capital, income and expenditure that underlie them. As far as I know, they are the first complete and consistent set of national accounts ever to have been made. Like all new inventions they are too simple, not to say crude: all the income is spent on consumption and that is that. The implication is that all taxes are indirect taxes and that all government expenditure is on goods and services and thus generates income for the factors of production. There are no direct taxes, no transfers, no saving, no investment, no provisions for depreciation. Still, the framework is there, ready for Petty's successors to build on.

4. An Economic Plan for Ireland

Not surprisingly, Petty wrote a good deal about Ireland. His *History of the Down Survey* was published in 1851 by Sir Thomas Larcom.[1] At his death Petty had several chests of books, maps and papers relating to the Survey, which in his will he valued at £2,000. It is fortunate that Larcom published the *History* when he did, for some of the maps had been damaged by a fire early in the eighteenth century and the remaining papers were lodged in the Dublin Public Records Office which was destroyed in 1921.

In *The Political Anatomy of Ireland*, written in 1672 but not published until 1691,[2] Petty attempts a socio-economic analysis of the country, drawing on his experience as a surveyor there in the 1650's. He uses his dissecting knife with his usual boldness and sometimes his hand slips, but his penetration is remarkable and his suggestions for remedying the ills which he reveals show a generous concern and great breadth of vision. He begins with an account of the lands and of the transfers of ownership which had taken place between the Rebellion of 1641 and the year 1672, by which time the rearrangements were more or less a *fait accompli*. With the help of the notes given by Hull the changes can be summarised as in table 1.3.

1. Irish Archaeological and Celtic Society Publication, vol. 15, Dublin University Press, 1851.

2. First published with *Verbum Sapienti*, London, 1691; reprinted in C. H. Hull (ed.), *op. cit.*

Table 1.3
THE LANDS OF IRELAND, 1641 AND 1672

	1641 Irish acres ('000)	1641 %	1672 Irish acres ('000)	1672 %
Waste land, rivers, roads	1 500	14.3	1 500	14.3
Rough land (unprofitable)	1 500	14.3	1 500	14.3
Good land				
Papists*	5 200	49.5	2 280	21.7
Protestants	2 000	19.0	4 820	45.9
Protestant Church	300	2.9	320	3.1
Unallocated	. . .	. . .	80	0.7
All good land	7 500	71.4	7 500	71.4
Total	10 500	100.0	10 500	100.0

* And sequestered protestants in 1641.
Source: William Petty, *The Political Anatomy of Ireland* (ed. Hull, vol. 1) pp. 135-38

This table shows how large the shift of ownership from catholics to protestants was, even though the harshness of the Cromwellian settlement had been somewhat tempered by Charles II's Act of 1662. Indeed, were the percentages worked out for 'good' land only, the catholic share would be seen to have fallen from 69 to 30 per cent. In view of Petty's direct involvement in both settlements, the figures in this table can I think be considered quite reliable.

He next discusses the composition and living standards of the population in 1672. He estimates there are about 800,000 catholic Irish, 100,000 presbyterian Scots, and 200,000 English of whom rather more than half conform to the Church of England and the rest belong to other protestant sects, making in all 1.1 million inhabitants. This population he distributes over 200,000 dwellings ranging from primitive cabins 'with no fixed hearth' to houses with 20 'smoaks' (chimneys). In addition there are twenty 'transcendental' houses belonging to the very rich and powerful. Some idea of the distribution of wealth as represented by the quality of housing can be gathered from table 1.4. The figures in this table must be taken with a large pinch of salt. For one thing, Petty has overlooked the institutionalised population such as soldiers, priests, inmates of workhouses and so on; not to speak of the homeless vagrants who must have been very numerous in a country so recently ravaged by a long and bloody war. For another, if we were to believe his figures all the catholic Irish would be living in cabins, which is implausible: he himself says elsewhere that only about 600,000 of the 800,000 live in cabins. However, 600,000 is still more than half the population.

Table 1.4
HOUSING IN IRELAND, 1672

Number of chimneys	Number of houses	Capital value (£)	Number of inhabitants: Average per house	Number of inhabitants: Total ('000)
None ('no fixed hearth')	160 000	50 000 or less	5	800
1	24 000	120 000	6	144
2-3	6 800	272 000	10	68
4-6	5 600	560 000	10	56
7-9	2 500	750 000	10	25
10-12	700	420 000	10	7
13-20	400	400 000	10	4
'Transcendental houses'	20	78 000	. .	. .
Total	200 020	2 650 000		1 104

Source: William Petty, *The Political Anatomy of Ireland* (ed. Hull, vol. 1) pp. 143-4.

This is only the beginning of Petty's description of a poverty-stricken country. His estimate of material wealth is a little less than £16 million, or about £14 per head as opposed to nearly £42 per head in England. His estimates of the national income and expenditure are not carefully worked out and are not consistent, but they suggest something rather less than £4 million, or under £4 per head per annum. He presents a grisly picture of the 160,000 'nasty cabins, full of smoke, damp and musty stenches, which cannot be kept free of beasts and vermin' and are quite unsuitable for any form of 'trade', his word for productive activity. He is strongly opposed to any redistribution of income which would lead to a levelling down of standards, as this would only increase the sordidness and squalor already too visible, and wants to see the 950,000 'plebeians' spend and consequently earn double what they do at present. As we might expect, he has a scheme to bring this about.

In order to explain his scheme he starts by drawing up an occupational classification of the population divided according to whether or not they are 'fit for trade' and whether or not they are already employed. This is shown in table 1.5. There are 320,000

Table 1.5
OCCUPATIONAL DISTRIBUTION OF THE POPULATION IN IRELAND, 1672
('000)

Not fit for trade		
Children under seven	275.0	
Incurables	2.0	
Soldiers	3.0	
Masters and mistresses in houses with more than 6 chimneys	7.2	
Their servants	14.4	
Servants in houses with 4-6 chimneys	11.2	
Servants in houses with 2-3 chimneys	6.8	
Clergy, students etc.	0.4	
Total		320.0
Already employed *		
Farmers and agricultural labourers	100.0	
Cowherds and shepherds	120.0	
Fishermen	1.0	
Foundry workers	2.0	
Smiths	22.5	
Tailors	45.0	
Carpenters and masons	10.0	
Shoemakers	22.5	
Millers	1.6	
Woodworkers	30.0	
Tanners and curriers	10.0	
Workers in trades of fancy and ornament	48.4	
Total		413.0 §
Publicans and brewers		
(i) needed to supply the drink at present consumed	60.0	
(ii) redundant	120.0	
Total		180.0
Gasherers and fait-neants		187.0 †
Grand total		1100.0

* The figures include wives and in some cases 'trade servants'.
§ Incorrectly given in the 1691 edition as 380,000.
† Incorrectly given in the 1691 edition as 220,000.
Source: William Petty, *The Political Anatomy of Ireland* (ed. Hull, vol. 1) pp. 144-6.

people not fit for trade and 413,000 already employed in useful occupations. Besides these there are 180,000 publicans and brewers which he considers largely redundant, since 'it is manifest that 2/3 of the alehouses may be spared, even although the same quantity of drink should be sold'. Finally there is a large group of 187,000 'casherers and fait-neants', that is discharged soldiers and idlers, all of whom could be put to productive work. Petty adds up the figures for the usefully employed incorrectly and reaches a total of 380,000 in place of 413,000; consequently his residual category numbers 220,000 in place of 187,000 as it should. In my table I have made the necessary corrections.

He then makes a list of projects which would occupy the unemployed and the wastefully employed without interfering with existing useful activities and would increase both local wealth and 'universal' wealth. The 120,000 redundant publicans and 187,000 idlers add up to 307,000 (he says 340,000) spare hands. If employment could be found for them at £7 a year this would represent a total cost of £2.15 million on my figures (or £2.38 million on his); in either case more than 50 per cent of the national income. To achieve this he proposes the programme of works shown in table 1.6. The figures in this table are as given by Petty.

This is an ambitious scheme. It has the merit of not setting the unemployed on work already being carried out, but one may wonder how all this useful activity could be obtained from the ex-publicans, casherers and fait-neants. Also it implies that the marginal propensity to consume is zero so that there would be no further expenditure out of the huge increase in national income. It might be expected therefore to bring about an immense inflation. A more modest programme would have been sufficient. But Petty's suggestion fell on deaf ears. Had it been taken up, even though in a modified form, much misery might have been avoided and the history of England and Ireland might have been very different.

Table 1.6
PETTY'S SCHEME FOR CURING UNEMPLOYMENT IN IRELAND
(cost in £ '000)

To increase local wealth		
Building 168,000 small stone-wall houses, with chimneys, doors, windows, gardens and orchards . . . instead of the lamentable sties now in use, at £ 3 each	544.0	
Planting 5 million fruit trees, at 4d each	83.3	
Planting 3 million timber-trees . . . at 3d each	37.5	
1 million perches* of inclosures and quicksets [fences and hedges], at 12d per perch	50.0	
Fortifying the city of Dublin	30.0	
Building a new palace for the chief Governor	20.0	
Making there a mole for shipping	15.0	
Making several rivers navigable and mending highways	35.0	
Building 100 churches, at £ 200 each	20.0	
Workhouses [factories] . . ., tan-yards, fishing crafts, rape-mills, allom and copperas§ works . . . etc.	50.0	
Total		884.8
To increase universal wealth		
For 10,000 tons of shipping	100.0	
For a stock of wool, hemp, flax and raw hides for one year's work	400.0	
For the labour of men to manufacture the same	1000.0	
Total		1500.0
Grand total		2384.8

* About 3125 miles.
§ Alum and sulphates of iron, copper and zinc.
Source: William Petty, *The Political Anatomy of Ireland* (ed. Hull, vol. 1) p. 147.

5. *Political Arithmetick*

In 1671 the publicist Roger Coke brought out a book on the political and economic conditions of England purporting to show that the power and trade of the country were in decline.[1] Petty, never a pessimist, set out to prove that things were not so bad as Coke said. The result was *Political Arithmetick*.[2] This book, begun probably in 1671 but not completed until 1676 and not published, again, until after Petty's death, brings together

1. Roger Coke, *A Treatise wherin is Demonstrated that the Church and State of England are in Equal Danger with the Trade of it*. London, 1671.
2. 1st edn, London, 1691; reprinted in C. H. Hull (ed.), *op. cit.*

all his economic and political beliefs and can be said to represent his manifesto for national prosperity.

He starts his preface by enumerating Coke's causes for concern and contrasting them with the signs of affluence which he maintains are everywhere visible, and goes on:

'These general observations, and that men eat, drink and laugh as they use to, have encouraged me to try if I could also comfort others, being satisfied myself, that the interest and affairs of England are in no deplorable condition.

The method I take to do this is not very usual; for instead of using only comparative and superlative words, and intellectual arguments, I have taken the course (as a specimen of the Political Arithmetick I have long aimed at) to express myself in terms of *number*, *weight* or *measure*; to use only arguments of sense, and to consider only such causes, as have visible foundations in nature; leaving those that depend upon the mutable minds, opinions, appetites and passions of particular men, to the consideration of others . . .

Now the observations or positions expressed by *number*, *weight* and *measure*, upon which I bottom the ensuing discourses, are either true, or not apparently false . . . and if they are false, not so false as to destroy the argument they are brought for; but at worst are sufficient as suppositions to show the way to that knowledge I aim at . . . I hope all ingenious and candid persons will rectify the errors, defects, and imperfections, which probably may be found in any of the positions, upon which these ratiocinations were grounded. Nor would it misbecome Authority itself, to clear the truth of those matters which private endeavours cannot reach to.'

In the first chapter, one of the most interesting in the book, Petty uses all his powers of ratiocination to demonstrate 'how a small country and few people, by its situation, trade and policy, may be equivalent in wealth and strength to a far greater people and territory'. He rests his argument on a comparison between Holland and France. Holland, having shaken off Spanish domination, was going through a period of great economic expansion and rapidly catching up on its powerful rival. The figures Petty quotes in proof of this are staggering and doubtless exaggerated, but from a comparison with the estimates made thirty years later by Gregory King and based on much more solid data, they would appear to be in the right direction. For land, Petty gives the ratio of France to Holland as 80 to 1; for population as 13 to 1; for wealth as 3 to 1; for exports as 5 to 21; and for shipping as 1 to 9. He attributes the success of the Dutch to two causes: the natural upsurge of a people freed from oppression and their high propensity to save, whereby in a hundred years they have decupled their wealth while the French have only doubled theirs.

Having thus set the stage for his argument he considers the natural advantages of Holland: a rich and fertile soil; a geographical formation which favours a high density of population and thus minimises the infrastructure needed; an abundance of inland waterways which make for cheap transport; and a coastline which encourages shipping, hence shipbuilding, hence a flourishing overseas trade.

He then describes how these advantages are enhanced by sensible policies in social, legal and financial matters. Top of the list he puts freedom of conscience, pointing out that it is usually the religious minorities, such as the Huguenots in France, the Jews in Venice and the Mahometans in India, that are the most productive groups in society, the heterodox being for the most part 'thinking, sober and patient men, and such as believe that labour and industry is their duty towards God'. The freedom they enjoy in Holland redounds both to that country's honour and to its benefit. Second he puts the Dutch system of land registration, which makes ownership secure and thus ensures that people make the best use of their property. Third he puts their well-developed banking system, which encourages saving and leads to a low rate of interest. Many other Dutch institutions are examined and given as examples of political wisdom which other countries would do well to imitate.

There follows a long chapter on fiscal policy, the purpose of which is to prove that taxes may increase rather than diminish the wealth of a country. The proceeds of most taxes are not simply destroyed or given away abroad but result in a transfer from one hand to another within the country. If money is taken from laborious and ingenious men and given to such as do nothing at all but eat, drink, sing, play and dance, 'nay to such as study the metaphysick or other needless speculation', the wealth of the community will be diminished. But if the money gets into the hands of those who buy durable goods or, better still, use it to improve some part of the productive system, wealth will be increased. Here the Dutch come in again for commendation. Taxes are higher in Holland than anywhere else in Europe, yet no other country has increased its wealth as much as Holland has. But then their taxes are higher on perishable than on durable goods. Further, as a rule they tax not according to what men gain but according to what they spend and, in particular, spend needlessly and without prospect of return.

The rest of the chapter is largely a reiteration of some of the arguments in the *Treatise of Taxes*. Among other points, he raises again the subject of unemployment, going as far as to say that even if the State cannot provide work for the unemployed it would be better to give them a modest income than put up with the crimes and disorders that follow if they are left to fend for themselves.

In the third chapter Petty gives arguments for thinking that France cannot be predominant at sea. His main reasons are: that France has no ports in the north suitable for large vessels of deep draught, such as are needed in a navy; that France has only a small merchant marine which could not spare enough men to man a fleet; and that it takes a long time to train a man for the navy, so that it would be many years before the French navy could reach any size.

In the fourth chapter he attempts to show that the peoples and territories of the king of England are nearly as strong and wealthy as those of the king of France. In terms of land area he grants that France has the superiority; although the British Isles as a whole probably cover an area nearly as large as that of France, if one adds in the two countries' possessions in the New World and elsewhere it could plausibly be argued that France's dominions were a seventh or even a fifth larger than England's.

Here he introduces, half in joke and half in earnest, one of his digressions: how would it be if all the moveables and people of Ireland and the Scottish Highlands were transferred to England,

Wales and the Scottish Lowlands. He admits that this is 'a wild conception', nevertheless he proceeds to demonstrate that it might actually prove a profitable dream.

Supposing the total population to be 9 million and the number to be transplanted 1.8 million, there would be no difficulty in feeding them on the area of England, Wales and the Scottish Lowlands, since when the immigrants were added to the 7.2 million there at present there would still be four acres per head, which is more than there is in Holland. Also there would be economies from having the population so densely concentrated. Further, few of the immigrants would be needed in agriculture and so most of them would be free to devote themselves to more profitable employment in handicrafts.

These benefits would far outweigh the costs of the operation. The land and housing vacated in Ireland and Scotland would not be worth more than £13 million and the cost of transplantation would not amount to more than £4 million, so the total cost would be £17 million. But rents in the rest of the country are about £9 million, and if these rose in proportion to the increase in population they would amount to £10.8 million and the number of years of purchase would rise from $17\frac{1}{2}$ years to 21. Thus the value of this land would rise by £$(10.8\times21)-(9\times17.5)=69.3$ million, which is over four times the estimated cost.

Finally, if any foreign prince were willing to extend his territories by buying the abandoned lands, the gain would be all the greater. Nor would this be dangerous, because the foreigner would be no nearer than he is and his territories would be divided. Petty does not seem at all troubled by a prospect which has frightened many later governments, and at this point seems to carry his optimism to an extreme. Perhaps the moral is that we should not try to make our dreams too profitable.

Coming back to reality, Petty thinks that despite its somewhat smaller population England is a match for France: it is more productive; is vastly superior as a marine power; does not devote so many resources to the pleasures of the king and court; and has not such an overabundance of clergy who, though they consume more than people in general, contribute nothing to production.

The fifth chapter contains a discussion of the impediments to England's greatness, which in Petty's opinion are contingent and remediable. They largely arise from the fact that the King's territories are spread out over a number of countries and islands with different legislative authorities which do not always act in harmony. Thus England, Scotland and Ireland with their separate legislatures frequently cross one another's interests and act as foreigners if not enemies to one another. Would it not be better if they were equally represented in a common parliament and, further, if the whole empire, including the New World, were managed by two councils, one chosen by the king and the other by the people. Similar criticisms can be made at the local level with its differences between shires, parishes, church livings, representations in parliament etc. These impediments are not natural but arise from historical causes. Their removal would bring many improvements to the operation of authority.

The sixth chapter, by contrast, describes the growth in the power and wealth of England in the last forty years. Among the signs of this, one need only consider the many improvements that have been made on the land and in agriculture: that the population has increased despite the 300,000 deaths from plague and war; that as for housing, London speaks for itself, the city showing perhaps double the value of forty years ago, and increases have taken place in many other towns; that the navy is now three or four times as large as it was forty years ago; that coasting and foreign trade have greatly increased; that the rate of interest, which was 10 per cent, is now down to 6 per cent thanks not to legislation but to the increase in the quantity of money; that the postage of letters has risen twentyfold, arguing a corresponding increase in business; and that the public revenue has nearly trebled, indicating an increase in the means to pay.

In the seventh chapter Petty goes back to his old contention that one tenth of the consumption expenditure of the King's subjects would be amply sufficient to meet all military and civil charges, presupposing a military establishment of 100,000 foot soldiers, 40,000 horse and 40,000 men at sea. If, he says, we put average consumption per head at £7 per annum and the population of the whole empire at 10 million, then total consumption is £70 million, a tenth of which is £7 million; and he remarks, as he had in *Verbum Sapienti*, that it would be no great hardship to work five per cent more and consume five per cent less. In any case a year's pay, winter and summer, for the above forces is only about £5 million and the civil expenditure in times of peace has never exceeded £600,000; so a revenue of £7 million would be more than enough. But he warns the reader that his figures presuppose a state of domestic harmony and would have to be changed if this condition were not fulfilled.

In the eighth he attacks the question of unemployment from a new angle, the loss it signifies for the nation in terms of wealth, arguing that there are spare hands enough to earn at least £2 million per annum more than is earned at present. Of the £70 million spent on consumption, about £30 million is income from property, leaving £40 million as labour income. But in a total population of 10 million, subtracting children under seven and the rich who do not work, there must be about $6\frac{1}{2}$ million fit for work; if these were all employed full time at the average wage of £10 per annum they would earn £65 million, or £25 million more than they spend on consumption. In other words they would be saving £25 million. Since it is quite obvious that saving falls far short of this figure, or else the nation would be much wealthier than it is, there must be a large number of unemployed. Yet there would be plenty of profitable work for them. To prove this, little more is needed than to compute: for instance, how much money is paid to foreigners for shipping; how much the Dutch get from fishing in our waters; how much we spend on imports which we could produce ourselves. Petty thinks these items alone would come to over £5 million per annum which, if not his £25 million, is well above the £2 million he originally suggested as possible.

In the ninth chapter he debates whether there is enough money to drive the trade of the nation. As in *Verbum Sapienti* he concentrates on England, saying that he does not doubt that similar conditions hold in the rest of His Majesty's dominions, and makes the same calculation as in that book. He estimates that there is £6 million of cash in England and considers the three sorts of circulation that this must meet. First, there is the national expenditure of £42 million per annum or about £800,000 per week. If everything were paid for weekly and the money could circulate within the week, then less than £1 million would answer the ends proposed. Second, the rent of land is £8 million per annum and paid half-yearly; so this kind of payment would require £4 million. Finally, the rent of housing is £4 million and paid quarterly; so this would require, again, £1 million. So he thinks that £6 million of cash is sufficient, at least until something better is advanced to the contrary.

In the final chapter he sets out to show that the King's subjects have enough stock to drive the trade of the whole commercial world. He estimates the value of world trade at £45 million per annum to which should be added perhaps £15 million of shipping engaged in it, making £60 million in all. So even without trust, if everything had to be paid for on the nail, £60 million at most would drive the whole trade. But in fact considerable credit is usually granted, so that perhaps half as much would be sufficient. And of this sum at least half is already in trade in the form of coin, shipping and stock. Suppose another £20 million is needed, this could be obtained by forming a land bank of £20 million worth of land as security for all the commodities bought on the account of the universal trade.

Some such institution would be desirable since nowadays many gentlemen and some noblemen put their younger sons to trade to enable them to live 'according to their birth and breeding'. The land of England being worth £8 million per annum suggests that there are about ten thousand families with an average annual income of £800. Suppose there is one younger brother to each of these families. He will need an income of £200 or £300 to maintain a suitable parity with his relatives. But positions at Court, in the army, the navy and the Church, earnings from the law and medicine and employment by noblemen and prelates cannot provide an income of £300 or so for more than three thousand of these younger brothers, so the remaining seven thousand must depend on trade. This means an expansion of trade, which in turn means an expansion of credit facilities to increase the stock.

He says in conclusion that he could go on *ad infinitum*,

> 'but what has been already said I look upon as sufficient, first to show what I mean by *Political Arithmetick*: and to show the uses of knowing the true state of the *people*, *land*, *stock*, *trade* etc. That the King's subjects are not in so bad a condition, as discontented men would make them. To show the great effect of *unity*, *industry* and *obedience*, in order to the common safety, and each man's particular happiness.'

One may think that Petty's arguments could be sharpened up in places and that the statistics available to him were deplorable, a point on which he would have been the first to agree. But in the breadth of his interests, the topics he thought important and his innovative use of quantitative data he seems to me to have shown a better understanding of what economics is all about than many of the well-known writers who have succeeded him.

6. Other Works

Petty's last substantial work, written in 1687 a few months before his death, was *A Treatise of Ireland*.[1] The book is an impassioned plea for sweeping reforms to bring peace to that unfortunate island. It was obviously written in great haste. A torrent of arguments and calculations pours forth, and at the centre of it all is Petty's favourite recipe for national harmony: mass migration. Ireland should be converted into a vast cattle ranch; 300,000 herdsmen and dairywomen would be needed to run it; and the rest of the inhabitants could be transplanted to England, where they would find well-paid work and would soon be peaceably absorbed by the native population. The book was dedicated to James II, who had come to the throne in 1685, and Petty hoped that it would be published, but too many factors conspired against this: the political situation was

1. First published in C. H. Hull (ed.), *op. cit.*

disastrous, the king's authority practically non-existent, Petty's health breaking down and the book itself too chaotic to be fit for publication as it stood. It finally saw the light two centuries later in Hull's collected edition.

An aspect of political arithmetic which Petty was always interested in was demography, particularly the demography of large cities. During the 1680's he published several essays on the subject, among them two sets of *Observations on the Dublin Bills of Mortality* which are interesting because of their connection with John Graunt's *Observations on the London Bills of Mortality.*[1] All these essays are brought together in the second volume of Hull, which also gives a complete bibliography of the works of Petty published before 1899.

Petty was a compulsive writer and at his death left a large number of manuscript notes on a wide variety of subjects. We are told that from his earliest days it was his habit when faced with a new problem 'to meditate and fill a quire with all that could in nature be objected, and to write down his answers to each, so that when any new thing started he was prepared as it were extempore to shoot them down'. A well-known example of this method is his 'Quantulumcumque concerning money', a dialogue on currency written in 1682 as a contribution to the ongoing debate on coinage.[2] A collection of Petty's miscellaneous notes and memoranda on economic and allied subjects was published by Lord Lansdowne in 1927.[3]

Whenever Petty returned to a subject, as he constantly did, he seems to have preferred to start again *de novo* rather than correct his earlier manuscripts. Consequently it is hard to tell whether any changes in the figures are meant to refer to a different date or whether they represent revisions. Interpretation is not made easier by the fact that items are often grouped differently in successive versions. For instance, his estimate of the material capital of the nation is raised from £250 million in *Verbum Sapienti* to £300 million in a note entitled 'A gross

1. See chapter 7 below.
2. First extant edn, London, 1695; reprinted in C. H. Hull (ed.), *op. cit.*
3. Lord Lansdowne (ed.), *The Petty Papers*. Constable, London, and Houghton Mifflin, Boston and New York, 1927.

estimate of the wealth of England'.[1] In this he values the £300 million of material capital at 5 per cent to give an income of £15 million as in *Verbum Sapienti* and applies 20 years purchase to the £25 million of labour income to give £500 million of human capital, which when divided by a population of 6 million, as before, is equivalent to £83 per head. In fact, his figures for the money value of a man increases from £69 in *Verbum Sapienti* to £80 in *Political Arithmetick*, £83 in 'A gross estimate' and £90 in 'Magnalia regni', a short paper written in the year of his death.[2]

The tendency for some of Petty's estimates to increase over time may be partly based on new information which came his way, though he does not produce evidence to this effect, and partly motivated by patriotic zeal. In his later years he was anxious to show that England was not going to the dogs and to assure the king that he had little to fear from the French. This intention is apparent in his books and papers from *Political Arithmetick* on. In the first of his *Five Essays in Political Arithmetick*, written in 1686,[3] he goes so far as to argue that London has more inhabitants than Paris, Rouen and Rome put together. His figures are: London, 696 thousand; Paris, 490 thousand; Rouen, 80 thousand; Rome, 125 thousand. Later estimates derived from other sources by Chandler and Fox for the year 1700 are 550, 530, 68 and 149 thousand respectively.[4] Even Charles Davenant, who was a great admirer of Petty and broadcaster of his ideas, admits that at times 'he rather made his court than spoke his mind'.

One of the leitmotifs that run through all Petty's writings is the need for better statistics. Among the papers published by Lord Lansdowne there are a number of notes and memoranda in which he sets out in detail the data he would like to see collected, perhaps with himself as the 'King's Accomptant'. Of one of these plans for the organisation of statistics he writes to his wife's cousin, Sir Robert Southwell, who preserved all he

1. *Ibid.*
2. *Ibid.*
3. London, 1687; reprinted in C. H. Hull (ed.), *op. cit.*
4. T. Chandler and G. Fox, *3000 Years of Urban Growth*. New York, 1974.

received from Petty: 'our Lord Lieutenant accepted its design kindly from me, and said the book should be forthwith made; but I hear no more of it'. Nobody heard much more of it until the nineteenth century, when in 1801 the first population census was taken and official statistics began to get under way in Britain. But had Petty's advice been attended to we should have for the end of the seventeenth century the contents of a modern statistical abstract complete with national accounts, vital statistics and the kind of information to be expected from censuses of population, housing and production.

Knowing the reluctance of the majority to accept innovation it is perhaps not surprising that Petty's far-sighted schemes were ignored by the practical world, but it seems a sad waste of good ideas. His intellectual peers recognised his excellence but they were not the kind of people in whose hands the implementation of policy lay. His contributions to economic theory have had better fortune: some of his spiritual descendants, among them Marx and Keynes, have delved into his rich mine and come up with a few nuggets and there are signs that a more widespread awareness of his importance is now on its way, witness Alessandro Roncaglia's recent interesting study of Petty as a theorist.[1] I have chosen to concentrate on his empirical work, which strikes me as a shining illustration of Gertrude Stein's aphorism, 'to begin you have to begin'.

1. Alessandro Roncaglia, *Petty: la nascita dell'economia politica*. Etas, Milano, 1977; Engl. transl., *Petty: the Origins of Political Economy*, New York, 1985.

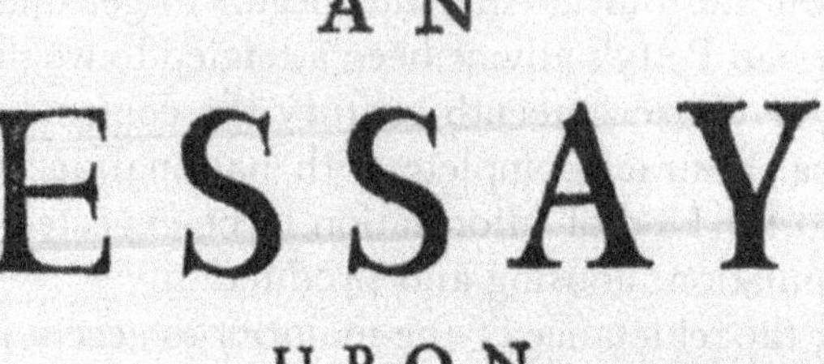

AN
ESSAY
UPON
Ways and Means
Of Supplying the
WAR.

The Second Edition.

LONDON:
Printed for *Jacob Tonson* at the *Judge's Head*, near the *Inner-Temple-Gate* in *Fleetstreet*. 1695.

Charles Davenant,
An Essay upon Ways and Means of Supplying the War.
Title page of the second edition, 1695.

CHAPTER 2

Charles Davenant and the Analysis of Taxes

1. Brief Life

Although Petty's proposals for economic policy, the relief of unemployment and the organisation of statistics were not acted upon by the politicians and administrators who alone could have put them into practice, his theories and his methods did not fall on barren ground. Political arithmetic became an established concept and found many advocates and one outstanding practioner in the younger generation. The practitioner was Gregory King, of whom I shall speak later. Among the advocates by far the most enthusiastic, fluent and persuasive was Charles Davenant, who did more than anyone else to keep the flag of political arithmetic flying.

Charles Davenant was born in London in 1656, the eldest son of the poet and playwright William D'Avenant, who was rumoured to be an illegitimate son of Shakespeare. William's mother, 'a very beautiful woman and of very good wit, and of conversation extremely agreeable', was married to an Oxford innkeeper, John D'Avenant, 'a very grave and discreet citizen'; and Shakespeare was in the habit of stopping at their inn on his journey between London and Stratford. William D'Avenant, who was very much a man of the theatre, did not mind being thought the bastard of such a father, in fact rather boasted of it. So, if we are to believe this typical bit of Aubrey gossip, Charles was Shakespeare's grandson. No wonder he became a writer and a prolific one at that, though his subject matter was very different from that of his father and putative grandfather.

Charles was educated at the grammar school of Cheam in Surrey and went up to Balliol College, Oxford, in 1671. He left without graduating in 1673, probably when he took over the management of his father's theatre, for which he wrote a play, *Circe*, and with which he remained associated until 1687. But his interest did not really lie in the theatre. In 1675 he obtained the degree of doctor of law 'by favour and money' – it is not sure from what university – and for a time practised law.

Things went well with him in the reigns of Charles II and James II, in whose first parliament he was member for St. Ives. From 1678 to 1689 he was commissioner of the excise, starting at a salary, of £500 a year which was raised to £1000 when tax farming was abolished and the collection of excise administered directly by the government. However, after the flight of James II and the advent of William and Mary he was not reappointed and held no official post in that reign, though he was again elected to parliament, this time for Great Bedwin, in 1698 and 1700. Politically he was not in sympathy with the new government. His polemical writings exposing ministerial abuses attracted a good deal of notice and provoked much public controversy. It was not until the reign of Queen Anne that he returned to government service, obtaining, first, a short-term post as secretary to the commissioners appointed to treat for a union with Scotland and, second, the position of inspector general of exports and imports, which he held at a salary of £1000 a year from 1705 until his death.

Davenant was married and had a son who followed a diplomatic career. This seems to have involved a financial drain on the father, who despite his not negligible salary ended his life largely dependent on the generosity of his friend James Brydges, later Duke of Chandos. He died in London on 6 November 1714. Further details about his life can be found in Watt[1] and in Waddell.[2]

2. *The Champion of Political Arithmetic*

Davenant was passionately interested in public policy and economic affairs and wrote extensively on taxation, war finance

1. Francis Watt, 'Charles Davenant'. *The Dictionary of National Biography*, vol. v, pp. 549-50.

2. D. A. G. Waddell, 'Charles Davenant - a biographical sketch'. *The Economic History Review*, 2nd ser., vol. xi, no. 2, 1958, pp. 279-88.

and foreign trade. He considered political arithmetic an indispensable tool for the policy-maker and his books are full of it. He was not very adept at figures, however, and left to himself his arithmetic would not have achieved the degree of consistency that Petty's did. Fortunately he had at his elbow Gregory King, who was a close friend of his and many of whose calculations he introduced, with due acknowledgements, into his own writings.

His *Discourses on the Publick Revenues, and on the Trade of England*, published in 1698, open with a discussion of Petty's work in which he gives his well-known definition: 'By political arithmetick we mean the art of reasoning by figures upon things relating to government'. He pays tribute to Petty for devising the name and being the first to bring this art 'into rules and method'; and, he continues,

'his excellent wit would have carried it very far if he had lived to this time; for his skilful hand did all along want right materials to work upon, with which he might have been furnished by the variety of new taxes that have been lately levied in this Kingdom.'

In all his enquiries Petty had taken as his guides the customs, excise and hearth money, but

'the accounts of those revenues were not fully stated and their produce was not known, at least to him, when his books were written. He endeavoured to compute the number of the people from the trade and consumption of the nation, into which the excise and customs were to give him an insight, and where the hearth-money might afford him yet better lights. He was to guess at our strength and wealth by the general stock employed in trade: and he might see a little into the quantity of money in the nation by the turnings it made into the exchequer in the payments of customs and excise; the number of houses in England showed him the number of families, from whence he was to gather how many inhabitants the Kingdom might contain.

But his chief schemes were calculated before the true produce of these three branches was fully known; for as to the excise, till the beginning of Mr. Vincent's farm, which was anno 1674, the farmers, in their several contracts, had never been obliged to give in a real state of their accounts and a true produce of the respective counties. And as to the hearth-money, its gross produce was likewise kept private till Mr.

Trant's farm (which began anno 1679) who was obliged by his contract to give it in. And we have yet never been able to meet with any true account of what the customs produced, till from the year 1671.

So that the very grounds upon which he built his calculations being probably wrong he must, in many instances, be mistaken in his superstructure; and the true produce of these branches being concealed from him, and indeed from everybody else but the parties concerned, in all likelihood he over-reckoned them in his mind and was thereby brought to over-rate the inhabitants of England and to under-rate the numbers and the strength and wealth of other countries: and this error in a fundamental, has led him into many others and has misled such as have followed him in these matters.

'Tis true, Sir William Petty had very much studied the Bills of Mortality, and the accounts of births and burials, not only in this Kingdom, but of other nations, which did certainly help him to very useful lights. But through the whole course of his writings it may be plainly seen, by any observing man, that he was to advance a proposition, not quite right in itself, but very grateful to those who governed.

The growth of the French king, and chiefly of his naval power, was a very unpleasant object for the Parliament, and the people of England to contemplate; and no doubt it did disquiet the mind of King Charles II. But this prince, delighted to be soothed in his ease and pleasures, and to have no anxious thoughts, was very glad to see one of Sir William Petty's repute for calculations of this nature, affirm, that France exceeded England very little in point of territory; that we came near 'em as to the numbers of men; and that our numbers were as effectual in point of strength; that the people of England had, head for head, thrice as much foreign trade, as the people of France; that France was under a natural and perpetual impediment of being powerful at sea; and, that the French had not above fifteen thousand seamen to manage their trade, out of which not above ten thousand could be spared for a fleet of war.

Every good Englishman does undoubtedly wish all this had been true; but we have lately had manifest proofs, that this great Genius was mistaken in all these assertions; for which reason we have grounds to suspect, he rather made his court, than spoke his mind.

The King was well pleased to be lulled asleep by a flattering council, which suggested, that the power of France was not so formidable, and could never be prejudicial to this Kingdom: for it excused his breach of the Triple Alliance, and all other measures which have since proved so pernicious to the interests of England.'

This is going a bit far. Petty can hardly be held responsible for Charles II's foreign policy. But Davenant was writing when England was smarting from a long and damaging war with France and seems to have forgotten that twenty-five years earlier, when Petty had made his estimates, France had not presented such an obvious threat. The enemy then was Holland, and Petty had certainly not under-estimated its resources.

In any case the fact that Petty had poor data and that many of his estimates were guesses and often biased guesses does not invalidate the usefulness of his method. To a statesman with the computing faculty, says Davenant, even a few data, provided they be reliable, can be quite revealing. In times of war, for instance, indicators such as population, trading activity and taxable capacity help to deduce the posture of allies and enemies alike. He continues:

'In the art of decyphering, 'tis said where three or four words, perhaps letters, can be found out, the whole cypher may be discovered; in a great measure, the same holds in the computations we are treating of: and very probable conjectures may be formed, where any certain footing can be found, to fix our reasonings upon.

This computing faculty may not only be useful to statesmen in the general and higher affairs, but it will likewise help them in the more subordinate and ministerial parts of government. It shall not only contribute to their well-guiding and conducting the nation's whole strength and wealth, trusted to their care; but if they rightly know how to reason upon things by figures, they shall commit very few errors in relation to their prince's revenues, or to the trade of the kingdom.

There are few places which afford better help for computation than England does at present. The excise is a measure by which we may judge not only of what the people consume, but, in some sort, it lets us into a knowledge how their numbers increase or diminish. The customs are the very pulse of a nation, from which its health, or decay, may be observed. The hearth-money has given us a view, certain enough, of the number of families, which is the very groundwork in such speculations; and these three revenues must be the better guide to computers, because the accounts of them are fairly kept and stated, and because the respective branches have been under so exact a management, that perhaps their utmost produce is known and understood.

The first poll tax, 1 Gul. & Mar., was paid with great alacrity and affection to the government, and very few avoided payment: so that from those books we may not only see the numbers, but divide the people into such proper classes and ranks, as may in a manner show the wealth and substance of the whole Kingdom . . .

The aid of 1 and 2 shillings per pound, in 1 Gul. & Mar., which was more carefully collected than any that has been since granted, has given a great insight into the rent of land and houses in England.

But as to the number of people, that matter is made yet clearer by the present duty on marriages, births and burials; and tho' the returns are very faulty and imperfect, Mr. Gregory King, by his general knowledge in political arithmetick, has so corrected these returns, as from thence to form a more distinct and regular scheme of the inhabitants in England, than peradventure was ever made concerning the people of any other country.

There is nothing of this kind 'scapes the comprehension and industry of that gentleman, who is a much better jewel to be in the cabinet of a statesman, than those wretched projectors and contrivers of deficient funds, who are always buzzing about the ministers. And the writer of these papers is desirous to take this occasion of owning himself obliged to that wonderful genius and master in the art of computing, for many lights and informations.'

This excursus in praise of King is followed by a long passage on the interpretation of data, ending with a list of the principles to be kept in mind by the political arithmetician:

'He who will pretend to compute, must draw his conclusions from many premises; he must not argue from single instances, but from a thorough view of many particulars; and that body of political arithmetick, which is to frame schemes reducible to practice, must be composed of a great variety of members.

He who will arrive at this art, must look into all the public revenues; he must understand something of their management; he must not be a stranger to the product and manufactures of every county and place; he must know what goods we export, and what foreign commodities are imported to us; and only from this general view, he must frame any scheme that may be useful to the public. A contemplation of one object, shall give him light into things perhaps quite of a different nature: for as in common arithmetick, one operation proves another; so in this art, variety of speculations are helpful and confirming to each other.

Nor is the faculty of computing less useful in matters relating to trade, than in what concerns the public revenues. The councils of a country are always inquisitive after truth, but to hide it from 'em, and to perplex things which have relation to trade, is the interest of so many, that in the greatest deliberations, wise men are often misled by such, as in all their actings, consult more their private profit than the common welfare.

There is hardly a society of merchants, that would not have it thought the whole prosperity of the kingdom depends upon their single traffic. There is hardly a commerce, but the dealers in it will affirm, we loose by all the rest. And yet 'tis evident, that in time of peace, the kingdom gets [gains] by trade in general.

A true account of the balance of trade would set all this aright, and show what traffics are hurtful, and what are beneficial to the nation; but probably this balance is no way to be found out, but by political arithmetick.

And perhaps this art alone can show the links and chains by which one business hangs upon another, and the dependence, which all our various dealings, have each upon the other.'

This, it seems to me, is a very good description of the data available at the time and of the problems facing the political arithmetician. Although the information existing today in most countries is vastly superior to what could be obtained three hundred years ago, anyone who has engaged in political arithmetick in the past generation will recognise the difficulty of prising information out of reluctant sources, the importance of economic interdependence, and the desirability of cross-checking by going at different totals from various points of view. The priorities and methodology sketched out by Davenant are sound and the main difference between him and us is that nowadays we start a bit higher up the scale than was possible for him.

After this introductory discourse the two volumes are largely concerned with Davenant's two favourite topics, public finance and the balance of trade. In the first volume he discusses credit, the administration and yield of each type of tax and the government debt. In the second he considers various aspects of foreign trade: how it increases wealth; what measures should be taken to protect it; and what shares our traffics with Europe, the western Plantations and the East India Company have in it.

He often mentions Petty and echoes many of his ideas. Like him, he draws frequent parallels with other countries; and after all his strictures on Petty's optimism it is amusing to find him in the second volume eagerly confuting, just as Petty had done a quarter of a century earlier, the prophets of doom who were seeking to show that the wealth and trade of England were in decline. As might be expected, he gives many numerical illustrations, often taken from other authors. Thus the estimates of foreign trade come from Fortrey[1] and the comparisons of income and expenditure in England, France and Holland from Gregory King, as we shall see later. On the other hand the figures for taxes appear to be mostly based on data collected by Davenant himself, often in the face of determined obstruction on the part of his colleagues in the civil service.

Davenant's work on taxes is his main contribution to the history of quantitative economics. When he wrote the *Discourses* he had already behind him his most interesting book on the subject, to which I shall now turn.

3. *The Regional Distribution of Taxes*

In 1695, three years before the appearance of the *Discourses*, Davenant had published a book entitled *An Essay upon Ways and Means of Supplying the War*. His motivation for writing it was the same as Petty's had been when he wrote *Verbum Sapienti*, namely to consider the best way of spreading the tax burden consequent on a war. The war in question was the War of the League of Augsburg and the enemy this time, as I have said, was France, England and Holland having sunk their differences in their common determination to resist the aggressive policies of Louis XIV. When Davenant published his *Essay* the war had been going on for six years and all sorts of expedients, fiscal and other, had been resorted to in order to finance it. Davenant examines each from three points of view: its effect on trade, its relative unpopularity and its regional distribution.

Many of his arguments anticipate what he said later in the *Discourses*. He thinks that as far as possible wars should be financed by taxation rather than by loans because public borrowing pushes up

1. SAMUEL FORTREY, *England's Interest and Improvement, Consisting in the increase of the Store and Trade of this Kingdom*. Cambridge, 1663.

the rate of interest and thus discourages trade. He thinks that poll taxes are so unpopular that even the tax farmers forbear to collect them, with the result that they yield much less than expected. He thinks it is a mistake to increase customs duties because, he says,

> ''tis now become indispensably our interest, to encourage foreign commerce and enlarge it as much as possible. Instead of loading that part of our strength, we ought to court it and nurse it with all imaginable art and care; 'tis a coy and fantastical lady, hard to win, and quickly lost.'

He thinks the poor rates are badly administered and are a sink of money which keeps the poor in idleness and would be much better employed in providing work for them. He thinks taxes on property, provided they be spread fairly, are a good source of revenue except that they lend themselves easily to evasion: they were generally assessed upon oath, 'but in matters of revenue, it has always been found that oaths are very little regarded'.

Above all, he thinks fairness and impartiality are the most important criteria of assessment. He discusses this at great length, tracing the origins of certain inequalities that persisted in his day though the reasons for them no longer obtained. Thus London and the ring of counties surrounding it were assessed relatively high and the rest of the country, especially the north and west, relatively low. This he attributes partly to the fact that London and the home counties, being under the eye of the government, were more easily controlled, and partly to a protective attitude towards the north and west that went back to the middle ages, when those regions were subject to depredations by the Scots and Welsh and incursions from the French; more recently they had also suffered from the Civil War more than the south-east had. But now circumstances had changed, the north and west had become more prosperous and there was no reason for this partiality.

He illustrates his discussion with a table in which he gives detailed estimates of the regional distribution of ten taxes from 1636 to the early 1690's. He provides information for England county by county and for Wales as a whole, adding three rows of subtotals, one for London, including Westminster and Middlesex, one for the eleven home counties and one for the rest of England and Wales. As a rough substitute for population he gives the number of houses as recorded in the Hearth Books of 1690, though he is aware that the size and distribution of the population had changed over the six decades covered by his table; and as a substitute for wealth he gives the number of hearths (or chimneys) at the same date. From this table I have derived my table 2.1.

In table 2.1 I have translated Davenant's figures into percentages in order to make his point clearer. I have also regrouped the counties according to his three main regions and rearranged the tax columns in chronological order. The first column relates to the ill-fated ship-money levied by Charles I. Davenant makes an interesting comment on this tax: in an effort to diminish its unpopularity the assessors had taken particular care to apportion it among the counties in as fair a manner as possible, 'for it would have been a double grievance to the people, if it had been imposed, both against the law and also with partiality'. So fair was their assessment thought to be that twenty-five years later it was taken as a model by the committee in charge of framing the first tax laws of Charles II's reign; the resulting apportionment is shown in the third column of the table. The fourth column shows the average annual yield of the poor rates towards the end of that reign. The next six columns are representative of the tax policies under William and Mary: there are two poll taxes, one excise and three 'aids', this term denoting a tax or complex of taxes voted to the king by parliament for some specific purpose and levied mainly on land.

Finally, the last two columns relate to houses and hearths in 1690 and give some indication of the standard of living in the different counties: the higher the ratio of hearths to houses the higher the standard. Davenant says in a later chapter that of the total of 1.3 million houses returned in the Hearth Books about half a million, or 38 per cent, were one-chimmey cottages whose inhabitants would be considered too poor to pay taxes. He does not give the regional distribution of these cottages but in view of his remark it might be supposed that tax yields would be roughly proportional to hearths, particularly for taxes levied around 1690. In fact this was not so. I have drawn some diagrams in which the proportion of hearths is plotted on the horizontal axis and the proportion of tax yields on the vertical. If the assessments were proportional to hearths each region would lie on the diagonal. A region lying above

Table 2.1

REGIONAL DISTRIBUTION OF TAXES, HOUSES AND HEARTHS IN ENGLAND AND WALES, 1636-1692

(percentages)

	Charles I		Charles II	
	Ship-money assessment	£ 400,000 assessment	£ 2 million apportionment (based on ship-money)	Poor r (annu averag
	1636-	1642-43	1660	c. 16
	a	b	c	d
1. London, Middlesex & Westminster	9.75	13.60	7.00	8.47
2-12. Home counties	27.93	33.28	31.29	32.18
2. Bedfordshire	1.45	1.08	1.4	1.04
3. Berkshire	1.93	1.40	1.7	1.47
4. Buckinghamshire	2.17	1.66	1.9	2.22
5. Cambridgeshire & Isle of Ely	1.69	2.11	1.8	1.37
6. Essex	3.87	4.48	4.8	5.6
7. Hertfordshire	1.93	1.87	1.8	1.62
8. Kent	3.87	5.23	4.8	4.49
9. Norfolk	3.77	6.07	4.8	6.94
10. Oxfordshire	1.69	1.59	1.7	1.19
11. Suffolk	3.87	5.11	4.8	3.87
12. Surrey & Southwark	1.69	2.68	1.8	2.34
13-39. Rest of England and Wales	62.32	53.12	61.71	59.35
13. Cheshire	1.45	0.79	1.4	0.87
14. Cornwall	2.66	2.51	2.4	1.39
15. Cumberland	0.39	0.16	0.4	0.75
16. Derbyshire	1.69	0.70	1.4	1.20
17. Devonshire	4.35	7.46	5.0	5.22
18. Dorsetshire	2.42	1.93	2.0	2.09
19. Durham, Northumberland & Berwick	1.11	0.59	1.4	2.05
20. Gloucestershire	2.66	2.75	2.5	2.95
21. Herefordshire	1.69	1.77	1.6	1.3
22. Huntingdonshire	0.97	0.88	0.9	0.88
23. Lancashire	0.48	1.08	1.6	1.08
24. Leicestershire	2.17	0.95	1.8	1.74
25. Lincolnshire	3.87	3.34	4.0	4.7
26. Northamptonshire	2.90	1.21	2.5	3.2
27. Nottinghamshire	1.69	0.75	1.4	1.7
28. Rutland	0.39	0.26	0.38	0.56
29. Shropshire	2.17	1.13	1.9	2.0
30. Staffordshire	1.45	0.95	1.4	1.0
31. Somersetshire & Bristol	4.35	4.42	4.25	4.55
32. Southamptonshire (Hampshire)	2.90	3.64	3.0	1.98
33. Sussex	2.42	2.71	2.6	2.8
34. Warwickshire	1.93	1.43	1.8	1.4
35. Westmoreland	0.29	0.14	0.3	0.2
36. Wiltshire	3.38	2.90	2.7	2.7
37. Worcestershire	1.69	1.53	1.8	1.6
38. Yorkshire	5.80	4.72	5.8	3.9
39. Wales	5.07	2.42	5.49	5.0
1-39. All England and Wales	100.00	100.00	100.00	100.0
Davenant's grand totals	£ 206 980	£ 403 160	£ 2 000 400	£ 665 3

* In summing the entries in this column Davenant made a mistake: their total is £ 298, 311 and I have calculated the percentages accordingly.

§ The correct total for this column is £ 1,566,647. The percentages are calculated accordingly.

Components do not always add up to totals because of rounding-off errors.

Source: Charles Davenant, *An Essay upon Ways and Means of Supplying the War*, 2nd edn, p. 76.

Taxes						Houses	Hearths (chimneys)
	William and Mary						
e poll	2nd & 3rd aids 1 & 2s. in the £	Excise on beer & ale	4th & 5th aids £ 137,642 monthly	Quarterly poll	6th & 7th aids 4s. in the £		
89	1689	1689	1690-91	1691-92	1692-	1690	
e	f	g	h	i	j	k	l
91	17.06	20.21	10.65	16.34	15.53	8.43	14.26
27	31.49	26.57	32.06	28.05	31.98	25.44	26.72
38	1.40	0.80	1.30	1.07	1.44	0.92	0.83
48	2.02	1.31	1.65	1.73	2.08	1.29	1.46
56	2.34	1.05	1.91	1.60	2.41	1.42	1.38
38	1.63	1.50	1.99	1.61	1.66	1.41	1.42
73	4.57	3.12	4.50	3.48	4.60	3.07	3.34
46	2.13	1.91	1.96	1.85	2.17	1.33	1.52
39	4.27	3.55	4.83	4.06	4.22	3.54	4.20
8	4.09	3.87	5.16	4.10	4.28	4.29	4.00
79	1.97	1.70	1.65	1.80	1.97	1.49	1.64
0	3.68	2.83	4.79	3.32	3.75	3.60	3.46
33	3.37	4.93	2.32	3.42	3.39	3.08	3.46
31	51.45	53.22	57.28	55.61	52.49	66.13	59.02
52	1.51	1.42	1.16	1.47	1.45	1.94	1.59
55	1.57	1.53	2.24	1.61	1.62	2.02	2.13
7	0.17	0.83	0.24	0.35	0.19	1.16	0.81
9	1.16	1.72	1.25	1.32	1.22	1.89	1.44
0	4.20	4.97	4.86	4.82	4.15	4.26	5.28
1	1.59	1.09	1.97	1.63	1.67	1.35	1.68
9	1.43	3.05	1.01	2.18	1.27	4.04	2.58
3	2.24	2.12	2.69	2.26	2.40	2.61	2.42
3	0.95	0.90	1.64	1.08	1.03	1.27	1.09
4	0.74	0.64	0.92	0.71	0.78	0.66	0.56
9	1.10	2.09	1.46	2.13	1.08	3.56	2.69
5	1.70	1.19	1.58	1.67	1.77	1.55	1.23
8	3.73	2.30	3.74	3.22	3.65	3.41	2.58
6	2.34	1.42	2.05	2.07	2.43	2.04	1.70
5	1.38	0.84	1.27	1.19	1.38	1.35	1.20
7	0.25	0.21	0.35	0.30	0.28	0.28	0.23
4	1.41	1.42	1.75	1.80	1.47	2.08	1.78
1	1.34	1.57	1.26	1.46	1.37	1.99	1.64
4	3.67	4.48	4.32	3.73	3.73	3.48	4.15
8	2.68	1.61	3.18	2.36	2.79	2.16	2.36
1	3.07	1.11	2.65	2.16	3.08	1.78	2.05
6	1.95	1.68	1.73	1.75	2.02	1.72	1.49
7	0.14	0.33	0.17	0.29	0.15	0.51	0.78
0	2.51	1.54	2.86	2.30	2.61	2.08	2.24
5	1.65	1.84	1.61	1.63	1.68	1.85	1.54
5	4.42	7.52	5.04	6.58	4.63	9.18	6.80
07	2.54	3.81	4.27	3.52	2.59	5.91	4.98
0	100.00	100.00	100.00	100.00	100.00	100.00	100.00
	£	£	£	£	£	Absolute numbers	
1*	1 566 628§	694 476	1 651 703	597 519	1 977 714	1 319 215	2 563 527

the diagonal might be considered to be over-assessed and one lying below the diagonal to be under-assessed. If a region, say London, had been growing relatively to the rest of the country one would expect it to lie below the line for a tax levied in say 1640, when its proportion of hearths would have been smaller than in 1690.

Diagram 2.1 shows the distribution of the ten taxes over the three major regional groups, which amply confirms Davenant's remarks about the erratic nature of some of the assessments. It is also consistent with the idea that London had been growing

Diagram 2.1

DISTRIBUTION OF DAVENANT'S TEN TAXES
OVER THE THREE MAJOR REGIONAL GROUPS
ENGLAND AND WALES, 1636-1692

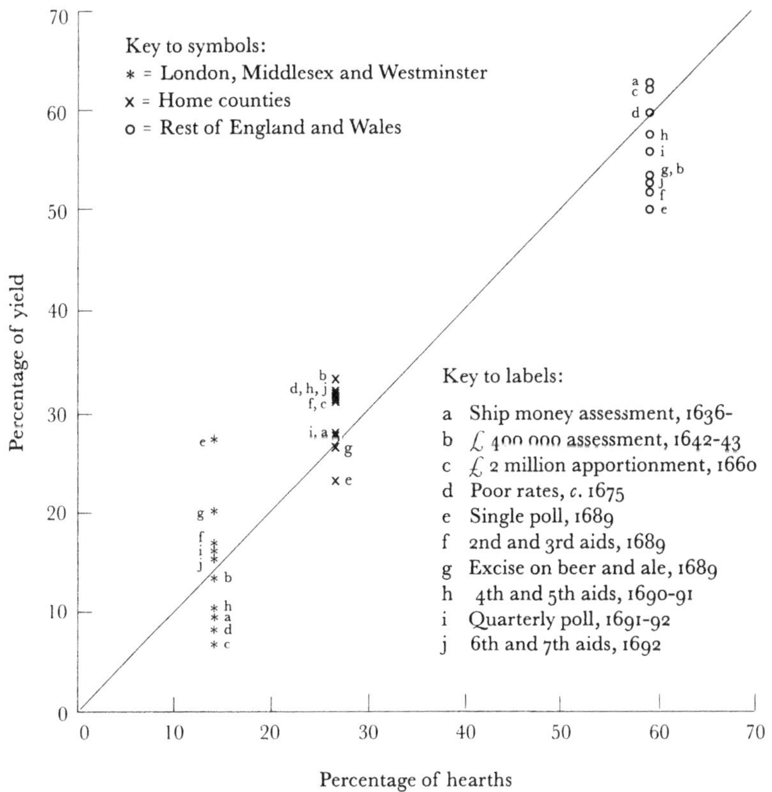

in relation to the rest of the country, since the lowest point on the scatter for London indicates a tax assessed in 1660, while the point for this tax in the other two regions lies above the line.

The next three diagrams show the county distribution of the three taxes levied in 1689, the first year of William and Mary's reign: the single poll tax, the second and third aids and the excise on beer and ale.

Diagram 2.2. relates to the poll tax. The point for London lies so high on the scale that it was not possible to include it in this

Diagram 2.2

COUNTY DISTRIBUTION OF THE SINGLE POLL TAX

ENGLAND AND WALES, 1689

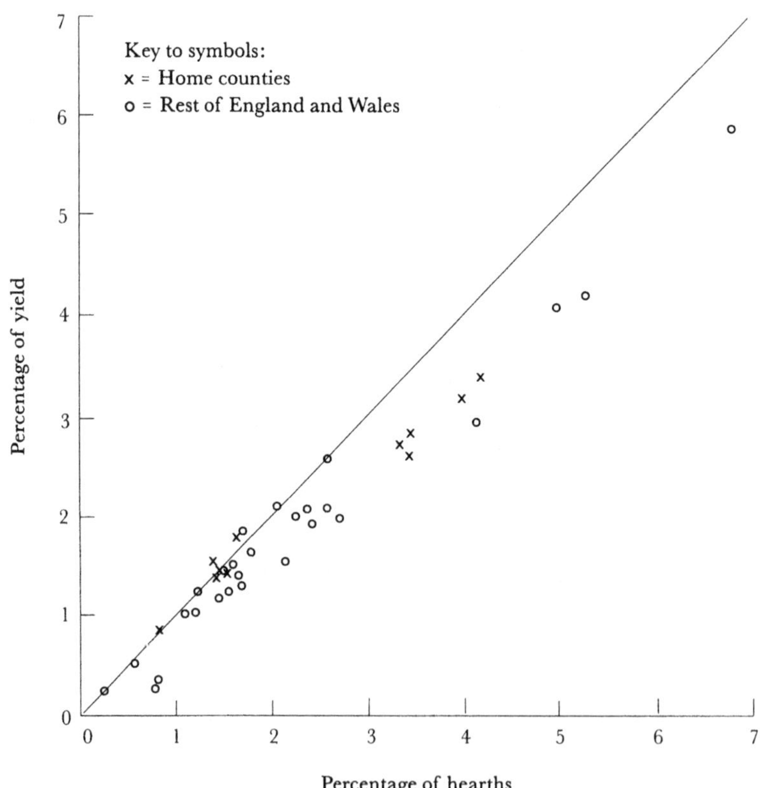

diagram but its position in relation to that of other taxes can be seen in diagram 2.1. Over and above the basic rate to be paid by all but the poorest, individuals were also assessed on their social status and wealth, so it is not surprising to find London, the place with the highest concentration of important and rich people, paying a very high proportion of this particular tax. These assessments were not mutually exclusive and an individual might find himself taxed under several heads. An actual instance of how heavily 'titles and offices' could be hit by a poll tax is given us by Pepys, who in 1667, when he was Clerk of the Acts to the Navy Office at a salary of £300 a year, had to pay about £50, he tells us, 'as an Esquire and for my office'. No wonder honours were not always accepted. Petty, as we know, twice declined a peerage; it would have added little to his social position, nothing to his self-esteem and less than nothing to his purse. Such refusals, however, were not always made with impunity: when Evelyn's father, under Charles I, declined a knighthood he was made to pay a fine of £50.

In contrast with London the country districts are let off very lightly: of the eleven home counties seven are below the line, and of the remaining twenty-seven, twenty-two are below it, some strikingly so. Again this is not surprising if we listen to Davenant:

> 'There is nothing can make it better apparent how displeasing poll-money is to the people, than the observation how ill it is brought in and answered to the King. For where taxes seem hard and oppressive, in particular to the poor, the country gentlemen proceed in the levying of them with no zeal or affection.'

Despite the unpopularity of poll taxes, however, the response to this one was exceptionally good. The reason was political. The troubled reign of James II had foundered on the rocks of religious intolerance. He had sought by high-handed methods to re-establish Roman catholicism in England, but England would have none of it. James, daughter Mary was a good sober anglican who could be trusted to steer a middle course between the extremes of popery on the one hand and fanatical presbyterianism on the other. Her husband William of Orange was just the man that was wanted to subdue the rebellious Irish and defend England from Louis XIV's attempts to restore James II. So the first poll tax of their reign was paid 'with great alacrity and affection to the government, and very few avoided payment', as Davenant himself says in the *Discourses*.

In the quarterly poll of 1691 the basic rate was quadrupled, rank was assessed less heavily and wealth was not taxed at all, so the tax was spread more evenly between London and the rest of the country; on the other hand the number of poor people exempted was much higher. The result, according to Davenant, was a yield of about half what could have been expected.

To continue with our diagrams. Diagram 2.3 shows the county distribution of the second and third aids. This is the double tax of 1 and 2 shillings in the pound mentioned by Davenant as having been 'more carefully collected than any that has been granted since' and providing 'a great insight into the rent of houses and land in England'. Its pattern suggests that the proportion of exemptions in the north and west was even higher than it had been in the poll tax: the great majority of the outlying counties appear under-assessed while all the home counties except one appear over-assessed. London is again out of the picture because of the high density of housing and the high value of rents; its position can be seen in diagram 2. 1.

Finally, diagram 2.4 relates to the excise on beer and ale and illustrates another source of variation in tax yield, which in this case depended not only on the amount of beer drunk but also on the amount of home brewing, which did not pay tax. No doubt the facilities for home brewing varied from region to region and were more widespread in rural than in urban districts: 'In London, almost all pay excise for their drink', says Davenant. Home brewing increased greatly during the war of the 1690's and Gregory King shows in his *Observation*[1] how much this affected the tax yield.

1. GREGORY KING, *Natural and Politicall Observations and Conclusions upon the State and Condition of England* (ed. G. E. Barnett), p. 40. See ch. 3 below for fuller bibliography.

Diagram 2.3

COUNTY DISTRIBUTION OF THE 2nd AND 3rd AIDS
ENGLAND AND WALES, 1689

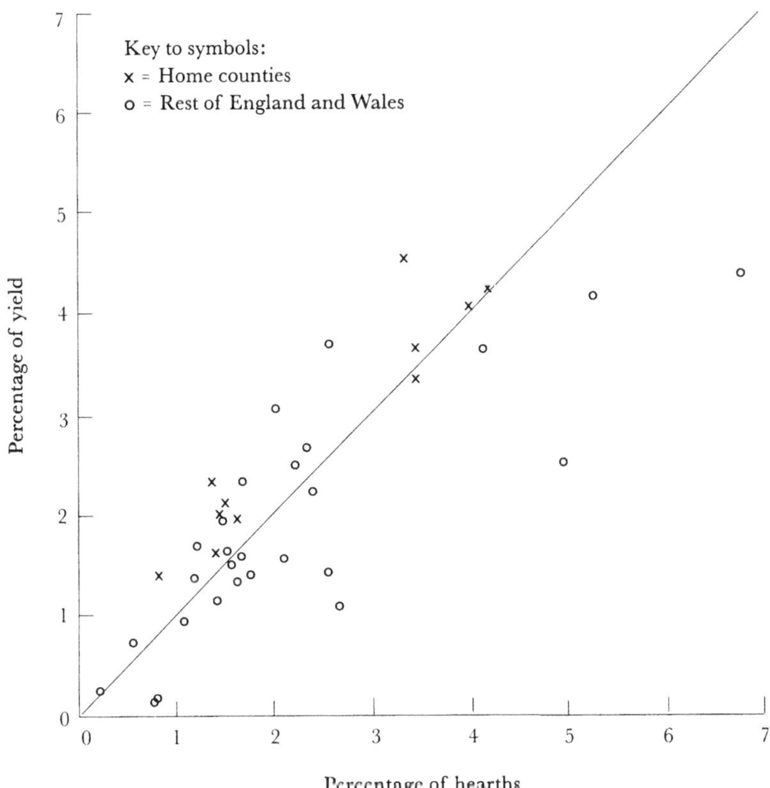

Diagram 2.4
COUNTY DISTRIBUTION OF THE EXCISE ON BEER AND ALE
ENGLAND AND WALES, 1689

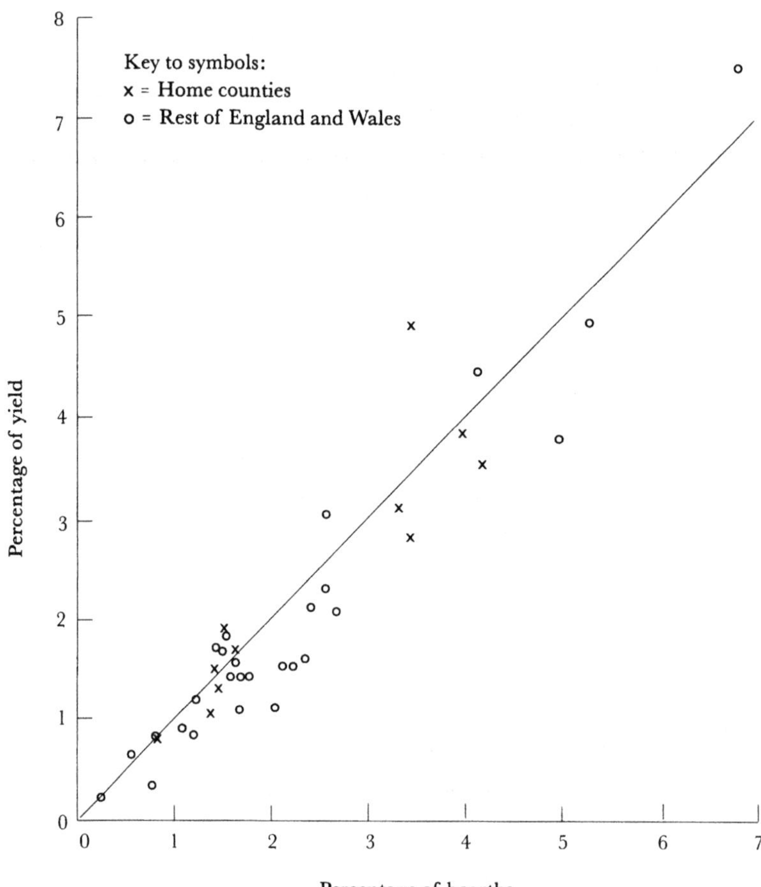

Davenant concludes this chapter by considering tax packages suitable for financing a long war. He suggests that

'a mixed aid, by a pound rate upon land and money, and by a quarterly poll, all carefully levied, might raise

by four shillings, pound rate, upon land	£3·0 million
by four shillings, pound rate, upon money	£0.2 million
by a quarterly poll	£0.5 million
Total	£3·7 million

which without any new *Ways and Means* would come very near raising that sum to which the expense of the war, has hitherto amounted.'

When all is said and done, however, he thinks that the best way of paying for the war is to broaden the range of excise and devotes his last chapter to a demonstration of this. Excise taxes are easy to pay and easy to collect. If properly graded they spread the tax burden over all sections of the community in proportion to their means. To counteract the adverse effect they may have on farmers and manufacturers by raising the price of commodities he advocates stricter control of the distributors, whose 'immoderate and unlawful gains' keep prices artificially high even in times of plenty. Retail prices should be kept in line with producers' prices, weights and measures regulated and any attempt at distorting the market severely penalised. Great care should be taken to avoid that the poor suffer. He discusses which commodities should be charged and which exempted and the criteria to be followed in fixing the rates of tax. Luxuries of course should be charged at very high rates, which incidentally might have salutary moral and physical consequences. Above all he would like to see brandy taxed out of existence; it discourages the consumption of other, less harmful drinks, destroys the appetite and thus hits at food production, and affects human fertility:

''Tis a growing vice among the common people and may, in time, prevail as much as opium with the Turks, to which many attribute the scarcity of people in the East. There is no way to suppress the use of it so certain, as to lay such a high duty, as it may be worth no man's while to make [? take] it, but for medicine.'

We may not like to follow Davenant all the way in his reforming zeal but we can agree with the gist of his argument, which he recapitulates at the end of the book. He is against loans. He does not want to see landowners over-taxed and does not want to force taxes on the poor beyond the amount they tax themselves by buying taxed commodities. On the other hand he would like to tax heavily the usurers, 'the true drones of the commonwealth, living upon the honey without any labour', and would like to arrange matters so that some taxes fell on various kinds of middlemen rather than on the producer or the consumer. And he wants to see the tax burden lightened as soon as the war is over because heavy taxation impoverishes a country and leads to disaffection and civil strife. In the never-ending debate about taxation his programme does not seem to me one of the worst.

4. Other Works

Davenant's third substantial book on economic matters is *An Essay upon the Probable Methods of Making a People Gainers in the Ballance of Trade*, published in 1699. Most of the political arithmetic in this book, however, is taken from King's *Observations*, so here I shall only touch on one point. In chapter III on the land of England and its product he sets out the demand schedule for corn usually referred to as 'Gregory King's law'. Some people consider that Davenant's part in the formulation of the law has been under-rated; I am inclined to think that the concept of the law was King's though I expect he discussed it with his friend Davenant, just as I believe that Graunt wrote the book generally attributed to him though I expect he discussed it with his friend Petty. However that may be, I shall deal with it when I come to Gregory King.

Davenant also wrote a pamphlet on the East India trade[1] in

1. *An Essay on the East India Trade*. Knapton, London, 1696; reprinted in C. WHITWORTH (ed.), *The Political and Commercial Works of Charles Davenant*, 5 vols., London, 1771.

which he opposed the protection of English textiles against Indian textiles on the ground that trade with India improved England's balance of trade. It is a well-written and persuasive essay though it does not provide much scope for calculations.

I have concentrated on the works of Davenant that are related to political arithmetic. He also wrote a large number of books and pamphlets of a purely political nature but these lie outside my field of interest. A collection of his writings both economic and political was edited by Whitworth in 1771.[1] More recently two unpublished manuscripts by him have been brought to light by Usher[2] and his work has been discussed by Waddell,[3] Coombs[4] and Hume.[5]

Davenant's contribution to political arithmetic, though not original, was invaluable. Without his 'zeal and affection' Petty's ideas might not have borne fruit and King's calculations never seen the light. His ability was not of the first order, but as he says himself in the *Discourses*,

'there is in this art a sphere for lower capacities to move in, who can presume no further than to find out and prepare materials to be made use of by abler hands, and who think it praise enough to them, if they can make tools for skilful artists to work withal: and of this rank is the writer of these papers'.

Such self-effacement is as endearing as it is rare.

1. C. Whitworth (ed.), *op. cit.*

2. A. P. Usher (ed.), *Two Manuscripts by Charles Davenant*: 'A Memoriall Concerning the Coyn of England' (1695) and 'A Memoriall Concerning Creditt' (1696). Johns Hopkins Press, Baltimore, 1942.

3. D. A. G. Waddell, 'The writings of Charles Davenant', *The Library*, 5th ser., no. 11, 1956, pp. 206-12; Id 'Charles Davenant and the East india Company', *Economica*, new ser., no. 23, 1956, pp. 261-4; Id 'Charles Davenant'. *International Encyclopaedia of the Social Sciences*, Macmillan and Free Press, 1968, vol. 4, pp. 14-16.

4. D. Coombs, 'Dr. Davenant and the debate on Franco-Dutch trade'. *The Economic History Review*, vol. 11, no. 10, 1957, pp. 94-103.

5. Leonard J. Hume, 'Charles Davenant on financial administration'. *History of Political Economy*, Winter 1974, vi (iv), pp. 463-77.

Gregory King, Rouge Dragon Pursuivant

CHAPTER 3

Gregory King and the Development of Economic Statistics

1. Brief Life

Economists, as I have said elsewhere, come in three types: the speculative, who construct theories; the active, who want to apply them; and the inquisitive, who want to test them. Petty was one of the rare cases in which all three are combined, Davenant was an activist and Gregory King was preeminently an inquirer. He processed vast quantities of data, both economic and demographic, and carried the practice of statistics to a high degree of sophistication apparently for his own amusement. He published none of his political arithmetic and had it not been for Davenant his work would have lain in archival obscurity until it was partially exhumed by Chalmers at the beginning of the nineteenth century. King himself, though he wrote an autobiography that covers three quarters of his life, is silent on the subject. And it is only recently, with the publication of his *Notebook* by Laslett, that the thoroughness of his enquiries and his technical inventiveness have been fully revealed.

Gregory King was born at Lichfield on 15 December 1648. His father, a surveyor and landscape gardener, had studied mathematics 'but with more attention to good fellowship than mathematical studies generally allow'. He was a good father, however, interested in his son's education, and Gregory says in his autobiography that he learnt as much from him as he did from his schoolteachers. At the age of two the child was sent to an infants' school where he learnt to read. At four he contracted some form of paralysis which luckily did not affect his intellect and from which he had recovered by the time he was six. He was then sent to the Free School at Lichfield, which he left at fourteen knowing Latin, Greek and Hebrew grammar and having at the same time acquired some mathematics from his father, who used him as an assistant in his surveying work.

Gregory was a bright boy and his precocity at learning was enhanced by the fact that he was very small for his age, possibly owing to his early illness. At school he seems to have been regarded as something between a genius and a mascot. On leaving school at the end of 1662 he became clerk to Sir William Dugdale, the antiquary and herald, at that time Norroy King at Arms. Dugdale liked his little clerk, who accompanied him on his visitations and was good at emblazoning armorial bearings on vellum and delineating 'the prospects of towns, castles and other remarquables'; he kept him four years in his service, inducted him into the methods of genealogical research and remained all his life a generous and dependable patron. In 1667 Gregory passed into the employment of Dugdale's friend Lord Hatton, who was forming a collection of the arms of the nobility, but in 1669 this project folded up and the young man returned to Lichfield. For a few months he earned his living by teaching writing and arithmetic, painting hatchments and coaches and giving instruction in the decypherment of ancient records, and then got a job as steward, auditor and secretary to the dowager Lady Gerard.

In 1672 he moved to London, which offered more scope for his many skills. Helped by an introduction from Dugdale to the famous engraver Hollar, he soon found plenty of work as a draughtsman, surveyor and map-maker. He was employed by John Ogilvy, the printer and publisher, on the production of some of his illustrated books and did the surveying for the great map of London which was subsequently engraved by Hollar. London was growing fast at that time, mostly westwards from the City, and King was also involved in the development of Soho Fields. Indeed the plan of the Soho of our day is his creation: he laid out its streets and squares and it is said that Greek Street is nothing but a corruption of 'Grig Street', after Gregory.

All this was useful to keep the wolf from the door but was not where King's real interest and ambition lay. Through Dugdale he was known and appreciated in heraldic circles and that was where he hoped to make a career for himself. His hopes were eventually fulfilled. He was called in to assist Francis Sandford, one of the heralds, in the compilation of his *Genealogical History of the Kings of England* and in 1677 succeeded him as Rouge Dragon Pursuivant in the College of Arms.

At first his emoluments as a herald were so meagre that he could not afford to give up his surveying. In 1674 he had got married and his wife brought him some money which he invested in house property, but as he says in his autobiography 'the continual care of his relations . . . joined to a generous way of living to which both his own and his wife's inclinations led them . . . kept him from laying up anything considerable'. Gradually, however, things improved. In 1680 he was given lodgings in the College of Arms, in 1684 he was made Registrar and in 1689 became Lancaster Herald, an office which carried with it many lucrative assignments.

King was obviously very proud of his position and relished its ceremonial side. At state functions such as the coronation of William and Mary he played his part to everybody's satisfaction, and between 1689 and 1693 was three times sent abroad to confer the Garter on foreign potentates. The last of these missions was to the Elector of Brandenburg, and on that occasion he was presented with '50 pieces of gold purposely coined, each of the value of 10 ducats, in an imbroidered crimson velvet purse, and in another curious purse of nuns' work 200 ducats as a compositition for his habit'. Unfortunately in January 1695 he was drawn into a dispute with the Earl Marshal over the arrangements for the funeral of Queen Mary and dismissed from the office of Registrar, though he retained his position as Lancaster Herald.

His autobiography stops here. We know, however, that in 1695 he was one of the commissioners in charge of the new tax on marriages, births and burials, in which capacity he issued for the use of tax collectors and taxpayers a broadsheet showing the rates of duty to be paid by individuals in the various ranks of society;[1] that between 1702 and 1712 he was alternately Secretary to the Commission of Public Accounts and Secretary to the Controllers of Army Accounts; and that in 1708 he was one of the three commissioners appointed to state the debts of King William III.

1. *A Scheme of the Rates and Duties Granted to His Majesty upon Marriages, Births and Burials, and upon Batchelors and Widowers, for the Term of Five Years, from May I. 1695.* Bill and Newcomb, London, 1695.

At the same time he kept up his connection with the College of Arms and in 1710 applied for the patent of Clarenceux King at Arms. By now he was one of the foremost genealogists of his day, in some people's opinion second only to Dugdale. Nevertheless to his great mortification Sir John Vanbrugh, the architect and playwright, who was a stranger to the College and knew nothing about heraldry, was preferred to him. As Chalmers puts it, 'Vanbrugh's wit, I fear, prevailed over King's arithmetic'.

King was twice married, the second time in 1701. He had three children by his second marriage but they all predeceased him. He died on 29 August 1712, leaving his widow in easy circumstances and bequeathing 'many legacies to his relations, to whom he was always kind, and to his friends, to whom he was ever obliging'. Further details about his life can be found in his autobiography[1] and in Chalmers,[2] Glass[3] and Cooper.[4]

2. *The Political Arithmetician*

The fact that King's autobiography breaks off in 1695 is particularly tantalising in my context because it is around this time that he seems to have turned his attention seriously to political arithmetic. Actually his first known statistical exercises are so sophisticated that it is obvious that he had already acquired some practice in this kind of work before he embarked on them. All the more surprising that he never mentions the subject in his account of his life.

The *Notebook* edited by Laslett, often referred to as 'the Burns Journal',[5] consists of about three hundred pages of closely

1. *Vitae Gregorij King Fecialis Armorum primo Rouge Dragon titulo deinde Lancastriensis occursus praecipui* (c. 1695). MS, Bodleian Library, Rawlinson C. 514; first printed in J. Dallaway, *Inquiries into the Origin and Progress of the Science of Heraldry*, Gloucester, 1793.

2. GEORGE CHALMERS, *An Estimate of the Comparative Strength of Great Britain. A New Edition... to which is now annexed Gregory King's Celebrated State of England*. Stockdale, London, 1804.

3. D. V. GLASS, 'Two papers on Gregory King'. In *Population in History* (eds D. V. Glass and D. E. C. Eversley), Arnold, London, 1965.

4. THOMPSON COOPER, 'Gregory King'. *The Dictionary of National Biography*, vol. XI, pp. 131-3.

5. GREGORY KING, *Notebook* ('The Burns Journal'). MS *c.* 1695, Greater London Record Office; facsimile in *The Earliest Classics - John Graunt - Gregory King* (ed. P. Laslett), Gregg International, 1973.

packed statistical material, both economic and demographic, and seems to belong almost entirely to the year 1695. For other years there are a few smaller miscellaneous notebooks and diaries containing the occasional set of data or page of calculations, some loose worksheets and a number of letters to various correspondents discussing points of political arithmetic. Taken all together, King's working papers and letters offer the historian a marvellous hunting ground that is still far from having been completely explored.

As to his 'finished' productions I know of only four, of varying importance, all dating from 1696 and 1697. The first is the *Natural and Politicall Observations Upon the State and Condition of England*, of which there are two manuscript copies extant; one is dated 1696;[1] the other, with marginal comments by Harley and answers by King defending the accuracy of his estimates, bears also the date 1697.[2] The *Observations* are King's most famous contribution to political arithmetic; though they were not published *in toto* in his lifetime, Davenant made them widely known by incorporating many of the calculations in his *Discourses*.

The second and third are two 'schemes' or tables which King submitted to the Board of Trade, one in September 1696 on the population of Gloucester[3] and the other in September 1697 on the hospitals and almshouses of England.[4] And the fourth, also dated 1697, is the short but very informative tract *Of the Naval Trade of England A° 1688 and the National Profit Then Arising Thereby*,[5] of which Davenant, again, made extensive use in the *Discourses*.

This is the sum total of King's known output as a political arithmetician, which I shall discuss in this chapter and in chapter 7 below. But before doing so I shall try to answer some

1. MS in British Library, Harley Mss 1898. First published as Appendix I in G. Chalmers, *op. cit.*; reprinted in *Two Tracts by Gregory King* (ed. G.E. Barnett), Johns Hopkins Press, Baltimore, 1936; facsimile in *The Earliest Classics* (ed. P. Laslett).

2. 'The Kashnoor MS', National Library of Australia.

3. *A Scheme of the inhabitants of the City of Gloucester* (1696). First published as Appendix II in G. Chalmers, *op. cit.*

4. *A Computation of the Endowed Hospitals and Alms -houses in England* (1697). First published as Appendix III in G. Chalmers, *op. cit.*

5. MS copy (undated), Bodleian Library, Rawlinson D919. First printed in *Two Tracts by Gregory King* (ed. G. E. Barnett).

questions it is natural to ask about King and his work: what led him to devote so much ingenuity and energy to the construction of elaborate tables of economic and demographic magnitudes; and why, having done so, did he never publish any of them.

From a perusal of his *Notebook* it seems clear that he was fascinated by numbers and their manipulation; so it may be that the first impulse came from a desire to spend his time agreeably on a new subject that was in the air. He had an inquisitive mind, as I have said, witness the aphorism from La Rochefoucauld which he inscribed on the fly-leaf of the *Notebook*:

'Pour bien savoir les choses, il faut savoir le détail, et comme il est presque infiny nos connaissances sont toujours superficielles et imparfaites.'

And having examined the estimates of Petty and the other early political arithmeticians he was not satisfied with them and thought he could do better.

But there is something else. When King undertook his work, England was engaged in a major war, and as a herald and public servant he was known in the corridors of power. It does not seem fanciful to suggest, as Laslett does, that he may have been invited to report on the economic conditions of the country and that the *Observations* and the *Naval Trade* were in effect State papers. This would account for the fact that they were not published though they were made available for quotation by Davenant.

I have given a conjecture as to why King may not have felt free to publish his estimates at the time he wrote them. But again there are other considerations. Davenant was a friend and also a publicist, and King may have been one of those people who prefer to remain in the background, an *éminence grise*, and allow others to undertake the work of publicity and public argument. Furthermore he was a busy man, with many other things to do, and may have preferred to spend his spare time making new calculations rather than writing up the old ones for the press. Data processing is time-consuming and King had no electronic machines to help him.

3. Sources and Methods

Another question one asks oneself is, how did King, given the conditions of statistics in his day, manage to produce his elaborate and consistent schemes. Again there is no simple answer. He obviously had access to tax returns, partly directly, partly through Davenant and partly perhaps through his own brother Thomas King, who was employed in the Excise Office. From the Hearth Office he would have got some assessments of houses and people on which to base his population estimates. Poll taxes and marriage, birth and death duties would give an indication of the socio-economic distribution of income. Land tax and excise returns, supplemented by what he may have observed in the course of his heraldic visitations, would give him data on agriculture and brewing. And customs duties would provide data on foreign trade.

Occasionally he would collect his own data, as when he made a house-by-house survey of the inhabitants of 'the Uplands in Southweald parish, Essex' or recorded the number of patients in St. Bartholomew's Hospital at a particular date. Occasionally he enlisted the help of friends, as when he wrote to George Stepney, English envoy to 'the Princes on the Rhine', for any information he could get on the land area of those principalities. Occasionally there would be a windfall of specialised data, such as the detailed breakdown of expenditure on clothing in 1688 which he wrote out on p. 203 of the *Notebook* and which can hardly be the product of his own imagination. But he must have relied to a large extent on his power of estimation based on a wide acquaintance with all kinds and conditions of man and a good understanding of how national accounting magnitudes should fit together.

An illustration of his method is provided in the *Notebook* by his estimates of consumers' expenditure in 1688, which are summarised in table 3.1 below. In this table the population is divided into twelve groups defined according to their average annual expenditure per head, the averages ranging from just under £3 to £1000. There are three main categories of expenditure: food and drink, clothing, and other expenses. Food and drink is subdivided into eight items, starting with bread and cereal products and ending with wine and spirits. Clothing and other expenses are not subdivided. There is evidence in the *Notebook* of a great deal of experimental calculation but the order of the operations can only be surmised.

Having reached, by means that I shall describe in chapter 7, an estimate of the total population but not of its distribution over expenditure groups, his next task was to form that distribution. He realised there were a great many poor and very few rich, so that the distribution would be highly skewed to the right: the numbers in each of his twelve groups drop rapidly as we go from the 2.25 million very poor who spend less than £3 per annum to the 40,000 fairly comfortably-off who spend £65, at which point the curve flattens out until it reaches the hundred very rich who spend £1000.

The next step was to work out the details. Although in his table total consumption per head is expressed in approximate terms, 'almost £3', 'about £9', 'above £42' and so on, King is quite precise in valuing its components: expenditure per head on all food and drink is given as an exact number of pounds; for clothing and other expenses shillings enter into some of the averages; and for the components of food and drink he finds it necessary to go down to pence. Thus his estimates look as if they were based on a very complete family expenditure survey which covered the very rich as well as the middle classes and the poor. But I think we can rule this out.

He probably started with the series of per head expenditures on all food and drink shown in the lower half of table 3.1: a simple progression of integers, £2, £3, £4 and so on, which he then subdivided into their component items. By multiplying these figures by the number of people in each group he obtained the groups' expenditures on food and drink. For clothing he used the table of 'the annual consumption of apparell A° 1688' which I mentioned above; it contains the prices, quantities and values of forty items and the values of four more. This gave him a total of about £10.4 million which he adjusted to £9.68 million before distributing it as seemed appropriate over the twelve groups. For other expenses

Table 3.1

'THE EXPENCE OF THE PEOPLE OF ENGLAND IN DYET, APPAREL AND INCIDENT CHARGES'

(*c.* 1688)

Population grouped by range of expenditure per head		Goods and services											
		Bread, cakes etc.	Milk, butter & cheese	Fruit & vegetables	Meat	Fish, poultry & eggs	Salt, oil, spices, sweets etc.	Beer & ale	Wines & spirits	All food & drink	Clothing & footwear	All other*	Totals
Serial no. of group	Number of people	Expenditure per group (£'000)											
1.	2 250 000	2 250	843.75	393.75	281.25	225	112.5	337.5	56.25	4 500	1 200	800	6 500
2.	1 200 000	1 380	570	300	390	240	150	420	150	3 600	1 600	1 300	6 500
3.	800 000	1 020	460	260	420	240	160	440	200	3 200	1 200	1 100	5 500
4.	500 000	700	325	200	362.5	200	137.5	387.5	187.5	2 500	1 000	1 000	4 500
5.	300 000	442.5	225	150	270	150	105	300	157.5	1 800	1 100	1 100	4 000
6.	200 000	320	200	140	245	155	100	280	160	1 600	900	1 000	3 500
7.	120 000	201	156	114	180	132	84	207	126	1 200	900	1 100	3 200
8.	80 000	146	170	116	180	164	108	192	124	1 200	900	1 300	3 400
9.	40 000	80	120	80	120	120	80	120	80	800	600	1 200	2 600
10.	9 000	20.25	33.75	22.5	45	45	27	36	40.5	270	200	530	1 000
11.	900	2.7	6.3	9	18	22.5	9	9	31.5	108	65	275	448
12.	100	0.4	1	3	4	7	3	1.6	10	30	15	55	100
1 to 12.	5 500 000	6 562.85	3 110.80	1 788.25	2 515.75	1 700.5	1 076.0	2 730.6	1 323.25	20 808	9 680	10 760	41 248
Serial no. of group	Percentage of total	Average expenditure per head (£)											
1.	40.91	1.0	0.375	0.175	0.125	0.1	0.05	0.15	0.025	2.0	0.53	0.35	2.8
2.	21.82	1.15	0.475	0.25	0.325	0.2	0.125	0.35	0.125	3.0	1.3	1.085	5.416
3.	14.55	1.275	0.575	0.325	0.525	0.3	0.2	0.55	0.25	4.0	1.5	1.375	6.875
4.	9.09	1.4	0.65	0.4	0.725	0.4	0.275	0.775	0.375	5.0	2.0	2.0	9.0
5.	5.45	1.475	0.75	0.5	0.9	0.5	0.35	1.0	0.525	6.0	3.6	3.6	13.3
6.	3.64	1.6	1.0	0.7	1.225	0.775	0.5	1.4	0.8	8.0	4.5	5.0	17.5
7.	2.18	1.675	1.3	0.95	1.5	1.1	0.7	1.725	1.05	10.0	7.5	9.16	26.6
8.	1.45	1.825	2.125	1.45	2.25	2.05	1.35	2.4	1.55	15.0	11.25	16.25	42.5
9.	0.73	2.0	3.0	2.0	3.0	3.0	2.0	3.0	2.0§	20.0	15.0	30.0	65.0
10.	0.16	2.25	3.75	2.5	5.0	5.0	3.0	4.0	4.5§	30.0	22.2	58.8	111.1
11.	0.02	3.0	7.0	10.0	20.0	25.0§	10.0	10.0	35.0§	120.0	72.2	305.5	497.7
12.	0.00	4.0	10.0	30.0	40.0	70.0	30.0	16.0	100.0	300.0	150.0	550.0	1000.0
1 to 12.	100.00	1.193	0.566	0.325	0.457	0.309	0.196	0.496	0.241	3.783	1.76	1.956	7.5

* Including consumers' durables and direct taxes.

§ Adjusted to agree with King's row total.

Notes: Shillings and pence have been converted to decimals of £.

Components do not always add up to totals because of rounding - off errors.

In this and subsequent tables England must be understood to include Wales.

Source: Gregory King, *Notebook*, p. 210.

he made a list of fourteen items 'relating to consumption only': eight types of good ranging from household durables to tobacco, pipes and snuff; five types of service including schooling of children and travelling; and one type of tax. The expenditure on durables includes their 'decay' or depreciation. Against most though not all of these items he put a round estimate of its total value, reaching a grand total of £11 million which he reduced to £10.76 million in making his distribution over the groups.

However reached, the results are plausible. Per head, the rich do not spend much more than the poor on bread but they spend very much more on wine and spirits. Expenditure on all food and drink is more evenly distributed than total expenditure. Clothing, on the other hand, is somewhat less evenly distributed than the total, but the Lorentz curves for these two series cross over at the extreme top-end of the range. The most uneven distribution occurs in other expenses, which of course would include a wide range of luxury goods lying outside the reach of the great majority of people. Total expenditure Engel curves show an elasticity of about 0.2 for bread, 0.8 for food and drink, 0.9 for clothing and 1.3 for other expenses.

These results suggest to me that King, in addition to having a good knowledge of the world, derived great strength from his practice of making detailed classifications and satisfying himself that the resulting numbers made reasonable sense in relation to each other. Thus instead of trying to guess the total expenditure of his population of 5.5 million, he divided this into the equivalent of twelve income groups, and their expenditures into ten commodity groups. In this way he got much nearer to items one could hope to know about. One could estimate what the average labourer consumed in the way of bread or dairy products or beer and what the average civil servant spent on clothing or furniture because one knew a number of labourers and civil servants. One also knew a few peers and rich landowners and could form an idea of what their standard of living would cost to maintain. Of course one's sample might not be representative but there was not much to be done about that. Without aiming at strict accuracy one could hope to talk sense, and the approach I have attributed to King would have been very helpful to that end.

Another example of King's method is his analysis of the poll tax of 1689. We have already met this tax in Davenant's discussion of the regional distribution of taxes and we know from him that the response to it was exceptionally good. As a consequence the returns provided a pretty full record of the socioeconomic composition of the population, and this has been preserved for us in King's *Notebook* in a table which gives details of the tax yield subdivided by rank, occupation and wealth. This table, which is an interesting counterpart to Davenant's regional analysis, is reproduced here, somewhat rearranged, as table 3.2.

Even allowing for the fact that King's estimates could not be very accurate, that his grouping is much simplified – tradesmen outside London, for instance, are not mentioned – and that his figures are rather cavalierly rounded off to approximate Davenant's total of £288,300, the table throws a great deal of light on the criteria of assessment and on the amounts yielded by the various elements of the tax. The basic rate was 1 shilling per head, in a population of 5.4 million registered in the returns, this element should have yielded £270,000, as indicated in row 1; but the exemptions on grounds of poverty were so numerous that the actual yield was only £162,500. The levy on rank or status, ranging from £50 for a duke to 10 shillings for a small merchant or artisan, yielded in all £65,400; that on official, professional and other earnings yielded £38,000; and that on financial holdings, £22,600.

The calculations leading up to these figures fill several pages and contain many details which King omitted in his final table, probably because he did not know how to reconcile them with his controlling totals. He often approached a problem of estimation from several angles, and not surprisingly obtained conflicting results. Modern statisticians have long been familiar with this situation and have dealt with it by openly introducing residual errors and statistical discrepancies into the accounts, which is honest but does not solve the problem. More recently a number of statistical techniques have been developed to balance out such discrepancies. But in King's day none of these expedients had been invented and so he had to devise his own adjustment methods: he subtracted a bit here, added a bit there and in the last resort, if

Table 3.2

'THE POLL BILL A° I° WILLIAM AND MARY, 1689'

			Tax yield £ Negative	Positive	Totals
1. The number of people as they answered in the 12d poll tax		5 400 000		270 000	
less: Persons receiving alms from the parish	– 600 000		– 30 000		
Their children under 16	– 300 000		– 15 000		
Children under 16 of day labourers	– 240 000		– 12 000		
Children under 16 of servants in husbandry	– 140 000		– 7 000		
Children under 16 of such poor people as do not pay to church and poor	– 600 000		– 30 000		
Children under 16 of such as have four or more and are not worth £ 50	– 180 000		– 9 000		
Omitted by neglect or otherwise deficient	– 100 000		– 5 000		
Discrepancy	+ 10 000		+ 500		
Insolvent population		– 2 150 000		– 107 500	
Solvent population paying basic rate of 1s		3 250 000			162 500
2. The nobility at £ 50 a Duke to £ 20 a Baron				4 000	
3. Their eldest and younger sons from £ 30 to £ 12				1 000	
4. Baronets and Knights of the Bath at £ 15 and Knights Bachelor at £ 10				16 000	
5. The King's Sergeants at Law at £ 20 and other Sergeants at £ 15				600	
6. Esquires or so reputed at £ 5				12 000	
7. Gentlemen or so reputed at £ 1				15 000	
8. Widows: the 3rd part of their husband's degree (except ecclesiastical persons)				6 000	
Yield from levy on social rank					54 600
9. Archbishops at £ 50 and bishops at £ 20				550	
10. Deans at £ 10 and archdeacons at 50s				500	
11. Canons and prebendaries at 50s				750	
12. Doctors of divinity (beneficed) and doctors of law or physic at £ 5				3 000	
Yield from levy on ecclesiastical and academic qualification					4 800
13. Every London merchant living within ten miles of London and not free* at £ 10				2 000	
14. Every merchant, tradesman or artificer living in a house of £ 30 per annum in London or within twenty miles, at 10s				3 000	
15. Every merchant-stranger and Jew at £ 10, except poor French protestants§				1 000	
Yield from levy on position in trade and industry					6 000
16. Offices, places and public employments (except in the army and navy): 1s per £ profit		[5%]		4 000	
17. Such offices as are not taxed in the monthly assessments: 3s per £ profit		[15%]		1 000	
18. Pensions, yearly stipends and annuities out of the King's revenue: 3s per £		[15%]		5 000	
19. Judges, judicial officers and other officers in places of profit, barristers and other practitioners in the law and medical practitioners: 3s per £ profit		[15%]		8 000	
20. Servants having £ 3 per annum or upwards (total wages £ 200,000): 1s per £°		[5%]		10 000	
21. Servants having under £ 3 per annum (total wages £ 400,000): 6d per £°		[2.5%]		10 000	
Yield from levy on professional and other earnings					38 000
22. Personal estate in money or debt (except from the King): 10s per £ 100, to be paid by the lender (total stock £ 2,000,000)		[0.5%]		10 000	
23. Every member of the East India Company: £ 2 per £ 100 of original stock		[2%]		8 000	
24. Every member of the Guinea and Hudson Bay Companies: £ 2 per £ 100 of original stock		[2%]		4 000	
25. Every sharer in the New River Water: 2s per £ of their dividend		[10%]		600	
Yield from levy on holding of financial assets					22 600
Total yield					288 500

* The freedom of the City carried a number of privileges, including exemption from certain taxes.

§ Huguenot refugees who had come to England after the revocation of the Edict of Nantes.

° This tax was often paid by the employer.

Source: Gregory King, *Notebook*, p. 70.

he still did not succeed, cut the Gordian knot by discarding what seemed to him the less plausible estimates.

The two examples I have given serve as illustrations of the thoroughness with which he prepared the groundwork for his two great economic surveys, the *Natural and Political Observations* and the *Naval Trade*. Let us now take a close look at these.

4. The English Economy, 1688-1698

King's purpose in writing the *Observations* was to draw up a comprehensive statement of the demographic and economic position in England, and in less detail France and Holland, over the decade 1688-1698 in order to see what bearing this had on the probable duration of the war. The tone is set in a short preface which should command the assent of all economists. In its entirety it runs as follows:

'If to be well apprized of the true state and condition of a nation, especially in the two main articles of its people and wealth, be a piece of political knowledge, of all others, and at all times, the most useful, and necessary; then surely at a time when a long and very expensive war against a potent monarch (who alone has stood the shock of an alliance and confederacy of the greatest part of Christendom) seems to be at its crisis, such a knowledge of our own nation must be of the highest concern. But since the attaining thereof (how necessary and desirable soever) is next to impossible, we must content ourselves with such near approaches to it as the grounds we have to go upon will enable us to make.

However, if having better foundations than heretofore for calculations of this kind, we have been enabled to come very near the truth; then doubtless the following observations and conclusions will be acceptable to those who have not entirely given up themselves to an implicit belief of popular falsehoods. But the vanity of people in overvaluing their own strength is so natural to all nations as well as ours, that as it has influenced all former calculations of this kind both at home and abroad, so if these, even these papers may be allowed not to have erred on that hand, I am of opinion they will not be found to have erred on the other.'

King chose as his benchmark years 1688, the last year of peace, and 1695, the sixth year of war. The two years are compared in considerable detail and some of the main totals are then extrapolated to 1698. The coverage is not uniform, doubtless because the available data were not uniform; on the whole, the estimates for 1688 are the more complete. The calculations take in practically all aspects of the economy except foreign transactions; for this we must turn to the *Naval Trade*.

The *Naval Trade* was written in 1697. King's purpose here was to evaluate the contribution of foreign trade to the wealth of the country. He starts by giving estimates of wealth in selected years from 1600 to 1698. He then examines the flows of exports, imports and re-exports in 1688, dividing the rest of the world into three regions: Europe, Africa and the Levant; the Plantations, namely the West Indies and mainland America; and the East Indies.

By combining the information given in the *Observations* and the *Naval Trade* it is possible to construct a consistent set of national accounts for the year 1688. I shall now describe the main calculations, beginning with income and outlay, the subject of King's most famous table.

5. *Income and Outlay*

After giving a great variety of demographic estimates, King opens the economic part of the *Observations* with a detailed account of income and outlay in England in 1688. The population is about 5.5 million distributed over about 1.36 million families. Income, expenditure and saving are divided among twenty-six social classes ranging from temporal lords to vagrants. Evidently King's main purpose in working out his balances was to find out the contributions made to the wealth of the kingdom by the various classes. His 'scheme' is reproduced here, with slight amendments, as table 3.3.

The first thing to notice in this table is the way the population is divided horizontally into two sharply contrasted groups: those who save, thereby increasing the wealth of the kingdom, and those who spend more than their income, or dissave, thereby decreasing the wealth of the kingdom. Petty, although he makes several references to saving, which he calls superlucration, does

'A SCHEME OF THE INCOME & EXPENCE OF THE SEVERAL FAMILIES OF ENGLAND CALCULATED FOR THE YEAR 1688'

Ranks, Degrees, Titles and Qualifications	Number of families	Heads per family	Number of persons	Income per family £	Income per head £	Expence per head £	Increase per head £	Totall income £'000	Totall expence* £'000	Totall increase £'000
Temporall Lords	160	40	6 400	2 800	70	60	10	448	384	64
Spiritual Lords	26	20	520	1 300	65	55	10	33.8	28.6	5.2
Baronets	800	16	12 800	880	55	51	4	704	652.8	51.2
Knights	600	13	7 800	650	50	46	4	390	358.8	31.2
Esquires	3 000	10	30 000	400	40	37	3	1 200	1 110	90
Gentlemen	12 000	8	96 000	240	30	27.5	2.5	2 880	2 640	240
Persons in greater Offices and Places	5 000	8	40 000	240	30	27	3	1 200	1 080	120
Persons in lesser Offices and Places	5 000	6	30 000	120	20	18	2	600	540	60
Eminent Merchants & Traders by Sea	2 000	8	16 000	400	50	40	10	800	640	160
Lesser Merchants & Traders by Sea	8 000	6	48 000	200	33.3	28.3	5	1 600	1 360	240
Persons in the Law	10 000	7	70 000	140	20	17	3	1 400	1 190	210
Eminent Clergy-men	2 000	6	12 000	60	10	9	1	120	108	12
Lesser Clergy-men	8 000	5	40 000	45	9	8	1	360	320	40
Freeholders of the better sort	40 000	7	280 000	84	12	11	1	3 360	3 080	280
Freeholders of the lesser sort	140 000	5	700 000	50	10	9.5	0.5	7 000	6 650	350
Farmers	150 000	5	750 000	44	8.8	8.55	0.25	6 600	6 412.5	187.5
Persons in Liberal Arts and Sciences	16 000	5	80 000	60	12	11.5	0.5	960	920	40
Shopkeepers and Tradesmen	40 000	4½	180 000	45	10	9.5	0.5	1 800	1 710	90
Artizans and Handicrafts	60 000	4	240 000	40	10	9.5	0.5	2 400	2 280	120
Naval Officers	5 000	4	20 000	80	20	18	2	400	360	40
Military Officers	4 000	4	16 000	60	15	14	1	240	224	16
	511 586	5¼	2 675 520	67	12.9	12	0.9	34 495.8	32 048.7	2 447.1
Common Seamen	50 000	3	150 000	21	7	7.5	−0.5	1 050	1 125	−75
Labouring People & outservants	364 000	3½	1 275 000	15	4.3	4.4	−0.1	5 460	5 587	−127
Cottagers & Paupers	400 000	3¼	1 300 000	5	1.5	1.75	−0.25	1 950	2 275	−325
Common Souldiers	35 000	2	70 000	14	7	7.5	−0.5	490	525	−35
	849 000	3	2 795 000	10.5	3.25	3.45	−0.2	8 950	9 512	−562
Vagrants	. .	. .	30 000	. .	2	4	−2	60	120	−60
	849 000	3¼	2 825 000	10.5	3.19	3.41	−0.22	9 010	9 632	−622

So the General Account is

Increasing the Wealth of the Kingdom	511 586	5¼	2 675 520	67	12.9	12	0.9	34 495.8	32 048.7	2 447.1
Decreasing the Wealth of the Kingdom	849 000	3¼	2 825 000	10.5	3.19	3.41	−0.22	9 010	9 632	−622
Neat Totalls [and averages]	1 360 586	$4\frac{1}{20}$	5 500 520	32	7.9	7.55	0.33	43 505.8	41 680.7	1 825.1

* This column does not appear in the original.

Notes: Shillings and pence have been converted to decimals of £.

Components do not always add up to totals because of rounding-off errors.

Source: Gregory King, *Observations* (ed. Barnett), p. 31. A few arithmetical errors which appear in the original have been corrected.

not include it in his calculations. With King it is one of the most important variables.

The second thing is the order in which the various social categories are listed. On the whole, social status is the organising criterion rather than income, as it would be today. Of course there was a lot of social mobility and interpenetration between classes, so this hierarchical arrangement should not be interpreted too rigidly. Still, it is quite revealing and holds a few surprises.

First come the nobility and gentry, then two classes of civil servants, then two classes of businessmen, one of lawyers and two of clergymen (other than bishops). There follow two classes of freeholders, which would have consisted largely of yeomen farmers who owned their own land but could not aspire to the rank of landed gentry. In spite of this they were an important category, partly because they were very numerous and partly because the right to vote depended on property qualifications. Below them come the tenant farmers, who constitute the largest group among the savers. Below the farmers come the artists and scientists, followed by shopkeepers, tradesmen and artisans. Bottom of the list, surprisingly, come the naval and military officers.

The dissavers, who are more numerous than the savers, are subdivided into five categories: common seamen; labourers and outservants; cottagers and paupers; common soldiers; and last of all, vagrants, though I cannot imagine how one could obtain data for this category. King, being nothing if not thorough, must have felt that he should include vagrants in his table since they existed in the population but his figures can be little more than a guess.

Now let us look at the columns of figures. The first gives the number of families in each category, adding up to about 1.36 million in all. The second gives the average number of persons in each type of family, which ranges from forty in a nobleman's family to two in that of a common soldier, the average over all families being 4.05. And the third gives the number of persons in each category, adding up to the population total of 5.5 million.

It must be understood that the term 'family' is the equivalent of what we now call household. It does not mean that noblemen had an average of thirty-eight children and bishops an average of eighteen. Infant mortality was very high and even the rich, however comfortably they lived, would not have had on average more than three or four surviving children. The rest of the household consisted of indoor servants and other unrelated inmates of the house. In a grand household these would have included secretaries, tutors for the children, possibly the artist who was decorating the state rooms with mythological scenes, and so on. In a merchant's household there would have been some clerks who lived in, and in that of an artisan probably an apprentice or two.

The fourth column shows income per household, which averages £67 for the savers and £10.5 for the dissavers. And the next three columns show income, expenditure and saving per head. The variations in these figures are striking. The households of temporal lords spend £60 per head and those of eminent merchants £40 per head but they save the same, £10 per head. Parsons save more than artists and scientists though they have a lower average income. The farmers do not seem to be as thrifty as the shopkeepers and artisans.

The last three columns show the total income, expenditure and saving of each of the categories. Here again, comparisons are interesting. For instance the temporal and spiritual lords, who are not very numerous but have high incomes, contribute between them about £70,000 to the wealth of the kingdom whereas the freeholders, who are considerably less rich but considerably more numerous, contribute as much as £630,000. As to the dissavers, one may ask where they found the money to pay for the excess of their expenditure over their income. The answer is poor relief and private charities, to which I shall return later.

From the lower panel of the table we can see the balances of national income and expenditure in a nutshell: total income, £43.5 million; total expenditure, £41.7 million; and total saving, £1.8 million. These figures, allowing for the appearance of saving, are not very far off the figure of £40 million which Petty had reached with very few data, a lot of painstaking calculation and a good deal of inspired guesswork thirty years earlier.

Table 3.4

WEALTH IN ENGLAND IN THE SEVENTEENTH CENTURY

(£ million)

	Capital stock (fixed assets)					'Actual stock' (moveable assets)					Total	Total material wealth	Human wealth	Total wealth
	Land	Housing	Other hereditaments	Personal estates etc.	Total	Coined gold & silver	Other gold, silver & jewels	Furniture & clothing	Shipping & stocks	Livestock				
1600 Elizabeth					72						25	97		
1630 Charles I					112						37	149		
1655 Commonwealth											53			
1660 Restoration: Charles II					168						58	226		
1664											62			
(1664-67 War with Holland; Great Plague; Fire of London)														
1667											50			
1670											53			
(1672-74 War with Holland)														
1676											62			
(1685 Accession of James II)														
1688	180*	36*	18*	18	252	11.5*	6.0*	10.5*	33.0*	25.0*	86.0*	338*	330*	668*
(1689-97 William & Mary; Irish War; War of League of Augsburg)														
1695					(257)§	7.5*	3.5*	8.0*	30.0*	24.0*	73.0*	(330)§		
(1697 Peace of Ryswick)														
1698 King's projections					(257.9)§	4.5*	2.0*	6.5*	26.5*	23.0*	62.5*	(320.4)§		

§ Calculated using King's series for saving in *Observations*, p. 47.

Sources: Gregory King, *Naval Trade* (ed. Barnett), p. 61 & 63; * *Observations* (ed. Barnett), pp. 30, 32, 35 & 48.

6. *Saving, Investment and Wealth*

King's treatment of saving and investment is at first sight somewhat disconcerting. In the *Observations* his figure for saving in 1688, after deduction of dissaving by the poor, is £1.8 million, as shown in table 3.3; in the *Naval Trade* he estimates investment in the same year at £2.4 million. Thus we must find some means of adding back the £0.6 million of dissaving to the £1.8 million of saving. This can be done, since the income from poor relief, which King does not take into account but which existed, would just offset the dissaving, and so we should be left with saving of £2.4 million as required. How all this works out in terms of a social accounting matrix I shall show in table 3.7 on p. 98 below.

Although in this way saving and investment can be equated, it seems probable that they are still too low. On the saving side nothing is said about the undistributed profits of trading companies or the surplus funds of private charities. On the investment side it seems likely that King underestimated the amount of domestically produced assets. He says in the *Naval Trade*: 'if the increase of the actual stock of wealth was anno 1688 £2,400,000, we may reasonably allow that the increase by foreign trade was £1,700,000 and by inland trade and labour £700,000'. It is odd that the greater part of additions to wealth should be said to consist of an increase in the stock of imported goods. But this is something for economic historians to look into; all I am trying to do is give a consistent picture of the position as King saw it.

Although King does not have much to say about investment he has quite a lot to say about the national wealth. The *Observations* contains estimates of wealth subdivided by type of asset for the years 1688 to 1695, with projections to 1698; and the *Naval Trade* gives the main totals for 1600, 1630, 1688, 1695 and 1698 with some interpolations for other selected years. King chose his dates so as to bring out the effects of political and other outside events on the economy. My attempt to put this material together and set it in its historical context is shown in table 3.4. I should make it clear, however, that no correction is made either by King or by me for changes over time in the value of money. The sources of the estimates are indicated in the notes to the table. The figures in brackets are my extrapolations based on a series for saving over the decade 1688-98 given in the *Observations*. From 1689 on, this series shows a progressive dissaving which in 1698 reaches the alarming figure of £4 million: by accumulating these dissavings on to the £338 million of material wealth in 1688 I obtained the corresponding totals in 1695 and 1698 and hence, residually, the subtotals for nonmoveable assets. Despite the war these subtotals show an increase on the position in 1688, which accords with what King says on p. 16 of the *Observations*, namely that there was some house-building during the war, though less than the normal amount. This increase partially offsets the decrease in moveable assets.

The estimate of human wealth in 1688 also comes from the *Observations*. King reaches it in much the same way as Petty had reached his. He estimates income from property at £13 million; he then subtracts this from total income and is left with £43.5−13.0=30.5 million of 'income by trade, arts, labour etc.'; and by capitalising the £30.5 million 'at near 11 years purchase' he obtains his figure of £330 million, which in a population of 5.5 million is equivalent to £60 per head. Unlike Petty, however, he does not distinguish between working and non-working population, and no comment is offered on Petty's remark that 'people may well be as perpetual as land, for aught we know'. It is noticeable that while his estimates of labour income and of the national income are higher than Petty's, all his other figures are substantially lower.

7. *Foreign Trade*

The final element in King's national accounting picture is the detailed analysis of foreign trade given in the *Naval Trade*. From this we can obtain English exports and imports on a FOB and a CIF valuation. Exports of goods are divided between English goods and re-exports; and exports of money, bullion etc., what King calls 'money and adequate treasure', are shown separately. Imports, valued CIF, are divided by their main uses in England. Domestic and foreign charges for freight etc., are shown separately. The balance of trade, the excess of English revenues from exports over English payments to foreigners for imports, is equal to the net inflow of money and adequate treasure into England, £5.12−4.42=1.25−0.55=0.7 million; it represents the amount England has lent abroad to enable foreigners to pay for the excess of English exports over English imports. This information is brought together in the three parts of table 3.5.

Table 3.5
ENGLISH FOREIGN TRADE IN 1688
(£ million)

Exports				
Cost to foreign buyers		Uses by foreign buyers		
Wares: English products	2.48	Wares		4.82
re-exports	1.28	Money, bullion, jewellery etc.		0.55
All wares	3.76			
Money, bullion, jewellery etc	0.55			
Value of exports FOB	4.31			
plus English freight etc.	0.81			
Revenue from exports	5.12			
plus Foreign freight etc.	0.25			
Value of English exports CIF	5.37	Value of English exports CIF		5.37
Imports				
Cost to English buyers		Uses by English buyers		
Value of imports FOB	4.02	Wares: re-exports		1.28
plus Foreign freight etc.	0.40	domestic consumption		3.59
Expenditure on imports	4.42	additions to stocks		1.00
plus English freight etc.	2.70	Money, bullion, jewellery etc.		1.25
Value of imports CIF	7.12	Value of imports CIF		7.12
Balance of trade				
Revenue from exports	5.12	Expenditure on imports		4.42
		Inflow of money etc.	1.25	
		less Outflow of money etc.	−0.55	
		Balance		0.70
Total	5.12	Total		5.12

Source: Gregory King, *Naval Trade* (ed. Barnett), pp. 64-76.

The last step in King's analysis was to show how much of England's profit from foreign trade came from operations in the three trading areas: Europe, Africa and the Levant; the Western Plantations; and the East Indies. This profit, which is calculated over and above the net consumption of imports, that is the difference between the amount of imported goods consumed and the amount of English goods exported, consists of £1 million of imported goods added to stocks and £700 thousand of net inflow of money etc., or £1.7 million in all. The results of these calculations are set out in table 3.6.

Table 3.6
THE NATIONAL PROFIT OF ENGLAND BY FOREIGN TRADE IN 1688
(£ million)

	Europe, Africa & the Levant	Western Plantations	East Indies	Total
Exports				
Exports of English products FOB to:	2.25	0.31	0.47	3.03
Re-exports FOB to:	1.19	0.04	0.05	1.28
Value of exports FOB	3.44	0.35	0.52	4.31
Imports				
Imports of area's own products CIF from:	2.87	0.95	1.70	5.52
Imports of area's re- exports CIF from:	1.40	0.12	0.08	1.60
Value of imports CIF	4.27	1.07	1.78	7.12
Additions to wealth				
Excess of imports CIF over exports FOB	0.83	0.72	1.26	2.81
Adjustment for source of gain from net imports*	– 0.30	0.15	0.15	0.00
True excess	0.53	0.87	1.41	2.81
less Freight etc.*	– 0.065	– 0.225	– 0.82	– 1.11
National profit	0.465	0.645	0.59	1.70

* As given on p. 71 of *Naval Trade*.
Source: Gregory King, *Naval Trade* (ed. Barnett), pp. 67-73.

In drawing up this table I have taken all the essential figures from King but I had to make some adjustments to the components of exports and re-exports in order to agree with his marginal totals. His table on p. 68 of the *Naval Trade* is somewhat confusing but I do not think I have done any serious damage to his intentions.

The only row in my table 3.6 which may seem a bit mysterious is the one I have termed 'adjustment for the sources of gain from net imports'. Its purpose is to attribute England's gain to the area of origin of imported re-exports rather than to the area of shipment to England. From King's table, which I repeat I find confusing, it should also be possible to break down the components of the national profit by area; but this defeated me.

8. A Reconstruction of the National Accounts for 1688

The examples I have given in the foregoing sections by no means exhaust the information contained in the *Notebook*, the *Observations* and the *Naval Trade*. For instance, I have said very little about King's work on taxes and nothing about his estimates of production. But I think I have said enough to show that he had the pieces for a consistent set of national accounts. Such a set was constructed a few years ago by Phyllis Deane[1] and her estimates, somewhat expanded by me, are brought together in the form of a matrix in table 3.7.

A few words of explanation as to the exact contents of this table may be useful. Professor Deane gives five accounts: production, households, government, capital transactions and the rest of the world. I have added to production an imputation for the services of indoor family servants. I have subdivided the household sector into 'rich' and 'poor': the rich are those who save in table 3.3 less an assumed 215,000 indoor servants, and the poor are those who dissave in table 3.3 plus the indoor servants. I have also subdivided government into central and local in order to show the financing and distribution of poor relief, which was one of the responsibilities of local government as represented by parish officers. And I have surrounded the accounts with very simple balance sheets.

1. 'The implications of early national income estimates for the measurement of long-term growth in the United Kingdom'. *Economic Development and Cultural Change*, vol. IV, no. 1, 1955, pp. 3-38.

Table 3.7

THE NATIONAL ACCOUNTS OF ENGLAND IN 1688 RECONSTRUCTED FROM GREGORY KING'S DATA

(£ million)

		0	1	2	3	4	5	6	7	8	00	Account totals
Balance sheet	0. Opening assets								338.0			
Pro-duction	1. Agriculture, manufacturing, trade etc.				30.3	11.2	2.3	0.1	1.7	5.1		50.7
	2. Indoor domestic service				1.6							1.6
Con-sumption	3. Rich		34.5									34.5
	4. Poor		9.0	1.6				0.6				11.2
	5. Central government		2.1		0.2							2.3
	6. Local government		0.7									0.7
Accumu-lation	7. Capital transactions	338.0			2.4						340.4	2.4
Rest of the world	8. Foreign transactions		4.4						0.7			5.1
Balance sheet	00. Closing assets								340.4			
	Account Totals		50.7	1.6	34.5	11.2	2.3	0.7	2.4	5.1		

Note: Material wealth in rows 0 and 00 is matched by net worth in columns 0 and 00.

Each row-and-column pair constitutes an account, with incomings in the row and outgoings in the column. For instance, row 1 shows the revenues of production, consisting of sales of consumption goods to the two types of household and the two branches of government, sales of tangible assets to the accumulation account and sales of exports to the rest of the world; and column 1 shows the costs of production, consisting of factor incomes paid to the two types of household, taxes paid to the two branches of government and purchases of imports from the rest of the world. Strictly speaking there should be another outgoing, namely provisions for the depreciation of tangible assets, which would be paid into the accumulation account; but King, although he gives some estimates of depreciation both in the *Notebook* and in the *Observations*, does not treat it as a separate item of outlay. Introducing it here would mean too much tampering with his figures.

The only tampering I have done is in the matter of indoor servants. King, as we saw in table 3.3, does not attribute to them a separate income for their services but treats them as members of the family. I have adopted Professor Deane's imputation of £1.6 million to cover the wages and keep of these servants and shown this as an expenditure of the rich in column 3, row 2; at the same time I have subtracted an amount equal to servants' income from the expenditure of the rich in column 3, row 1, and added it to the expenditure of the poor in column 4, row 1. I have also accommodated Professor Deane's £0.2 million of hearth money (treated as a direct tax) by reducing the consumption of the rich by the same amount, thus balancing accounts 1 and 3.

The £2.4 million of saving shown in the seventh row is the saving of the rich in table 3.3; and the dissaving of the poor is removed by the receipt of £0.6 million of poor relief Assuming, as I have, that indoor servants are 'poor' we can say that in 1688 there were in England 2.46 million rich with an average annual income of £14 per head and 3.04 million poor with an average annual income of £3.70 per head.

The balance sheets show on the assets side (rows 0 and 00) what I have termed material wealth and on the liabilities side (columns 0 and 00) what is usually called net worth. There are no revaluations, I am afraid, and what is perhaps a worse omission no financial claims. These certainly existed, for example bills of exchange, mortgages and government debt, but for a closed economy with a single capital account they would cancel out. Raymond Goldsmith[1] gives figures for mortgages, corporate stock and trade credit in 1688. These amounted to 11 per cent of national assets but I have not attempted to work them into the picture.

9. *War Finance*

Towards the end of the *Observations* King summarises the results of his calculations for the ten years 1689-98. He divides the decade into two periods and gives the main aggregates for each period and for the decade as a whole. He also gives a table showing the components of the national income and outlay account year by year from 1688 to 1698. He then uses this material to analyse the sources of war finance and discuss the question of how long the war can continue.

He enumerates three sources. First, greater industry, by which he means the excess of annual income in wartime over the income of the last peacetime year; this ceased to be a positive source of finance after 1693. Second, greater frugality, by which he means the reduction in annual private expenditure, current and capital, and public civil expenditure from their levels in 1688. And third, 'decrease', by which he means the annual using up without replacement of material wealth existing at the outbreak of war. He accumulates these changes over his three periods and obtains the figures shown in table 3.8. The significance of the time spans is obvious: when King was writing, the estimates in the first column related to the past, those in the second to a forecast period and those in the final column to the decade as a whole.

He then subdivides disinvestment into the five types of moveable assets specified in table 3.4 above: coined gold and silver; other gold and silver; consumers' durables; shipping and stocks of merchandise; and livestock. He concludes that the reduction

1. *Comparative National Balance Sheets*. University of Chicago Press, 1985.

in these items by 1698 is the greatest that can be contemplated, so that the war cannot be sustained beyond that date. He was quite right: the war dragged on languidly through 1696 and part of 1697 and finally came to an end with the Peace of Ryswick in the summer of 1697.

Table 3.8
SOURCES OF WAR FINANCE IN ENGLAND, 1689-98
(£ million)

	1689-95		1696-98		1689-98	
Industry, that is increase in income generated		– 0.4		– 10.2		– 10.6
Frugality, that is reduction in:						
private consumption	1.7		5.5		7.2	
public civil expenditure	2.3		1.7		4.0	
private investment	12.6		5.4		18.0	
In all		16.6		12.6		29.2
Decrease, that is disinvestment		12.8		10.6		23.4
War expenditure		29.0		13.0		42.0

Source: Gregory King, *Observations* (ed. Barnett), p. 7.

10. International Comparisons

King concludes the *Observations* with a comparison of the economies of England, France and Holland in 1688 and 1695. He starts by giving estimates of the area, population, income, private and public expenditure, taxes and saving in France and Holland in each of the two years. He points out that while France has lost on all counts, Holland 'by more than ordinary frugality and industry' has actually managed to save £6 million over the seven years, equivalent to £850,000 per annum. He then divides private expenditure into food and drink, clothing, and other expenses, with food in the year 1695 further subdivided into eight items as in table 3.1. Finally he summarises his results in a table which gives in parallel the income and outlay accounts of the three countries. This is reproduced here, transposed, as table 3.9. King does not include the details of consumption in his summary table but I have added them in as it seemed a pity to lose them.

Table 3.9

'THE GENERAL ACCOUNT OF ENGLAND, FRANCE & HOLLAND FOR THE YEARS 1688 & 1695'

	Totals (£ million)						Per head (£'s)					
	1688			1695			1688			1695		
	England	France	Holland	England	France	Holland	England	France	Holland	England	France	Holland
Bread . . . & all things made of Meal or Flower				4.3	10.1	1.40				0.79	0.75	0.63
Beef, Mutton, Veal . . . Venison, Conies				3.3	5.3	0.80				0.61	0.39	0.36
Butter, Cheese & Milk				2.3	4.0	0.60				0.42	0.30	0.27
Fish, Fowle & Eggs				1.7	3.7	1.10				0.31	0.27	0.49
Fruit, Roots & Garden Stuff				1.2	3.4	0.40				0.22	0.25	0.18
Salt, Oyl, Pickles . . . & confectionery Ware				1.1	2.8	0.30				0.20	0.21	0.13
Beer & Ale				5.8	0.1	1.20				1.06	0.01	0.54
Wine, Brandy Spirits . . . & made Wines				1.3	8.6	0.40				0.24	0.64	0.18
Dyet [food and drink]	21.3	41.0	6.40	21.0	38.0	6.20	3.87	2.93	2.91	3.85	2.82	2.78
Apparell [clothing and footwear]	10.4	18.5	3.00	10.2	16.0	2.80	1.89	1.32	1.36	1.87	1.19	1.25
Incident Charges [expenditure n.e.s.]	10.0	21.0	6.35	14.3	26.0	8.40	1.82	1.50	2.89	2.62	1.93	3.75
Increase [saving]	1.8	3.5	2.00	-3.0	-6.0	0.85	0.33	0.25	0.91	-0.55	-0.44	0.38
General Expence	43.5	84.0	17.75	42.5	74.0	18.25	7.91	6.00	8.07	7.80	5.49	8.15
Rent of Land, Buildings & other Hereditaments	13.0	32.0	4.00									
Produce of Trade, Arts & Labour	30.5	52.0	13.75									
General Income	43.5	84.0	17.75	42.5	74.0	18.25	7.91	6.00	8.07	7.80	5.49	8.15
Consumption besides Taxes	39.7	70.0	11.00	39.0	62.5	10.50	7.22	5.00	5.00	7.16	4.63	4.69
Publick Revenue & Taxes	2.0	10.5	4.75	6.5	17.5	6.90	0.36	0.75	2.16	1.19	1.30	3.08
Increase	1.8	3.5	2.00	-3.0	-6.0	0.85	0.33	0.25	0.91	-0.55	-0.44	0.38
General Expence	43.5	84.0	17.75	42.5	74.0	18.25	7.91	6.00	8.07	7.80	5.49	8.15
Population (millions)	5.5	14.0	2.2	5.45	13.5	2.24						

Shillings and pence have been converted to decimals of £.
Components do not always add up to totals because of rounding-off errors.

Source: Gregory King, *Observations* (ed. Barnett), p. 55.

This table is a mine of information. It contrasts totals with per head figures. It shows three alternative definitions of income and outlay: as the sum of consumption at market prices plus saving; as the sum of property income plus labour income; and as the sum of consumption at factor cost plus taxes plus saving. And by presenting the data within a unified framework and expressed in a common unit of account, the £, it enables all sorts of interesting and amusing comparisons to be made both over space and over time.

Thus France, with its relatively large population, has by far the largest total income while Holland has the smallest; in terms of income per head, however, the position is reversed. In England and France income falls in wartime but in Holland it increases. Taxes are much higher in Holland than in the other two countries and in all three they increase greatly in wartime, most of all in England. In all three countries saving falls, though in Holland it remains positive. The English appear as great consumers of meat and beer; the frugal Dutch eat more poultry and fish and drink less; the French naturally consume more wine than beer but on the whole they drink less than the Dutch and much less than the English. And so on.

It may be asked where King got his information from. The wording of his preliminary calculations suggests that though he had data for some of the components the majority were reached by deduction. Obviously he could not aspire to absolute accuracy. His intention was to give an idea of the orders of magnitude involved: his totals are rounded off to the nearest ten thousand and the per head figures are simply the totals divided by the population. There is no reason to think, however, that he was very wide of the mark. In any case his table of international comparisons is a *tour de force* which as far as I know has only been emulated in this century.

11. *Private and Public Medicine and the Care of the Poor*

A constant feature of King's political arithmetic, in which he follows Petty's lead, is the interplay of demography and economics.

Indeed many of his economic estimates are offshoots of his interest in demography. A case in point, and a very interesting one, which is tied to his estimates of mortality, is his calculation of private expenditure on health which is to be found on p. 206 of the *Notebook*.

His approach is characteristic. In a population of 5.5 million, he says, yearly burials are one in thirty, or 180,000, of which an eighteenth part, or 10,000, have died of some serious illness with an average duration of three weeks. In a lifetime, people have on average four such fits of illness, the first three of which do not prove fatal, giving another 30,000 cases of illness per year. Apart from these acute cases, 20,000 people take 'physick' as a matter of course or for prevention but do not need the assistance of a physician or apothecary. Thus he reaches a total of 60,000 people annually undergoing some sort of medical treatment. He distributes these 60,000 over six population groups distinguished by total expenditure per head and then estimates their expenditure on medical care, both per head and per group. Finally he divides this expenditure into four types of treatment ranging from 'kitchen physick' to doctors and quacks. The result of his calculation is set out in table 3.10.

It is noticeable that in all but the two poorest groups the highest proportion of expenditure went in apothecary's physick. Apart from making and dispensing medicines, apothecaries were employed much more than they are now as medical advisers. Only the rich could afford to call in the doctor when they were ill. In King's table, incidentally, doctors are bracketed with quacks; this may seem somewhat cynical to us, but in those days it was not always easy to tell them apart. The poor relied almost entirely on home-brewed remedies, King's 'kitchen physick'; for proper medical attention they depended on charity. This was not lacking, however, and some information on it is provided by King himself.

King's estimates of what I have called public medicine are much less detailed and made in quite a different way, being based on institutional rather than medical criteria. A few words of explanation may help to understand them better.

After the dissolution of the monasteries under Henry VIII the

Table 3.10

'ESTIMATED ANNUAL EXPENCE IN PHYSICK, PHYSICIANS & SURGEONS'
(*c.* 1695)

Total expenditure				Expenditure on private medicine							
Population grouped by range of expenditure per head		Exp. per head	Exp. per group	People taking physick	Exp. per head	Exp. per group	Type of treatment				
Serial no. of group	People in group						Kitchen physick	Apothecary's physick	Surgeons & plasters	Doctors & quacks	Total
	('000)	(£)	(£'000)	('000)	(£)	(£'000)	(£'000)				
1.	1 000	2	2 000	6.0	0.1	0.6	0.5	0.08	0.02	0.0	0.6
2.	1 000	3	3 000	7.0	0.2	1.4	0.9	0.4	0.1	0.0	1.4
3.	1 000	5	5 000	8.5	0.45	3.8*	1.6	1.8	0.35	0.05	3.8*
4.	1 000	8	8 000	11.0	1.25	13.75	4.0	8.0	1.3	0.45	13.75
5.	1 000	13	13 000	15.5	4.0	62.0	10.0	43.77	4.23	4.0	62.0
6.	500	24	12 000	12.0	12.5	150.0	13.0	87.5	14.0	35.5	150.0
1 to 6.	5 500	8*	43 000	60.0	3.925	231.55	30.0	141.55	20.0	40.0	231.55

* Rounded off as in the original.

Shillings and pence have been converted to decimals of £.

Source: Gregory King, *Notebook*, p. 206.

care of the poor, which had been largely the concern of the monastic orders, devolved on the State. This charge was met by the poor rates. Davenant, as we saw in table 2.1, estimated the poor rates in the period 1660-80 at an average of £665,000 per annum. Allowing for the costs of collection this can be rounded off to £600,000, which is the figure I imputed for poor relief in my social accounting matrix for 1688. It represents about 1.4 per cent of the national income.

Poor relief was quite generously supplemented by private charities of which there were many hundreds, ranging from modest almshouses to splendid institutions like Chelsea Hospital, founded by Charles II as a home for war veterans and built by Wren. Hospital and almshouse were generic terms that could denote three types of institution. Some were medical hospitals in the modern sense of the word. Some were what would now be called hospices, whose function was to give shelter, food and when necessary medical attention to those members of the community who needed care and had nobody to look after them. And some were intended simply to provide housing, often accompanied by a small income, for people who though destitute were able to look after themselves.

The *Computation of the Endowed Hospitals and Alms-houses in England*[1] which King prepared for the Board of Trade in 1697 gives, in very round figures, estimates of the number of such institutions, the number of people they could house at any one time and the annual cost of running them, both in total and per head. As might be expected from a report intended for civil servants who knew what it was about and needed no explanation, it is a dry document, in fact nothing but a set of figures unaccompanied by the elaborate reasonings with which King usually presents his estimates. Its contents are shown in table 3.11.

The only institutions specified separately are the four great London hospitals, St. Bartholomew's, St. Thomas', Christchurch and Bridewell, which could house an average of two hundred and fifty patients each. They were medical hospitals and consequently the most expensive to run, having the highest-paid staff

1. First published as Appendix III in G. CHALMERS, *An Estimate of the Comparative Strength of Great Britain*.

Table 3.11

'A COMPUTATION OF THE ENDOWED HOSPITALS AND ALMS-HOUSES IN ENGLAND'
(*c.* 1697)

	London		Other cities and market towns	Rest of the Kingdom	Totals
	Great hospitals	Lesser institutions			
General information					
Number of institutions	4	100	500	500	1 104
Average number of poor maintained in each	250	14	12	10	
Total number of poor maintained	1 000	1 400	6 000	5 000	13 400
Total population of area	530 000		870 000	4 100 000	5 500 000
Percentage of population in care	0.45		0.69	0.12	0.24
Number of officers, assistants etc. in each area	200	120	300	250	870
Incomings (£'000)					
Rents [income from property]	10.0	. .	. .	. .	. .
Gifts and subsidies	15.0	. .	. .	. .	. .
Total incomings	25.0	20.0	70.0	50.0	165.0
Outgoings (£'000)					
Charge of the poor [food, clothing, medicaments etc.]	16.0	15.4	60.0	42.5	133.9
Charge of the officers, assistants etc. [wages and salaries]	6.0	2.4	4.5	3.0	15.9
Repairs, maintenance etc.	3.0	2.2	5.5	4.5	15.2
Total outgoings	25.0	20.0	70.0	50.0	165.0
Average cost per head (£)	25.0	14.29	11.6	10.0	12.31

Source: Gregory King, *A Computation of the Endowed Hospitals* . . . (ed. G. Chalmers), pp. 72-3.

and the highest proportion of staff to inmates. King puts the annual cost of these four hospitals at £25,000 in all, or £6,250 per hospital and £25 per patient. Besides these, he says, 'there may be' within London about one hundred other hospitals or endowed almshouses, each costing about £200 per annum and with an average capacity for fourteen people; in other urban centres about five hundred institutions costing about £140 per annum and with a capacity for twelve people; and in the rest of the country another five hundred costing £100 per annum and with a capacity for ten.

Some of the figures in this table were based on precise information. King's unpublished 'Stafford Diary'[1] contains a list, ward by ward, of the patients present in St. Bartholomew's Hospital on two separate dates in 1696. This is shown here as table 3.12. On the first date there were 225 patients, of whom one third were seamen and soldiers, one third male civilians and one third women. On the second there were fewer in-patients, the proportion of women was lower, that of seamen and soldiers higher and there were also fifty soldiers listed as out-patients. Such a degree of detail suggests that King collected the information in person. It is very probable that he also collected data on costs, but of this there is no record. Nor is it known whether he carried out similar surveys in the other three great hospitals or whether he extrapolated for them from the St. Bartholomew's figures.

In any case it would seem that the estimates for the four hospitals in table 3.11, though given in round figures, were pretty good approximations. Those for the lesser institutions, on the other hand, were guesses. Still, King was a level-headed man and I think we can accept his guesses as indicators of the orders of magnitude involved. Thus if we add to the total cost of hospitals and almshouses the £600,000 of poor relief we obtain an expenditure on the poor of £765,000, or nearly 1.8 per cent of the national income. And if, guess for guess, we assume that two thirds of the cost of hospitals and almshouses were spent simply on housing and feeding the destitute, we are left with

1. Miscellaneous notes on blank pages of *ΕΦΗΜΕΡΙΣ, or a Diary Astronomical, Astrological and Meteorological for 1696*. Stafford Record Office.

£55,000 spent specifically on medical care; if this is added to the £232,000 spent on private medicine, we obtain an expenditure on health of £287,000, or nearly 0.7 per cent of the national income.

Table 3.12

'A VIEW OF ST. BARTHOLOMEW'S HOSPITAL' AT TWO DATES IN 1696

	27 March 1696				10 September 1696			
	Seamen	Soldiers	Other men	Total men and women	Seamen	Soldiers	Other men	Total men and women
Men								
Long ward	5	..	8	13	4	1	5	10
Cloister ward	8	1	6	15	5	2	4	11
Charity ward	7	1	6	14	6	1	3	10
Soldier ward	3	2	8	13	5	1	5	11
Gardin dormitory ward	3	..	9	12	4	1	5	10
New ward	8	..	4	12	6	1	4	11
Naples ward	3	2	4	9	6	1	2	9
Dyet ward	5	1	4	10	4	1	3	8
King's ward	4	1	5	10	4	..	5	9
Queen's ward	8	..	6	14	6	..	5	11
Martha ward	9	1	14	24	4	..	15	19
Katherine ward	..	..	..	..	9	..	4	13
Total men	63	9	74	146	63	9	60	132
Women								
Katherine ward				14				..
Mary ward				14				12
Magdalen ward				14				10
Elizabeth ward				16				13
Curtin ward				17				9
Total women				75				44
Both sexes								
Cutting ward				4				5
All in-patients				225				181
Out-patients	..	..	..	..	..	50	..	50
'In ye lock'	..	16 or 18	..	16 or 18	..	..	..	..

Source: Gregory King, 'Stafford Diary', June 1696, 3rd blank page.

12. Consumers' Behaviour: the Demand for Corn

King was probably a pioneer also in another field of quantitative economics, the analysis of market demand. I say probably because we have no firm proof that the formulation of what has become known as 'King's law of demand' was in fact all his own work, though all internal and some external evidence suggest that it was. Opinions differ on this point, but before I go further into the debate let me lay out the facts of the case.

In his *Essay upon . . . the Ballance of Trade* Davenant gives a little table showing the relationship between a deficiency in the corn crop and the associated rise in the price of corn: as the crop falls below normal the price rises more and more above normal. For instance, a 10 per cent deficiency in the crop is associated with a 30 per cent rise in price, and a 50 per cent deficiency with a 450 per cent rise. This table is shown here in modern form as table 3.13.

Table 3.13

QUANTITY AND PRICE VARIATIONS IN THE CORN CROP

Quantity variations in percentages (0 = normal)	Price variations in percentages (0 = normal)
0	0
−10	30
−20	80
−30	160
−40	280
−50	450

Source: Charles Davenant, *Essay Upon . . . the Ballance of Trade*, p. 38.

Davenant was concerned only with the price effect of a poor harvest. However, it turns out that the figures given in his table are exactly fitted by a cubic equation which makes it possible to extrapolate the curve so as to show what would happen to demand as a consequence of a bumper harvest. If we write q for quantity variations in percentages and p for the corresponding price variations, then the numbers in table 3.13 are exactly expressed by

$$p = -2.\dot{3}q + 0.05q^2 - 0.001\dot{6}q^3$$

This equation can be solved for different values of q and, without deriving the inverse function, the data in table 3.13 can be put in the form of q as a function of p interchanging the axes, as illustrated in diagram 3.1.

Diagram 3.1

GREGORY KING'S DEMAND CURVE FOR CORN

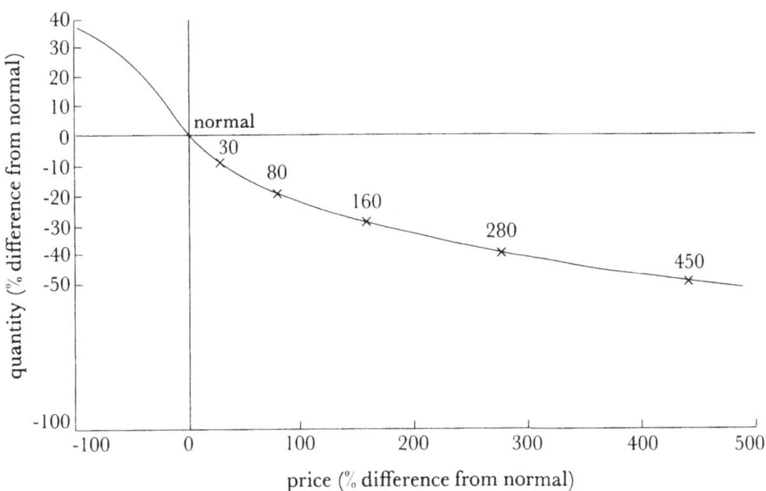

The data given by Davenant appear in the lower part of the diagram. The upper part is my extrapolation showing the effects of an above-normal harvest. The result is rather interesting and quite realistic. The demand curves drawn in textbooks often assume that as the price falls towards zero the demand rises indefinitely. In fact for most goods there is a saturation level beyond which a good will not be bought no matter how cheap it is. The equation fitted to Davenant's data implies that if the price fell to zero the demand would only rise to about 35 per cent above normal.

Two questions have been discussed in connection with this early piece of demand analysis. First, is it right to attribute it wholly to King or should some of the credit go to Davenant; and second, should the numbers be regarded as purely hypothetical or do they rest on a basis of observations.

The attribution to King goes back to Lauderdale, who in his *Inquiry into . . . Public Wealth* published in 1804 refers to it as 'Gregory King's Calculation, published by Davenant'.[1] Of the many writers who have subsequently worked on the law, among them Whewell, who first made the connection with a cubic function,[2] Jevons,[3] Wicksteed,[4] Pareto[5] and Yule, who wrote out the equation as I have given it,[6] some have accepted this attribution, some have ignored it and some have challenged it. The claim of Davenant to be considered at least joint author of the schedule was put forward in 1967 by Evans.[7] He argues that Davenant, usually scrupulous in his acknowledgements to his friend, does not specifically mention him in this case; and though on page 234 of King's *Notebook* there are some calculations of quantity-price relationships for corn, they do not include the schedule as printed in Davenant's *Essay*.

This and the second question, whether the figures are real or imaginary, were considered in 1986 by Creedy in his admirable analysis of the law and of the comments made on it by the writers mentioned above.[8] The fact that the numbers follow exactly a third degree polynomial may be fortuitous, which would

1. LORD LAUDERDALE, *An Inquiry into the Nature and Origins of Public Wealth*... Edinburg, 1804; Italian transl., *Biblioteca dell'economista*, vol. V, 1st ser., 1854, pp. 1-139.

2. WILLIAM WHEWELL, 'Mathematical exposition of some doctrines of political economy: second memoir' (1850). *Transactions of the Cambridge Philosophical Society*, vol. 9, pt. 1, 1856, pp. 1-7.

3. W. S. JEVONS, *The Theory of Political Economy*. London, 1871.

4. P .H. WICKSTEED, 'On certain passages in Jevons's *Theory of Political Economy*'. *The Quarterly Journal of Economics*, vol. III, Apr. 1889, pp. 293-314.

5. VILFREDO PARETO, 'La legge della domanda'. *Giornale degli economisti*, 2nd ser., vol. X, 1895, pp. 59-68.

6. G. UDNY YULE, 'Crop production and prices: a note on Gregory King's law'. *Journal of the Royal Statistical Society*, vol. LXXVIII, pt. II, 1915, pp. 296-8.

7. G. H. EVANS JR., 'The law of demand - the roles of Gregory King and Charles Davenant'. *The Quarterly Journal of Economics*, vol. 81, no. 3, 1967, pp. 483-92.

8. JOHN CREEDY, 'On the King - Davenant "law" of demand'. *Scottish Journal of Political Economy*, vol. 33, no. 3, 1986, pp. 193-212.

strengthen the view that they were hypothetical. On the other hand, as Creedy points out, Whewell's discovery that they lie on this particular curve was made using the method of differences which had been invented by the mathematician James Gregory in 1670 and published by Newton first in 1672 and later in the 1687 edition of the *Principia.* Thus by the time Davenant brought out his *Essay* the Gregory-Newton formula would have been known to anyone interested in mathematics and might very well have been used to fit a cubic to observations. If so, it is more than ever likely that King was the author of the schedule, since Davenant was no mathematician. But this is a matter of speculation, so Creedy very fairly entitles his paper 'The King-Davenant "law" of demand'. And there the matter must rest until some new piece of evidence comes to light.

13. Conclusions

As I have said, I have left King's demographic work for discussion in my third lecture and have here concentrated on his economic writings and in particular have tried to show how far he could have got with his national accounting. But he did not pursue the matter, he had no followers in the younger generation and after his brilliant start all thoughts of balanced accounts seem to have evaporated. Although he was much quoted in the eighteenth century, presumably on the evidence of Davenant's published tables, nobody attempted to emulate him. The nineteenth century seems to have confined itself to refining estimates of income and wealth to the neglect of spending and saving.

At last about fifty years ago the subject was revived by Colin Clark, who in his *National Income and Outlay*[1] estimated the principal macro-economic accounting magnitudes for selected years in the 1920's and 30's and devoted a considerable amount of space to King's political arithmetic. Deane and Cole took King's national accounts as the starting point for their great work on

1. London, 1937.

British economic growth.[1] My own admiration for him will be clear from what I have said in this lecture.

Apart from the national accountants, writers whose main interest lies in the distribution of occupations, income and wealth have also gone back to King's work, but in a more critical spirit. Holmes[2] emphasises the fact that King underestimated both the numbers and the incomes of the upper and middle classes. Lindert and Williamson, who have examined King's income figures in the light of recent research,[3] have come to similar conclusions. In brief, their findings are: first, an increase in the number of people and the income of many categories of the nobility and gentry; second, an increase in the number of people in the commercial and industrial classes with incomes above the average level; and third, a reduction in the number of the poor. They reach a figure for total income which is about 25 per cent higher than that reached by King and which they think may still be on the conservative side. At the end they say modestly that all they have done is replace old rough tentative guesses with new rough tentative guesses.

I am not sure that this is quite fair either to King or to themselves. King produced a clear and plausible picture of the English social and economic scene which is remarkably coherent in spite of its complexity. A change in one part of it inevitably throws the rest out of balance. So a new balance must be found and this cannot be done arbitrarily but must be based on solid proof, which is not easy to establish. On the demographic side, for instance, Glass's estimate of the population of England and Wales[4] is a little less than King's, but the recent back-projection by Wrigley and Schofield[5] lies between the two and is in fact rather closer to King than to Glass, as we shall see in chapter 7

1. PHYLLIS DEANE and W. A. COLE, *British Economic Growth, 1688-1959*. Cambridge University Press, 1962.

2. G. S. HOLMES, 'Gregory King and the social structure of pre-industrial England'. *Transactions of the Royal Historical Society*, 5th ser., vol. 27, 1977, pp. 41-68.

3. P. H. LINDERT and J. G. WILLIAMSON, 'Revising England's social tables, 1688-1812', and 'Reinterpreting Britain's social tables, 1688-1913'. *Explorations in Economic History*, vol. 19, 1982, pp. 385-408, and vol. 20, 1983, pp. 94-109.

4. D. V. GLASS, 'Two papers On Gregory King'.

5. E. A. WRIGLEY and R. S. SCHOFIELD, *The Population History of England, 1541-1871*. Arnold, London, 1981.

below. On the economic side, I have found that King's estimates of personal consumption stand up well to modern statistical analysis.

All this is not to say that King is infallible. If information can be found to revise his picture and preserve its coherence I think the effort would be well worth while. But it will be an uphill job.

SECOND LECTURE
PROGRESS IN ECONOMIC STATISTICS

William Fleetwood (1656-1723)
Arthur Young (1741-1820)
Patrick Colquhoun (1745-1820)

William Fleetwood, Bishop of Ely

CHAPTER 4

William Fleetwood and the Birth of Index-Numbers

1. Brief Life

When commenting on Gregory King's estimates of total wealth through the seventeenth century in section 6 of the preceding chapter, I remarked that his figures were not adjusted for changes in the value of money. This is such an important element in any comparison over time, especially over a long period of time, that it is surprising that King, who thought of most things, did not think of it, or if he did, did not introduce it explicitly in his calculations. The first man who saw its importance and gave it formal expression was not in fact a political arithmetician but a churchman, William Fleetwood. Fleetwood's favourite pastime was the study of history, and his analysis of price movements since the Middle Ages, which is considered the first step towards the construction of index-numbers, was a by-product of this pastime.

William Fleetwood was born on 1 January 1656 in the Tower of London, where his father, Captain Geoffrey Fleetwood, was one of the officers in charge. William obtained a scholarship first to Eton and then to King's College, Cambridge, where he graduated in 1679. In due course he became a fellow of the college and took orders.

As a fellow of King's he was involved in 1689 in an incident typical of the time. His uncle James Fleetwood, provost of the college from 1660 to 1675, had been nominated to the provostship by Charles II. So had his successor, Provost Page. The next provost, John Copleston, was James II's nominee. This use of the royal prerogative, though in accordance with established custom, was contrary to the statutes of the college founder, Henry VI, which vested the right of electing the provost in the fellows. When Provost Copleston died in 1689, William III put forward the name of Isaac Newton for the vacancy. But Newton was an outsider, a Trinity College man; the fellows had their own candidate and decided that the time had come to resist the royal intervention. A group of them, including William Fleetwood, were deputed to assert the right of the college and after a stormy debate at Hampton Court with the Crown lawyers they won their case. And so the college lost Newton but recovered in perpetuity its right of free election.

The choice of William Fleetwood as one of the spokesmen for the college was apt. He was already beginning to make his mark as a gifted and persuasive preacher; politically he held liberal views and had welcomed the advent of William and Mary; and the king liked him, so much so that soon after his accession he made him one of his chaplains.

At the end of 1689 Fleetwood moved to London to take up the rectory of St. Augustine's, to which was added the lectureship of St. Dunstan's-in-the-West. Here he had full scope for his gifts as a preacher and he soon became one of the most celebrated of his day. People flocked to his sermons, which were characterised by 'the fine vein of casuistry which ran through most of them, wherein he displayed a peculiar talent, and gave ease to many weak and honest minds', and he was often chosen to speak before the royal family and the Houses of Parliament on State occasions.

In 1702 the king nominated him to a canonry at Windsor but died before the nomination could be ratified, and Fleetwood's political adversaries tried to take the opportunity to elbow him out. But William's successor, Queen Anne, would not allow it. Anne, who was Mary's younger sister, was married to Prince George of Denmark, a nonentity who took no part in public affairs, and all decisions pertaining to the Crown rested ultimately with her. She was one of Fleetwood's warmest admirers, was in the habit of attending his sermons, and in 1708, of her own personal act, made him bishop of St. Asaph's in Wales, thereafter often referring to him as 'my bishop'.

Throughout this time Fleetwood had remained a convinced Whig. After more than fifty years of bitter political and religious dissension, culminating in James II's attempt to re-establish

Roman catholicism in England, William III had been seen by the more liberally minded as the guarantor of civil liberties and of the protestant succession, and his prolonged war against Louis XIV, who wanted to put James II back on the throne, as a sort of crusade. For no sooner had the War of the League of Augsburg been concluded than the king of Spain had died, and this had been the signal for the start of the War of the Spanish Succession. William III had led the English and Dutch forces, and after his death his place had been taken by the almost invincible Marlborough.

But now the political wind had changed. Louis XIV was an old man, James II was dead. The Tories were in the ascendant, they wanted to pull out of the war, and the queen and most of the country were behind them. Marlborough was displaced and soon after that, in 1711, England signed a separate peace with France, to the indignation of all good Whigs.

Fleetwood's protest took the form of a sermon he was expected to preach before the House of Lords early in 1712 and for which he had chosen for his text a passage from the Psalms, 'the people that delight in war'. He was prevented from delivering it but this did not stop his publishing it. What is more, he followed it up with the publication of four sermons he had preached on royal occasions, which were significant in themselves and were prefaced by an outspoken attack on what he regarded as a dangerous concession to political and religious authoritarianism. The House of Commons, by a large majority, sentenced the preface to be burnt by the common hangman. It was at once issued, on 21 May 1712, as no. 384 of the *Spectator*, which, as Fleetwood wrote to a friend, 'conveyed above fourteen thousand copies into people's hands, who would otherwise never have seen or heard of it'. An early instance of the power of the media.

In 1714 Queen Anne died. All her children had died before her, and the next in succession on the protestant side was the Elector of Hanover, whose mother was a Stuart and who duly became George I of England. The Whigs were now back in power and three months after the accession of the new king Fleetwood was raised to the bishopric of Ely, which he held for the rest of his life.

In spite of his political opinions, which included a wide tolerance of nonconformists and thus ran counter to the views of most of the ecclesiastical establishment, Fleetwood secured in both his dioceses the affection and respect of his clergy, whom he assisted liberally with gifts of books and money. He also had a good business head and could give them sound advice on financial matters, as we shall see. He believed in advancing the most worthy and avoided personal controversy. When attacked he would say, 'I write my own sense as well as I can. If it be right, it will support itself; if it be not, it is fit it should sink'.

He died on 4 August 1723, leaving a widow and one son. A fuller account of his life will be found in Powell[1] and Venables.[2]

2. *The First Index-Numbers of Prices*

It is apparent from the subject matter of his sermons and other writings that as a churchman Fleetwood was much more concerned about the moral implications of social and individual behaviour than about the finer points of theology. In other words, he was an honest exponent of practical Christianity. He was also a scholar of wide and accurate learning. It is on these two tickets that he comes into my story.

In 1707 he published anonymously *Chronicon Preciosum: or an Account of English Money, the Price of Corn and other Commodities, for the last 600 years.*[3] After his death the book was included in the 1737 edition of his collected works and re-issued, with the author's name on the title page, in 1745. It is this third edition that my quotes come from.

Fleetwood is the least ponderous of writers. His tone is conversational and friendly, his style clear and unpretentious. One can see why he was such a popular preacher. In his preface he says:

1. W. Powell, Preface to *A Complete Collection of the Sermons, Tracts and Pieces of all kinds that were written by . . . Dr. William Fleetwood* (W. Powell ed.). London, 1737.

2. Edmund Venables, 'William Fleetwood'. *The Dictionary of National Biography*, vol. VII, pp. 269-71.

3. Harper, London, 1707; reprinted in W. Powell (ed.), *op. cit.;* reissued with the author's name, a longer title and an *Appendix Containing an Historical Account of Coins . . . from William the Conqueror to the Restoration,* Osborne, London, 1745.

'When I had set down, in *the first chapter*, the reason and occasion of writing this little book; and, *in the following ones* had given the proofs of my determination; and, *in the last*, had shewn the use and application of them, I thought I had made an end of my business.

But the *Bookseller*, it seems, is of the opinion, that I should not shew myself respectful enough to you, unless I introduced you by the way of *a Preface*. To comply, therefore, with his desires, I must needs think of saying something, tho' it be but to discover some of the imperfections of this book.'

The main imperfection, for which he apologises to the reader, he considers to be the lack of illustrations to the chapters on coins (an omission made good in the 1745 edition). He continues:

'As to the *chapter* of *prices*, it will be in everybody's power to make it more complete by reading in the old *computus's* [account books] that he shall chance to light upon, and insert what he finds wanting, or differing from the *accounts* that I have given; but most specially the gentlemen of each *University* will have it in their hands to make what amendments they shall see good out of their old *rolls* and *bursars accounts*; which I look upon as the most sure guides in enquiries of this nature; because our general histories do mostly give us the prices of things which are *extraordinary* either for *cheapness* or for *dearness*; whereas the *college accounts* deliver faithfully the *ordinary* and *common* price of most commodities and provisions.

One thing more I must observe to you; that the nature of the work obliged me, I thought, to set down the names of the *authors* out of which I collected the materials of this book; as well as to justify myself, as that you may recur to the originals whenever you please; as also to avert, a little, that scorn with which some, in their supercilious gravity, may pursue the collectors of such light and trivial matters; when they shall find that no *English historian* of any tolerable esteem among us hath failed to make observation of the like nature. Nay, some considerable ones have made it so much of their business, that they seldom conclude a year without informing us whether it were a *dear* or a *cheap* one.

This remark will also help to remove the ostentation of *much reading*, because there is no need of reading an *author* throughout to find what I have here discovered; the method of many of them making it easier to do so, by setting down (as I said) the price of corn and other provisions at the end of every year. But so far I must needs ostentate my reading as to assure you, that I have viewed with my own eyes, and transcribed from all the *originals*, whatever I have set down.'

Having thus established his credentials as a historian, Fleetwood proceeds in the first chapter to explain his motive for writing the book. He had written it in response to a question of conscience put to him by a student in the University of Oxford. He does not say which college his correspondent was attached to, but only that it had been founded between 1440 and 1460; Edgeworth, who was a fellow of All Souls, founded in 1438, thought that might be it. In any case the statutes of the college required that a fellow should vacate his fellowship if he came in possession of an estate by inheritance or of a perpetual pension worth £5 per annum. The question was, could a man who owned an estate yielding £6 per annum in 1706 honestly swear on oath that he was conforming to the statutes if (i) he made he estate over in trust to a friend but retained the income for himself; or (ii) he had inherited the estate only after being admitted to his Fellowship; or (iii) he thought that £6 in the circumstances of 1706 were worth less than £5 had been when the statute was made. Fleetwood disposes summarily of the first alternative:

'The answer to your *first* question may be easily had by your asking yourself another, *viz*, Whether that estate, tho' made over to another, be not still yours, as to the profits of it for the present, and as to the disposal of it for the future? If it be, how can you safely swear it is not yours when you have it to all intents and purposes? And such an oath as yours has not respect to the *title* alone, but to the *title* with the *profits* of an estate. They who make over the title of an estate and yet reserve the profits are, in the sight of God (as well as their own) as much masters of the estate as if they had the *titles* of them also in their cabinets.'

The second alternative, though morally less reprehensible, is fundamentally a quibble:

'Your *second* question seems to require more pains to answer it than the first. But it only *seems so*, for there is, in truth, but little difficulty in it if you consider never so little the plain and visible intention of your Founder: which was, Nobody worth five pounds *per annum* should be fellow of his college: why else should he require you to declare, under an oath, you would obey that statute? The having that estate therefore must of necessity hinder you, by the Founder's visible intention, from being *admitted* fellow; will not the same intention therefore hinder you from *continuing* fellow? I do not, however, directly charge with perjury such continuation unless you deny, or do industriously conceal, your having such an estate; because I am not sure you are obliged (by virtue of your general oath) to vacate, of your own accord, your fellowship. But yet I think it is such a violation of that statute as I would not counsel you to venture on.'

Coming to the third alternative, he says:

'Your third and last question will cost me more pains, and you more patience, before we come to the conclusion; if we can come to any satisfactory one at last. It will require both a good casuist and a pretty good historian to answer it absolutely and to your purpose. A better casuist, I own, you might easily have found. But it may be you could not so easily have found one who hath in his readings made more observations on the price of corn and other commodities at different times, as you will perceive by reading this long letter. And when you shall find that many a single line of this letter has cost me the looking over a great book, you will think I wanted not good will to do you service. But I am now come to your question and I must premise, before I speak to it, that whereas you say your statutes were made betwixt the years 1440 and 1460, I must, to save labour, call this space of time *the reign of Henry VI*, tho' his reign began 18 years sooner.

I do affirm then, with the best judgement I have, that I am seriously persuaded that, altho' you are actually possessed of an estate of 6*l* *per an.* as money and things go now, you may safely take that oath, upon presumption that 6*l* *now* is not worth what 5*l* was *then*, when that statute was first made. Because whoever swears, swears to *things* that are signified by words, and not to *mere words* . . . A *pound* (for instance) will buy either more or less corn *now* than it would in Henry VI's time. A *pound* is therefore of more or less value *now* than it was *then*; and the *value* of a *pound* is truly a *pound*, and not its mere *name*. It is not therefore the same thing *now* that it was in Henry VI's time.

And if it be said that I must needs take the words of my oath in their *plain, literal* and *grammatical* sense, I answer, That so I must, wherever I can; but in this case the *plain, literal* and *grammatical* sense of 5*l* is not the same with what it was 260 years ago. What shall I do then? Shall I prefer the *plain, literal* and *grammatical* sense of words at this present [time] before the *plain, literal* and *grammatical* sense of the same words as it stood 260 years ago; which, I am sure, was the sense of the Founder? I grant that if it were *a case in law* I should be determined by the sense which the words bear at present; but as it is *a case of conscience*, I do roundly affirm that 5*l* is not the same thing at present that 5*l* was in the reign of Henry VI.

And that I may very honestly have regard to the value of five pounds 260 years ago will, I believe, appear evident from what I am going to say; That the Founder intended the same ease and favour to those who should live in his college 260 years after his decease as to those who lived in his own time. Now, they who lived in his time might with 5*l* purchase so much bread, so much drink, meat, cloth, firing, books, and other necessaries or conveniencies: I know not exactly how much, nor is it material: I only say, the Founder intended I might keep such an estate as would suffice to procure the same bread, drink, meat, cloth, books &c. as the other might have procured for 5*l*, 260 years ago. But this I cannot possibly do with 6*l* as things go *now*, nor it may with four times as much . . .

They who are the guardians of your college statutes . . . have it in their power . . . to judge according to the *letter*, and to determine that 5*l* as pounds do *now* go shall be the limited sum which shall not be exceeded . . . If they *should*, you would be obliged to abide by their judgement. And therefore all I have said, or can say on this head, is only to shew you what I think may be safely done with respect to equity and a good conscience. Not to exempt you from the jurisdiction of your superiors but to shew you what you may do as an honest man, tho' what you do does not agree exactly with the *letter* of the statutes to which you are obliged; nay (if you will), to shew you what you may innocently do even when you may be punished for so doing.

Supposing, therefore, that you are convinced that you may innocently swear to the observation of the statutes . . . altho' you have an estate of 6*l per annum* . . . I am now at liberty to proceed to an historical account of money and of the different price of corn and other commodities; that by understanding both, and comparing one with the other, you may be the better able to determine what proportion a *pound*, a *mark*, a *shilling*, or a *penny*, now, bears to the same denominations many years ago.'

There follow four scholarly chapters full of numerical data on gold coins, silver coins, the prices of commodities and the levels of wages, salaries, pensions etc. over the past six centuries; and finally the conclusion, in which Fleetwood explains how to use this information and gives the decisive answer to the Oxford student's dilemma:

'To apply the chapter on *corn*, and make it useful to your present purpose, you must in the first place remember that during the whole reign of Henry VI excepting the first and last years of it the ounce of silver was at 2s 6d [£0.125]; 'tis *now* at 5s 2d [£0.258]. So that the 5*l* which is the sum you are concerned with did *then* contain 40 ounces; and 5*l* *now* does not contain above 19$\frac{1}{3}$ ounces. From whence you may safely conclude that 5*l* in the reign of Henry VI was of somewhat better value than 10*l* nowadays is. In the next place, to know somewhat more distinctly whereabouts an equivalent to your ancient 5*l* will come, you are (as before hinted) to observe how much corn, meat, drink or cloth might have been purchased 260 years ago with 5*l*, and to see how much of the modern money will be requisite to purchase the same quantity of corn, meat, drink or cloth nowadays. To this end you must neither take a very dear year, to your prejudice, nor a very cheap one, in your own favour, nor indeed any single year to be your rule; but you must take the price of every particular commodity for as many years as you can (20, if you have them) and put them all together; and then find out the common [mean] price; and afterwards take the same course with the price of things for these last 20 years; and see what proportion they will bear to one another; for that proportion is to be your rule and guide.'

He then proceeds to demonstrate his method by giving the average prices of five commodities in the two periods and calculating their ratios in the manner described in the preceding paragraphs: if the average price of a quarter of wheat was 6s 8d in Henry VI's time and is now £2,

''tis plain that 5*l* in H. VI's time would have purchased 15 quarters of wheat, for which you must have paid for these last 20 years 30*l*. So that 30*l* *now* would be no more than equivalent to 5*l* in the reign of H. VI.'

He repeats this operation for oats, beans, ale and cloth, and concludes:

'I think I have good reason to believe, that beef, mutton, bacon and other common provisions of life were six times as cheap in Henry VI's reign as they have been for these last 20 years. And therefore I can see no cause why 28*l* or 30*l* *per annum* should *now* be accounted a greater estate than 5*l* was heretofore, betwixt 1440 and 1460 . . . Nor does my kindness and concern for you bias my judgement in this affair; for I have thought the same thing long before your question was put . . . And if so, 28*l* or 30*l* may be enjoyed with the same innocence and honesty together with a fellowship, according to the Founder's will.'

Thus did Canon Fleetwood (for he was not yet a bishop) by a fine vein of casuistry give ease to a weak and honest mind, and in so doing take the first step towards the formulation of index numbers.

A summary of his estimates, with their decimal equivalents, is given in table 4.1.

Table 4.1

FLEETWOOD'S PRICE COMPARISONS

Commodity	Unit	Average price				Ratio
		1440-60		1686-1706		
		shillings and pence	decimal equivalents £	shillings and pence	decimal equivalents £	
Wheat	quarter	6s 8d	0.33	40s	2.00	6
Oats	quarter	2s	0.10	12s	0.60	6
Beans	quarter	5s	0.25	30s	1.50	6
Ale	gallon	0s 1½d	0.006	0s 8d	0.03	5⅓
Cloth	yard	3s 7½d	0.181	18s	0.90	5
Meat & other	..	..	..	..	..	6

Source: William Fleetwood, *Chronicon Preciosum* (1745 edn), pp. 136-7.

The book does not quite end here. On the strength of his findings Fleetwood questions the validity of any law or regulation based on the application of specific money criteria and cites in support of his view the opinion of a famous legal historian and antiquary of a previous generation:

'Sir H. Spelman (a very competent judge and estimator of these matters) complains, That the laws have not sufficient regard to the different price of things when they condemn people to death for stealing things to the value of *twelve pence* . . . And he instances a *quarter of wheat*, which in the *assize of bread*, 51 Henry III [*c.* 1250], was rated at *twelve pence*, but in his time [*c.* 1610] often sold for 40 shillings and upwards.'

Another example Fleetwood cites is the level of income which entitled freeholders to vote in parliamentary elections. By an act passed in 1430, only those who had an income of no less than £2 per annum 'free of all incumbrances' had the right to vote. Since £2 at 1430 values were equivalent, at a conservative estimate, to at least £8 at 1706 values, it was obvious that the act had been originally framed so as to 'cut off many hundred thousand voices, and consequently many occasions of tumults and disorders'. Clearly, then, a man who in 1706 swore that he was entitled to vote because he had an income of £2 did not swear according to the intention of the original law-givers, but so long as parliament did not change the figure that man could not possibly be said to have commited perjury.

Fleetwood concludes by giving his correspondent a useful piece of advice. If he intends to obtain a position in the Church, he should be careful how he makes 'any composition or agreement, for any long space of years' to receive a fixed sum in lieu of the corn that is due to him as a tithe, 'altho' for the present it may seem a profitable exchange'; and he gives examples of some bad bargains reached by ignoring this precaution.

Although in his price comparisons Fleetwood did not go so far as to think of weighting his individual items according to their importance in a shopping basket, he did see the need to have a single magnitude, however approximate, as an index of change. If we do what in essence he advised his correspondent to do, namely take the average of the ratios shown in table 4.1, we obtain 5.75. It is interesting to set this figure in the context of modern scholarship. Phelps Brown and Hopkins, in their excellent study of price changes over seven centuries,[1] provide an annual index of the prices of consumables in southern England from 1264 to 1954, covering farinaceous foods, meat and fish, butter and cheese, drink, fuel and light, and textiles. Their base period is 1451-75=100. If we compare their average indices for 1440-60 and 1686-1706, the periods taken by Fleetwood, we obtain $\frac{609.6}{99.8}=6.1$. So, it seems, Fleetwood was not far off the mark in the answer he gave to the Oxford student.

1. E. H. Phelps Brown and Sheila V. Hopkins, 'Seven centuries of the prices of consumables, compared with builders' wage-rates'. *Economica*, vol. XXIII, no. 92, 1956, pp. 296-314.

3. Developments Abroad

As with the work of the political arithmeticians, it was many years before anyone in England embarked again on comparisons over time in the value of money. Two notable attempts were made on the Continent, however, one by the Frenchman Dutot (as he is now known) and the other by the Italian Carli.

Charles de Ferrare du Tot, to give him his full name, was for a time associated with the Compagnie des Indes, the great French trading company formed by the English financier John Law. What happened to him when Law's fortunes crashed in 1720 is not known, but in 1738 he published his *Réflexions politiques sur les finances et le commerce*,[1] in which he contended that the great increase in taxes that had occurred in France chiefly under Louis XIV was more apparent than real because of the decline in the purchasing power of money.

This being eighteenth-century France, Dutot presents his arguments in terms of the products of agriculture to the exclusion of all other commodities. In his own words,

> 'The question is, whether Louis XV, with a revenue of 100 million livres, is richer today than Louis XII was [in 1508] with a revenue of 7,650,000 livres. To know the answer we must look at the price of food under those two reigns; and he who with his revenue will be able to obtain the greater quantity of food at the prices of his time will be the richer.'

He then compares a variety of agricultural prices in three regions, Auvergne, Champagne and Bourbonnais, in 1508 and 1735. His data for the earlier year are taken from various historical sources, principally Bodin, and those for the later one are collected by himself. His basket of commodities, which varies with the regions, includes farm animals, corn, hay, oil, wine, vineland, woodland, a day's labour in summer, a day's labour in winter and so on. He sums the unit prices, without weighting them, in each region separately and then over all three regions and thus obtains two totals, 171.3 *sous* in 1508 and 3771 *sous* in 1735. The ratio of these two totals is $\frac{3771}{171.3}=22.1$. He concludes that the value of

1. 2 vols, Prévost, The Hague, 1738; reprinted (ed. HARSIN), Droz, Paris, 1935.

money has declined by a factor of more than 22 to 1 and therefore Louis XV is worse off in 1735 with 100 million than Louis XII was in 1508 with 7.65 million. Indeed, $\frac{100}{7.65}=13.11$.

Dutot's index of price change is very rough, in fact quite unreliable because he adds together three heterogeneous baskets, he takes the prices of two isolated years instead of the average prices of a series of years, and his prices are not weighted. On the other hand it has two merits over Fleetwood's: it includes services in the form of a day's labour and it allows for regional variations.

Count Gian Rinaldo Carli-Rubbi was born in 1720 at Capodistria, which was then part of the Venetian Republic. At the age of 24 he became professor of astronomy at Padua, but his interest gradually turned to economic and financial matters and in 1751 he published the first volume of his monumental work on coins and minting.[1] In 1753 he moved to Milan, where he was appointed president of the board of finance by the Austrian government, thus becoming a member of that brilliant group of economists and public servants which included Beccaria and Verri. He took an active part in the economic debates of the time and exercised a considerable influence on the economic and monetary policies of that administration. He died in 1795.

Carli's contribution to the development of index-numbers appears in the third volume of the work mentioned above, which came out in 1760. His purpose was to see whether in Italy too there had occured over the centuries a change in the value of money analogous to those calculated for England and France by Fleetwood and Dutot, whose works he knew well. He took as his base period the half century 1450-1500 and as his current period the 'decade' 1744-55. His motives for choosing that particular half century as his base were three, one economic, one political and one demographic: America and its gold mines had not yet been discovered; Italy had been relatively free of political upheavals; and he had reason to think that the size of the popula-

1. Gian Rinaldo Carli, *Delle monete e della istituzione dalle zecche in Italia*. Vol. i, The Hague (Venice), 1751, and Mantova, 1754; vol. ii, Pisa, 1757; vol. iii, Lucca, 1759-60. Abridged reprint in P. Custodi (ed.), *Scrittori classici italiani di economia politica*. Parte moderna, vol. xiii, Milano, 1804.

tion, at least in some of the regions he proposed to analyse, had been near the size it was in his own time.

For each period he calculated the average prices of three basic commodities, corn, wine and oil, in seven selected regions ranging from Friuli in the Venetian Alps down to Naples. His coverage, however, is not uniform, since not all three commodities were produced in every region. As with Fleetwood, his preferred sources were institutional records such as the account books of convents and hospitals.

He summarises his findings very clearly in a table similar to the one I have drawn up to illustrate Fleetwood's calculations. Corn appears in all seven regions, wine in five and oil in four only. For each commodity he gives (i) the prices in the two periods region by region, (ii) the ratios of these prices and (iii) the arithmetic average of these ratios. His results are: corn, $3\frac{5}{6}$ to 1; wine, $4\frac{1}{2}$ to 1; oil, $3\frac{1}{4}$ to 1. The mean of these averages is approximately $3\frac{5}{6}$, from which he concludes that if in the fifteenth century an income of 2,000 *lire* was enough to support an average family, then in the current period that family would need 7,467 *lire*.

Carli's method is far from ideal, partly because of the restricted range of commodities included and partly, again, because of the lack of weighting. Nevertheless it represents an important step forward in that it is independent of the units in which the different commodities are expressed. His seven regions belonged politically to different states and though the currency used in most of them was called the lira its purchasing power was not necessarily the same everywhere. By reducing his prices to ratios Carli dealt effectively with one of the first problems encountered when making international comparisons.

4. *Developments in England*

After Fleetwood the next writer I know of in England to attempt a systematic analysis of price changes over time was Sir George Shuckburgh-Evelyn (1751-1804). Shuckburgh, who added his wife's surname to his own when he married a Miss Evelyn in 1783,

Table 4.2

THE PRICES OF VARIOUS ARTICLES FROM THE CONQUEST TO THE PRESENT TIME

Year	Miscellaneous items: Horse	Ox	Cow	Sheep	Hog	Goose	Hen	Cock	Butter per pound	Cheese per pound	Ale per gallon	Small beer per gallon	Mean of the preceding entries	Wheat per bushel	Beef and mutton per pound	Labour in husbandry per day	Mean of all entries
	Prices (£, shillings and pence)																
1050	1.17.6	0. 7.6	0. 6.0	0. 1. 3	0. 2.0	..	..	..	..	..	..	..		0.0. 2¼	..	..	
1150	0.12.5	0. 4.8¼	..	0. 1. 8	0. 3.0	..	0.0. 3	..	..	..	..	..		0.0. 4½	..	0.0. 2	
1250	1.11.0	1. 0.7	0.17.0	0. 1. 7	..	0.1.0	0.0. 3	0.0. 4½	..	..	..	..		0.1. 7¾	..	..	
1350	0.18.4	1. 4.6	0.17.2	0. 2. 7	0. 2.6	0.0.9	0.0. 2	0.0. 3¾	..	..	..	..		0.1.10½	..	0.0. 3	
1450	..	1.15.8	0.15.6	0. 4.11½	0. 5.1	0.0.6¼	..	..	..	..	..	..		0.1. 5	..	0.0. 3¾	
1550	2. 2.0	1.16.7	0.16.0	0. 4. 3¾	0. 5.6	0.1.0	0.0. 8¼	0.1. 0	0.0. 5	0.0.2	0.0. 1½	0.0.1		0.1.10½	0.0.1⅛	0.0. 4	
1600	..	..	..	..	..	..	..	..	..	..	0.0. 4	0.0.2		0.4. 0½	0.0.1½	0.0. 6	
1625	..	..	..	..	..	0.2.0	..	0.1. 6	..	..	..	..		0.4.11	..	0.0. 6½	
1650	..	..	..	..	..	..	..	..	..	..	0.0. 4	0.0.2		0.5. 6	..	..	
1675	5.10.0	3. 6.0	2.17.0	0.11. 0	0.14.0	0.3.0	0.1. 3	0.1. 3	0.0. 4½	0.0.2	0.0. 8	0.0.2½		0.4. 6	0.0.1⅞	0.0. 7½	
1700	..	..	..	..	..	..	..	..	..	..	0.0.10	0.0.3		0.4. 9½	..	..	
1720	..	..	..	..	..	..	..	..	..	..	0.1. 0	0.0.3		0.4. 4½	0.0.2½	0.0. 8	
1740	10. 0.0	8. 0.0	7. 7.0	1. 6. 0	1.15.0	0.3.6	0.1. 6	0.1. 6	0.0. 9	0.0.3½	0.1. 0	0.0.3		0.3. 8	0.0.3	0.0.10	
1760	14. 0.0	8.10.0	7. 0.0	1. 7. 0	1.15.0	0.5.0	0.1.10	0.1.10	0.0.10	0.0.5½	0.1. 2	0.0.3		0.3. 9¾	0.0.4½	0.0.11	
1780	..	..	..	..	..	..	..	..	..	..	..	..		0.4. 5½	..	0.1. 2	
1795	19. 0.0	16. 8.0	16. 8.0	1.18. 0	5. 8.0	0.3.0	0.1. 6	0.1. 6	0.0.11½	0.0.5	0.1. 2½	0.0.2¾		0.7.10	0.0.5¾	0.1. 5¼	
	Index-numbers (1550=100)																
1050	89	20	37	29	36	..	..	..	..	..	..	..	42	10	..	..	26
1100	..	..	..	..	..	..	..	..	..	..	..	..	..	..	..	..	34
1150	..	..	..	..	..	..	..	..	..	..	..	..	..	..	..	..	43
1200	..	..	..	..	..	..	..	..	..	..	..	..	..	..	..	..	51
1250	..	..	..	..	..	..	..	..	..	..	..	..	..	..	..	..	60
1300	..	..	..	..	..	..	..	..	..	..	..	..	..	..	..	..	68
1350	43	66	106	61	45	75	24	31	..	..	..	..	56	100	..	75	77
1400	..	..	..	..	..	..	..	..	..	..	..	..	..	..	..	..	83
1450	..	..	..	..	..	..	..	..	..	..	..	..	..	..	..	..	88
1500	..	..	..	..	..	..	..	..	..	..	..	..	..	..	..	..	94
1550	100	100	100	100	100	100	100	100	100	100	100	100	100	100	100	100	100
1600	..	..	..	..	..	..	..	..	..	..	..	..	..	..	..	..	144
1625	..	..	..	..	..	..	..	..	..	..	..	..	..	..	..	..	..
1650	..	..	..	..	..	..	..	..	..	..	..	..	..	..	..	..	188
1675	250	184	345	256	254	300	182	125	90	100	530	250	239	246	166	188	210
1700	..	..	..	..	..	..	..	..	..	..	..	..	..	..	..	..	238
1720	..	..	..	..	..	..	..	..	..	..	..	..	..	..	..	..	257
1740	476	437	884	602	634	350	218	150	180	175	800	300	434	197	266	250	287
1750	..	..	..	..	..	..	..	..	..	..	..	..	..	..	..	..	314
1760	667	465	874	626	634	500	266	183	200	262	930	300	492	203	400	275	342
1770	..	..	..	..	..	..	..	..	..	..	..	..	..	..	..	..	384
1780	..	..	..	..	..	..	..	..	..	..	..	..	..	..	..	..	427
1790	..	..	..	..	..	..	..	..	..	..	..	..	..	..	..	..	496
1795	904	890	2000	882	1960	300	218	150	230	250	969	275	752	426	511	436	531
1800	..	..	..	..	..	..	..	..	..	..	..	..	..	..	..	..	562

Source: G. Shuckburgh-Evelyn, An account of some endeavours . . ., *Philosophical Transactions of the Royal Society of London*, vol. CXIII, pt. 1, 1798.

was a gentleman of means, a member of parliament and a Fellow of the Royal Society, who cultivated mathematics and was particularly interested in standards of measurement. In 1789 he communicated to the Society a paper mainly concerned with apparatus for the measurement of length and weight, at the end of which he brings up the subjest of 'the price of provisions, and of necessaries of life, &c., at different periods of our history, and, in consequence, the depreciation of money'.[1]

His price series extend over the period 1050-1795 and relate to agricultural production only: farm animals, beer and ale, wheat, meat, and farm labour. He gives the prices in pounds, shillings and pence and as index-numbers with the year 1550=100. As his table is perhaps not very well known I reproduce its contents in table 4.2.

The top part of the table shows prices and the lower part shows the corresponding series expressed as index-numbers, which Shuckburgh carries on to 1800. The average indices for each year, shown in columns 13 and 17, are obtained from the items for which prices were available in that year. Thus the index for the twelve miscellaneous items in 1050 is based on the prices of the five farm animals only, and that for all items is based on the average of these and wheat. From these scattered observations for 1050, 1350, . . . 1795, the price index for other years is obtained by interpolation.

In concluding his paper Shuckburgh seems to think that some sort of apology is needed, saying 'however I may appear to descend below the dignity of philosophy, in such oeconomical researches, I trust I shall find favour with the historian, at least, and the antiquary'. I have introduced his calculations to show how far the construction of index-numbers had got in the century after Fleetwood, but as a 'historian and antiquary' I must utter a *caveat* as to their validity. If we look at his indices for the years 1450 and 1700, which are roughly the mid-points of Fleetwood's two periods, we find a price increase of $\frac{210}{88}$=2.39; Fleetwood's increase, it will be remembered, comes to 5.75. The divergence is

1. GEORGE SHUCKBURGH, 'An account of some endeavours to ascertain a standard of weight and measure'. *Philosophical Transactions of the Royal Society of London*, vol. CXIII, pt. I, 1798, pp. 132-76.

striking, but there is no doubt that Fleetwood's figure is the more reliable. Not only does he bring an impressive mass of documentary evidence in support of his estimates but he has the acumen to use prices averaged over twenty years and homogeneous baskets of goods. By contrast, Shuckburgh's list of sources is scanty; his indices refer to isolated years, which can lead to great distortions especially where agricultural products are concerned; and the composition of his baskets varies with the dates. If Fleetwood has the superiority for quality of data and soundness of method, Shuckburgh must be allowed the merit of having tried to compare a long series of years rather than being content with only two points in time as his predecessors had been. Unfortunately he did not think of weighting any more than they had.

The realisation that weighting was an indispensable element in time comparisons was not far to come, however. At first Shuckburgh's table appears to have been well received, but in 1812 the whole idea of a 'table of appreciation' was severely criticised by Arthur Young, an undoubted expert on agricultural prices, who considered such tables tissues of errors and deceptions: 'They take for granted the question in dispute, and assign any rise in price, whatever may be the real cause, to depreciation, even in cases where none whatever is to be discovered'.[1] His specific criticisms include the lack of weighting and the failure to allow for improvements in quality, a matter which still gives rise to difficulties.

Young makes some suggestions about the criteria that should be followed to weight the various commodities that enter into a shopping basket: wheat, for instance, should be repeated five times 'on account of its importance'; barley and oats twice; meat, butter, cheese 'or whatever is the produce of grass land' four times; labour five times, and so on. His suggestions may be sensible but are too dependent on personal judgement to amount to a method.

The first man to devise an objective method for constructing weighted index-numbers of prices was Joseph Lowe. I have been unable to find any biographical information about Lowe. All I

1. Arthur Young, *An Inquiry into the Progressive Value of money in England. Annals of Agriculture*, vol. 46, pt. 2, Macmillan, London, 1812.

can say is that he wrote on economic topics and that his writings attracted a good deal of attention. In 1822, during the period of recession which followed the Napoleonic wars, he published a book entitled *On the Present State of England in regard to Agriculture, Trade and Finance*; a second, enlarged edition came out in 1823, and in the same year a German translation was published at Leipzig. The book can be summed up as a long, detailed and somewhat chaotic discussion of the causes and effects of fluctuations in the value of money. All the English writers who had attempted to measure them are passed in review, among them Fleetwood, Shuckburgh and Young. Fleetwood gets high marks for his accuracy. Shuckburgh is dismissed as being 'far from correct, even in the fundamental points'. Young receives qualified praise:

'In 1811, the late Arthur Young . . . entered into researches of great extent, both as to the past and current prices of commodities, and published [in 1812] the whole in a pamphlet, entitled "An Inquiry into the Progressive Value of Money in England". This tract, however inaccurate in a theoretical sense, has a claim to attention, as well for the value of its materials, as for a correction of the mistakes of Sir George Shuckburgh.'

Throughout his book Lowe illustrates his arguments with a large number of comparative tables, among them some interesting family budgets. His historical estimates are expressed at current prices but he makes it abundantly clear that he does this not from choice but because the scarcity of data makes the calculation of constant prices impossible. And at the very end of the book he gives an example of how he would proceed in ideal circumstances. His verbal explanation is not a model of clarity, but when taken in conjunction with his two pro-forma tables, one representing a base period and the other a current period, his intention becomes evident.

He would set up a statement for all the products entering into the national expenditure in the base year. The statement would contain the quantity and price of each commodity, though there would doubtless be a number of unimportant items that would not need to appear separately. Expenditure would be shown as price times quantity for each of the specified commodities and as a lump sum for the unspecified ones. He would then set up a parallel statement for the current period. By revaluing the base-year quantities at current prices and dividing their sum by the sum of the base-year expenditures he would obtain a weighted measure of the average change in prices, and hence of the change in the value of money.

When Lowe's cryptic explanation is translated into modern terms, it can be seen that his method is quite simply the method which many years later was expressed by Laspeyres in the familiar formula

$$P_{01}=\Sigma p_1 q_0/\Sigma p_0 q_0$$

But Lowe did not know the language of modern economics and was no mathematician and so his discovery of how to construct a weighted index number of prices passed unnoticed until quite recently. Jevons, for instance, mentions 'among valuable books, which have been forgotten' Lowe's *Present State of England* and refers particularly to the 'scheme for giving a steady value to money contracts', but it is apparent from his brief description of it that even he did not grasp its significance.[1] So the honours of the field have gone to Lowe's more articulate successors.

5. *Summing up*

After I had written this chapter I had the curiosity to glance at the International Statistical Institute's revised *Bibliography of Index Numbers*,[2] which goes up to 1968 and lists about 2600 entries. I found that Fleetwood, Dutot, Carli, Shuckburgh, Young and Lowe are the first in the list. Granted that the bibliography is not complete, there is no doubt that between them my six authors roughed out the basic principles of index-number theory and practice. Being pioneers they had no ready-made terminology or evolved mathematical techniques to help them sort out their ideas, which makes their achievement all the more remarkable.

1. W. Stanley Jevons, *Money and the Mechanism of Exchange*. London, 1875, ch. xxv.
2. W. F. Maunder, *Bibliography of Index Numbers*. International Statistical Institute, London, 1970.

I have given a fairly full account of Fleetwood's contribution, but for the other five I have limited myself to very condensed summaries. Anyone who wishes to know more about them without wading through the originals, which anyhow are pretty difficult to come by, should read Parenti's excellent critical essay in *Economia*,[1] which covers the ground from Fleetwood to Shuckburgh and includes some tables that I have not given, and Kendall's lucid survey in the *Review* of the I.S.I.,[2] which carries the story of price index-numbers to the end of the nineteenth century and illustrates it step by step with the appropriate mathematical formulae.

It took more than two centuries for people to realise what Fleetwood had done. As Professor Parenti reminds us, Irving Fisher called Jevons 'the father of index-numbers', Jevons gave the priority to Shuckburgh, Walsh gave it to Carli or Dutot. It was Edgeworth who first noticed *Chronicon Preciosum* as 'the oldest and one of the best treatises on index-numbers'. Nothing so far has come to light to gainsay this pronouncement.

1. Giuseppe Parenti, 'La tecnica e il significato dei primi numeri indice dei prezzi'. *Economia*, new ser., vol. xxv, no. 6, 1940, pp. 1-31.

2. M. G. Kendall, 'The early history of index numbers'. *Review of the International Statistical Institute*, vol. 37 no. 1, 1969, pp. 1-12.

Arthur Young

CHAPTER 5

Arthur Young and the Concept of Value Added

1. Brief Life

When in 1812 Arthur Young intervened in the debate on the measurement of price movements he could speak with some authority: he was Secretary of the Board of Agriculture, was recognised as one of the leading figures in the agricultural revolution of the eighteenth century and had to his credit the first production accounts for agriculture. Thus the method he proposed for weighting index-numbers, though not as rigorous as that devised by Lowe, was grounded on a lifetime's study of agricultural practices and agricultural prices. Yet he was by training neither a farmer nor an economist. Apart from a smattering of accountancy he had no formal training of any kind, a fact he deplores in his autobiography when describing his frivolous youth. However, he more than made up for it in later life.

Young was born in London on 11 September 1741. He was the second son of a clergyman of some distinction, rector of Bradfield in Suffolk, prebendary of Canterbury, chaplain to the Speaker of the House of Commons Arthur Onslow, and author of a number of books on theological subjects. The boy grew up in an atmosphere of cultured ease and one gets the impression that everyone around him concurred in spoiling him. He was sent to a school in Lavenham, near his father's rectory, 'where he received more indulgence than instruction'. A bright and precocious boy, much more interested in life than in books, he got all the stimulus he needed from his family and their friends. In fact he could have said with Osbert Sitwell that he was educated in the holidays from school. He loved music, he loved the theatre, he had a passion for dancing and an even greater passion for flirting. His elder sister in her letters kept him abreast of London society gossip. Speaker Onslow, a politician of liberal views, was his godfather and gave him the *entrée* into the more progressive political circles. His upbringing is well epitomised by a visit to London at the age of twelve, when he was taken to hear Handel's *Messiah*, saw the great Garrick on stage and met 'more than once' the already notorius free-thinker John Wilkes.

The result of it all was that on leaving school in 1758, instead of going to the university as would have been natural for a clergyman's son, he was sent to learn accountancy with a firm of merchants in Lynn in order to equip himself for a business career. At Lynn he danced and flirted more than ever and 'his great foppery in dress for the balls' ran away with the money he was supposed to spend on books. So, being gifted with a fluent pen, he took to writing in order to earn some money: between the ages of seventeen and eighteen he published two political pamphlets and four novels. In 1759 his father died and Arthur left Lynn 'without education, profession or employment', as he says in his autobiography.

For the next two years he remained at Bradfield with his mother, of whom he was very fond. Then in 1761 he moved to London and threw himself into a whirl of activities. Clever, lively, good looking, charming, all doors were open to him and he made a large number of friends especially in the literary, theatrical and musical world. In 1763 he was offered a commission in a cavalry regiment which he would have liked to accept, but his mother was so averse to the idea that he renounced it and at her suggestion returned to Bradfield and took up the management of the family estate. Without realising it he had at last found his vocation.

In 1765 he married a Miss Allen but the marriage turned out badly. His wife had an ungovernable temper and quarrelled with his mother, so after the birth of his first child he thought it best for the sake of peace to leave Bradfield. He bought a farm in Essex, lost money in unsuccessful experiments and decided to try somewhere else. Eventually he settled for a farm in Hertfordshire. As a farming venture this proved equally unsatisfactory but the search for it had unexpected and important consequences: while going round to inspect various properties that were up for sale he had taken copious notes of what he had observed, visiting farmers wherever he went and questioning them closely on their methods, and in 1768 he published the results under the title *A Six Weeks' Tour through the Southern Counties of England and Wales.*[1] He wrote well and knew how to combine solid technical information with amusing anecdotage. The book was an immediate success. The booksellers asked for more and Young, who had become really interested in agriculture and was always short of money, was only too glad to oblige: in 1770 there appeared *A Six Months' Tour through the North of England*[2] and this was followed in 1771 by *The Farmer's Tour through the East of England.*[3]

These were only some of the books he wrote at this time. Indeed from 1767 to 1774 he seems never to have stopped writing: farming manuals, books and essays on political and economic topics, even parliamentary reports for the press. In particular, he wrote in 1771 a pamphlet on the desirability of a census of population,[4] a suggestion which was not adopted until the census of 1801; and in 1774 he published his *Political Arithmetic*,[5] an intelligent if not very original treatise on economic policy of which he was extremely proud. In the same year he was elected a Fellow of the Royal Society.

His books ran to many editions, were translated into several languages and brought in a substantial income. But it was an anxious time. In his memoirs, written many years later, he records that in 1771 his receipts had been £1,167 but adds ruefully: 'No carthorse ever laboured as I did at this period, spending like an idiot, always in debt'. And elsewhere he says: 'What would not a sensible, quiet, prudent wife have done for me? But had I so behaved to God as to merit such a gift?'. Reading between the lines it is easy to see that he was extremely susceptible to women, impulsive, restless, excitable, impatient of restraint,

1. Nicoll, London, 1768.

2. 4 vols, Strahan, Nicoll, London 1770.

3. 4 vols, Strahan, London, 1771.

4. ARTHUR YOUNG, *Proposals to the Legislature for Numbering the people*. Nicoll, London, 1771; facsimile in *The Development of Populations Statistics* (ed. D.V. Glass), Gregg International, 1973.

5. Pt. I, Nicoll, London, 1774; pt. II, Cadell, London, 1779.

one minute on top of the world, the next down in the dumps. On the whole, however, the positive, cheerful side of his nature prevailed. Life may have been depressing at home but the world was full of interesting people, stirring events and amusing incidents and, above all, agriculture was fascinating.

In 1776, at the instigation of Petty's great-grandson the Earl of Shelburne (later first Marquis of Lansdowne), Young embarked on a tour of Ireland, and this led the following year to an invitation from Lord Kingsborough to become his agent in County Cork at a very good salary. So he sold his Hertfordshire farm and brought his family over to Ireland, only to find himself after a short time eased out of his post by a designing rival. He returned to England dispirited and at a loose end, toyed with the idea of emigrating to America, was dissuaded by his mother, and finally bought some land near Bradfield and resumed his farming there. In 1780 his *Tour in Ireland*[1] came out.

The 1780's were an important decade in Young's life. His perseverance was bringing its rewards. For more than fifteen years he had been experimenting on his own land, collecting specimens of plants and soils wherever he went, comparing methods of cultivation, observing conditions of work, getting information on production costs, on markets, on the effects of taxation, and broadcasting his findings in book after book. He was now regarded both in England and abroad as the foremost authority on all aspects of agriculture and also as someone worth listening to on economic matters. In 1784 he started his *Annals of Agriculture*, a monthly journal which continued regulary until 1809 and attracted over the years many distinguished contributors.[2] Among the people who wrote for it, besides Young himself, were Sir Frederick Eden, Jeremy Bentham, Joseph Priestly, whose help Young enlisted for some of his chemical experiments on soils, the Sicilian agricultural economist Paolo Balsamo and, under the pseudonym of Ralph Robinson, King George III, 'Farmer George' as he was called, who was one of Young's warmest admirers.

1. Cadell and Dodsley, London, 1780.

2. Arthur Young (ed.), *Annals of Agriculture*. Monthly from 1784 to 1809; the final volume, no. 46, is incomplete: pt. 2 was issued in 1812, pt. 3 in 1818 (pt. 1 is missing).

Around the time when Young was starting his *Annals*, a French nobleman of progressive views, the Duc de Liancourt, a descendant of the great La Rochefoucauld, sent his two young sons on a riding tour of England so that they might get a first-hand knowledge of English agriculture and economic conditions generally. The boys were in the charge of a Monsieur de Lazowski and the trio sought the acquaintance of the famous Mr. Young. A friendship sprang up and in 1787 Young received from Lazowski an invitation to join him and the duke's eldest son, the young Count de La Rochefoucauld, in a riding tour to the Pyrenees.

This was a wonderful opportunity to see for himself what was going on in a country which had always interested him particularly. So in May 1787 he crossed from Dover with his mare, joined his friends in Paris, went with them as far as Barcelona, paid a visit to Liancourt on his way back and returned home in November. In the following year he made another riding trip to France by himself. In 1789 he went over again, this time travelling by carriage. He spent the troubled month of June in Paris, leaving shortly before the fall of the Bastille and proceeding on to Nice and thence to Venice and Florence. In 1792 he published his *Travels during the Years 1787, 1788 and 1789*,[1] the best of all his *Tours* and the one on which his reputation as a writer chiefly rests.

Before he went to France, Young's political opinions had predisposed him to sympathise with revolutionaries and what he observed while he was there confirmed him in his inclinations. But his revolutionary ardour was damped by the scenes of violence he witnessed on his last journey, and quite extinguished by the Terror. Years later Sir John Sinclair told him a story that must have pleased him greatly; Sinclair had it from the secretary of the French Royal Society of Agriculture whom he had recently met in Paris. During the Revolution this gentleman had been arrested and at his trial had been told that his life would be spared if he could show that he had done something useful for the Republic. He replied that he unquestionably had: convinced that Arthur Young's *Travels* contained highly useful information, he had published a cheap abridged edition which was much read and had had important

1. 2 vols, W. Richardson, Bury St. Edmunds, 1792; 2nd edn, W. Richardson, London, 1794; Irish edn, Cross, Wogan and others, Dublin, 1793.

effects. At this he was released. 'Tell your friend Mr Young,' he said to Sinclair, 'that he was thus the means of saving my life'.

In 1792 Young bought a large estate of 4,400 acres in Yorkshire with the intention of leasing his Suffolk farms and moving to his new property which would give him greater scope for experiments. However, in the following year he was offered the secretaryship of the newly established Board of Agriculture and accepted it. In many ways he repented his decision. He had looked forward to Yorkshire and regretted having to sell his new estate; he disliked having to spend so much time in London; and he did not get on with the president of the Board, Sir John Sinclair.

All this sounds very negative, and there is no doubt that as the years went by the pessimistic side of his nature took the upper hand. In 1790 he had had a severe illness and on his recovery had written what he called 'a melancholy review of his past life', which he published in the *Annals*[1] and which is indeed very melancholy. In spite of his depression he was still very active, however, writing books and papers, carrying on tours of inspection as required by his post, receiving a stream of admirers from all over the world and maintaining a vast correspondence with some of the most famous men of his time; among them, to mention only a few, were Pitt, Burke, Priestly, Malthus, Wilberforce, Washington, Lafayette, the Empress Catherine of Russia, who sent him a gold snuffbox and ermine cloaks for his wife and daughters, and Count Rostopshine, governor of Moscow, who sent him a snuffbox studded with diamonds and inscribed 'from a pupil to his master'.

In 1797 a blow fell from which his spirits never recovered: his favourite daughter, Martha Ann, died of consumption in her fourteenth year. After this, though he continued to write and fulfil his duties at the Board of Agriculture, Young was a broken man. His melancholy deepened into religious obsession, he cut down his correspondence and gave up social life altogether. In 1807 he became aware that his eyesight was failing and in 1811 he went completely blind. His diary ends in 1818. He died in London on 20 April 1820 and is buried at Bradfield.

1. ARTHUR YOUNG, 'Memoirs of the last thirty years of the *Editor's* farming life'. *Annals of Agriculture*, vol. XV, 1791, pp. 152-7.

Further details about his life and work will be found in his *Autobiography*,[1] in Higgs[2] and in Gazley.[3]

2. *The First Production Account Based on Value Added*

Of Young's voluminous writings I shall confine myself to his tours and travels, to which he owes his reputation as a minor classic. In addition to detailed descriptions of agricultural practices they are full of anecdotes of the many people he met in his perambulations. They broaden out into political arithmetic and contain a great deal of numerical data. Beyond this, they throw a penetrating light on the political and social scene. They are as entertaining as a novel and as informative as an encyclopaedia. Since it is impossible to review them all here, I have selected the three which seemed to me the most interesting: the *Tour through the North of England* because it introduces a new concept in economic accounting, the *Tour in Ireland* because it can be taken as a sequel to Petty's *Anatomy of Ireland*, and the *Travels in 1787, 1788 and 1789* because it gives a vivid first-hand impression of France at that critical time.

The *Tour through the North of England* gives a good idea of the vivacity and spontaneity of Young's style. He does not bite his pen trying to find the *mot juste*, he just writes down what strikes him as it strikes him, whether it be a landscape, a conversation with somebody he meets, the cooking at an inn, the character of a town or the way a particular farmer grows his turnips; the whole interspersed with quantities of numerical information on farming costs and revenues in the various areas he visits. I shall let his prose speak for itself when I come to his tours of Ireland and France. Here I shall concentrate on his political arithmetic, and more specifically on the estimate of the national income with which he summarises his findings in the fourth volume of the work.

1. Edited by M. Bethan-Edwards. Smith & Elder, London, 1898.

2. HENRY HIGGS, 'Arthur Young'. *The Dictionary of National Biography*, vol. XXI, pp. 1272-8.

3. JOHN G. GAZLEY, *The Life of Arthur Young*. American Philosophical Society, Philadelphia, 1973.

This estimate is of special interest as being the first based essentially on value added. It begins with a detailed production account for agriculture which is shown here as table 5.1.

Table 5.1

A PRODUCTION ACCOUNT FOR AGRICULTURE, ENGLAND *c.* 1770

(£'000)

Costs					
Materials and maintenance					
Renewal of stock of draught cattle				780	
Maintenance of horses and other draught cattle				7 024	
Equipment of horses and vehicle maintenance				8 195	
Tenants' repairs of buildings				279	
Seed				4 873	
Other				2 284	
Total material costs					23 436
Value added					
Labour					
Farm servants: men	wages	1 893			
	board	2 007			
			3 900		
maids	wages	577			
	board	836			
			1 413		
boys	wages	346			
	board	725			
			1 071		
Regular labourers			6 160		
Extra (seasonal) labourers			2 053		
Total labour costs				14 597	
Taxes					
Tithes			5 500		
Poor rates			867		
Other parish rates			200		
Total taxes				6 567	
Rent				16 000	
Interest				4 400	
Profit				18 238	
Total value added					59 801
Total costs					83 238

Revenues		
Arable Crops		
Wheat and rye	17 476	
Barley	9 856	
Oats	7 714	
Pease	4 520	
Beans	3 111	
Turnips	4 111	
Clover	1 449	
Potatoes, cabbages etc	. .	
Total from arable crops		48 238
Livestock and hay		
Product of cows	7 108	
Profit on sheep	14 495	
Value of wool	695	
Profit on fatting cattle	7 024	
Profit on young cattle	2 230	
Profit on pigs	2 509	
Profit on poultry	334	
Hay sold to towns	605	
Total from livestock and hay		35 000
Total revenues		83 238

Note: Components do not always add up to totals because of rounding-off errors.
Source: Arthur Young, *A Six Months' Tour Through the North of England*.

In this table, apart from slightly modernising the terminology, I have left Young's presentation alone. The table shows on one side the revenue from crops, livestock and hay, and on the other the costs divided between material inputs and value added. The latter includes not only wages in cash and kind, rent, interest and farmers' profits but also tithes, poor rates and parish rates which provided income for the clergy, the poor and the parish officers. Profit is obtained as the excess of revenue over all outgoings.

For his estimate of total national income Young rounded up the income generated in agriculture to £60 million and added to it rough estimates of the revenue from forestry, fisheries and mines, and from the principal branches of manufacturing, trade, transport and other services. The result is shown in table 5.2.

Table 5.2
THE NATIONAL INCOME OF ENGLAND *c.* 1770

(£ million)

Agriculture, mining and fishing		
Products specified in table 5.1 above	60.0	
Woods, timber, inland fisheries, parks and mines	6.0	
		66.0
Manufactures		
Wool	7.0	
Leather	4.0	
Metals	6.0	
Flax, hemp, glass, paper and porcelain	2.0	
Silk and cotton	1.5	
Construction, furniture-making and retail trade	6.5	
		27.0
Commerce, shipping and shipbuilding		10.0
Professional activities		5.0
Public revenue net of interest paid abroad		9.0
Interest n.e.s.		5.0
Total income of England		122.0

Source: Arthur Young, *A Six Months' Tour through the North of England.*

His comment to these figures is typical:

'Now the most inattentive eye must be able, at the slightest glance, to specify abundance of various kinds of income omitted in this table;

but I by no means aim at accuracy in a matter that requires it not. All I would endeavour to show is that the income of the whole people is a very considerable sum compared to all public wants! and that it, in all probability, amounts to considerably more than an hundred millions.'

Young made a second estimate of the national income in his *Farmer's Tour through the East of England*, and a third in part II of his *Political Arithmetic*. An up-to-date version of his calculations is given in Deane[1] and a comparison of his industrial breakdown of the national products with King's analogous estimates is attempted in Deane and Cole.[2]

3. The Tour of Ireland

In 1776, when Young was returning to London from his first visit to Ireland, an unfortunate thing happened: his trunk was stolen, and with it went not only all the specimens of plants and soils he had collected but also his travel diary. As a consequence the *Tour in Ireland* lacks the wealth of numerical data that one finds in his other books and so does not lend itself to the construction of tables that could be compared with Petty's tables in the *Anatomy of Ireland*. Neverthless it makes interesting reading. Though much had happened in the past hundred years, Young describes a country that Petty would have recognised. But while Petty's point of view is strictly that of an economist, Young's is more that of a social anthropologist interested in the behaviour, customs and attitudes of the people he observes. In the following generation Maria Edgeworth, aunt of the famous economist, who lived most of her life in Ireland and was the author of several important books on Irish social conditions, said of Young's *Tour* that 'it presented the most faithful portraiture of the Irish peasantry that had yet appeared'.

1. Phyllis Deane, 'The implications of early national income estimates for the measurement of long-term growth in the United Kingdom'. *Economic Development and Cultural Change*, vol. IV, no. 1, 1955, pp. 3-38.

2. Phyllis Deane and W. A. Cole, *British Economic Growth, 1688-1959*, p. 156.

In reading Petty's description of the cabins in which the Irish peasants lived in his time I was somewhat surprised that he put the average number of occupants as high as five, but in fact he was right. Young collected information on this point from three estates he visited. He gives data on 99 cabins of harvesters and labourers which turned out to contain 615 souls, or an average of over six per cabin. These cabins, which swarm with children and farmyard animals, 'generally consist of a single room with only a single door which serves also as a window to let in the light and as a chimney to let out the smoke. But in stone cottages built by improving landlords, I have seen the windows and chimney stopped to keep in the warm smoke'. So Petty's plan to replace the cabins by neat cottages might not have had the advantages he intended.

The poor in Ireland lived mainly on milk and potatoes. Young does not consider this a diet inferior to the bread and cheese of the English labourer:

'If anyone doubts the comparative plenty which attends the board of a poor native of England and Ireland, let him attend to their meals: the sparingness with which our labourer eats his bread and cheese is well known; mark the Irishman's potato bowl placed on the floor, the whole family upon their hams around it, devouring a quantity almost incredible, the beggar seating himself to it with a hearty welcome, the pig taking his share as readily as the wife, the cocks, hens, turkies, geese, the cur, the cat, and perhaps the cow – all partaking of the same dish. No man can have been a witness of it without being convinced of the plenty, and I will add the cheerfulness, that attends it.'

Young gives the budget of four of these families. The annual incomings are in the range of £9 to £16, which may include the sale of animals and produce as well as wages; the man earns £5 or £6 and the total is made up by other members of the family. On the outgoing side only the main expenses, including materials and animals for resale, are given. In three out of the four budgets there is a positive balance which in one case Young terms 'remains for whiskey etc., etc.'. He asks the fourth man, whose account shows a deficit and considerable expenditure on clothing, how he will meet the deficiency and find money for whiskey and the priest; 'I must either not eat my geese and pig or else not dress so well', is the reply. In general, however, 'except on Sundays and holidays their clothing is deplorable and gives an impression of universal poverty'.

From his observations Young concludes that the supposed laziness of the Irish is more apparent than real; it usually disappears when they are working for themselves or playing games. Dancing is a favourite pastime. Dancing masters travel through the country from cabin to cabin, with a piper or blind fiddler; and the pay is sixpence a quarter. There is also a measure of education in what are called 'hedge schools' though, says Young, 'they might as well be called ditch schools, as I have seen many a ditch full of scholars where reading and writing are taught'. Grown men too go to school, with the intention of becoming priests.

Nowadays Irish labourers do not live in one-room cabins, their clothes are not deplorable and their children go to proper schools. But affluence has not bred stuffiness, and the itinerant dancing master is still a feature of the countryside. What is even more remarkable, the memory of past miseries has not bred rancour, and in independent Eire the English visitor is still greeted with smiling faces and open hospitality.

Although Young's *Tour in Ireland* did not have as much success with the general public as his other travel books, his championship of the Irish peasantry made an impression in the right quarters, and one of the tax reforms he advocated to lighten the fiscal burden on Irish agriculture was implemented by the government within a year of the publication of the book.

4. The First Continental Tour

The *Travels* through France, northern Spain and northern Italy cover the three journeys undertaken in 1787, 1788 and 1789. Between May 1787 when he left for his first trip and January 1790 when he returned from his last, Young spent about seventeen months on the Continent. He travelled thousands of miles, slept in hundreds of inns, met a vast number of people, witnessed many dramatic events and collected an innumerable quantity of data. When he sat down to arrange his notes into a book he was not quite sure what shape to give it: should it be a journal recounting his experiences as they had occured; or should it be a treatise setting out the results of his enquiries into French agriculture, the main purpose of his travels. It would not be easy to combine the two into a running narrative. In the end he decided to devote the first part to a journal of his itinerary and the second to a systematic account of his findings grouped by topic, not confining himself to agriculture but dealing also with matters of economic and political relevance.

The journal starts on 15 May 1787, when Young crosses the Channel. After stopping one day in Calais to let his mare recover from sea-sickness he sets off for Paris, where he is expected by Lazowski and the Duc de Liancourt. His first impressions are of a rich country badly cultivated by a depressed peasantry. However,

'if the French have not husbandry to show us, they have roads; nothing can be more beautiful, or kept in more garden order, . . . which would fill me with admiration, if I had known nothing of the abominable *corvées*, that make me commiserate the oppressed farmers, from whose extorted labour this magnificence has been wrung.'

He reaches Paris on the 25th, spends a breathless day under Lazowski's guidance sightseeing and shopping for necessaries as his luggage has not arrived from Calais, and is then whisked off to Versailles as the guest of the duc de Liancourt in order to watch the following morning Louis XVI invest his nephew, a boy of ten, with the order of the *Saint Esprit*. Young is not impressed: 'pompous folly', is his verdict. After the investiture

'the King and the knights walked in a sort of procession to a small apartment in which he dined. . . . The ceremony of the King's dining in public is more odd than splendid. The Queen sat by him with a cover before her, but ate nothing; conversing with the Duke of Orléans, and the Duke of Liancourt, who stood behind her chair . . .

The whole palace, except the chapel, seems to be open to all the world; we pushed through an amazing crowd of all sorts of people to see the procession . . . But the officers at the door of the apartment in which the King dined, made a distinction, and would not permit all to enter promiscuously.'

In the evening Young goes back to Paris, and the following day he departs with Lazowski and the Count de La Rochefoucauld for their ride south.

Their destination is Bagnères-de-Luchon, a fashionable watering place in the Pyrenees, to join a contingent of La Rochefoucauld relatives who are spending the summer there. They travel at a leisurely pace, covering between twenty and forty miles a day, and what they see in the countryside confirms Young's first impressions:

'. . . the fields are scenes of pitiable management, as the houses are of misery. Yet all this country highly improveable, if they knew what to do with it: the property, perhaps, of some of those glittering beings, who figured in the procession the other day at Versailles. Heaven grant me patience while I see a country thus neglected. . . . All the country girls and women are without shoes or stockings: and the ploughmen at their work have neither sabots nor feet to their stockings. This is a poverty, that strikes at the root of national prosperity; a large consumption among the poor being of more consequence than among the rich: the wealth of a nation lies in its circulation and consumption, and the case of poor people abstaining from the use of manufactures of leather and wool ought to be considered an evil of the first magnitude. It reminded me of the misery of Ireland.'

Another sign of poverty is the squalor of the country inns, which compare very badly with their English counterparts in everything except food.

In spite of these drawbacks he enjoys the journey very much. His travelling companions are the nicest of people, intelligent, amusing and informative. They go through Orléans, Chateauroux, Limoges, Souillac, Montauban, visiting cathedrals and manufactures, calling on friends and acquaintances, sampling wines, chatting with the locals, making an occasional detour to view some particularly fine prospect. Young is everywhere impressed by the scale of public engineering: excellent roads, magnificent bridges, noble canals. The inns, dirty and awful as they are, usually succeed in producing good food. And in some districts farming shows signs of good management. When they come in sight of the Pyrenees his admiration overflows; and the grandeur of nature is made even more delightful to his eye by the sight of well-tilled land and prosperous-looking farmsteads: vines on the hills, maize and corn in the plain, 'the whole scenery one vast sheet of cultivation; everywhere chequered with these well built white houses . . . The peasants are for the most part land proprietors', he remarks.

The travellers reach Bagnères-de-Luchon on 17 June. Here Young spends three extremely enjoyable weeks in beautiful surroundings and comfortable lodgings among the cream of French society:

'Those who bathe, or drink the waters, do it at half after five or six in the morning; but my friend [Lazowski] and myself are early in the mountains, which are here stupendous. . . . Cultivation is here carried to a considerable perfection in several articles, especially in the irrigation of meadows: we seek out the most intelligent peasants, and have many and long conversations with those who understand French, which however is not the case with all, for the language of the country is a mixture of Catalan, Provençal and French. . . . The ramble of the morning finished, we return in time to dress for dinner, at half after twelve or one: then adjourn to the drawing room of Madam de La Rochefoucauld, or the Countess de Grandval alternately, the only ladies who have apartments large enough to contain the whole company.'

In the afternoon there are games, cards and music. In the evening

'the company splits into different parties, for their promenade, which lasts till half an hour after eight; supper is served at nine: there is, after it, an hour's conversation in the chamber of one of our ladies; and this is the best part of the day, – for the chat is free, lively and unaffected; and uninterrupted, unless on a post-day, when the duke [de La Rochefoucauld] has such packets of papers and pamphlets, that they make us all politicians. All the world is in bed by eleven.'

As part of their holiday in the Pyrenees Young and Lazowski had planned an excursion into Spain. Accordingly, on

10 July they set off on muleback. Their conductor marches on foot, 'boasting that his legs are good for fifteen leagues a day . . . but we are not a little disappointed to find his French is pretty much that of a Spanish cow, if I may use a common French expression'. After an exhausting journey through a poverty-stricken countryside, stopping at miserable inns, 'dog holes' Young calls them, they reach Barcelona on the 16th. Here they find a bustling commercial and manufacturing town, much of it modern, with good houses, grandiose public buildings, well-lit streets and a splendid quay beautifully designed and 'most solidly erected in hewn stone, and finished in a manner, that discovers a true spirit of magnificence'. In the evening they go to the theatre:

'A Spanish comedy was represented, and an Italian opera after it. We were surprized to find clergymen in every part of the house . . . In the centre of the pit on benches the common people seat themselves. I saw a blacksmith, hot from the anvil, with his shirt sleeves tucked above his elbows, who enjoyed the entertainment equally with the best company in the boxes, and probably much more.'

On the next day, the 18th, they leave for France, this time on horseback, and on the 21st they are at Perpignan. Here Young parts with his friend in order to make a tour of Languedoc. He goes to Narbonne and then to Béziers where he visits the Abbé Rozier, the editor of the *Journal Physique*, whom he knows to have an experimental farm there, but learns to his disappointment that the Abbé had left two years ago and sold his farm. And why did the Abbé leave, he asks at the table d'hôte of his inn. Because, he is told,

'the bishop of Béziers cutting a road through the Abbé's farm leading to his (the bishop's) mistress, that occasioned such a quarrel, that Mons. Rozier could stay no longer in the country. This is a pretty feature of a government: that a man is to be forced to sell his estate, and is driven out of a country, because bishops make love – I suppose to their neighbours wives, as no other love is fashionable in France. Which of my neighbours wives will tempt the bishop of Norwich to make a road through my farm, and drive me to sell Bradfield?'

These few weeks riding through a sun-baked countryside along splendid but empty roads leading as often as not to unspeakable inns, have given Young a different opinion of French roads and their usefulness:

'The roads here are stupendous works. I passed a hill, cut through to ease a descent, that was all in the solid rock, and cost 90,000 livres (£3,937) yet it extends but a few hundred yards. Three leagues and a half from Sejean to Narbonne cost 1,800,000 livres (£78,750). These roads are superb even to a folly . . . The traffic on the way, however, demands no such exertions . . . In 36 miles, I have met one cabriolet, half a dozen carts, and some old women with asses. For what all this waste of treasure? – In Languedoc, it is true, these works are not done by *corvées*; but there is an injustice in levying the amount not far short of them. The money is raised by *tailles*, and, in making the assessment, lands held by a noble tenure are so much eased, and others [held] by a base one so burthened, that 120 *arpents* in this neighbourhood, held by the former, pay 90 livres, and 400 possessed by a plebeian right, which ought proportionally to pay 300 livres, are, instead of that, assessed at 1,400 livres . . . At St. Gironds go to the Croix Blanche, the most execrable receptacle of filth, vermin, impudence and imposition that ever exercised the patience, or wounded the feelings of a traveller . . . What can be the circulating connection between towns and countries, that can be held together and supported by such inns? There have been writers who look upon such observations as arising merely from the petulance of travellers, but it shews their extreme ignorance. Such circumstances are political data . . . Bridges that cost £70 or 80,000 and immense causeways to connect towns, that have no better inns than such as I have described, appear to be gross absurdities. They cannot be made for the mere use of the inhabitants, because one-fourth of the expence would answer the purpose of real utility. They are therefore objects of public magnificence, and consequently for the eye of travellers.'

Adam Smith, who had spent almost three years in France in the mid-1760's, makes a very similar comment in *The Wealth of Nations*:

'In France . . . the great post-roads, the roads which make the communication between the principal towns of the kingdom, are in general kept in good order; and in some provinces are even a good deal superior to the greater part of the turnpike roads in England . . . The proud minister of an ostentatious court may frequently take pleasure in executing a work of splendor and magnificence, such as a great highway which is frequently seen by the principal nobility, whose applauses, not only flatter his vanity, but even contribute to support his interest at court.'[1]

It is odd that neither Smith nor Young seem to have realised the military implications of these great highways.

On getting back to Luchon on 6 August Young finds that the party are not yet ready to leave for another ten days, so he decides to make use of the time in a tour of the south-west as far as Bayonne. From there, crossing Béarn and the *landes*, he rejoins his friends at Auch and with them goes back through Bordeaux, the Loire and Paris to Liancourt's estate near Chantilly, where he has been asked to stay with the family.

Young's observations since he had set foot in France had convinced him that the only districts where agriculture flourished were those where the farmers owned their own land; 'whenever you stumble on a Grand Seigneur, even one who was worth millions, you are sure find his property a desert'.

Of course there were exceptions, and the duc de Liancourt was one of them. His estate was a model of good farming, and in order to provide employment for the villagers not working on the land he had set up a textile factory with twenty-five looms, a number which he intended to increase. The daughters of the poor were taught to read and write and to spin cotton, they were employed until they were marriageable and were then given a part of their earnings as a marriage portion. He also had an establishment for training the orphans of soldiers to be soldiers themselves. Young says it is very well conducted but that personally he would rather see those hundred and twenty boys educated to the plough and to good farming methods.

He is interested in the menagerie and dairy that the duchess has built near the château and is delighted to find that her sister, the Vicomtesse du Pont, is actually a farmer: 'A French lady, young enough to enjoy all the pleasures of Paris, living in

1. Adam Smith, *The Wealth of Nations*. Glasgow edn, Clarendon Press, Oxford, 1976, vol. 2, p. 729.

the country, and minding her farm, was an unlooked for spectacle'. He comments at many points in his diary on his admiration for the position of women in France: invited by the duke to dine with the provincial assembly, he finds there twenty-five or six men, including three rich farmers, and two ladies, 'a thing that could never have happened in England'.

Young had come to Liancourt with the intention of staying three or four days but everyone is so agreeable and pressing that he remains more than three weeks. It is with regret that he leaves on 9 October to go back to Paris. There he spends about a fortnight, seeing the principal sights and meeting many people of note. Among these he visits Lavoisier and his wife, 'a lively, sensible, scientific lady', who works with her husband in his laboratory and is translating an English book on chemistry. One entry is of particular interest:

'Dined today with a party, whose conversation was entirely political... One opinion pervaded the whole company, that they are on the eve of some great revolution in the government: that everything points to it: the confusion in the finances great; with a *deficit* impossible to provide for without the states-general of the kingdom, yet no ideas formed of what would be the consequences of their meeting: no minister existing, or to be looked to in or out of power, with such decisive talents as to promise any other remedy than palliative ones... a great ferment amongst all ranks of men, who are eager for some change, without knowing what to look to, or hope for; and a strong leaven of liberty, increasing every hour since the American revolution... It is very remarkable, that such conversation never occurs, but a bankruptcy is a topic: the curious question on which is, *would a bankruptcy occasion a civil war, and a total overthrow of the government*? All agree, that the states of the kingdom cannot assemble without more liberty being the consequence; but I meet with so few men who have any just ideas of freedom, that I question much the species of this new liberty that is to arise.'

On 28 October Young leaves Paris and on 4 November he is at Lille, where his free-trade convictions are ruffled:

'The cry here for a war with England amazed me... It is easy enough to discover, that the origin of all this violence is the commercial treaty [promoted by Pitt to liberalise trade between England and

France], which is execrated here, as the most fatal stroke to their manufactures they ever experienced. These people have the true monopolizing ideas; they would involve four-and-twenty millions of people in the certain miseries of war, rather than see the interest of those who consume fabrics, preferred to the interest of those who make them. The advantages reaped by four-and-twenty millions of consumers are supposed to be lighter than a feather, compared with the inconveniences sustained by half a million of manufacturers.'

On 8 November he is back at Calais and a few days later he arrives home, 'and have more pleasure in giving my little girl a French doll, than in viewing Versailles'.

5. *The Second Continental Tour*

Young's second visit to France, undertaken with the intention of touring the north-western provinces, began on 4 August 1788. Compared with his first, it proved disappointing. To begin with, after barely fifty miles his mare went half blind. Finding another good horse was not easy and in any case he did not like to part with her: 'A plague on a blind horse! – But I have worked through life with her; and she TALKS'. So he continues on his ride, but not in the best of tempers: Normandy exhibits the usual mismanagement of good land; the only sources of prosperity are manufacture and commerce, to his mind no compensation for the neglect of agriculture; the inhabitants are cheeseparing and unfriendly; their inns starve you and then fleece you.

Gradually his ill humor subsides. Le Havre is fine; the Pays d'Auge full of opulent pastures; the Benedictine Abbey at Caen magnificent; 'in the evening to the play-house, and I could not but remark an uncommon number of pretty women'. He has introductions to many distinguished and learned people, all very hospitable and informative. At Le Havre it is 'Mons. l'Abbé Dicquemarre, the celebrated naturalist, and Messrs. Hombergs, who are ranked amongst the most considerable merchants of France'. At Caen it is the Marquis de Turgot, 'elder brother of the justly celebrated comptroller general'. That same night 'supped at the Marquis d'Ecougal, at his château *à la Frénaye*. If these French marquesses cannot show me good crops of corn and turnips, here is a noble one of something else – of beautiful and elegant daughters, the charming copies of an agreeable mother'.

Two days later he notes: 'Found at last a horse to try in order to prosecute my journey a little less like Don Quixotte, but it would by no means do . . . so my blind friend and I must jog on still further.' Accordingly they jog on to Bayeux and Cherbourg and on 31 August reach Brittany.

The first impression is disastrous: 'There is a long street in the episcopal town of Dol, without a glass window, a horrid appearance. My entry into Bretagne gives me an idea of its being a miserable province.' He makes a complete circuit of the peninsula and all along the way it is the same story: some of the larger towns, Rennes, Brest, Lorient, are civilised, and here and there one finds an estate properly run by a sensible landowner, but in between there is nothing but wilderness and wretched poverty.

Finally on 21 September he enters Nantes. The contrast is dramatic:

> 'Arrive – go to the theatre, new built of fine white stone . . . Within all is gold and painting, and a *coup d'oeil* at entering, that struck me forcibly. *Mon Dieu!* cried I to myself, do all the wastes, the deserts, the heath, ling, furze, broom, and bog, that I have passed for 300 miles, lead to this spectacle? What a miracle, that all this splendour and wealth of the cities in France should be so unconnected with the country!'

The town is up to the standards of its theatre. The tone is set by the *haute bourgeoisie*, the rich merchants, who could not be more polite and eager to do their English visitor the honours of their city. Here as in some of the other towns he had crossed, especially Rennes, there is great political ferment: 'Nantes is as *enflammée* in the cause of liberty, as any town in France can be; the conversations I witnessed here prove how great a change is effected in the minds of the French . . . The American revolution has laid the foundation of another in France, if government does not take care of itself.'

After four enjoyable days Young strikes the road again. He goes to Angers, where he is entertained by a Monsieur de la Livonière, Perpetual Secretary of the local Society of Agriculture:

'Mons. Livonière conversed with me much on the plan of my travels which he commended greatly, but thought it very extraordinary, that neither government, nor the Academy of Sciences [? the Royal Society], nor the Academy of Agriculture, should at least be at the expence of my journey. This idea is purely French; they have no notion of private people going out of their way for the public good, without being paid by the public; nor could he well comprehend me, when I told him that every thing is well done in England, except what is done with public money.'

Young was now nearing the end of his tour. He crossed Maine, went back to Rouen and on 15 October was in Dieppe, where he embarked for England:

'I was lucky enough to find the passage-boat ready to sail; go on board with my faithful sure-footed blind friend. I shall probably never ride her again, but all my feelings prevent my selling her in France. Without eyes she has carried me in safety above 1500 miles, and for the rest of her life she shall have no other master than myself; could I afford it, this should be her last labour; some ploughing, however, on my farm, she will perform for me, I dare say, cheerfully.'

6. *The Third Continental Tour*

Young's third and last Continental tour was much the longest and most eventful of the three. This time he did not ride but travelled post, intending to go down the eastern provinces of France and spend about two months in Italy. But first he wanted to go to Paris and see for himself what was happening there. He landed at Calais on 5 June 1789 and on the 8th reached Paris where he spent the next three weeks as the guest of the La Rochefoucauld Liancourt family. His detailed reportage of events, at times breathless with excitement, adds many vivid scenes to the picture painted by historians.

'Paris is at present in such a ferment about the States General, now holding at Versailles, that conversation is absolutely absorbed by them . . . While I remain at Paris, I shall see people of all descriptions, from the coffee-house politicians to the leaders in the States; and the chief object of such rapid notes as I throw on paper will be to catch the ideas of the moment.'

Pamphlets pour out the whole time: on the 9th Young reports that 'thirteen came out today, sixteen yesterday and ninety two last week, and the duc de Liancourt has them all'. Soap-box orators make inflammatory speeches in the Palais Royal. On the 15th Young and Lazowski go to Versailles to hear the important debate on 'the state of the nation':

'Mons. l'Abbé Syeyès opened the debate. He is one of the most zealous sticklers for the popular cause . . . being in fact a violent republican . . . He speaks ungracefully, and uneloquently, but logically, or rather reads so, for he read his speech . . . Mons. de Mirabeau spoke without notes, for near an hour, with a warmth, animation, and eloquence, that entitles him to the reputation of an undoubted orator . . . They adjourned for dinner. Dined ourselves with the Duc de Liancourt, at his apartment in the palace, meeting twenty deputies . . . they all speak with equal confidence of the fall of despotism.'

On the 18th he writes, 'Yesterday the commons decreed themselves, in consequence of the Abbé Syeyès's motion, the title of *Assemblée Nationale*'. And on the 20th,

'News! News! – A message from the king to the president of the three orders, that he should meet them on Monday; and, under pretence of preparing the hall for the *séance royale*, the French guards were placed with bayonets to prevent any of the deputies entering the room . . . The circumstances of doing this ill-judged act of violence have been as ill-advised as the act itself . . . the deputies met at the door of the hall, without knowing that it was shut . . . The resolution taken on the spot was a noble and firm one; it was to re-assemble instantly at the *Jeu de Paume*, and there the whole assembly took a solemn oath never to be dissolved but by their own consent, and to consider themselves, and act as the National Assembly, let them be wherever violence or fortune might drive them . . . When this news arrived at Paris, the Palais Royal was in a flame, the coffee-houses, pamphletshops, corridors, and gardens were crowded – alarm and apprehension sat in every eye – the reports that were circulated eagerly, tending to shew the violent intentions of the court... are perfectly incredible for their gross absurdity: yet nothing was so glaringly ridiculous, but the mob swallowed it with indiscriminate faith.'

On the 22nd the deputies, while waiting for the *séance royale*, meet in the church of Saint Louis to take the oath of those who had not been present at the *Jeu de Paume*. Young of course is in the crowd, and when the session is over goes to dine at the palace with Liancourt and a large party of the nobility and deputies, including the duc d'Orléans and the Abbé Syeyès. After the stormy scenes in the streets and in the church Young is amazed by the behaviour of his fellow guests:

'There were not, in thirty persons, five in whose countenance you could guess that any extraordinary event was going forward... they ate, and drank, and sat, and walked, loitered, and smirked and smiled, and chatted with that easy indifference, that made me stare at their insipidity. Perhaps there is a certain *nonchalance* that is natural to people of fashion from long habit... but... the present moment, which is beyond all question the most critical that France has seen from the foundation of the monarchy... was such as might have accounted for a behaviour totally different. The presence of the Duc d'Orléans might do a little, but not much; his manner might do more; for it was not without some disgust, that I observed him several times playing off that small sort of wit, and flippant readiness to titter, which, I suppose, is a part of his character, or it would not have appeared today. From his manner, he seemed not at all displeased. The Abbé Syeyès has a remarkable physiognomy, a quick rolling eye, penetrating the ideas of other poeple, but so cautiously reserved as to guard his own.'

On the 23rd the king makes his long awaited speech, which seems reasonable to Young but is not acceptable to the majority of the deputies. Finally on the 26th the king acceeds to their demands: he merges the three orders into a single unified chamber and thus sanctions the take-over of power by the popular party.

On the 27th Young concludes that 'The whole business seems over, and the revolution complete'. To us, with hindsight, this may seem an amazing statement but in fact it was not. Mob riots in Paris had been a recurrent feature in French history for centuries. They had always died down fairly quickly. The new National Assembly was run by the champions of the people; it had full powers and doubtless would exercise them in favour of the people. What more could the people want?

Buoyed by these optimistic thoughts Young packs his bags and leaves Paris on 28 June to go to Nancy, visit Lazowski's father at Lunéville and then proceed on his journey down the eastern provinces.

His optimism does not last long. Everywhere in Champagne and Lorraine there are signs of unrest and talk of subversion; at Nancy he gets news of fresh tumults in Paris; and at Strasbourg on 20 July he hears of the fall of the Bastille. The following evening, passing through the square of the *hôtel de ville*, he sees a mob breaking the windows with stones, notwithstanding a detachment of soldiers in the square. He stops to watch, clambering onto the roof of a low building to be out of their way:

'In about a quarter of an hour, which gave time for the assembled magistrates to escape by a back door, they burst all open, and entered like a torrent with an universal shout of the spectators. From that minute a shower of casements, sashes, shutters, chairs, tables, sophas, books, papers, pictures, & c. rained incessantly from all the windows of the house, which is seventy or eighty feet long, and which was then succeeded by tiles, skirting boards, bannisters, framework, and every part of the building that force could detach. The troops, both horse and foot, were quiet spectators . . . I was for two hours a spectator at different places of the scene, secure myself from the falling furniture, but near enough to see a fine youth crushed to death by something, as he was handing plunder to a woman, I suppose his mother, from the horror that was pictured in her countenance.'

It must have taken courage to travel in France at that time. In the towns, confusion and violence; in the country, châteaux in flames, their owners hunted by the peasantry now in open revolt; and everywhere the intimidatory rule of the *garde bourgeoise*. After being more than once threatened with arrest

Young found it desirable to wear a cockade of the *tiers état* and necessary at one point to have a passport, which eventually with some difficulty he got.

His progress south is punctuated by alarming and sometimes ludicrous episodes. Near Ferrand he wants to see some springs in the mountains and takes a woman to conduct him there. When they return to the village the *garde bourgeoise* arrest her for guiding a stranger without permission, though they say they have no quarrel with him. They march her off to the castle and Young decides to go along to explain what had happened. Eventually he succeeds in getting the woman off by saying that if they imprison her, they should do the same by him, and answer it as they can. On another occasion his curiosity about farming matters arouses the suspicions of the rustics, who decide he must be a surveyor sent by the queen and the Count d'Entragues (their landlord) to measure their fields in order to double their taxes; it is touch and go that they do not arrest him.

By 5 September he is at Marseilles where he seeks out the Abbé Raynal, author of a notorious treatise on colonial policy which in 1770 had had the distinction of being burnt by the public executioner.[1] Young finds the abbé at the house of his friend Monsieur Bertrand and is received with great cordiality by them both. In the course of a long conversation,

'Mons. l'Abbé Raynal remarked, that the American revolution had brought the French one in its train: I observed, that if the result in France should be liberty, that revolution had brought a blessing to the world, but much more so to England than to America. This they both thought such a paradox, that I explained it by remarking, that I believed the prosperity which England had enjoyed since the peace [with America], not only much exceeded that of any other similar period, but also that of any other country, in any period since the establishment of the European monarchies: a fact that was supported by the increase of population, of consumption, of industry, of navigation, shipping, and sailors; by the augmentation and improvement of agriculture, manufactures, and commerce; and . . . [by] the rising

1. G. T. F. Raynal, *Histoire philosophique et politique des établissements et du commerce des Européens dans les deux Indes*. Geneva, 4 vols, 1770; 10 vols, 1781.

ease and felicity of the people... these circumstances... unquestionably form one of the most remarkable and singular experiments in the science of politics that the world has seen; for a people to lose an empire – thirteen provinces, and to GAIN, by that *loss*, an increase of wealth, felicity, and power! When will the obvious conclusions, to be drawn from that prodigious event, be adopted? That all transmarine, or distant dominions, are sources of weakness: and that to renounce them would be wisdom.'

On the 8th Young leaves Marseilles and on the 16th he enters Italy, greatly excited at the prospect of seeing a country 'so long and so justly celebrated, that has produced those who have conquered, and those who have decorated the world ... our faculties are expanded ... and then all is attention, and willingness to enjoy'. The first Italian town he comes to is Nice, which was then part of the Kingdom of Savoy. From Nice he goes to Turin, which is full of French refugees, including members of the royal family, and it is with difficulty that he finds room in a hotel.

His reputation has preceded him here too and he meets several distinguished people, sees all the important sights in and around the city, visits a country estate, spends a morning at the university, shops for books and goes three times to the opera. He leaves Turin on 2 October and two days later is in Milan.

Milan is delightful. A good hotel, polished company, opulence arising from an intelligent use of the land, a great opera house, what more could one wish for? As a foreign member of the local Society of Agriculture, known as the Patriotic Society, he is welcomed with great cordiality by his fellow members, who go out of their way to entertain him. He attends a meeting of the Society, chaired by Marchese Visconti. He is taken by two of the members to a dairy belonging to Visconti to watch 'the method of making the Lodesan cheese [grana] ... which is so totally different from what we use in England, that skill in making may have a great effect in rendering this product of Lombardy so superior to all others'. In the evening he invites his new friends to dine with him in his hotel and a band of itinerant musicians gives a serenade to the '*illustrissimi, eccellentissimi, nobili signori Inglesi*'. He is asked to stay at Mozzate with Count Castiglioni, a charming and clever man and, what pleases Young very much, 'a practical farmer'. And he goes three times to the Scala, 'a most noble theatre; the largest as well as handsomest I have seen . . . the three best rows [of boxes] let at 40 louis d'or a box. This is marvellous for an inland town, without commerce or great manufactures. It is the PLOUGH alone that can do this.'

On his last evening at the opera one of his friends asks him if he would like to be introduced to one of the prettiest ladies of Milan. '*Senza dubbio*'; and he is taken to the box of Signora Lamberti,

'a young, lively, and beautiful woman, who conversed with an easy and unaffected gaiety, that would make even a farmer wish to be her *cicisbeo*. The post, however, is in the hands of another, who was seated in his post of honour *vis-à-vis* the lady . . . The custom seems to flourish at Milan; few married ladies are without this necessary appendage to the state . . . I asked an Italian gentleman, why he was not in his post as a *cicisbeo*? He replied he was not one. How so? *If you have either business or other pursuit, it takes too much time*. They are changed at pleasure, which the ladies defend, by saying, that when an extension of privileges not proper to give is expected, to part with is better than to retain them.'

He concludes his stay in Lombardy with a four-day tour of the great dairy farms of Lodi, Codogno and Crema 'through miles of such amazing exertions in irrigation, that we can have in England no idea of it'. Still more amazing, these small towns have each its opera house, with good singers performing in it. On the 15th Young resumes his journey towards Venice. In Bergamo he has an introduction to a Dr. Maironi da Ponte, the secretary of the local academy:

'I mounted a steep hill into the city . . . and searched hard for the doctor; after examining several streets, a lady from a window, who seemed to pity my perplexity . . . informed me that he was in the country but that if I returned in the morning, I should have a chance of seeing him . . . The next morning . . . I repaired to the street where the lady gave me information the night before; she was luckily at her window, but the intelligence cross to my wishes, for both the [Maironi] brothers were in the country . . . The darkness of the evening had last night veiled the fair *incognita*, but looking a second time now, I found her extremely pretty . . . She asked me kindly after my business, *spero che non è un gran mancamento?* words of no import, but uttered with a sweetness of voice that rendered the poorest monosyllable interesting. I told her that the bosom must be cold, from which her presence did not banish all feeling of disappointment. It was impossible not to say something a little beyond common thanks. She bowed in return; and I thought I read in her expressive eyes, that I had not offended; I was encouraged to ask the favour of Signore Maironi's address in the country. – *Con gran piacere ve lo darò*. – . . . I took a card from my pocket; but her window was rather too high to hand it. I looked at the door; *Forse è aperta*. – *Credo che sí*, she replied. If the reader be an electrician, and have flown a kite in a thunderstorm, he will know, that when the atmosphere around him becomes highly electric, and his danger increases, if he do not quickly remove, there is a cobweb sensation in the air, as if he was inclosed in an invisible net of the filmiest gossamer. My atmosphere, at this moment, had some resemblance to it: I had taken two steps to the door, when a gentleman passing, opened it before me, and stood upon the threshold. It was the lady's husband: she was in the passage behind, and I was in the street before him; she said, *Ecco un Signore Inglese che ha bisogno di una direzione al sig. Maironi*. The husband answered politely that he would give it, and, taking paper and pencil from his pocket, wrote and gave it to me. Nothing was ever done so concisely: I looked at him askance, and thought him one of the ugliest fellows I had ever seen.'

Young continues his journey via Brescia, Verona, Vicenza, Padua. He is now in the territory of Venice and the contrast with Lombardy is depressing: bad roads, squalid country inns, villainous *vetturini*. 'From Brescia to Verona, but especially to Desenzano, I believe there are fifty crosses by the side of the road for deaths. When a person is murdered, they set up a cross for the good of his soul. They had better institute a police for that of his body.' In the towns the inns are good but the streets are unlit and the stucco is peeling off the magnificent palaces by Sammicheli and Palladio. The countryside, festooned with vines, looks reasonably well farmed however.

On 30 October he reaches Venice. His reactions are mixed. Yes, it is beautiful, it is unique; the Renaissance buildings are unrivalled, the pictures splendid, the women 'of a distinguished beauty'; and there are seven theatres. For all this, 'I think I would not be an inhabitant to be Doge, with the powers of the Grand Turk. Brick and stone, and sky and water, and not a field or a bush even for fancy to pluck a rose from!' Furthermore there is an uncomfortable sense of decay about the place and disconcerting traits of grossness in the manners of its inhabitants. The Italians, like the French, have few inhibitions about performing certain physical functions in public, but the Venetians carry this regrettable custom to revolting extremes:

'There is between the front row of chairs in the pit and the orchestra, in the Venetian theatre, a space of five or six feet without floor: a well dressed man, sitting almost under a row of ladies in the side boxes, stepped into this place, and made water with as much indifference as if he had been in the street; and nobody regarded him with any degree of wonder but myself.'

This does not prevent Young from going to see a play or an opera every night of his stay and enjoying them.

On 7 November, he embarks on a ghastly boat that is to take him to Bologna *via* Ferrara; the less said about this experience the better. He arrives in Bologna on the 11th and, apart from the only execrable inn that he has so far experienced in an Italian city, has a pleasant few days there. The Bolognese are as hospitable and informative about agricultural matters as the Milanese. One of the nicest, the Marchese Marescotti, is married to an Englishwoman and is 'a singular instance at Bologna, of going into company with his wife, and consequently superseding the necessity of a cicisbeo. He is regarded by his countrymen for this, pretty much as he would be if he walked on his head, instead of his feet'.

From Bologna Young goes to Florence, where he remains a whole fortnight. This is perhaps the most successful of his Italian halts. The works of art, especially the Greek sculptures, above all the Medici Venus, are beyond anything he has ever seen. Florentine society is cosmopolitan and intellectually alive. Natural philosophy flourishes encouraged by the Grand Duke Leopold, the wisest prince in Europe. The English envoy, Lord Hervey, pays him every attention and invites him to a splendid dinner party. The Florentines do not give dinner parties but hold *conversazioni* at which one meets everybody worth meeting in the literary and scientific world, including several agronomists of international reputation. One of them, Signor Fabbroni, has a charming, intelligent and beautiful wife: 'if Titian were alive, he might form from her a Venus not inferior to those he has immortalized on his canvass . . . Signora Fabbroni is here, but where is Titian to be found?'

One feature of Florence and other Italian cities which puzzles Young is the degree of opulence attained by them in the fifteenth and sixteenth centuries:

'. . . all here reminds one of the Medicis . . . that splendid and magnificent family. How commerce could enrich it sufficiently, to leave such prodigious remains, is a question not a little curious; for I may venture, without apprehension, to assert that all the collected magnificence of the House of Bourbon, governing for eight hundred years twenty millions of people, is trivial, when compared with what the Medici family have left, for the admiration of succeeding ages – sovereigns only of the little mountainous region of Tuscany, and with not more than one million of subjects . . . Would Mr Hope, of Amsterdam, said to be the greatest merchant in the world, be able in this age, to form establishments, to be compared with those of the Medicis? We have merchants in London, that make twenty, and even thirty thousand pounds a year profit, but you will find them in brick cottages, for our modern London houses are no better, compared with the palaces of Florence and Venice, erected in the age of their commerce; the paintings, in the possession of our merchants, a few daubed portraits; their statues, earthen-ware figures on chimney-pieces; their libraries – their cabinets – how contemptible the idea of comparison! . . . This is inexplicable, and demands inquiries from the *historical* traveller.'

On 2 December, with much regret, Young starts on his return journey. 'Renew my connection with that odious Italian race, the *vetturini* . . . To step at once from an agreeable society, into an Italian *voiture*, is a kind of malady which does not agree with my nerves.' He goes back to Bologna and thence to Parma, where he views the Correggios, inspects a factory of Parmesan cheese and visits the Bodoni printing works. He meets Bodoni himself 'who shewed me many works of singular beauty, and buys Tasso's *Aminta* 'as a specimen of this celebrated press, which really does honour to Italy'. He proceeds through Piacenza and Alessandria to Turin, crosses the Alps by the Mont Cenis and descends into Savoy, which was then still part of the Kingdom of Sardinia. On Christmas day he crosses the French frontier and on the 27th arrives at Lyon;

'and there, for the last time, see the Alps... leaving Italy, and Savoy, and the Alps, probably never to return, has something of a melancholy sensation. For... what country can be compared with Italy? to please the eye, to charm the ear, to gratify the enquiries of laudable curiosity, whither would you travel?... To the theatre; a musical thing, which called all Italy by contrast to my ears! What stuff is French music!'

However, what was interesting in France was not opera but politics. In Lyon, centre of the silk industry, the political situation had had disastrous repercussions:

'All those I have conversed with in the city, represent the state of the manufacture as melancholy to the last degree. Twenty thousand people are fed by charity, and consequently very ill fed, and the mass of distress, in all kinds, among the lower classes, is greater than ever was known – or than anything of which they had an idea. The chief cause of the evil felt here, is the stagnation of trade, occasioned by the emigration of the rich from the kingdom, and the general want of confidence in merchants and manufacturers; whence, of course, bankruptcies are common.'

Nevertheless both in Lyon and in the surrounding countryside the revolutionary violence of the summer has to all appearances died down.

Things are very different in Paris, where he arrives on 3 January 1790. The royal family, forced to leave Versailles, are now living under close guard in the Tuileries, where the National Assembly also hold their sessions. Young goes with Lazowski for a walk in the gardens of the palace and sees the king and queen walking there too, each with an escort of grenadiers of the *milice bourgeoise*. As long as the king is in the garden only people with passes are allowed in, but when he goes indoors the gates are thrown open to the crowd even though the queen is still outside. 'A mob followed her, talking very loud, and paying no other apparent respect than that of taking off their hats whenever she passed . . . In a little garden railed off. . . the Dauphin . . . was at work with his little hoe and rake, but not without a guard of two grenadiers.' The duc de Liancourt, as Master of the Wardrobe, has an apartment in the palace, where twice a week he gives a great dinner to thirty or forty of his fellow deputies. At these dinners 'most of the deputies, especially the younger ones, were dressed *au polisson*, without powder in their hair, and some in boots; not above four or five were neatly dressed. How times have changed!'

The meetings of the Assembly are stormy and disorderly and made more so by the audience in the galleries, who 'clap, when anything pleases them, and have been known to hiss; an indecorum which is utterly destructive of freedom of debate'. The moderates can hardly make themselves heard. The violent democrats, the *enragés*, 'have a meeting at the Jacobins, called the revolution club, which assembles every night . . . and they are so numerous, that all material business is there decided, before it is discussed by the National Assembly'. Riots flare up the whole time, checked with difficulty by the militia under the orders of La Fayette. Insistent rumours of plots to rescue the king, of disorders fomented by English money, of plans for a counterrevolution add to the state of alarm.

Young is accepted everywhere and by everyone, royalists, moderates and *enragés* alike. He has long arguments with them, trying to persuade them to model their new constitution on that of England, but they will not hear of it: England is not a democracy, it is an aristocratic oligarchy masquerading as a democracy, and this is emphatically not what France wants. One does not sense any animosity in these discussions, however. In fact, far from resenting his propaganda, they arrange a flattering surprise for him: on the 18th, two days before his intended departure,

'Mons. Decretat, and Mons. Blin, carried me to the revolution club at the Jacobins . . . There were above one hundred deputies present, with a president in the chair; I was handed to him, and announced as the author of the *Arithmétique Politique*; the president standing up, repeated my name to the company, and demanded if there were any objections – None; and this is all the ceremony, not merely of an introduction, but an election: for I was told, that now I was empowered to be present when I pleased, being a foreigner.'

On the 19th he takes leave of the duc de Liancourt, for whom he has come to feel great admiration and affection:

'a nobleman, to whose uninterrupted, polite and friendly offices I owe the agreeable and happy hours which I have passed in Paris... his conduct in the revolution has been direct and manly from the very beginning... From the first assembling of the States General, he resolved to take the party of freedom... He is, undoubtedly, to be esteemed one of those who have had a principal share in the revolution, but he has been invariably guided by constitutional motives; for it is certain, that he has been as much averse from unnecessary violence and sanguinary measures, as those who were most attached to the ancient government.'

The duke and Young were never to meet again, although they continued to correspond. In 1792, under the Terror, the duke was forced to emigrate and went to America. When he left France his establishments at Liancourt gave employment to 1000 people and he had set up an 'English farm', complete with English tools, English cattle and an English farmer as a manager, to encourage English methods in his neighbourhood; when he came back from exile he found his establishments destroyed and his improvements laid waste by the very people they were intended to benefit. He lived until 1827.

Young spends his last evening in Paris with Lazowski, 'he endeavouring to persuade me to reside upon a farm in France, and I enticing him to quit French bustle for English tranquillity'. Neither succeeds. The next day, 20 January, Young leaves Paris, reaches London on the 25th, and on the 30th is back at Bradfield. The journal closes with the words,

'however pleasing it may be to hope for the ability of giving a better account of the agriculture of France that has ever been laid before the public, yet the greatest satisfaction I feel, at present, is the prospect of remaining, for the future, on a farm, in that calm and undisturbed retirement, which is suitable to my fortune, and which, I trust, will be agreeable to my disposition.'

7. The Wine Accounts of France

The second, technical part of the book is over twice as long as the travel journal and is preponderantly devoted to France. Each chapter deals with a specific topic: extent of territory, climate, population, capital employed in agriculture, farming costs and revenues, wages and prices, manufactures, commerce, taxes, foreign trade. The various types of produce are separately distinguished and there is even a chapter on waste lands, on which Young held strong opinions. The section on Italy is arranged by region and is much less detailed. The book ends with a very brief section on Spain.

To help him in his survey of France Young read much in the writings of the French economists and in official publications, but he relied for his detail largely on his own observation and on conversations with landowners and farmers. This is a good way of collecting information but has the drawback that the results do not lend themselves to neat and comparable tabulation. In his chapter on vines, which I have chosen as an example of his method, he comments on 'the difficulty of reducing the infinite variety of French measures, of lands and liquids, to a common standard, added to an unavoidable uncertainty in the information itself'.

His aims were to find out the value given to the soil by viticulture, the amount of the annual produce and the degree of profit attending it. He soon came to realise that wine is one of the most variable of products. Corn lands and meadows have their good and bad years but they always yield something and the variation in yield is not very great. But with vines the differences are enormous; in some years they yield nothing, in others there are not enough casks to contain the exuberance of the vintage. So even the proprietors can seldom tell accurately the average for their own land, let alone the average for their district.

Although he gives a vast number of data showing proceeds, costs and profit, he is not very proud of his labours but hopes they are free from gross errors, remarking that 'considerable variations from place to place is not a proof of error'. In all cases the price of the product is that obtaining in the same autumn as the vintage. If the wine can be kept even three or six months before sale, the price is much higher but this excess he regards as a return on dealing rather than on growing.

Young describes about eighty wine districts, some very summarily, some in great detail, and for eleven vineyards presents his data in the form of accounts. I have tried to set out these cost structures in table 5.3. In each case Young shows profit as a residue and I have followed his practice. Since the accounts differ considerably both in the number of items distinguished and in the units of measurement used, in order to make them comparable I have translated money values into percentages.

It is hardly necessary to say that this table is not based on a standardised system of accounting but is derived from what Young understood his informants to have told him and my understanding of what he passed on to us. The accounts are intended to relate to an average year but do not altogether succeed in this aim. Intermediate inputs exist in the form of casks, props and manure. In some of the accounts they may also include a certain amount of labour and in such cases the percentage for labour should be correspondingly increased, but it is impossible to tell by how much; what is certain is that in most of the other cases the share of labour is larger, sometimes much larger than that of profit. Interest is intended to relate to the use of land and buildings. Taxes and dues were of many kinds and varied widely not only from district to district but also according to the status of the landowner: in general, the higher the status the lower the tax.

In concluding his chapter on vines Young controverts the opinion which he describes as prevalent in France 'that the wine provinces are the poorest, and that the culture is mischievous to the national interests.' He considers this view to be the reverse of the truth and examines it from a social point of view in terms of the produce and from an individual point of

Table 5.3

PRODUCTION ACCOUNTS FOR ELEVEN FRENCH VINEYARDS, *c.* 1787-89

(percentages)

	Verson, Sologne	La Roche Guyon, Anjou	Epernay, Champagne	Rheims, Champagne	Metz, Loraine	Pont au Mousson, Loraine	Besançon Franche Comtée	Nuits, Bourgoge	Izoire, Auvergne	Montélimar, Dauphiné	Tour d'Aigues, Provence	Average
Intermediate inputs												
Props	2.73	10.00	5.00	2.86	3.08	2.22	3.33	3.43	11.90	..	..	
Manure	..	2.67	3.33	2.86	2.31	4.44	..	..	0.48	..	..	
Casks	..	12.00	2.50	4.29	2.31	8.89	..	3.43	..	4.00	..	
Total	2.73	24.67	10.83	10.01	7.70	15.55	3.33	6.86	12.38	4.00	..	8.91
Taxes												
Taille & capitation	5.45	1.67	} 1.50		5.00		} 1.25		2.86		6.67	
Vingtième	2.27	..		} 1.90	1.54	} 1.67			..	} 2.67	..	
Tithe	..	..	..		3.85		..		..		..	
Droits d'aide	..	..	5.00	9.52	..	..	..	} 4.57	..	..	..	
Droits de gabelle	..	..	..	..	..	5.56	..		..	..	..	
Seigneurial duty	..	..	..	..	..	..	..		..	..	1.07	
Total	7.72	1.67	6.50	11.43	10.38	7.22	1.25	4.57	2.86	2.67	7.73	5.82
Labour												
Culture by contract	18.18	20.00	9.16	9.52	18.46	16.67	16.67	41.14	38.10	40.00	32.00	
Hoeing, planting &c.	..	..	5.33	1.43	..	..	1.25	..	1.90	..	8.00	
Manure spreading	..	..	..	1.67	..	..	..	..	..	..	..	
Vintage	15.00	2.67	8.00	4.29	6.15	1.67	16.67	3.43	..	8.00	6.67	
Pressing	..	..	..	1.90	3.46	1.11	..	..	..	..	..	
Cellarman	..	..	..	2.38	..	..	..	..	..	2.67	..	
Total	33.18	22.67	22.49	21.19	28.07	19.44	34.58	44.57	40.00	50.67	46.67	33.05
Interest & rent												
Interest on land	..	16.00	25.00	28.57	23.08	25.00	50.00	28.57	23.81	20.00	20.00	
Interest on buildings	..	..	3.33	7.14	..	..	..	..	11.43	..	10.00	
Interest on labour	..	..	..	4.29	..	..	..	..	..	..	..	
Rent	27.27	..	..	..	..	..	..	..	..	..	..	
Total	27.27	16.00	28.33	40.00	23.08	25.00	50.00	28.57	35.24	20.00	30.00	29.41
Total costs	70.90	65.01	68.15	82.62	69.23	67.22	89.17	84.57	90.48	77.33	84.40	77.19
Profit	29.10	35.00	31.85	17.38	30.77	32.78	10.83	15.43	9.52	22.67	15.60	22.81
Total revenue	100.00	100.00	100.00	100.00	100.00	100.00	100.00	100.00	100.00	100.00	100.00	100.00

Note: Components do not always add up to totals because of rounding-off errors.

Source: Arthur Young, *Travels During the Years 1787, 1788, 1789*, 2nd edn., vol. II, pp. 3-19.

view in terms of the profit. From a sample of twenty-three vineyards he excludes those in which the land is worth more than £100 an acre and the produce is above £21 an acre, and from the remainder works out the following annual averages per acre:

	£	s	d	
Value of land	45	1	0	(45·05)
Value of produce	9	2	0	(9.10)
Cost of labour	2	12	6	(2.625)

He thinks that net profit on capital employed probably ranges between 7 and 10 per cent. He cannot say how far those estimates are accurate but believes they may not be too far from the truth. If so, a produce of £9 an acre averaged over good and bad years is high; even in the richest counties of England wheat does not yield more than £6 or £7 an acre. Also, £30 to £40 an acre, let alone £45, is a good price for land especially when it is realised that while some vines are grown on good land, many flourish on sandy or stony soil and on rocks and declivities too steep for the plough.

He is astonished to hear it questioned whether it is nationally more advantageous that wine should be a common drink rather than beer, as in England. The English, he points out, are obliged to have recourse to their best lands to grow barley for their drink, whereas the French, under a good government, could have all theirs from soils which in England are only fit to feed rabbits. Indeed England would be better off if it were not necessary to grow so much barley. If it be true, he says, that the common people of England have more bodily vigour than those of France,

'it proves nothing against wine. Are the French poor as well fed as ours? Do they eat an equal quantity of animal flesh? Were they as free? These common prejudices, for or against certain liquors, are usually built on very insufficient observation.

But the enemies of vineyards recur to the charge; *the vine provinces are the poorest of the kingdom: and you always see misery among the poor proportional to the quantity of vines.*'

In so far as there is some truth in this, Young is convinced that it arises not from the unprofitability of wine-growing but from the excessively small properties into which vineyards are often divided. To succeed in this form of culture a man needs an ample capital so that he can afford to store his wine and thus get a much better price and be indifferent to the uncertainty of the crop, concentrating on average results rather than living from hand to mouth as the poor proprietor is forced to do. However, since wine-growing depends almost entirely on labour, requiring no expensive equipment such as carts, ploughs or cattle, it is superficially very attractive to the poor farmer. The desire of possessing landed property is universal in France and when indulged in by the poor leads to small farms which have often to be neglected from the necessity to earn money by working for richer neighbours; and, as generation succeeds generation, the land gets more and more subdivided and the individual holdings become minute and quite unable to support a family. This is the reason for the apparent poverty of wine districts. In fact,

'A poor man can nowhere be better situated than in a wine province, provided he possess not a plant. Whatever may be the season, the poor are sure of ample employment among their richer neighbours, to an amount as we have above seen, thrice as great as any other arable lands afford . . . What an apparent contradiction that property should be the parent of poverty, yet there is not a clearer or better ascertained fact in the range of modern politics.'

8. Summing up

When he published the results of his French survey Young was well aware that the data he had collected could not in themselves be taken as an analysis of the economic situation in France but only as the raw material for such an analysis. The chapter on vines ends with a caveat which puts his attitude in a nutshell:

'To investigate such questions fully, would demand dissertations expressly written on every subject that arises, which would be inconsistent with the brevity necessary to the register of travels: I attempt no more than to arrange the facts procured; it belongs to the political arithmetician fully to combine and illustrate them.'

The case was different when he was dealing with English agriculture, about which he knew so much more. His production account for English agriculture, shown in table 5.1 above, is remarkable for its clarity and degree of detail and provides a solid foundation for his estimates of total agricultural income in table 5.2. If, as he says himself, the income totals for other activities are rough and incomplete we cannot hold this against him. Since he had to collect most of his data himself, had many other things to do and only one lifetime, he naturally concentrated on the branch of production that interested him most. Here he had no hesitation in acting as his own political arithmetician, and in so doing he made one important methodological step forward: he is the first, as far as I know, to have calculated output as the excess of revenue over costs and to have done this on a national scale.

Patrick Colquhoun

CHAPTER 6

Patrick Colquhoun and the Accounts of the British Empire

1. Brief Life

In the decades that intervened between Gregory King and Arthur Young very little original work was done on estimating the national income. Writers on economic matters were for the most part content with using Petty's and King's figures somewhat updated. Young gave a fresh impulse to the subject with his estimates of agricultural output, which constituted about half of the national total; but his estimates of the other half were, as we have seen, pure guesswork. Another step forward was made at the turn of the century by a number of authors who took as their starting point the official estimates of income occasioned by Pitt's recently imposed income tax. An excellent survey of these developments can be found in Studenski.[1] Here I shall not go into them but shall pass on to the first man who can rightly be compared with Gregory King, the Scottish businessman and lawyer Patrick Colquhoun.

Colquhoun was born on 14 March 1745 in Dumbarton, where his father was Register of the Records of the county and a local judge. After attending the grammar school there, he went before he was sixteen to try his fortune in Virginia. Intelligent, upright and energetic, he soon made his way in the society of the colony. To earn his living he engaged in trade and at the same time schooled himself in the law by reading, frequenting the company of lawyers and attending the law courts. Although his biographers are not specific about the nature of his 'commercial pursuits' we can guess from their location and from his subsequent activity that they were connected with the cotton trade.

1. Paul Studenski, *The Income of Nations*. New York University Press, 1958.

In 1766 he returned to Scotland and settled in Glasgow, continuing in business and becoming a considerable figure in the local community: in 1780 he became a member of the Glasgow city council and was appointed justice of the peace; he initiated many schemes of local improvement, among them in 1783 the Glasgow Chamber of Commerce of which he was the first chairman; not surprisingly, he was elected three years in succession Lord Provost of Glasgow. By now he was well known also in London, and throughout the 1780's exerted his influence in government circles to stimulate a series of measures helpful to the trade and commerce of Glasgow and to the British cotton industry in general, writing several papers to publicise its needs and paying visits to the Continent to promote the exports of its products.

In 1789 he moved with his family to London, and there his career took an entirely different turn. In 1792 a long-overdue act of parliament was passed to reform the administration of justice in the capital and Colquhoun was chosen to be one of the magistrates serving on it. He was not new to this type of office, having been for many years justice of the peace in Glasgow, and he 'immediately turned his attention to the subject of police, to the errors and imperfections of the then existing system, and to the means of improvement'. He brought together the results of his findings in a book entitled *A Treatise on the Police of the Metropolis*, published anonymously in 1796, in which he analysed the social causes of crime and laid stress on the importance of prevention as opposed to punishment. The book was widely read and in some cases acted upon not only in England but also abroad, being hailed in the United States as 'one of the most valuable books to the legislature that ever was published'. Indeed, it went into three editions in its first year, and by 1806 has reached a seventh. It also earned its author a doctorate *honoris causa* from the University of Glasgow.

Colquhoun's humanitarian bent led him to take an active interest in the poor. Thus in 1795, when food prices were high, he helped to establish a soup kitchen in Spitalfields, the first of its kind; in 1796 he started a society to redeem the pledges of 'honest industrious families' who had been compelled to pawn their goods and working-tools for subsistence; in about 1803 he promoted in

Westminster an elementary school for poor children; and in his will, being a good Scots and a staunch Colquhoun, he left £200 the interest on which was to be distributed among poor people named Colquhoun in certain parishes of his native county.

From his experiences among the London poor another excellent book was born, *A Treatise on Indigence*, published in 1806, which can be regarded in some sense as a sequel to the *Treatise on the Police*. The greater part of both these volumes is taken up with a discussion of the problems of poverty and crime and of various methods of alleviation and prevention. I shall return to this aspect of Colquhoun's work when I come to talk about Fredrick Eden. Here I shall concentrate on its economic side.

Colquhoun was well-read in political economy, and from his business training was familiar with the principles of accounting. Thus he possessed the two basic ingredients needed to make a good political arithmetician, and he did not waste them. Already in the *Treatise on the Police* he had used numbers to reinforce his arguments. In the *Treatise on Indigence* he went much further, setting his study against a background of national income estimates. And in his next book, *A Treatise on the Wealth, Power and Resources of the British Empire in Every Quarter of the World*, first published in 1814,[1] economic statistics are no longer used in an accessory capacity but take the centre of the stage. This monumental exercise in national income accounting was the culmination of Colquhoun's many-sided output and was the last book he wrote. In 1818 he retired from his position as city magistrate and two years later, on 25 April 1820, he died. In 1775 he had married a Miss Colquhoun, from whom he had seven children; she died in 1810.

A full account of his life and work up to his retirement, written by his son-in-law Dr. Yeats under the pseudonym of 'Ιατϱος, appeared in 1818 in *The European Magazine*.[2] A more accessible biography is that by Espinasse.[3]

1. 2nd edn, with additions and corrections, 1815.

2. Dr. Yeats ('Ιατϱος), 'Memoir of Patrick Colquhoun, Esq., L. L. D.'. *The European Magazine and London Review*, 1818, pp. 187-92, 305-10, 409-13 and 497-503;

3. Francis Espinasse, 'Patrick Colquhoun'. *The Dictionary of National Biography*, vol. iv, pp. 859-61.

2. *The National Income in 1803*

It was his concern for the poor, especially the unemployed poor, that stimulated Colquhoun to study in some depth the economic conditions of the England of his day. As he says in the *Treatise on Indigence*,

'Looking at the various resources which England possesses exceedingly beyond any country in Europe for the employment of her population, and considering that these resources are increasing in consequence of the progressive, and in some instances the rapid accumulation of her *agricultural*, *commercial* and *manufacturing* capitals, it should seem that the evil is to be traced to other causes besides those which simply apply to the want of the means of employment; and while it is admitted that occasional pressures may produce indigence, even where the greatest resources exist, it is the object of the author, in the course of this work, to investigate the other sources of evil and misfortune from which has sprung this gangrene in society.

But in order more clearly to comprehend the subject, and to afford the necessary aids to an accurate discussion, it will be necessary to look back to the state of society a century ago, and to compare it with the present era: this perhaps will best be effected by introducing the following table, framed in the year 1688, by Mr. Gregory King (who has been acknowledged by all political arithmeticians to have been extremely accurate in his researches), and to contrast this general view with the state of society in England at the present period.'

There follows the table which I have reproduced in my chapter on Gregory King (table 3.3, p. 87 above) and side by side with it a table showing the distribution of income in England and Wales in 1803, modelled on King's table but with King's classification expanded to reflect the economic and social changes that had occurred in the interval. This is shown in my table 6.1.

After giving his income table Colquhoun proceeds to discuss 'the different sources from whence the national income is derived; which, notwithstanding its numerous and intricate ramifications, are, in fact, confined solely to *five branches of industry*, aided by capital, skill, and labour; namely, *Land*, *Manufactures*, *Fisheries*, *Foreign Commerce*, and *Colonial and East India Remittances*'.

Table 6.1

AN ATTEMPT TO EXHIBIT A GENERAL VIEW OF SOCIETY AND TO ESTIMATE THE NATIONAL INCOME ENGLAND AND WALES, 1803

Ranks, degrees, titles and descriptions	Population			Income	
	Recipients of income	Families	Total number of persons	Total per group £'000	Average per family £
Temporal peers, including the princes of the blood		287	7 175	2 296.0	8 000
Bishops		26	390	104.0	4 000
Baronets		540	8 100	1 620.0	3 000
Knights		350	3 500	525.0	1 500
Esquires		6 000	60 000	9 000.0	1 500
Gentlemen and ladies living on incomes		20 000	160 000	14 000.0	700
Persons in higher civil offices		2 000	14 000	1 600.0	800
Persons in lesser offices		10 500	52 500	2 100.0	200
Eminent merchants, bankers etc.		2 000	20 000	5 200.0	2 600
Lesser merchants trading by sea		13 000	91 000	10 400.0	800
Persons of the law, incl. judges, barristers, clerks etc.		11 000	55 000	3 850.0	350
Eminent clergymen		1 000	6 000	500.0	500
Lesser clergymen		10 000	50 000	1 200.0	120
Freeholders of the better sort		40 000	220 000	8 000.0	200
Lesser freeholders		120 000	600 000	10 800.0	90
Farmers		160 000	960 000	19 200.0	120
Liberal arts & sciences: doctors, writers, artists		16 300	81 500	4 238.0	260
Shopkeepers and tradesmen		74 500	372 500	11 175.0	150
Artisans and labourers in manufacture and construction		445 726	2 005 767	24 514.9	55
Naval officers including surgeons	7 000	3 000	15 000	1 043.0	149*
Military officers including surgeons	13 064	5 000	25 000	1 815.9	139*
Common soldiers, incl. non-commissioned officers	190 000	50 000	200 000	5 510.0	29*
Common seamen etc. in the navy and customs	130 000	38 175	150 000	4 940.0	38*
Seamen in the merchant service, fisheries etc.	180 000	67 099	299 663	7 200.0	40*
Agricultural labourers		340 000	1 530 000	10 540.0	31
Labourers in mines, canals etc.		40 000	130 000	1 600.0	40
Paupers	1 040 716	260 179	1 040 716	6 868.0	26†
Vagrants, thieves etc.	222 000	..	222 000	2 220.0	10*
Description of persons not included in Mr. Gregory King's estimate					
The King and the royal household		1	50	2 000.0	200 000
Shipowners letting for freight		5 000	25 000	2 500.0	500
Manufactures		25 000	150 000	20 000.0	800
Principal wholesalers		500	3 000	400.0	800
Shipbuilders		300	1 800	210.0	700
Master tailors, dressmakers, army clothiers etc.		25 000	125 000	3 750.0	150
Builders and engineers		5 000	25 000	1 000.0	200
Clerks and shop-assistants	90 000	30 000	150 000	6 750.0	75*
Dissenting clergymen		2 500	12 500	300.0	120
Teachers in universities and chief schools		500	2 000	300.0	600
Other teachers		20 000	120 000	3 000.0	150
Actors and musicians	2 000	500	2 000	400.0	200*
Hawkers, pedlars etc.	2 500	800	4 000	100.0	40*
Immates of debtors prisons	3 510	2 000	10 000	87.8	25*
Persons keeping houses for lunatics		40	400	20.0	500
Lunatics in private and public asylums	2 500	..	2 500	75.0	30*
Innkeepers and publicans		50 000	250 000	5 000.0	100
Half-pay officers (army and navy)	4 015	2 000	10 000	180.7	45*
Pensioned seamen and soldiers	30 500	10 000★	70 500	610.0	20§
Institutional and other unallocated income	50 000	..	..	5 056.0	..
Total	..	1 905 823	9 343 561	222 000.0	..

Per recipient.

Consisting of £10 earnings and £10 pension per recipient.

ource: Patrick Colquhoun, *A Treatise on Indigence.*

† Consisting of £10 earnings and £16 poor relief.

★ Deduced from other figures.

He recapitulates his discussion in a summary table which shows the amounts of income generated in each of his five branches of production and which I reproduce here as table 6.2.

Table 6.2
THE NATIONAL INCOME
ARISING IN PRODUCTIVE ACTIVITIES
ENGLAND AND WALES, 1803
(£ million)

Agriculture and mines etc.	106
Manufactures of all kinds*	86
Fisheries	1
Foreign trade and shipping	25
Income from possessions abroad	4
National income	222

* Including distribution.
Source: Patrick Colquhoun, *A Treatise on Indigence.*

Colquhoun constructed his estimates for 1803 from a variety of sources, ranging from the 1801 population census to insurance estimates and information supplied by 'an intelligent farmer'. His ingenuity in piecing them together into a coherent whole and getting the totals of the two tables to balance is remarkable, and so is his conception of how to set his subject within a broad quantitative framework. But they pale when compared with his next effort, the *Treatise on the Wealth, Power and Resources of the British Empire.*

3. The Income and Wealth of the Empire in 1812

Colquhoun's views on colonial expansion were diametrically opposed to those of Arthur Young. Young, like Adam Smith, saw it as an economic drain on the mother country and a cause of wasteful and bloody wars. Colquhoun, more conventionally perhaps, saw it as a source of wealth and glory. In 1778, when Britain was trying to resist the American drive for independence, he had been one of the principal contributors to the fund for raising the

Glasgow regiment. And in 1812 he wrote with pride that 'it may be averred with truth that the sun never sets on the flag of the United Kingdom'. The first expression of this sentiment is usually attributed to the publicist Christopher North, whose phrase 'His Majesty's dominions, on which the sun never sets' hit the limelight in 1829. North's phrase may be more quotable than Colquhoun's but it was not the first.

Whether one sympathises with Colquhoun's imperial pride or agrees more with Smith's and Young's sober, practical views, the *Treatise on the Wealth, Power and Resources of the British Empire* remains a statistical *tour de force* and a notable contribution to economic history. In what follows I shall refer to it for short as the *Treatise* without qualification.

The *Treatise* covers a wide range of topics. Colquhoun begins with fairly detailed estimates of the population, tangible assets (which he terms 'property') and net output (which he terms 'new property') in Britain and her possessions. He then further disaggregates the figures for Great Britain and Ireland to give ampler details of population, income originating and income distributed. He follows this up with three chapters giving an historical account of public income and expenditure and the public debt, which is particularly full when he comes to the reign of George III. He then devotes six chapters to a circumstantial description, complemented by elaborate tables, of the different parts of the empire. In a final chapter he discusses the demobilisation crisis to be expected at the end of a war in which despite the unprecedented demands for military manpower there had always been an adequate supply of labour for civilian purposes. He sees emigration to different parts of the empire as one means of solution deserving the encouragement and generous assistance of the government.

In table 6.3 I have attempted to summarise Colquhoun's statistical picture of the British Empire in 1812 as set out in the second edition of the *Treatise*. In condensing the immense number of details he provides I have tried to arrange them so that they will be traceable in his table by anyone who wishes to consult the original. Almost every entry in my table comprises several items in his. For instance, he lists nine dependencies in Europe, of which Gibraltar and Malta are the most important; the islands

Table 6.3

AN ATTEMPT TO ESTIMATE THE POPULATION, PROPERTY AND NEW PROPERTY CREATED ANNUALLY IN THE BRITISH EMPIRE, 1812

Region	Population '000				Property (Tangible assets) £'000			New property (National income) £'000
	Europeans	Free persons of colour	Negro labourers	Total	Private	Public	Total	
Great Britain and Ireland								
England	9 538.8	..	..	9 538.8	} 1 814 900	32 000	1 846 900	..
Wales	611.8	..	..	611.8				..
Scotland	1 805.7	..	..	1 805.7	278 080	3 000	281 080	..
Ireland	4 500.0	..	..	4 500.0	554 660	9 000	563 660	..
Army, navy, marines etc.*	640.5	..	..	640.5	..	45 000	45 000	..
Totals	17 096.8	..	..	17 096.8	2 647 640	89 000	2 736 640	430 521
Dependencies in Europe	180.3	..	..	180.3	14 861	7 300	22 161	1 818
Dependencies in America								
Canada	486.1	..	..	486.1	45 125	1 450	46 575	13 215
British West Indian colonies	65.0	33.1	634.1	732.2	96 822	3 193	100 015	18 517
Newly conquered West Indian territories								
a) to be retained by Britain	6.0	3.7	136.0	145.7	30 378	660	31 038	3 980
b) to be restored	29.9	22.6	236.8	289.3	41 872	2 310	44 182	6 216
Totals	586.9	59.3	1 006.9	1 653.2	214 197	7 613	221 810	41 928
Dependencies in Africa								
British settlements	20.0	101.9	..†	121.9	3 300	1 000	4 300	708
Newly conquered territories, to be restored	0.7	6.4	..†	7.1	400	70	470	92
Totals	20.7	108.3	..†	129.0	3 700	1 070	4 770	800
Dependencies in Asia and the Indian Ocean								
British colonies and settlements	32.7	800.0	70.0	902.7	18 592	2 900	21 492	3 381
Newly conquered territories, to be restored	28.4	1 007.5	70.5	1 106.4	15 629	1 600	17 229	2 814
East India Company territories*	25.2§	40 033.2	..	40 058.4	1 041 031	31 397	1 072 428	211 966
Totals	86.3	41 840.6	140.5	42 067.4	1 075 252	35 897	1 111 149	218 161
Foreign corps	30.7	..	..	30.7	..	..	..	..
Grand totals	18 001.8	42 008.3	1 147.3	61 157.4	3 955 650	140 880	4 096 531	693 228

Including troops in the dependencies but excluding 20,000 troops in the service of the East India Company and 30,700 'foreign corps'.

No reliable estimates existed of the black population in the hinterland.

Including St. Helena.

Including 20,000 troops.

ource: Patrick Colquhoun, *A Treatise on the Wealth, Power and Resources of the British Empire*, 2nd edn, tables 1-3 and 7-12.

in the West Indies are treated individually; private property is greatly subdivided, often in a way which enables productive property such as land, buildings, ships and stores to be distinguished from unproductive property such as furniture and clothing. He also gives a considerable amount of information on foreign trade. The inclusion of even a small part of this material, interesting as it is, would have led to a highly indigestible table and I have resisted the attempt.

4. The National Income in 1812

Colquhoun's estimates of income and output for Great Britain and Ireland in 1812 are conceived on the same lines as his estimates for 1803 but are much more thorough. On the output side he distinguishes about eighty activities; and on the income side, although he lists only fifty groups of recipients he is at pains to specify their occupational composition.

He sets about estimating income originating and its distribution in a manner which makes use of Adam Smith's distinction between productive and unproductive labour, though he points out that the 'unproductive' workers such as professional men, civil servants, soldiers and sailors are highly useful in their different stations in society since 'in addition to the benefits derived from personal exertions, they eminently tend to promote, invigorate and render more productive the labour of the creating classes'. These classes consist of those employed in agriculture, mining and quarrying, manufactures, domestic and foreign trade, shipping and fisheries, though it should be recognised that commerce includes banking and that allowance should be made for foreign income. The 'new property' is the value added in the above branches and this is to be distributed between the productive sectors and the unproductive ones. Thus income originating is arranged on an industrial classification which though detailed is incomplete by modern conventions, and income distributed is arranged on a socio-occupational classification almost identical with that given in table 6.1 above. I shall set out his calculations for 1812 in three tables, 6.4, 6.5 and 6.6.

Table 6.4

THE STRUCTURE OF THE ECONOMIC SYSTEM ACCORDING TO COLQUHOUN GREAT BRITAIN AND IRELAND, 1812

Sectors	Population		Income		
	Number of families	Total number of persons	Originating	Distributed	Transferred to the unproductive sector
	'000	'000	£ million	£ million	£ million
Productive sector					
Agriculture and mining	1 302	6 129	225.8	107.2	118.6
Manufacturing	975	4 624	114.2	100.0	14.2
Inland trade and transport	72	406	31.5	28.1	3.4
Foreign commerce, shipping, banking etc.	465	2 067	59.0	57.2	1.8
Totals	2 814	13 226	430.5	292.5	138.0
Unproductive sector					
Royalty, nobility and gentry	47	417	0.0	58.9	..
Civil service	22	115	0.0	8.8	..
Army and navy	130	941	0.0	25.2	..
Clergy, law, medicine and education	92	495	0.0	25.2	..
Other	398	1 903	0.0	19.8	..
Totals	688	3 871	0.0	138.0	..
Grand totals	3 502	17 097	430.5	430.5	138.0

Source: Patrick Colquhoun, *A Treatise on . . . the British Empire*, 2nd edn, tables 3 and 4.

Table 6.5

AN ATTEMPT TO ESTIMATE THE NEW PROPERTY CREATED ANNUALLY IN GREAT BRITAIN AND IRELAND, 1812

(The National Income by Industry of Origin)

Activities and industries	Value added: In each activity £'000	Value added: In each industry £'000	Value added: In each sector £million
Agriculture and mining			
Agriculture		216 818	
Mining			
Coal mining	4 000		
Other mining and quarrying	5 000		
Total		9 000	
Total agriculture and mining			225.8
Manufactures			
Food			
Meat and dairy products	1 100		
Salt and alum	300		
Refined sugar	250		
Millers and maltsters	2 500		
Butchers, bakers etc.	750		
Total		4 900	
Drink and tobacco			
Beer and porter	2 100		
Cider, perry etc.	300		
Spirits	1 050		
Tobacco and snuff	300		
Total		3 750	
Textiles			

Activities and industries	Value added: In each activity £'000	Value added: In each industry £'000	Value added: In each sector £million
Brought forward		316 348	225.8
Manufactures (continued)			
China and glass			
Earthenware, china, porcelain etc.	2 500		
Glass	2 000		
Total		4 500	
Metal and metalware			
Jewellery, plate and watches	2 000		
Hardware and cutlery	6 500		
Total		8 500	
Instruments, ships and vehicles			
Musical instruments, toys etc.	200		
Steam engines, machinery etc.	500		
Ships	2 000		
Coaches, carriages etc.	800		
Total		3 500	
Construction			
Building materials	700		
Construction	6 000		
Total		6 700	
Fine arts		500	
Total manufactures			114.2

Silk	2 000		
Total		56 000	
Clothing and haberdashery			
Tailors, dressmakers etc.	2 500		
Haberdashery	1 500		
Straw products	500		
Furs, feathers etc.	50		
Gold and silver trimmings	500		
Total		5 050	
Leather, footwear, saddlery etc.		12 000	
Timber and hair products			
Furniture	500		
Cooperage	500		
Turnery ware	100		
Hair products	500		
Floor cloth	30		
Total		1 630	
Paper and printing			
Paper etc.	2 000		
Books, newspapers, printing etc.	2 000		
Total		4 000	
Chemicals			
Painters colours, white lead, turpentine etc.	1 000		
Soap	450		
Candles	450		
Gunpowder	300		
Drugs and chemical preparations	500		
Dyestuffs	500		
Total		3 200	
Carried forward	. .	316 348	225.8

Wholesalers and retailers	15 000		
Innkeepers and publicans	7 500		
Total		22 500	
Transport			
Water transport	7 000		
Road transport	2 000		
Total		9 000	
Total inland trade			31.5
Foreign commerce, shipping, banking etc.			
Overseas activities			
Foreign commerce	23 340		
Shipping	22 000		
Marine insurance	1 034		
Total		46 374	
Coastal trade		2 000	
Fisheries		2 100	
Other			
Banking	3 500		
Foreign income	5 000		
Total		8 500	
Total foreign commerce, shipping, banking etc.			59.0
Grand total	. .	430 521	430.5

Source: Patrick Colquhoun, *A Treatise on . . . the British Empire*, 2nd edn, table 3.

Table 6.6

AN ATTEMPT TO EXHIBIT A GENERAL VIEW OF SOCIETY
GREAT BRITAIN AND IRELAND, 1812
(The National Income by Type of Recipient)

Ranks, degrees and description	Sector	Population: Families	Population: Total number of persons	Income: Total per group £'000	Income: Average per family £
1. The Prince Regent	U	1	50	172.0	172 000
2. The King	U	1	50	146.0	146 000
3. Other royalty	U	10	200	183.0	18 300
4. Temporal peers	U	516	12 900	5 160.0	10 000
5. Bishops	U	48	720	240.5	5 010
6. Baronets	U	861	12 915	3 022.1	3 510
7. Eminent merchants, bankers etc.	P	3 500	35 000	9 100.0	2 600
8. Knights and esquires	U	11 000	110 000	22 000.0	2 000
9. Persons in higher civil offices	U	3 500	24 500	3 430.0	980
10. Lesser merchants by sea	P	22 800	159 600	18 354.0	805
11. Shipbuilders	P	500	3 000	402.0	804
12. Manufacturers	P	44 000	264 000	35 376.0	804
13. Principal wholesalers	P	900	5 400	723.6	804
14. Gentlemen and ladies living on incomes	U	35 000	280 000	28 000.0	800
15. Eminent clergymen	U	1 500	9 000	1 080.0	720
16. Teachers in universities and chief schools	U	874	3 496	524.4	600
17. Shipowners letting for freight	P	8 750	43 750	5 250.0	600
18. Persons keeping houses for lunatics	U	70	700	35.0	500
19. Persons in the law	U	19 000	95 000	7 600.0	400
20. Physicians, surgeons, apothecaries etc.	U	18 000	90 000	5 400.0	300
21. Persons in lesser civil offices	U	18 000	90 000	5 400.0	300
22. Builders, architects, engineers etc.	P	8 700	43 500	2 610.0	300
23. Artists, sculptors, engravers etc.	P	5 000	25 000	1 400.0	280
24. Freeholders of the better sort	P	70 000	285 000	19 250.0	[illegible]

28. Lesser clergymen	U	17 500	87 500	3 500.0	200
29. Actors and musicians	U	875	3 500	175.0	200
30. Shopkeepers and tradesmen	P	140 000	700 000	28 000.0	200
31. Master tailors, dressmakers, army clothiers etc.	P	43 750	218 750	7 875.0	180
32. Farmers	P	280 000	1 540 000	33 600.0	120
33. Half-pay officers' widows (army & navy)*	U	2 500	14 500	856.6	100
34. Dissenting clergymen	U	5 000	20 000	500.0	100
35. Lesser freeholders	P	210 000	1 050 000	21 000.0	100
36. Innkeepers and publicans	P	87 500	437 500	8 750.0	100
37. Clerks and shop-assistants	P	42 500	262 500	6 750.0	70†
38. Umbrella makers, embroideresses, laundresses etc.	P	500★	150 000	3 500.0	50†
39. Artisans and labourers in manufacture & construction	P	1 021 974	4 343 389	49 054.8	48
40. Agricultural labourers and miners	P	742 151	3 154 142	33 396.8	45
41. Hawkers, pedlars etc.	P	1 400	5 600	63.0	45
42. Seamen in the merchant service, fisheries etc.	P	80 000	400 000	8 100.0	45†
43. Petty officers and seamen in the navy, revenue etc.	U	50 000	320 000	7 204.7	42
44. Lunatics	U	..	4 000	160.0	40§
45. Non-commissioned officers and soldiers*	U	70 000	450 000	9 800.0	35
46. Inmates of debtors' prisons	U	3 500	17 500	105.0	30
47. Pensioned seamen and soldiers* (army and navy)	U	..	92 000	1 050.0	25
48. Paupers	U	387 100	1 548 400	9 871.0	25
49. Vagrants, thieves etc.	U	..	308 741	3 704.9	12§
50. Institutional and other unallocated income	..	..	..	5 211.1	..
Totals	U & P	3 501 781	17 096 803	430 521.4	..
Income received by the unproductive sector	U	687 856	3 870 672	137 966.3	..
Income received by the productive sector	P	2 813 925	13 226 131	292 555.2	..

* See table 6.7
§ Per head.
† Per earner.
★ Should read 37 500, and the total at the foot of the column should be altered accordingly.

Source: Patrick Colquhoun, *A Treatise on . . . the British Empire*, 2nd edn, table 4.

Table 6.4 provides a framework, constructed by me, for the more detailed estimates which follow. It gives in summary form the amounts of income generated in the productive sector, the amounts retained in it and the amounts transferred to the different groups in the unproductive sector. These transfers are shown twice; once in the upper part of column 5, classified by productive branch of origin, and once in the lower part of column 4, classified by unproductive group of retention.

Table 6.5 gives an industrial subdivision of income originating in the productive sector. It is obtained by aggregating and rearranging the data in table 3 of the *Treatise* according to a modern industrial classification, excluding of course the activities which Colquhoun treats as unproductive.

Finally, table 6.6 gives a socio-occupational classification of income distributed. It is taken directly from table 4 of the *Treatise* but with the classes rearranged in order of family income and the productive and unproductive groups indicated by the letters P and U.

As can be seen by comparing the various totals and subtotals in my three tables, Colquhoun's system is numerically perfectly consistent. Conceptually, however, it is not altogether so. Colquhoun follows Adam Smith in the distinction between productive and unproductive sectors and the dividing line is at times somewhat blurred, just as it is in Adam Smith. On the whole, labour and business income seems to be retained in the productive sector and income derived from taxes and rent seems to accrue to the unproductive sector, but this is not the whole story. Shipowners who let ships for freight are productive but landowners, namely the nobility and gentry, who let lands for farming are not. 'Freeholders', however, are productive, presumably because the word is restricted to yeomen who farm their own land (as opposed to 'farmers' who farm rented land). Again, farmers, who produce the raw materials for millers, butchers etc., are productive but writers, who produce the raw material for printers, are not. Artists on the other hand, presumably because they add value to material products such as marble, canvas and metal, are included in manufacturing.

Since Colquhoun does not attempt to estimate expenditure we

Table 6.7

LEVELS OF PAY IN THE ARMY AND NAVY, 1812

	Number of persons	Average pay £	Total income £'000
Naval officers, surgeons etc.			
Married	3 000	250	750.0
Single	5 380	250	1 345.0
Total drawing pay	8 380		
plus Dependents	16 620		
Group totals	25 000		2 095.0
Army officers, surgeons etc.			
Married	5 000	200	1 000.0
Single	16 000	200	3 200.0
Total drawing pay	21 000		
plus Dependents	19 000		
Group totals	40 000		4 200.0
Half-pay officers' widows (army and navy)			
Heads of families	2 500	100	250.0
Single	6 066	100	606.6
Total drawing half pay	8 566		
plus Dependents	5 934		
Group totals	14 500		856.6
Petty officers and seamen in the navy, revenue service etc.			
Married	50 000	42	2 100.0
Single	121 540	42	5 104.7
Total drawing pay	171 540		
plus Dependents	148 460		
Group totals	320 000		7 204.7
Non-commissioned officers and soldiers			
Married	70 000	35	2 450.0
Single	210 000	35	7 350.0
Total drawing pay	280 000		
plus Dependents	170 000		
Group totals	450 000		9 800.0
Pensioned soldiers and seamen			
Heads of families	20 000*	25	500.0
Single	22 000	25	550.0
Total drawing pension	42 000		
plus Dependents	50 000		
Group totals	92 000		1 050.0
Totals for all services	941 500		25 206.3

*This figure is not stated explicitly in Colquhoun.

Source: Patrick Colquhoun, *A Treatise on . . . the British Empire*, 2nd edn, table 4, notes A and B.

cannot see who pay the taxes which provide the income for the armed and civil services or the rents which provide much of the income of the unproductive rich, or the parish rates which provide relief for the poor. As a consequence we cannot carry out a detailed to-whom-from-whom analysis and can only check the consistency of the totals as shown in my tables.

Apart from these general points there are in table 4 of the *Treatise* a few slips and omissions that call for some comment. Most of them are misprints easily detectable with the help of the voluminous notes appended to the table, but some are due to a conceptual lacuna in that Colquhoun, like Gregory King, did not recognise explicity the existence of one-person families. In most groups he smoothed out this difficulty by averaging the population over the estimated number of families but in some groups this was not possible, either because the data on the number of families were non-existent, as in the case of lunatics and vagrants, thieves etc., or because they were too precise to justify wholesale averaging, as in the case of the army and navy.

In my table 6.6 I have treated lunatics and vagrants as one person families and ordered them by reference to Colquhoun's average annual income of £40 and £12 respectively. As to the different groups in the army and navy, whether active or retired, Colquhoun solved his problem by including the unmarried in the total population but excluding them from the number of families and setting out the data about marital status in a footnote. In my table the number of persons and the number of families appear as Colquhoun gives them and the order is based on average income per earner, which is the same for married and single, as shown in his footnote. The information given in this note is summarised in my table 6.7.

5. Conclusion

In discussing his estimates of the national income of Great Britain and Ireland, which he hopes are conservative, Colquhoun expresses regret that 'the official materials are so scanty'. He goes on:

'A period may perhaps arrive after the author of this work shall be mouldered in the dust, when the same ground may be gone over by some abler pen under those superior advantages which the progress of society with respect to official facts may afford, so as to exhibit to future generations views *which shall be official* of the value of the new property created every year from the labour of the people, in all the different occupations in which they may be employed. Such estimates, were it possible to publish them annually, would prove a most correct barometer by which the resources of the State could be measured, and its power and opulence ascertained.

It is by such efforts . . . embracing the whole range of political economy, that the statesman is enabled to form just conceptions of what constitutes the true interest of a country. It is a subject which never can be contemplated partially, far less acted upon without hazarding some collateral interest, and disturbing the harmony of the great whole.

Of all branches connected with this most interesting subject the ascertainment of the national income, or the property created yearly from the labour of the people, is the most important; since on the produce of this labour everything depends which constitutes the existence, the comfort, the power, and the security of the sovereign and the people.'

As far as possible I have left Colquhoun's figures as they stand, since my aim is to show his world as he saw it rather than as it might appear to modern scholarship. His work has been looked at from a modern point of view by Deane[1] and Deane and Cole[2] on the economic side, and by Lindert and Williamson[3] on the social side. I shall not go further into the matter beyond saying that while Colquhoun's way of arranging his data might have seemed more natural to Adam Smith than it does to us, I do not think he should be accused of incoherence or considered a less competent statistician than Gregory King. It would have been interesting if he could have

1. PHYLLIS DEANE, 'The implications of early national income estimates for the measurement of long-term growth in the United Kingdom'. *Economic Development and Cultural Change*, vol. IV, no. 1, 1955, pp. 3-38.

2. PHILLYS DEANE and W. A. COLE, *British Economic Growth, 1688-1959*. Cambridge University Press, 1962.

3. PETER H. LINDERT and JEFFREY G. WILLIAMSON, 'Revising England's social tables, 1688-1812'. *Explorations in Economic History*, vol. 19, 1982, pp. 385-408.

worked into his account the voluminous information on public income and expenditure set out in his chapter VI of the *Treatise*, but in order to do this he would have had to estimate not only the national income but also the national expenditure. Considering what he did, it would be churlish to blame him for what he did not do.

THIRD LECTURE
DEMOGRAPHY AND VITAL STATISTICS

John Graunt (1620-1674)
Edmond Halley (1656-1742)
William Farr (1807-1883)

Natural and *Political*

OBSERVATIONS

Mentioned in a following INDEX,

and made upon the

Bills of Mortality.

BY

Capt. *JOHN GRAUNT*,

Fellow of the *Royal Society*.

With reference to the *Government*, *Religion*, *Trade*, *Growth*, *Air*, *Diſeaſes*, and the ſeveral Changes of the ſaid CITY.

—— *Non, me ut miretur Turba, laboro,*
Contentus paucis Lectoribus. ——

The Fourth Impreſſion.

OXFORD,

Printed by *William Hall*, for *John Martyn*, and *James Alleſtry*, Printers to the *Royal Society*, MDCLXV.

John Graunt, *Observations upon the Bills of Mortality.*
Title page of fourth edition, 1665.

CHAPTER 7

John Graunt and the Birth of Demographic Statistics

1. Brief Life

Demographic statistics, like national accounting, has its origins in the seventeenth century. It is in fact the twin to national accounting, the other child of political arithmetic, and like its twin was fashioned out of nothing by the ingenuity of its begetter, the London merchant John Graunt. Graunt was a great friend of Petty's and may easily have caught from him his enthusiasm for 'reasoning with figures'. Or they may have caught it from each other. Graunt, who had great scientific integrity, was better at it than Petty; Petty on the other hand had inexhaustible inventiveness. One can imagine them eagerly discussing ideas and methods and deciding to put them to the test in the true spirit of experimental science.

John Graunt was born in 1620, three years before Petty. He was the son of a London draper whose family came from Hampshire. We do not know much about his boyhood except that on leaving school he was apprenticed to a haberdasher. He became a haberdasher himself, a member of the Drapers Company and a substantial figure in the City, serving on the Common Council and as a captain and later major in the City militia, the trained bands. By the age of thirty he had sufficient influence to secure for Petty a professorship of music at Gresham College. Aubrey says of him:

'he was a very ingeniose and studious person and rose early in the morning to his study before shop-time. He understood Latin and French . . . A man generally beloved, a faithful friend. Often chosen for his prudence and justness to be an arbitrator; and he was a great peace-maker. He had an excellent working head, and was very facetious and fluent in his conversation.'

And Anthony Wood adds: 'But above all his excellent working head was much commended, and the rather for this reason, that it was for the public good of learning, which is very rare in a trader or mechanic'.

Pepys shows us another side of Graunt, the art lover. On one occasion he notes: 'I went forth, by appointment, to meet Mr. Grant [*sic*], who promised to meet me at the coffee house, to bring me acquainted with Cooper, the great limner'. Another time

'to Mr. Grant's. There saw his prints, which he showed me, and indeed are the best collections of any things almost that ever I saw, there being the prints of most of the greatest houses, churches and antiquities in Italy and France, and brave cuts. I had not time to look them over as I ought, which I will take time hereafter to do.'[1]

Graunt seems also to have been a very religious man. He had been brought up a Puritan and was a supporter of Cromwell, but later was attracted by Socinianism and eventually converted to Catholicism, 'and then', says Aubrey, 'laid down trade and all other public employment for his religion . . . of which he died a great zealot'.

His conversion caused him some trouble. Religious feelings ran high in those days and Roman Catholics were viewed with suspicion. After the Fire of London in 1666 there was much talk of sinister plots by 'fanatics' and it was maliciously rumoured that as a trustee of the New River Company Graunt had managed to stop the supply of water to the City the night before the fire broke out; apart from the fact that such an act would have been completely out of character and would have damaged him financially, it is known that he did not receive the key which would have enabled him to turn off the water until three weeks after the fateful night. He did indeed suffer serious financial losses in the fire, a misfortune which Petty is said to have done much to alleviate.

No better conclusion can be written to Graunt's life than that written by Aubrey:

1. Samuel Pepys, *Diary* (ed. H. B. Wheatley). London, 1893, vol. v, p. 94.

'Major John Graunt died on Easter-eve 1674, and was buried in St. Dunstan's church in Fleetstreet . . . under the pews (alias huggstics) of the north side of the middle aisle (what pity 'tis so great an Ornament of the City should be buried so obscurely !) *aetatis anno 54°*.

His death is lamented by all good men that had the happiness to know him; and a great number of ingeniose persons attended him to his grave. Among others (with tears) was that ingeniose great Virtuoso, Sir William Petty, his old and intimate acquaintance.

He was my honoured and worthy Friend – *cuius animae propitietur Deus. Amen.*'

Graunt was married and his wife survived him. They had a number of children, among them a son who died in Persia and a daughter who became a nun.

Further details of his life can be found in Aubrey,[1] Wood,[2] Cooper,[3] Pearson[4] and Glass.[5]

2. *The Population of London Around 1660*

Graunt was virtually a one-book man but this book, which I shall call for short *Observations on the Bills of Mortality*,[6] has won him permanent fame as a pioneer of statistics and demography. It first appeared in 1662, attracted immediate attention and led to Graunt's election to fellowship of the Royal Society. No more flattering distinction could be wished for by a man of Graunt's cast of mind than to be thought worthy of inclusion in the famous Gresham College group. The choice had the wholehearted

1. JOHN AUBREY, *Brief Lives* (ed. O. Lawson Dick). Penguin, 1972.

2. ANTHONY WOOD, *Athenae Oxonienses*. London, vol. I, 1691, vol. II, 1692; 2nd edn, revised, 1721. The reference to John Graunt appears in the 2nd edn, vol. I, 'Writers', p. 311, under the entry for Edward Grant.

3. THOMPSON COOPER, 'John Graunt'. *The Dictionary of National Biography*, vol. VIII, pp. 427-8.

4. KARL PEARSON, *The History of Statistics in the 17th and 18th Centuries*. London, 1978, pp. 10-29.

5. D. V. GLASS, 'John Graunt, and his *Natural and political observations*'. *Proceedings of the Royal Society*, ser. B, vol. 159, 1963, pp. 2-37.

6. JOHN GRAUNT, *Natural and Political Observations . . . made upon the Bills of Mortality*. 1st edn, London, 1662; reprinted (ed. F. W. Willcox), Johns Hopkins Press, Baltimore, 1939; facsimile in *The Earliest Classics* (ed. P. Laslett), Gregg, Farnborough, 1973. 5th edn (revised), 1676; reprinted in *The Economic Writings of Sir William Petty* (ed. C. H. Hull), Cambridge, 1899.

approval of Charles II: 'His Majesty', we are told, 'gave this particular charge to his Society, that if they found any more such tradesmen, they should be sure to admit them all, without any more ado'.[1]

Graunt does not seem to have had the ebullient self-assurance of his friend Petty and opens his book in a systematic and cautious manner by describing the history of his sources and the way in which the information they contain was collected. The Bills for London had started at the end of the sixteenth century in times of plague, and after the great plague of 1603 they were printed and published every week and an annual summary, made up to the Thursday before Christmas, was produced at the end of each year. They contained information on christenings and burials, deaths from the plague being distinguished; from 1629 onwards other causes of death were specified and males and females were shown separately. They related to the 97 parishes within the Walls, 16 parishes and the pest-house outside the Walls but within the Liberties of London, and nine out-parishes adjoining London in Middlesex and Surrey; eight more parishes were added in 1636. Similar bills were prepared for many other towns in the Kingdom and the system continued until about 1840 when the registration of births, marriages and deaths was taken over by the newly-established office of the Registrar General.

The information on causes of death was obtained for each parish by the 'Searchers', 'ancient Matrons, sworn to their office', who when anyone died repaired to the place, viewed the corpse, made enquiries of relatives and the physician and reported the cause of death to the parish clerk. The Bills were kept by the Company of Parish Clerks and could be obtained on payment of a subscription of four shillings a year. Graunt remarks that subscribers to the Bills made little use of them except to take them 'as a text to talk upon in the next company' and in plaguetime to see if they should leave town or, if tradesmen, what the immediate prospects were likely to be for their business.

1. THOMAS SPRAT, *The History of the Royal Society of London for the Improving of Natural Knowledge*. London, 1667.

What induced him to take a closer look at them was something quite else. He had often heard 'men of great experience' talk of millions of people in London, and was quite prepared to believe it until one day he was told by 'one of eminent reputation' that in 1661 there were two million more people than in 1625. This made him sit up and decide to check the figure: 'casting mine eye upon so many of the General *Bills* as next came to hand', he says in his preface,

'I found encouragement from them to look out all the *Bills* I could, and to furnish my self with as much matter of that kind, even as the Hall of the *Parish-Clerks* could afford me; the which, when I had reduced into Tables . . . so as to have a view of the whole together . . . I did then begin not onely to examine the conceits, opinions and conjectures which upon view of a few scattered *Bills* I had taken up; but did also admit new ones, as I found reason and occasion from my Tables.

Moreover, finding some *truths*, and not commonly believed opinions, to arise from my meditations upon these neglected *Papers*, I proceeded further to consider what benefit the knowledge of the same would bring to the world; that I might not engage myself in idle useless speculations, but like those noble *Virtuosi* of *Gresham-College* (who reduce their subtile disquisitions upon Nature into downright mechanical uses) present the world with some real fruit from those ayrie blossoms.'

He had imagined that what his informant had told him would imply that there were now six or seven millions in London. But from the Bills he found that not above 15,000 were buried each year, or about 1 in 400 if the population were really six million. This was palpably absurd.

To get the right order of magnitude he began with the number of christenings, about 12,000 a year, and considered that the number of women of childbearing age, that is between 16 and 40, would be about twice as many, or 24,000, 'forasmuch as such women . . . have [on average] scarce more than one child in two years'. He thought there might be twice as many families again, or 48,000, since there might be twice as many women between 16 and 76 as there were between 16 and 40. Allowing on average eight persons in a family (household), namely the man, his wife, three children and three servants or lodgers, would give a total of 48,000×8=384,000 people.

A second approach was to find that in a sample of parishes three people died each year out of eleven households. In the whole of London, deaths averaged 13,000 per annum, and so the number of households should be $(13{,}000 \times 11)/3 = 47{,}667$. And $47{,}667 \times 8 = 381{,}336$, which checks out well with the estimate based on christenings.

Lastly, he took a recent map of London drawn on a scale of yards. He thought that in every 100-yards square there might be 54 households. There were 220 such squares within the Walls, and the housing within the Walls was about a quarter of the whole. This would give $54 \times 220 \times 4 = 47{,}520$ households, and $47{,}520 \times 8 = 380{,}160$, which again checks out pretty well.

Although Graunt does not specify how many parishes these calculations refer to, it seems clear that they do not include the eight 'distant' parishes which were added to the original 122 in 1636; this is shown by his statement in another part of the book that 'in the 97, 16, 10 and 7 parishes usually comprehended in our Bills . . . in and about London, there are 460,000 souls'.

So there were no millions of people in London, any more than there were three women to one man, as most people believed, but rather fourteen men to thirteen women, this being the sex ratio apparent from both the christenings and the burials. A comparable estimate made by Gregory King in 1695, when London had grown much larger, gave a total population of 527,600 and a sex ratio of 14 females to $13\frac{1}{2}$ males. King as we shall see had much better data than Graunt had, but Graunt reached much the same conclusions by sheer force of induction.

Graunt was well aware of the shortcomings of his data. Early in the book he remarks on the complications introduced into the statistics by the relative neglect of christening in recent years. This mattered, since christenings stood for birth registrations. Up to 1642 burials and christenings were nearly equal; but in 1648 the christenings were only two-thirds of the burials; and in 1659 less than half, 5,670 compared with 14,720 burials. From the numbers of women dying in childbed in the two years 1631 and 1659 he deduces that the true number of births in 1659 was about 11,500, half of which were not recorded.

The reasons he gives for this change were three. The first was the growth of a religious opinion against the baptizing of infants. The second was the scruples of many ministers about the worthiness of certain parents to have their children baptized; 'whereat the parents would take the child to another minister who, however, might not be able to require the names of the baptized to be entered on the Register', so that the existence of these children would not be recorded. And the third was that a small fee had to be paid for the registration, which discouraged poor people.

3. An Analysis of Morbidity and Mortality

A large part of Graunt's book is devoted to a discussion of the causes of death, their distribution over age groups, and their medical, social and environmental implications. The causes of death as reported by the searchers were comparatively easy to sort out. His 'Table of casualties' listing 81 causes and showing their incidence in the years he selected for analyis is reproduced in the fold-out facing p. 216 and the facsimile in the pocket of the back cover.

In the twenty years he analyses, 1629-36 and 1647-58, he finds 229,250 deaths recorded. He begins by grouping causes of death under broad headings such as infantile, chronic and acute diseases, the plague, accidents and murders, and old age, and considering what proportion each group bears to the total. He points out that the distinction between chronic and acute is important because

'chronical diseases show (as I conceive) the state and disposition of the Country (including as well its *food* and *air*) in reference to health or rather longaevity: for as the proportion of *acute* and *epidemical* diseases shows the aptness of the air to suddain and vehement impressions, so the *chronical* diseases show the temper of the place, so that upon the proportion of *Chronical* diseases seems to hang the judgement of the fitness of the Country for *long life*.'

He also distinguishes a number of sub-groups and gives a table of 'some of the more formidable and notorious diseases' of which 'many persons live in great fear and apprehension', showing the numbers that died from them so that 'those persons may better understand the hazard they are in'; and he gives a similar list for accidental and violent deaths.

This much was apparent from a first examination of the searchers' reports. The question was, how far did the searchers know what they were talking about? As he says,

> 'In many of these cases . . . such as drowning, scalding, bleeding, vomiting, making-away themselves, lunatiques; sores; small-pox &c. their own senses are sufficient, and the generality of the world are able prettie well to distinguish the gowt, stone, dropsie, falling-sickness, palsie, ague, pleurisy, ricketts &c. one from another,'

but other cases were not so clear for a number of reasons. One was the ignorance of the searchers themselves and the obscurity of the nomenclature they used. Another was the uncertainty surrounding the nature of some complaints. Yet another was the reluctance of families to disclose the presence of shameful or dangerously infectious diseases. In particular Graunt thinks it likely that in plague years 'a quarter more die of that disease than are reported'; certainly, plague-stricken families would have had a strong incentive to get a death from plague recorded otherwise in order to avoid being confined to their dwellings. The age distribution of deaths presented another problem. The Bills contained no information about age: the searchers mentioned 'infants', and Graunt says he wishes he knew what they meant by the term, remarking that 'it is somewhat to know how many die usually before they can speak, or how many live past any assigned number of years'; similarly they referred to 'aged' and Graunt supposes that they must mean 'the same that David calls so, *viz.* 70'. In order to introduce even a little and perhaps not very accurate information about age, he had to consider what could be regarded as specifically childish diseases, interpret the terms used by the searchers and make a number of assumptions.

Out of the 229,250 deaths recorded, he finds that 71,124, or about 1/3 of the whole, were from children's diseases. To estimate total deaths under the age of six, he adds half the deaths from a range of not specifically infantile diseases and about a third of the deaths from plague. To get the deaths for the age group 6-69 he considers acute diseases (other than plague), 'about 50,000', and chronic diseases, 'about 70,000'. Deaths from plague, other than those ascribed to children, must be added in and so must accidents, murders, suicides and cases of starvation. Deaths over the age of 69 are subsumed under the category 'aged', of whom there are 15,757.

These figures are very tentative. In describing how he reached them Graunt puts all his cards on the table so that with the help of his explanations it is possible to draw up a summary statement of the age distribution of deaths which checks out fairly well with the total given in his table of casualties. No doubt a medical historian, with the information given, could get the sums right. My own amateur attempt is set out in table 7.1 below, as I have not seen a similar calculation in other commentators on Graunt and some insight into the information available to him is relevant when we come to discuss his attempt to construct a table of survivors to different ages of life.

Table 7.1

A SUMMARY OF LONDON DEATHS IN THE TWENTY YEARS 1629-36 AND 1647-58

Ages 0-5		
Children's diseases	71 124	
Plague (about 1/3)	5 296	
Specified other diseases (1/2)	6 110	
Total		82 530
Ages 6-69		
Plague	11 088	
Other acute diseases	45 471	
Chronical diseases	70 872	
Accidents, murders etc.	3 146	
Executed	384	
Total		130 961
Ages 70+		
Causes unspecified		15 757
Discrepancy		2
Graunt's total		229 250

Source: John Graunt, *Observations*, 4th edn., pp. 27-32.

After giving this general view of the situation Graunt goes on to consider particular causes of death. He notices first that very few are starved, so there is no sign of a want of food. He further observes that 'the vast number of beggars, swarming up and down this city' seem mostly healthy and strong. He suggests it might be better 'for the State to keep them, even although they earned nothing; that so they might live regularly, and not in that debauchery, as many beggars do', and might eventually be taught to work and fitted for labour. There is no need to worry that the objects of charity would be removed, since in Holland, 'although nowhere fewer beggars appear to charm up commiseration in the credulous, yet nowhere is there greater or more frequent charity; only indeed the magistrate is both the beggar and the disposer of what is gotten by begging; so as all givers have a moral certainty, that their charity shall be well applied'. In other words, Graunt suggests the dole where Petty suggests the creation of employment. Most people, he says, will laugh to hear him say this, but the answer is that if the work available 'be already being done by the not-beggars, then to employ the beggars about it, will but transfer the want from one hand to another; nor can a learner work so cheap as a skilful practised artist can'.

He then remarks that very few people are murdered, only 86 out of 299,250, very unlike Paris 'where few nights escape without their tragedy'. He gives two reasons: first, that 'the *government and guard* of the city is by the citizens themselves' (namely the trained bands in which he was an officer); and, second, the Englishman's hatred of bloodshed as proved by the fact that 'of all that are *executed* few are for *murther*'.

Lunatics also seem to be few, 158 in 229,250, but he thinks there are many more. The only ones entered in the Bills are those who die in Bedlam, and they all seem to die of their lunacy; but then not all lunatics are in Bedlam. Conversely, lunatics may die of many other things whether or not they are in Bedlam.

He next considers why so few are recorded as dying of venereal disease, 'the French-pox', only 392 out of 229,250. He had found that all those explicity mentioned as dying of this disease came from two parishes which contained the 'vilest and most

The '*Table of Casualties*' is available as a download from
www.cambridge.org/9780521128452

miserable houses of uncleanliness'. Those dying of it in certain hospitals were returned as dying of ulcers and sores; but in general they were recorded as dying of consumption since they died emaciated and lean. 'The old-women searchers', he goes on, 'after the mist of a cup of ale, and the bribe of a two-groat fee, instead of one, given them', cannot tell what the emaciation is due to.

He then speculates at some length on the rise and fall of diseases. He has noticed that while the frequency of some is increasing, others seem to be on the way out and he wonders whether these inverse trends are in any way correlated; whether, for instance, ricketts is a new disease or a new name for 'livergrown' and 'spleen'; whether 'stopping of the stomach' is the same as 'rising of the lights' and 'mother fits'. The 'learned physicians' may have answers to these questions, nevertheless the data he presents may be of interest: 'I had not meddled so far', he explains,

'but that I have heard that the first hints of the circulation of the blood were taken from a common person's wondering what became of all the blood which issued out of the heart.'

The plague gets two chapters to itself. Although this terrible disease was endemic it rose to epidemic levels only at intervals. Graunt gives statistics of the four most severe outbursts recorded in the Bills, starting with the great plague of 1592-3 and ending with that of 1636, both in absolute terms and as a proportion of all burials. By comparing one year with another he is able to detect mistakes and omissions in the Bills and to make the necessary adjustments. He also discusses the effects of the plague on fertility and migration. Fertility in general is another subject which he considers important enough to fill two more chapters.

What I have described is only a part of the information which Graunt managed to extract from the London Bills. I shall add one more example: his calculation of survival rates, the precursor of Halley's life table.

4. Graunt's Table of Survivors

All Graunt had to go on in making his table of survivals was that out of 100 births 64 survived to age 6 and seven were still alive at age 70. When it comes to the point he gives up the second piece of information and assumes instead that by age 76 the survivors will be reduced to one. He then seeks seven (he says six) mean proportional numbers which will interpolate at ten-year intervals his 64 survivors at age 6 and his one survivor at age 76. He does not say how he does this but gives the results shown in table 7.2.

Table 7.2
SURVIVORS TO DIFFERENT BIRTHDAYS AND DEATHS BETWEEN BIRTHDAYS, (*c.* 1660)

Birthday	Survivors	Deaths between birthdays
0	100	36
6	64	24
16	40	15
26	25	9
36	16	6
46	10	4
56	6	3
66	3	2
76	1	1
86	0	..

Source: John Graunt, *Observations*, 4th edn., pp. 124-6.

A number of writers in this century have discussed these results. Walter F. Willcox in his edition of the *Observations*[1] gives what seems to me a highly plausible conjecture. He suggests that having estimated that 64 per cent of births survived to age 6 and that 7 per cent of the deaths took place at age 70 or more, Graunt felt he had shot his bolt and turned the problem over to his friend Petty who may have experimented with a uniform rate of decrease of survivors. Had he chosen 5/8, and it seems certain that

1. WALTER F. WILLCOX, Introduction to *Natural and Political Observations made upon the Bills of Mortality by John Graunt*. Johns Hopkins Press, Baltimore, 1939.

he would have used fractions expressible as the ratio of integers, he would have produced the survivors up to age 56 correctly. After that his numbers would have been 1 percentage point too high and it might be supposed that he scaled down these very small figures to accord with his assumption of 1 per cent of survivors at age 76.

Other writers have suggested values for the rate of decrease of survivors. Thus Greenwood suggests 0.62,[1] Ptoukha (64-1)/100=0.63.[2] Karl Pearson discussed the matter in his lectures on the history of statistics, mentioning a suggestion by Ethel Newbold that Graunt may have got the deaths first and obtained the numbers living by subtraction.[3] Glass suggests that Graunt used a method of diminishing differences to distribute the 64 deaths over age 6[4] and this method appeals to Sutherland as an arithmetical approach of a kind that might have occurred to Graunt.[5]

Whoever was really responsible for the figures in table 7.2, it is a remarkable production as the first known survival table. It is interesting that Petty, who was always prepared to guesstimate though preferably on as solid a basis of facts as he could command, and Graunt, who was much less speculatively inclined, were not brought up short by the very large death rates in youth implied by their results. Thirty years later Halley, when he was analysing the data for Breslau, found very much lower figures for youthful mortality and, on checking on deaths at the Blue Coat school, found his data confirmed.

1. MAJOR GREENWOOD, 'Graunt and Petty'. *Journal of the Royal Statistical Society*, vol. XCI, pt. 1, 1928, pp. 79-83.

2. MICHEL PTOUKHA, 'John Graunt, fondateur de la démographie, 1620-1674'. *Congrès International de la Démographie*, vol. 2, Paris, 1937, pp. 61-74.

3. KARL PEARSON, *The History of Statistic . . .*, pp. 38-9.

4. D. V. GLASS, 'Graunt's life table'. *Journal of the Institute of Actuaries*, vol. 76, 1950, pp. 60-4.

5. IAN SUTHERLAND, 'John Graunt: a tercentenary tribute'. *Journal of the Royal Statistical Society*, ser. A, vol. 126, pt. 4, 1963, pp. 537-56.

5. A Comparison Between Town and Country

Towards the end of the book Graunt discusses the changes that are taking place in the capital and the relationship between its numbers and those in the rest of the country. The Court was now established at Westminster and many of the nobility were moving their houses westward, their old mansions being converted into tenements and the gardens built over. Trade followed this movement. Formerly Ludgate was the only western gate to the city, but when Holborn started to grow, Newgate was made. But now, he says, both the gates are not sufficient for the communication between the walled city and its enlarged western suburbs, 'as daily appears by the intolerable stops and embarrasses of coaches near both these gates, especially Ludgate'. Pepys too complains of traffic jams, especially at the gates. *Plus ça change . . .*

London was growing despite the fact that deaths exceeded births. The net increase in numbers was due to a constant immigration from the country. Indeed the inflow from the country enabled London to make a quick recovery from a severe epidemic of the plague, which in an exceptional year might carry off as many as 30 or 40,000 Londoners: after one of the great plagues, says Graunt, the city had been repeopled by the second year.

Graunt then turns from the London Bills to the country Bills, which he illustrates by those for a parish in Hampshire, in fact Romsey, Petty's birthplace. Just as he set out fully his data for London so he gives for Romsey figures of burials, christenings and weddings for the ninety years 1569-1658, distinguishing males and females.

From this information he concludes that in Romsey every wedding produces on average four children; that 15 females are born for 16 males (though there is a good deal of variation), whereas in London there are 13 for 14, so that London is more apt to produce males than the country and it would be interesting to know if there are places where the ratio goes the other way; that in the whole period the burials of males and females were exactly equal though in some decades the preponderance went sometimes one way and sometimes the other; that in the whole period there was in Romsey an excess of births over deaths, namely 1059 or not quite 12 a year; that as the place only grew by about 300 and it is known that 400 went to the New World in the last forty years, it is likely that 3-400 more went to London.

He tried to calculate the population by following the rules he had used for London: he multiplied the mean annual deaths, 58 by 4 to get 232 families and was surprised that so considerable a place should only have 232 houses; he then multiplied 232×8 to obtain 1,856 inhabitants. He then discovered that there were normally about 1,500 communicants and nearly as many children under 16, so that in fact there must have been 2,700 or 2,800 souls in the parish. From this he reaches the conclusion that the country, where about one dies in fifty, is healthier than London, where about one in thirty-two dies apart from the plague.

He thinks that before 1600 London may have shown an excess of births over deaths, like the country, and wonders why the position should have changed. It may be that as it becomes more populous it becomes more unhealthy; a further factor may be the widespread use of coal. In any case all this confirms that the great increase in the population, from 2 to 5 in the last fifty-four years, can only be the result of immigration from the country.

6. *Graunt's* Observations *Concluded*

This is a very orderly book and so it begins with a detailed table of contents and ends with a conclusion recapitulating the book's subject matter and its aims, followed by the tables and an explanation of their construction. The conclusion, in its salient points, says:

'It may be now asked, to what purpose tends all this laborious buzzling and groping? . . . To this I might answer in general by saying that those who cannot apprehend the reason of these enquiries are unfit to trouble themselves to ask them . . . But I answer more seriously by complaining that whereas the art of governing and the true politiques is how to preserve the subject in peace and plenty that men study only that part of it which teacheth how to supplant and overreach one another . . . Now, the foundation or elements of this honest harmless policy is to understand the land and the hands of the territory to be governed according to all their intrinsic and accidental differences . . . But whether the knowledge thereof be necessary to many, or fit for others than the Sovereign and his chief Ministers, I leave to consideration.'

Although the sober ending is like Graunt, there is a strong whiff of Petty about this chapter. When the *Observations* appeared in 1662 no one expressed a doubt that Graunt was the author, but some years later a few writers ascribed the authorship to Petty. This started a controversy which continued almost to the present day. In 1895 Hull went carefully into the evidence. I do not propose to discuss the matter beyond saying that I fully agree with Hull and that nothing that has appeared since has led me to change my mind; Graunt was the author of the book associated with his name. More than likely, he discussed it with his friend; Petty may have encouraged him to write it, contributed certain passages, helped in obtaining the Bills for the country parish from the register of the Abbey of St. Mary and St. Ethelfleda at Romsey, the church in which Petty's baptism is recorded and in which he is buried; he may even have suggested the means of interpolating the numbers of survivors between childhood and old age. But all this does not amount to joint let alone sole authorship.

7. Gregory King on the Population of England in 1695

About a generation after Graunt's book appeared Gregory King wrote his *Observations on the State and Condition of England.* In chapter 3 above I concentrated on King's economic estimates but he was equally active in demography and this seems a suitable place at which to introduce his work in that field. It covers a wide range, from the population of England classified in all sorts of ways to the population of the world. He also has something to say about the historical growth of London and the country as a whole; and about the future population of the world should our planet in the course of millennia ever become 'fully peopled'.

In estimating the population of England and Wales King starts with the number of houses in 1695. According to the books of the Hearth Office, at Lady Day 1690 the number taxed was 1,319,215. Normally the annual increase would have been 2,000 but with the war then raging he thinks that there cannot have been much more than 1000 new houses built each year, so that by 1695 the total number taxed would be about 1,326,000. About 3 per cent would be either empty or used as workshops, so he deducts 36,000, leaving 1,290,000 or in a round number 1,300,000 inhabited houses.

He then turns to another source with which he was very familiar, the assessments for the 1695 tax on marriages, births and burials for which he was one of the commissioners. From this he derives the average number of souls per house and hence the population covered by the assessments. But this, he says, does not add up to the whole population, partly because of omissions in the assessments themselves and partly because of the many transitory people such as seamen, soldiers and vagrants to whom the assessments do not apply. After making the necessary adjustments he comes up with the figures set out in my table 7.3.

Table 7.3

HOUSING AND PEOPLE IN ENGLAND AND WALES, 1695

Locality	Inhabited houses ('000)	Population ('000)			
		People in assessments	Assessments adjusted for omissions	Transitory people not in assessments	Totals after adjustment
	(1)	(2)	(3)	(4)	(5)
97 parishes within the Walls	13.5	72.9	80.2	..	..
16 parishes without the Walls	32.5	149.5	164.5	..	..
15 parishes in Middlesex and Surrey	35.0	154.0	169.4	..	..
7 parishes in Westminster	24.0	103.2	113.5	..	..
All London and suburbs	105.0	479.6	527.6	2.4	530.0
Other cities and market towns	195.0	838.5	855.0	15.0	870.0
Villages and hamlets	1 000.0	4 000.0	4 040.0	60.0	4 100.0
Totals	1 300.0	5 318.1	5 422.6	77.4	5 500.0

Source: Gregory King, *Observations* (ed. Barnett), p. 17.

The population total of 5,500,000 given in this table raises a question. There is no doubt that the calculations are intended for the year 1695; and this is borne out by repeated statements in the *Observations*, in particular one on p. 27 where it is explicitly said that, whereas in 1688 'the Nation . . . did contain . . . 5,550,000 souls', in the intervening seven years the war had caused an abnormal rise in the death rate and an abnormal drop in the birth rate, so that by 1695 'it do . . . contain 5,500,000 souls'. However, in the economic accounts (tables 3.3 and 3.7 above) these totals are scaled down to 5,500,000 in 1688 and 5,450,000 in 1695. There is some confusion here which I cannot explain. Having said this, I shall leave King's figures as I find them.

The estimates shown in table 7.3 are only the first step in King's analysis of the population structure. His next subdivisions are by sex and by marital status. His results are summarised with some amendments in table 7.4.

Table 7.4

THE POPULATION OF ENGLAND AND WALES IN 1695 CLASSIFIED BY MARITAL STATUS, LOCALITY AND SEX ('000)

Status	London and suburbs (1)	Other cities and market towns (2)	Villages and hamlets (3)	Totals (4)	Males* (5)	Females* (6)
Husbands and wives	196.0	313.2	1 394.0	1 903.2	951.6	951.6
Widowers	10.6	17.4	61.5	89.5	89.5	-
Widows	37.1	52.2	184.5	273.8	-	273.8
Children	174.9	348.0	1 927.0	2 449.9	1 275.0	1 174.9
Servants	68.9	95.7	410.0	574.6	267.0	307.6
Sojourners etc.	42.4	43.5	123.0	208.9	99.5	109.4
Totals	529.9	870.0	4 100.0	5 499.9	2 682.6	2 817.3

* Adjusted to agree with the totals in column 4. The series as given by King are as follows: males, 950, 90, 1300, 260, 100, total 2700; females, 950, 240, 1200, 300, 110, total 2800.

Source: Gregory King, *Observations* (ed. Barnett), p. 22.

The figures in the first three columns of this table are as given by King and their totals are shown in the fourth column. The figures for the two sexes, which King rounds off to the nearest 10,000, are modified to agree with these totals. The series given by King are shown in the note to the table.

In another table King gives a classification of the population by age and sex which I have rearranged as shown in table 7.5.

Table 7.5
AGE AND SEX COMPOSITION OF THE POPULATION OF ENGLAND AND WALES, 1695
('000)

Age Group	Males	Females	Totals
Under 1	90	80	170
1-4	325	325	650
5-9	349	351	700
10-15	358	362	720
Total under 16	1 122	1 118	2 240
16-20	278	282	560
21-24	150	150	300
25-59	880	920	1 800
Total 16-59	1 308	1 352	2 660
60 and over	270	330	600
Total population	2 700	2 800	5 500

Source: Gregory King, *Observations* (ed. Barnett), p. 23.

From this information he derives the number of communicants, namely the population over the age of 16, and the number of fighting men, namely the males between the ages of 16 and 60. He then calculates the average age of the population from the average ages of the categories in table 7.4. above weighted by their relative importance in the total. The derivation of the answer, $27\frac{1}{2}$ years, is set out in table 7.6 below.

The final topic treated by King in this section of his *Observations* is the growth of the population in England and Wales and in London since the coming of the Romans in 53 B.C. He makes the population of the country as a whole grow exponen-

Table 7.6
AVERAGE AGE OF THE POPULATION OF ENGLAND AND WALES, 1695

Status	Average age years	multiplied by	Percentage in population	equals	Total years
Husbands	43		17¼		742
Wives	40		17¼		690
Widowers	56		1½		84
Widows	60		4½		270
Children	12		45		540
Servants	27		10½		284
Single persons and sojourners	35		4		140
Total or average	27½	equals	100	divided into	2750

Source: Gregory King, *Observations* (ed. Barnett), p. 23.

tially, which is the same as the initial part of a logistic curve. But London he makes get off to a much quicker start, suggesting a Gompertz curve,[1] which is the same as the final part of a logistic. It would be amusing to bring his figures up to date with the help of census data and see how well these curves would fit over the two millennia.

King's demographic estimates have been studied by a number of modern statisticians and demographers. Karl Pearson in his lectures on the history of statistics quoted them extensively, drawing comparisons with the corresponding estimates for his own period. An example is the average age of the population which he gives as 28.7 around 1930 as against King's figure of 27.5 around 1695.[2]

David Glass reworked King's figures for England and Wales, reaching a somewhat lower total, 4.913 million as against King's 5.5 million. He also adjusted them to give an estimate for England alone (without Wales) of 4.632 million. Another point he

1. Benjamin Gompertz, 'On the nature of the function expressive of the law of human mortality'. *Philosophical Transaction of the Royal Society*, vol. XXXVI, 1825, pp. 513-85.
2. Karl Pearson, *op. cit.*, p. 109.

made was that King's age distribution seems much too young even though the proportion of over-sixties is high.[1]

These calculations have been further investigated by Wrigley and Schofield in their monumental *Population History of England.*[2] For England alone their estimate, obtained by back projection, is 4.951 million as opposed to Glass' 4.632 million. They compare these figures with a figure of 5.183 million derived directly from King with the aid of Davenant's list of houses by county (table 2.1 above). They also present an age distribution in quinquennial age groups, again obtained by back projection, and compare it with King's distribution expressed in similar age groups by Glass. Their results are summarised in table 7.7.

Table 7.7

AGE DISTRIBUTION OF THE POPULATION OF ENGLAND, *c.* 1695

(percentages)

Age group	King (after Glass)	Wrigley and Schofield
Under 15	38.36	31.28
Ages 15-59	50.91	59.53
Over 59	10.73	9.18
Total	100.00	100.00

Note: Components do not always add up to totals because of rounding-off errors.
Source: Wrigley and Schofield, *The Population History of England*, p. 218.

8. The Population of the World According to King

Besides his estimates of the population of England and Wales, King also made estimates of the population of the world. In his *Notebook* he begins by saying 'Sir William Petty computes the number of people in the world about the year 1670 or 1680 to be 320 million'. He is quoting, I suppose, the estimates given in

1. D. V. Glass, 'Two papers on Gregory King'. In *Population in History*, London, 1965.
2. E. A. Wrigley and R. S. Schofield, *The Population History of England, 1541-1871*, Arnold, London, 1981.

Petty's *Essay Concerning the Growth of the City of London*[1] of the dates at which the population might have doubled, starting with the eight people saved from the Flood in Noah's ark. But, continues King, 'my computation is about 630 millions' and he adds a marginal note: 'But as Sir W. Petty endeavoured to magnify England so he lessened the world and all other countries'.

Petty's approach is methodical and leads to definite numerical results but it is highly speculative. One must take the Bible very seriously, know the date of the Flood and estimate the periods of doubling of the population subsequently. Anyway, on this basis, Petty estimates the world's population at 16 million in Moses' time, 32 million about David's time, 128 million about the birth of Christ and 320 million in his own day, though at this point he gets rather mixed up about his chronology.

King's approach is quite different. He begins by calculating the surface area of the earth, divides it between sea and land, and finally fills up the land with people. By putting together various calculations in the *Observations* and the *Notebook* we can compare his estimates with those available today.

The circumference of the world, he says, is 360 degrees at 69.5 miles to a degree, or 25,020 miles. The diameter is very near 8000 miles and so the superficial area, the product of the two, is, in round numbers, 200 million square miles. This is the figure given in the 1967 *Times Atlas of the World*. King then multiplies this figure by 640, the number of acres in a square mile, to give 128,000 million acres and does all his calculations in acres. I shall not follow him in this but instead shall multiply by 4.0468 and work in square kilometres, which gives the surface area of the world as km^2 518 million.

Having calculated the total surface area, King apportions it between land and sea in two ways. First, in the *Observations*, by making the assumption common in his day that the earth's surface was equally divided between land and sea; on this assumption each would occupy 259 million square kilometres.

1. William Petty, *Another Essay in Political Arithmetick Concerning the Growth of the City of London, 1682*. London, 1683; reprinted in C. H. Hull (ed.), *op. cit.*

Second, in the *Notebook*, by working out with the help of maps the land and sea areas in each of four pairs of latitudinal bands into which he divides the globe; in this way he reaches the more realistic figure of 194.2 million square kilometres of land, equivalent to 37.5 per cent of the whole. The modern figure is about 30 per cent. His ingenious calculation is shown in table 7.8.

Table 7.8

KING'S ESTIMATES OF SEA AND LAND AREAS IN LATITUDINAL BANDS ROUND THE GLOBE

(km² million)

Latitude	Land	Sea	Totals
Equator to ± 30 degrees	101.2	129.5	230.7
± 30 to ± 55 degrees	64.7	113.3	178.1
± 55 to ± 70 degrees	16.2	68.8	85.0
± 70 to ± 90 degrees	12.1	12.1	24.3
Totals	194.2	323.7	518.0

Note: Components do not always add up to totals because of rounding-off errors.
Source (converted to km²): Gregory King, *Notebook*, p. 2.

He thus has two distinct estimates of the total land area, that in the *Notebook* being by far the better of the two. Each total is then subdivided among the four known continents plus an ample allowance for unknown lands. The two sets of estimates are shown in table 7.9 side by side with my own, which are based on a combination of the data in *The Times Atlas* and the UN *Demographic Yearbook* for 1984.

In the *Notebook* King also gives the areas of the countries of Europe but I shall not reproduce them here as in many cases the boundaries have changed, and to give a meaningful account would require more knowledge of historical geography and of the maps that King used than I have.

King fills up the land tracts of the world in a variety of ways. Although he does not specify his sources, rough estimates of population existed for many countries, both European and extra-European, some based on tax assessments, some on registers of

Table 7.9

KING'S ESTIMATES OF SEA AND LAND AREAS GROUPED BY CONTINENTS COMPARED WITH MODERN ESTIMATES

(km² million)

	King's estimates		Modern estimates	
	Observations assuming equal land & sea areas	*Notebook* based on latitudinal bands		
Europe	6.9	12.1	10.5	Europe
Asia	27.5	36.4	44.4	Asia
Africa	24.7	24.3	30.3	Africa
America	34.0	48.6	42.1	America
Uninhabitable zones	..	20.2		
Known lands	93.1*	141.6	127.3	Known in 1695
Terra incognita	165.9§	52.6	28.1	Oceania etc.
Total land area	259.0	194.2	155.4	
Sea area	259.0	323.7	362.6	
Total world surface	518.0	518.0	518.0	

* Of which 80.9 habitable and 12.1 uninhabitable.

§ Of which 101.2 'perhaps inhabitable' and 64.7 'perhaps uninhabitable'.

Note: Components do not always add up to totals because of rounding-off errors.

Sources: Gregory King, *Observations* (ed. Barnett), pp. 20-21; *Notebook*, pp. 1-2. *The Times Atlas of the World*, 1967. *UN Demographic Yearbook 1984*.

births and deaths, some on partial enumerations, some on the descriptions of travellers. He condensed this disparate material into three alternative sets of estimates, somewhat different from one another but each consistent in itself and each adding up to a grand total in the region of 640 million, which by his computations he believed to be the population of the world in 1695.

In the first set, which appears in the *Observations*, he builds up his population figures for the four continents from estimates of density: total area divided by number of acres per head equals number of inhabitants. In the second set, which appears in the *Notebook*, he follows an inverse order: number of inhabitants divided into total area equals acres per head. These two sets are shown side by side in Table 7.10 together with some modern estimates for 1700 which I derived from Carr-Saun-

Table 7.10

KING'S ESTIMATES OF CONTINENTAL POPULATIONS IN 1695 COMPARED WITH MODERN RETROSPECTIVE ESTIMATES FOR *c.* 1700

	King's estimates for 1695				Modern estimates for 1700	
	Observations assuming equal land & sea areas		*Notebook* based on latitudinal bands			
	km² per head* (averages)	Population (millions)	km² per head* (averages)	Population (millions)	Population (millions)	
	(1)	(2)	(3)	(4)	(5)	
Europe	0.069	100	0.105	115	120.0	Europe
Asia	0.081	340	0.107	340	404.5	Asia
Africa	0.260	95	0.347	70	97.5	Africa
America	0.523	65	0.540	90	12.7	America
Known lands	..	600	..	615	634.7	Known in 1700
Terra incognita	1.659 (perhaps)	100 (perhaps)	2.287	11	2.0	Oceania
Totals or averages	0.432-0.370	600-700	0.304	626	636.7	

* When the acre is used as the unit of measurement the areas per head are simple numbers.

Sources: Gregory King, *Observations* (ed. Barnett), p. 21; *Notebook*, pp. 1-2. A.M. Carr-Saunders, *World Population*, p. 42.

ders' *World Population*[1] by averaging his retrospective estimates for 1650 and 1750.

In this table the figures in columns 1 and 2 are reproduced as they stand in the *Observations*. In the *Notebook* there are a lot of crossings out and minor variations but the upshot seems approximately as shown in columns 3 and 4. The total for Europe is the sum of the populations of all the European countries. It is not clear how the total for Asia is reached but it seems to have given King some trouble. First he puts it at 225 million, which would make the population of the world 500 million in all. This does not satisfy him and so he adds in another 115 million, thus bringing the total for Asia up to the 340 million given in the *Observations*, where he remarks on the populousness of India, Persia and China and suggests that there should be at least 230 million in

1. A. M. Carr-Saunders, *World Population: Past Grouth and Present Trends*. Clarendon Press, Oxford, 1936.

China alone. The totals for Africa and America are no more than reasoned guesses. A comparison of column 4 with column 5 shows that apart from America and terra incognita he was not too far off the mark.

King's third set of estimates, also in the *Notebook*, distributes the population of the world not over continents but over latitudinal bands, as shown in table 7.11. As a curiosity I have added to it a projection he made to a time when the world would be 'fully peopled', which by some elaborate calculations he expects to occur around A.D. 5,000 or 5,500.

Table 7.11

KING'S ESTIMATES OF THE PRESENT AND FUTURE POPULATION OF THE WORLD IN LATITUDINAL BANDS

Latitude	Land area (km² million)	Distribution of population			
		1695		If fully peopled	
		km² per head* (averages)	Population (million)	km² per head* (averages)	Population (million)
	(1)	(2)	(3)	(4)	(5)
Equator to ± 30 degrees	101.2	0.364	278	0.03643	2 778
± 30 to ± 55 degrees	64.7	0.202	320	0.02023	3 200
± 55 to ± 70 degrees	16.2	0.405	40	0.06475	250
± 70 to ± 90 degrees	12.1	..	0	0.40469	30
Totals or averages	194.2	0.304	638	0.03103	6 258

* When the acre is used as the unit of measurement the areas per head are simple numbers.
Source: Gregory King, *Notebook*, p. 2.

So in King's opinion the world would be fully peopled with ten times the population of 1695. Moreover, he says, it would not be possible to maintain more than double that number, a maximum that might be reached between A.D. 10,000 and 61,000 depending on what rates of growth obtained in the future.

I need hardly say that this projection is not to be taken very seriously. It is one of several which King made, experimenting with rates of growth from the Creation (2 people) to the Flood and from the Flood (8 survivors) to his day, and extrapolating from then on to the year 2,639,310. Like Petty, indeed like all his contemporaries, he was conditioned to think of history in terms of the Bible so that his projections though more rigorous than Petty's are no more valid. They are another example, however, of his dexterity in devising computational methods appropriate to solving whatever statistical problem he set himself.

As far as I know this is the only case in which King was swept off his feet by his arithmetical virtuosity. As long as he stuck to his own time his feet did not leave the ground and modern historians, as we have seen, still keep an eye on his estimates when making their own.

Edmond Halley

CHAPTER 8

Edmond Halley and the First Life Table

1. Brief Life

It may be wondered why Edmond Halley, an astronomer, should come into my story. The answer is simple. Both Graunt and Petty had seen the need for a survival table showing the proportions of a given number of births likely to survive to successively older ages. They tried to construct such a table but with the information at their disposal could not really succeed. They would have needed to know the age at death, which the Bills of Mortality did not provide, and to have been dealing with a stable population in a stable environment, conditions which were not satisfied by London partly on account of the plague and partly because the city was subject to considerable net immigration. The importance of the problem was recognised and the Royal Society was on the look-out for a solution. This solution, unexpectedly, was provided by Halley.

Edmond Halley was born on 8 November 1656 at Haggerston in the parish of St. Leonard's Shoreditch, a suburb of London. His father was a wealthy soap boiler in the City. He sent his only son to St. Paul's School, where the boy distinguished himself in classics and mathematics and very early revealed where his vocation lay: 'he studied the heavens so closely' that it was said of him by a well-known globe maker 'that if a star were displaced in the globe he would presently find it out'. In 1673 he went up to Queen's College, Oxford, knowing Greek, Latin and Hebrew and taking with him a collection of instruments. While at Oxford, he pursued his astronomical observations and before he was twenty had contributed three papers to the *Philosophical Transactions* of the Royal Society.

In November 1676 he left the university without taking a

degree in order to sail to St. Helena 'purely upon the account of the advancement of astronomy, to make the globe of the southern hemisphere right, which before was very erroneous, as having been done only by the observations of ignorant seamen', as Wood puts it. Charles II got the East India Company to give him a passage on one of their ships and his father made him an allowance of £300 a year. He arrived at St. Helena after a three-month voyage and remained there for eighteen months.

St. Helena was not an ideal place for his work, being so damp that the object-glass of his telescope had to be dried every few minutes and paper became so wet that he could not write down his measurements with ink. He also found that the pendulum of his clock had to be shortened to keep time. The first of these observations led him to realise the circulatory process by which the moisture in rivers which is continually flowing into the sea gets back into the rivers; and the second, on being reported to Newton, was attributed by him to the change in gravity being due to the fact that the earth was an oblate spheroid and not a perfect sphere. Thus even as an undergraduate his acute observation and imagination led him to interesting results outside his main objective.

Despite the handicaps of the climate he succeeded in cataloguing over 340 stars and returned home in October 1678, shortly before his twenty-second birthday, to be hailed by Flamsteed as 'the Southern Tycho'. In November he presented his *Catalogus Stellarum Australium* to the Royal Society and was immediately elected into a fellowship, and in December the university of Oxford, by command of the King, conferred on him the degree of Master of Arts. Six months later the Society sent him to Danzig to arbitrate in a dispute between Hooke and Hevelius on the respective merits of telescopic and plain sights, which he resolved by testifying to the accuracy of Hevelius' telescopic observations.

In 1680 he went on a continental tour with a friend and in 1682 he married Mary Tooke, the daughter of an Auditor of the Exchequer, with whom he lived happily until her death fifty-five years later. She was, we are told, 'a young lady equally amiable for the gracefulness of her person and the beauties of her mind'.

Shortly after these events, Halley provided some ingenious

assistance to John Houghton, a regular writer on agriculture and trade and a Fellow of the Royal Society. On being asked the acreage of England and Wales, Halley took a map, cut out the land area and weighed it 'in nice scales'. He then cut out from the middle of the map a circle having a diameter of 2° of the meridian which lay wholly within the land area. He found that the land map weighed just four times as much as the circle, which would give England and Wales an area of about 38.7 million acres on the presumption that 'a million or two acres will break no squares'. The modern estimate is 37.3 million acres. He used the same method to estimate the acreage of each county. His description of his method and the accompanying county estimates were published some ten years later by Houghton in his periodical.[1] Some interesting comments on the acreage measurements of Halley, King and Petty can be found in McCulloch's *Statistical Account of the British Empire*.[2]

In 1687 Newton's *Principia* was published. Its appearance owed a great deal to Halley. Indeed it is probable that but for Halley the book would not have existed. His suggestions originated it, he averted the threatened suppression of the third book, undertook the printing costs, corrected the proofs and laid aside his own work to press forward with the printing. For this, posterity must be grateful, as all who have read Maynard Keynes' account of Newton's strange, neurotic personality will appreciate.[3]

Halley's paying for the printing was particularly meritorious as his father had died in 1684 in bad financial circumstances, leaving him a relatively poor man. I am glad to say that he was eventually refunded by the sale of copies.

I do not propose to discuss Halley's astonishing scientific achievements but it is perhaps of interest to mention the varied positions he held at different times. From 1685 to the beginning of 1693 he was assistant secretary of the Royal Society and editor of its *Transactions*. In 1692 these had been renewed after several

1. Edmond Halley, 'Letter to John Houghton concerning the number of acres in England and Wales'. In *A Collection of Letters for the Improvement of Husbandry and Trade* (ed. J. Houghton), no. xxiv, 20 Jan 1693, pp. 68-70, and no. xxv, 27 Jan 1693, pp. 71-3.

2. 2nd edn. London, 1839, vol 1, p. 4.

3. John Maynard Keynes, 'Newton, the man'. In *Essays in Biography*, vol. x of *The Collected Works*, pp. 363-74.

years of suspension and Halley had undertaken to provide five sheets in twenty for the new series. For a short time at the end of the century he was deputy controller of the Chester Mint. In 1698-1700 he was in command of the *Paramour*, a war sloop put at his disposal by William III for scientific purposes, and was again involved in scientific navigation in 1701-2. In 1703 he became Savilian Professor of Geometry at Oxford in succession to Wallis. He engaged, among other things, with David Gregory, in the translation into Latin of some of the works of Apollonius from Arabic and Greek. In 1713 he was appointed Secretary of the Royal Society but gave it up on succeeding Flamsteed as Astronomer Royal in 1721.

For most his life Halley enjoyed health and spoke and acted with unusual sprightliness and vivacity. He was disinterested and upright, an affectionate husband and father and, though he had his differences with Flamsteed and Newton, a good friend, free from rancour or jealousy. In 1737, the year of his wife's death, his right hand became affected with paralysis. He did not stop working and continued for some years to attend the Thursday meetings of the Royal Society, but from 1740 on his bodily powers deteriorated though his memory, judgement and cheerfulness remained intact. On 14 January 1742, in his eighty-sixth year, weary of the cordials prescribed by his doctor, he asked for a glass of wine, drank it and died. He was buried near his wife in the churchyard of Lee near Greenwich. Out of a numerous family only two daughters survived him.

Further details of his life and work will be found in Wood,[1] Clerke[2] and Armitage.[3]

2. *Halley's Table of Survivors*

Two of Halley's salient traits were his versatility and his readiness to help people. The trouble he took over the publication of

1. Anthony Wood, *Athenae Oxonienses*, 2nd edn, vol II, 'Writers', pp. 981-3, and 'Fasti', p. 210.

2. Agnes Mary Clerke, 'Edmond Halley'. *The Dictionary of National Biography*, vol. VIII, pp. 988-93.

3. Angus Armitage, *Edmond Halley*. London, 1966.

Newton's *Principia* and his estimation of the area of England for Houghton are two instances of this. A third, which also had remarkable results, was his calculations of the first statistically correct life table, which he constructed on the basis of data provided by Caspar Neumann for the town of Breslau.

Neumann was a scientifically-minded clergyman, a few years older than Halley, born in Breslau, who after studying theology, oriental languages, philosophy and mathematics at Jena took his master's degree there in 1670. After teaching in his university for a time, he was appointed in 1673 Chaplain to Prince Christian and travelled with him extensively. In 1678 he returned to Breslau where in 1692 he became Pastor of the Church of St. Elizabeth. Wishing to test some current superstitions concerning the influence of the moon on health, he made a systematic study of the Breslau registers of births and burials over a period of years and sent his analysis to Leibnitz. Probably at Leibnitz's suggestion he then got in touch with Justell, a fellow of the Royal Society, who passed the matter on to Halley. There followed a correspondence with Neumann, at the end of which Halley possessed monthly records of births by sex and deaths by age and sex in Breslau for the five years 1687-91. He got to work on these data and in 1693 published his results in the revived *Philosophical Transactions.*[1]

He opens his paper with a tribute to Petty and Graunt for their attempt to calculate survival rates from the very defective information at their disposal. 'This defect', he continues, 'seems in a great measure to be satisfied by the late curious tables of the Bills of Mortality of the city of Breslau . . . wherein both the ages and sexes of all that die are monthly delivered, and compared with the number of the births, for five years last past, *viz.* 1687, 88, 89, 90, 91'. Further, all evidence suggests that Breslau has an almost stationary population. The only missing element is the size of the population, but this can be estimated from the information contained in the Bills.

1. Edmond Halley, 'An estimate of the degrees of mortality of mankind drawn from curious tables of the births and funerals at the city of Breslaw'. *Philosophical Transactions of the Royal Society of London*, vol. xvii, no. 196, 1693, pp. 596-610; reprinted in *Degrees of Mortality of Mankind by Edmund Halley* (ed. L. J. Reed), Johns Hopkins Press, Baltimore, 1942.

In all, 6,193 births and 5,869 deaths are recorded. When averaged over the five years, the births are 1,238 and the deaths 1,174 per annum. The excess of births over deaths is only 64 per annum, or about 5 per cent, which 'may perhaps be balanced by the levies for the Emperor's service in his wars'. Of the 1,238 infants born each year, 348 die in their first year of life, so that only 890 survive to their first birthday. A further 198 'do die in the five years between 1 and 6 compleat, taken at a medium; so that but 692 of the persons born do survive six whole years. From this age the infants being arrived at some degree of firmness, grow less and less mortal'.

He then gives a summary table, classified partly by single ages and partly by age groups, showing the average number of deaths per annum at each age up to 100. The series is very irregular but Halley thinks that the irregularities would be smoothed out if the data extended over a longer period, twenty years, say, instead of five. He concludes that the very low mortality apparent in the teenage group 'seems rather to be attributed to chance'; that 'from 25 to 50 there seem to die from 7 to 8 and 9 per annum of each age; and after that to 70 . . . the mortality increases, and there are found to die 10 or 11 of each age per annum. From thence the number of the living being grown very small, they gradually decline till there be none left to die'.

After this brief *exposé* he presents the table of survivals which I reproduce here without alterations as table 8.1.

It is not quite clear how Halley reached the estimates shown in this table. He gives no explanation of his method, and since most of the original material is lost it is not possible to reconstruct his calculations with precision. To get the number of survivors in each year of age, which he terms 'age current', he appears to have taken as the benchmark for each age not the birthday but the midpoint between two consecutive birthdays; nowadays this is usually represented by L, as opposed to l which denotes age at birthday. If this interpretation is correct, the first entry in the table, 1,000, shows the number surviving to the middle of their first year: in modern notation $L_0=1{,}000$ infants six-month old as opposed to $l_0=1{,}238$ births. This implies that out of the 348 deaths in the first year of life, 238, or 68 per cent, took place in the first

Table 8.1

HALLEY'S TABLE OF SURVIVORS FOR BRESLAU, 1687-91

Age Curt.	Persons	Age Curt.	Persons	Age Curt.	Persons	Age Curt.	Persons	Age Curt.	Persons	Age Curt.	Persons
1	1000	8	680	15	628	22	586	29	539	36	481
2	855	9	670	16	622	23	579	30	531	37	472
3	798	10	661	17	616	24	573	31	523	38	463
4	760	11	653	18	610	25	567	32	515	39	454
5	732	12	646	19	604	26	560	33	507	40	445
6	710	13	640	20	598	27	553	34	499	41	436
7	692	14	634	21	592	28	546	35	490	42	427
Age Curt.	**Persons**	**Age Curt.**	**Persons**	**Age Curt.**	**Persons**	**Age Curt.**	**Persons**	**Age Curt.**	**Persons**	**Age Curt.**	**Persons**
43	417	50	346	57	272	64	202	71	131	78	58
44	407	51	335	58	262	65	192	72	120	79	49
45	397	52	324	59	252	66	182	73	109	80	41
46	387	53	313	60	242	67	172	74	98	81	34
47	377	54	302	61	232	68	162	75	88	82	28
48	367	55	292	62	222	69	152	76	78	83	23
49	357	56	282	63	212	70	142	77	68	84	20

Age	Persons
7	5 547
14	4 584
21	4 270
28	3 964
35	3 604
42	3 178
49	2 709
56	2 194
63	1 694
70	1 204
77	692
84	253
100	107
Sum Total	34 000

Source: Edmond Halley, 'An estimate of the degrees of mortality of mankind', p. 599.

six months, which is plausible. Similarly, out of the 1,238 births we know that l_1=890 survived to their first birthday and the table shows that L_1=855 survived to age $1\frac{1}{2}$; continuing down the table, L_2=798 survived to age $2\frac{1}{2}$, L_3=760 survived to age $3\frac{1}{2}$ and so on. In the column by the side of the table Halley gives the age composition of the population, which adds up to 34,000 inhabitants.

It is interesting to compare Halley's estimates with those made by Graunt thirty years earlier. The two curves are shown in diagram 8.1, where the circles represent Graunt's figures and the crosses Halley's.

Diagram 8.1

SEVENTEENTH CENTURY SURVIVAL CURVES

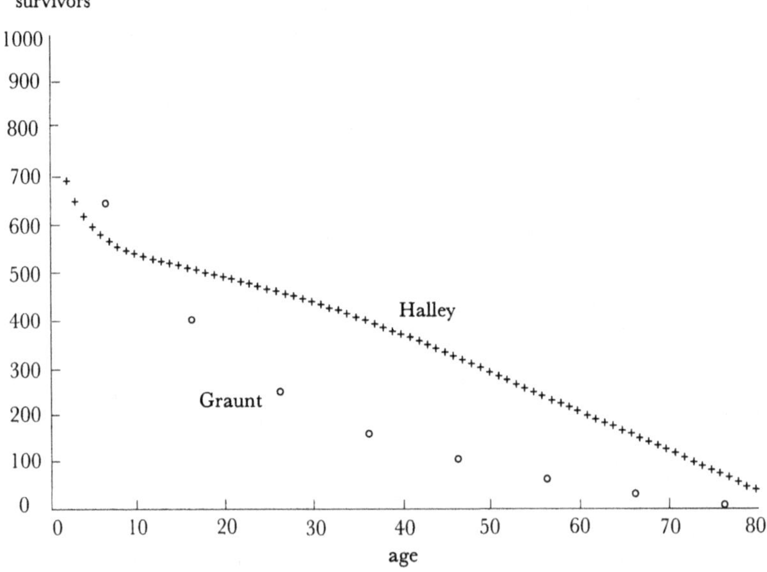

As can be seen, Graunt's figures imply a very high death rate in youth; it is curious that neither he nor Petty seem to have been worried by this. Also, there are no survivors beyond the age of about 80. Halley's curve, though still not quite right, is much more realistic: after high rates in infancy and early childhood, mortality slows down to very low rates in youth and gradually accelerates with age as the number of survivors fall; and 80 is by no means the extreme limit of life.

After giving his table of survivals Halley proceeds to illustrate its uses.

First, he calculates the proportion in the population of men able to bear arms, that is men between 18 and 56, a question that interested also Graunt. He calculates the number of inhabitants under 18 as

$$5{,}547+4{,}584+628+622+616=11{,}997$$

and the number over 56 as

$$1{,}694+1{,}204+692+253+107=3{,}950;$$

he then subtracts their sum, 15,947, from 34,000 to give 18,053; finally, allowing one half to be males, he reaches 9,027, or say 9,000. So the proportion of 'fencible men, as the Scotch call them', is 9/34 or somewhat more that a quarter of the number of souls.

Second, he uses the table to calculate 'the differing degrees of mortality, or rather vitality', at any age. For instance, we can see that 'a person of 25 years of age has the odds of 560 to 7, or 80 to 1, that he does not die in a year'. The same method can be used to calculate 'the odds that any person does not die before he attain any proposed age'. For instance, what are the odds that a man of 40 lives 7 years. The number surviving at age 47 is 377; if we subtract this from the number, 445, surviving to age 40 we obtain 68. Thus the odds are 377 to 68, or $5\frac{1}{2}$ to 1, that a man of 40 survives 7 years.

Third, the table can be used to calculate 'at what number of years it is an even lay that a person of any age shall die'. Consider a person aged 30. According to the table there are 531 survivors at this age. One half of this number, 215, is reached between the ages of 57 and 58. So a man of 30 may reasonably expect to live another 27 or 28 years.

Fourth, the price of life insurance ought to be regulated according to the probability of death at different ages. For instance, it is 100 to 1 that a man of 20 does not die within a year but it is only 38 to 1 for a man of 50.

Fifth, the value of annuities upon lives can be calculated from the table since the purchaser ought to pay for only that part of the value of the annuity as he has chances to live. Halley explains how to do this, and as the amount of calculation is considerable he gives a table of the value of annuities, expressed in years purchase, for each fifth year of age up to the seventieth. This is reproduced here as table 8.2.

Table 8.2

VALUE OF ANNUITIES FOR EVERY FIFTH YEAR OF LIFE UP TO THE SEVENTIETH

Age	Years Purchase	Age	Years Purchase	Age	Years Purchase
1	10.28	25	12.27	50	9.21
5	13.40	30	11.72	55	8.51
10	13.44	35	11.12	60	7.60
15	13.33	40	10.57	65	6.54
20	12.78	45	9.91	70	5.32

Source: Edmond Halley, 'An estimate of the degreees of mortality of mankind', p. 602.

The value at the usual rate of interest drops from nearly 13½ years purchase at age 10 to a little over 11 years purchase at age 35. This, he says, shows the advantage of putting money into the present government fund which yields 14 per cent per annum, equivalent to 7 years purchase. He goes on to deal with annuities on two or three lives.

Although the method is general the results depend on the expectations, which vary with the salubrity of different places. Halley finds that in Breslau about 1 in 30 die annually, 'as Sir William Petty has computed for London'. If so, Breslau cannot be very salubrious, a surmise confirmed by the high infant mortality. It is to be desired, he concludes, 'that in imitation here of the curious in other cities would attempt something of the same nature, than which perhaps nothing can be more useful'.

Table 8.3

SURVIVALS OUT OF 10,000 BIRTHS AND THE COMPLETE EXPECTATION OF LIFE AT DIFFERENT AGES BASED ON HALLEY'S NUMBERS FOR BRESLAU, 1687-91

Age at birthday x	Number of survivors l_x	Complete expectation of life $\mathring{e}_x$	Age at birthday x	Number of survivors l_x	Complete expectation of life $\mathring{e}_x$	Age at birthday x	Number of survivors l_x	Complete expectation of life $\mathring{e}_x$	Age at birthday x	Number of survivors l_x	Complete expectation of life $\mathring{e}_x$	Age at birthday x	Number of survivors l_x	Complete expectation of life $\mathring{e}_x$
0	10 000	27.54	20	4 806	33.93	40	3 557	22.05	60	1 914	12.33	80	290	..
1	7 192		21	4 757		41	3 485		61	1 834		81	250	
2	6 624		22	4 705		42	3 408		62	1 753		82	202	
3	6 269		23	4 651		43	3 328		63	1 672		83	170	
4	6 011		24	4 603		44	3 247		64	1 591		84	154	
5	5 816	41.47	25	4 552	30.69	45	3 167	19.47	65	1 511	9.96	85	137	..
6	5 656		26	4 496		46	3 086		66	1 430		86	121	
7	5 534		27	4 439		47	3 005		67	1 349		87	105	
8	5 453		28	4 383		48	2 925		68	1 268		88	89	
9	5 371		29	4 322		49	2 840		69	1 188		89	73	
10	5 307	40.25	30	4 257	27.64	50	2 751	17.05	70	1 103	7.74	90	61	..
11	5 242		31	4 193		51	2 663		71	1 014		91	53	
12	5 194		32	4 137		52	2 574		72	925		92	44	
13	5 146		33	4 063		53	2 485		73	836		93	36	
14	5 097		34	3 994		54	2 400		74	751		94	28	
15	5 049	37.19	35	3 921	24.78	55	2 319	14.75	75	670	7.30	95	20	..
16	5 000		36	3 849		56	2 238		76	590		96	12	
17	4 952		37	3 777		57	2 157		77	509		97	8	
18	4 904		38	3 704		58	2 076		78	427		98	4	
19	4 856		39	3 631		59	1 995		79	363		99	..	

Source: R. Böckh, 'Halley als Statistiker', pp. 20-21.

3. A Modern Version of Halley's Table

Halley's conception furnished the prototype on which all later life tables have been based, so that the results set out in table 8.1 above can easily be converted into the form of a modern table. Thus, given that $l_0=1{,}238$, $L_0=1{,}000$ and $l_1=890$, we can calculate l_x for higher ages, since there is little error in assuming that after infancy and until very high ages are reached deaths are spread evenly through the year. Thus

$$\begin{aligned} l_{x+1} &= L_x - \tfrac{1}{2}(l_x - l_{x+1}) \\ &= 2L_x - l_x. \end{aligned}$$

We can then calculate what is usually called the expectation of life at age x, e_x (not Halley's even lay), from

$$e_x = \sum_{t=1}^{\infty} l_{x+t}/l_x.$$

This gives the number of exact years of life that may be expected after birthday x. However, since deaths may take place at any time and not just at exact ages, the so-called 'complete' expectation of life, $\mathring{e}_x$, is half a year longer, that is

$$\mathring{e}_x = e_x + \tfrac{1}{2}.$$

This can be compared with Halley's even lay, which is given by the value of t for which

$$l_{x+t} = \tfrac{1}{2} l_x.$$

In 1893, to mark the bicentenary of Halley's table, Böckh wrote a paper on Halley as a statistician[1] in which he calculated from Halley's figures the series for l_x and for $\mathring{e}_x$ shown in table 8.3. In this calculation Böckh adopted the modern convention of starting from 1,000 births (instead of Halley's 1,238), scaling

1. R. Böckh, 'Halley als Statistiker'. *Bulletin of the International Statistical Institute*, vol. VII, no. 1, 1893, pp. 1-34.

down all the subsequent figures proportionately. Thus all the l_x's become numbers per mille, which makes it easier to take in the relative orders of magnitude. In table 8.3 I have multiplied Böckh's l_x's by 10 in order to avoid decimal points.

A few years earlier what survived of the Neumann-Halley correspondence and other documents had been published by Graetzer,[1] so that Böckh had at least some of the original material to help him in his reconstruction. Further comments on Halley's work will be found in Pearson[2] Greenwood,[3] and Reed.[4]

4. A Postscript

Shortly after the publication of his paper Halley added a note in another issue of the *Transactions*[5] in which he expressed the hope that Neumann would be kind enough to continue his observations for some years more, so that chance irregularities in the table could be corrected. If we had observations for a great many years, 'it would be very well worth the while to think of methods for facilitating the computation of the value of two, three or more lives; which as proposed in my former, seems (as I am informed) a work of too much difficulty for the ordinary arithmetician to undertake'. He has tried, he says, to find a theorem which would simplify the calculations, but in vain. He offers to prepare a table of the sums of logarithms that enter into the calculations with examples of their use. Small wonder that computing was a problem at a time when the latest tool in the arithmetician's kit-bag was a table of logarithms.

The note ends with two philosophical reflections. How unjust it is, he says, to repine at the shortness of our lives and think

1. J. Graetzer, *Edmund Halley und Caspar Neumann: ein Beitrag zur Geschichte der Bevölkerungs-statistik*. Breslau, 1883.

2. Karl Pearson, *The History of Statistics in the 17th and 18th Centuries*.

3. Major Greenwood, *Medical Statistics from Graunt to Farr*. Cambridge University Press, 1948.

4. Lowell J. Reed, Intoduction to *Degrees of Mortality of Mankind by Edmund Halley*.

5. Edmond Halley, 'Some further considerations on the Breslaw bills of mortality'. *Philosophical Transactions of the Royal Society of London*, vol. XVII, no. 198, 1693, pp. 654-56; reprinted in L. J. Reed (ed.), *op. cit.*

ourselves wronged if we do not attain old age. If we look at the table we can see that half of those born are dead in seventeen years, time; so we should 'account it as a blessing that we have survived, perhaps by many years, that period of life, whereat the one half of the whole race of mankind does not arrive'.

The second reflection is in quite a different strain. Like Petty and many other writers of the time, Halley would like to see a larger population in England. The lack of growth is not to be attributed to natural causes but to the delay of marriage due to poverty arising partly from the unequal distribution of possessions, whereby the labourer must work not only to feed his own family but also 'for those who own the ground that feeds them', and partly from unemployment, which it should be the care of the State to provide against.

Thus even in this scientific context we find a sympathy for the difficulties of the poor and a recognition that something could be done about them which is characteristic of the group of writers I am describing.

William Farr

CHAPTER 9

William Farr and the Development of Vital Statistics

1. Brief Life

Although William Farr, my third demographer, received his early training as a doctor he only practised as one for a very short time. Instead, he used his medical knowledge to create and develop a national system of vital statistics which drew attention to sanitary problems and played an important role in the health progress of the nineteenth century.

William Farr was born at Kenley, a village in Shropshire, on 30 November 1807. His grandfather was a small farmer. His parents, who were young and poor, moved early in their married life to Sorrington, a village six or seven miles from Shrewsbury, and little William was adopted when only two by Joseph Pryce, the benevolent and well-to-do squire of Dorrington. He did not remember his infancy with his parents but his father, who died in 1864, spent the last years of his life with him. He had happy memories of his benefactor: 'to him I owe my education, the most constant and tender care, and an example of benevolence and integrity'.

The local schools were very poor and Farr's classical and mathematical knowledge was mainly due to his own reading. As he grew up his interest turned to medical studies, and fortune again favoured him. One day, when he was nineteen, Dr. Webster, a physician of Shrewsbury, paid Mr. Pryce a visit and fell into discussion with the young man on some works which were lying on a table. The doctor was impressed: it was arranged that William should study with him in Shrewsbury and 'act as a dresser for Mr. Sutton at the infirmary'. Through the summer of 1826 Farr walked daily into Shrewsbury and back, as his old benefactor did not like him to be out of sight for more than a day, but as the winter came on a mare was bought for him so that he was able to make his daily trip on horseback. For the next two years he read medical works with Webster and at the same received good practical training in surgery from Sutton. As a diversion, he and Webster read the Italian classics with an Italian political refugee, 'a carbonarist from Turin, a Roman patriot'.

At the end of 1828 Pryce, a bachelor, died at the age of ninety and left his protégé a legacy of £500 to promote his education and advancement. In the following year Farr left Shrewsbury to pursue his medical studies at the University of Paris where he spent two years. His dominant interest in public health and medical statistics dates from this period. On his return he held for a time a temporary position in the Shrewsbury infirmary, which might have been made permanent if he had had any medical qualifications. However, he had none. This was a serious handicap, so he decided to enter himself as a student at University College, London. Here again, possibly for lack of funds, he remained only two years, long enough to become a Licentiate of the Society of Apothecaries, which he did in 1832.

Modest as this qualification was, it enabled him to marry and set up a practice in London. He also offered to give lectures on his favourite subject, the science of hygiene, which he called 'hygiology'. The practice did not flourish, the patients did not come; and nobody in those days was interested in public health and the prevention of diseases. But Farr persevered. He wrote for various medical journals. including a series of papers in the *Lancet*, recently founded by Dr. Wakley; two long papers on the history of medicine, full of medical and mortality statistics, in the *British Medical Almanac*; and an outstanding chapter on vital statistics in McCulloch's *Statistical Account of the British Empire*. In 1837 he lost his second benefactor, Dr. Webster, who left him £500 and his library.

1837 was the year when the General Register Office was established, with T.H. Lister as the first Registrar General. At this point Farr's reputation as a writer on medical subjects paid off and he was appointed in 1839 to the post of Compiler of Abstracts.

He remained at the General Register Office until shortly

before his death. During his forty years there he wrote an immense number of reports, was in charge of the population censuses of 1851, 1861 and 1871, and was responsible for the first three British life tables based on census data. He was repeatedly called in by the government to give advice on medical, sanitary and actuarial matters such as the preparation of army medical statistics, the sanitary conditions of the army in India, the condition of miners, the control of the water supply, the pensions of the Metropolitan Police, the setting up of a state insurance scheme and many others. He carried on an unremitting campaign for the introduction of public health measures and eventually had the satisfaction of seeing many of his views ratified by the sanitary legislation of 1872 and 1875.

He must have had uncommon powers of persuasion to make such an impression on the British establishment. He was indeed very persistent, worked very hard, paid great attention to detail and his statistical evidence was impressive both for quantity and for quality. On top of this he wrote clearly and vividly and had by all accounts an engaging personality. In the words of one of his colleagues in the Register Office, N.A. Humphreys,

> 'Those who had the privilege and pleasure of his friendship, or even of his acquaintance, enjoy and treasure the memory of the man, quite apart from the inevitable respect and admiration they feel for his talents and his services. With scarcely an exception, Dr. Farr has been invariably spoken of with respectful appreciation. It would be hard indeed to believe that he could have had a private enemy, for he was not only essentially modest and unassuming in his manner, but he was always ready to see and appreciate merit, being especially free from jealousy of the success or suspicion of the motives of others.'

In financial matters this candour made him an easy prey to unscrupulous speculators and he lost a lot of money thereby. He was also extremely absent-minded, often with ludicrous results. But these characteristics added to his charm.

In the statistical community both at home and abroad Farr achieved a high standing. He was early a Fellow of the Statistical Society of London, a frequent contributor to its journal and president in the years 1871-73. He was active in many other learned societies and at the International Statistical Congresses from 1853 on. In 1855 he was elected a Fellow of the Royal Society and soon after a Corresponding Member of the French *Institut*. He received honorary degrees from New York and Oxford and a diamond ring from Tsar Alexander II.

In the course of his career Farr was frequently referred to by the press and the public as the Registrar General. In fact he never held that office. In 1842 T.H. Lister retired and was followed by Major Graham, who remained in the post until his retirement in 1879. Graham and Farr made a very effective team. Graham was a good administrator, well able to organise the three thousand or so registration officers and the central staff of nearly a hundred. Farr was free to devote himself to the development of vital statistics and to the writing of the endless reports in which they were embodied. The two men were on very good terms. In the valedictory conclusions of his last *Annual Report* Graham wrote of Farr: 'to his scientific researches I attribute any reputation that may have accrued to the General Register Office of England and Wales from the time I accepted office in the Department'.

In 1879 Farr was 72 and not in very good health but he hoped to hold the post of Registrar General, if only for a short time, before he retired. He applied for it but was refused. One Sir Brydges Henniker, a political protégé of Disraeli's, was appointed and Farr resigned. 'A very general feeling of surprise and even of annoyance was evoked in scientific circles', says Hare, 'when it became known that Dr. Farr was not to be promoted, some attributing the fact to there having "arisen a new king over Egypt which knew not Joseph". The award of a Companionship of the Bath was a poor compensation for his bitter disappointment. His career ended on 1 February 1889 and soon after he had a stroke from which he never recovered. Later in the same year the British Medical Association awarded him a gold medal, the highest honour they could confer, but he was too ill to receive it in person. He died three years later, on 14 April 1883.

After his retirement a testimonial fund had been opened in recognition of the value of his services. A particularly generous contributor was Florence Nightingale, to whom he had given much help in her work on the health of the army and the sanitary condition of hospitals. Having contributed ten guineas when the fund was opened, she made a further donation of £100 before it closed. A grant of £400 from the government brought the balance up to £1,734, which at Farr's request was used to supplement the modest provision he had been able to make for his three unmarried daughters.

Farr was twice married, first in 1833 to a Miss Langford, a farmer's daughter from his part of the world, who died of consumption four years later, and second, in 1842, to a Miss Whittall, who bore him eight children of whom five survived him.

A large selection of Farr's works were brought together in a memorial volume edited by Humphreys,[1] who also wrote the very informative biographical notice prefixed to it. Further details of Farr's life will be found in Hare,[2] Bettany[3] and Greenwood.[4]

2. *Vital Statistics*

I shall begin my account of Farr's work with the chapter on vital statistics which he contributed to McCulloch's *Statistical Account.*[5] This chapter, which he wrote before joining the Office of the Registrar General and which Greenwood ranks for importance almost as high as Graunt's *Observations*, is in effect a seventy-page survey of the information available on mortality and morbidity drawn from a variety of sources in England and abroad. He brings together for recent periods death rates in different age-groups in England and Wales, Belgium and Sweden; and by sex and age-group in the individual counties of England. He also gives information for groups of counties and for individual towns and stresses the high rates of mortality in towns compared with that in the country as a whole.

1. William Farr, *Vital Statistics* (ed. N. A. Humphreys). London, 1885.
2. F. A.C. Hare, *William Farr, F.S.S., M.D., F.R.S., C.B., &c. &c.* London 1884.
3. G. T. Bettany, 'William Farr'. *The Dictionary of National Biography*, vol. vi, pp. 1090-1.
4. Major Greenwood, *The Medical Dictator and Other Biographical Studies.* London, 1936.
5. William Farr, 'Vital statistics'. In J. R. McCulloch, *Statistical Account of the British Empire*, 2nd edn, London, 1839, vol. ii, pp. 521-90.

He goes on to consider the mortality experience of the Army in different parts of the world, both in peace and in war conditions and divided between officers and men. He shows from the statistics of the Peninsular War that the soldiers had more to fear from disease than from the enemy: for privates he obtained annual percentage death rates of 4.2 in battle and 11.9 from other causes; for captains the corresponding figures were 6.6 and 3.7. Thus though the risk from battle was greater for field officers than for their men, the risk of death from other causes was almost three times as high for the men as for their officers, pointing to some combination of bad sanitary conditions, bad food and bad water. It was her experience of these conditions in the Crimea that led Florence Nightingale to undertake her vigorous campaign on behalf of the British soldier.

Before leaving the subject of war, Farr provides an interesting table of annual death rates classified by age and sex for Sweden over the years 1801 to 1830, distinguishing the years of civil war, 1806 to 1810, from the earlier and later periods. Mortality rates in the two peace-time periods were similar and the civil war had raised them by about 25 per cent: the effect of the war was felt by the population generally and not simply by the able-bodied men engaged in fighting.

Deaths at sea are often associated with shipwreck, battle and other external causes. Farr shows the role played by insanitary conditions on board and how the death rate could be immensely reduced by taking appropriate measures. Captain Cook, who had been highly successful in this respect, read a paper to the Royal Society in 1776 describing in detail the measures he had taken to secure the health of his crew, but little use was made of his experience by the Admiralty until much later. Farr says that to maintain a force of 60,000 to 70,000 seamen, 170,910 were recruited in the years 1776-80; 1,243 were killed in action and 18,545 died from disease.

After dealing with mortality in prisons and workhouses, Farr turns to sickness. Information was available from the records of friendly societies, government dockyards, the East India Company and elsewhere. Some of these sources are very detailed and enable a classification by age and sex of the average duration of sickness per annum for all employees and for every person sick. Though not relating to the population as a whole and varying from source to source, these records provide a considerable amount of information on the incidence of sickness at the time.

The next section of the paper relates to the history of deaths from different diseases and accidents. Farr brings together statistics from several sources and authors for a classification of deaths in London for selected runs of years from the early seventeenth century to his day. For each period he arranges this information to show the contribution of each cause to 1000 deaths and the mortality rate for each of twenty classes of disease. A proper understanding of these tables requires medical knowledge and an ability to interpret the vague and often obsolete terminology used in the Bills of Mortality; even so, they are an interesting link between Farr's own time and the London about which Graunt was writing.

The earlier part of these historical tables contains no breakdown by age, but for more recent times Farr was able to give data on deaths classified by age and cause, the diseases being grouped by their nature and by their site. His information came from the observations of Dr. Heysham at Carlisle in the 1780s and from the experience of the Equitable Society in the first three decades of the nineteenth century.

In conclusion he offers suggestions on the means of promoting public health. Among these he mentions the provision of comparative information on the state of health in different circumstances, educating the public in health matters, and giving the medical profession an interest in preventing disease from developing as opposed to attempting to cure it once it has developed.

3. The Classification of Diseases

The vagaries of medical nomenclature deplored by Graunt nearly two centuries earlier had seen only partial improvement by the time Farr came to deal with mortality statistics. The systematic classification of diseases had been undertaken in the eighteenth century by Sauvages,[1] Linnaeus[2] and Cullen[3] but was still far from being complete and consistent. In particular, the classification of William Cullen, the one in use in the British public services, had never been revised and Farr did not consider it satisfactory for statistical purposes. As is clear from his 'Letters' in the *Annual Reports of the Registrar General*, nomenclature and classification received his constant attention. In the first of these Letters he wrote:

'The advantages of a uniform statistical nomenclature, however imperfect, are so obvious, that it is surprising no attention has been paid to its enforcement in Bills of Mortality. Each disease has, in many instances, been denoted by three or four terms, and each term has been applied to as many different diseases; vague, inconvenient names have been employed, or complications have been registered instead of primary diseases. The nomenclature is of as much importance in this department of inquiry as weights and measures in the physical sciences, and should be settled without delay.'[4]

The need for a uniform classification of the causes of death was so strongly felt at the first International Statistical Congress in 1853 that Farr and Dr. Marc d'Espine of Geneva were asked to prepare 'une nomenclature uniforme des causes de décès applicable à tous les pays'. At the next Congress two separate lists were received based on different principles, and a compromise list of 139 rubrics was adopted. In 1864 this list was revised at Paris 'sur le modèle de celle de W. Farr'. It has been revised many times since then and although there was never any universal acceptance of this classification, the general arrangement, including the principle proposed by Farr of classifying diseases by anatomical site, has survived as the basis of the International Classification of Diseases.[5]

1. Pierre Augustin Sauvages, *Nosologia Methodica Sistens Morborum Classes, Genera et Species*. Amsterdam, 1763.

2. Carl Linnaeus, *Genera Morborum*. Uppsala, 1759.

3. William Cullen, *Synopsis Nosologiae Methodicae*. Edinburgh, 1769.

4. William Farr, 'Statistical nosology'. *First Annual Report of the Registrar General*, H.M.S.O., London, 1839.

5. World Health Organisation, *Manual of the International Statistical Classification of Diseases, Injuries and Causes of Death*. 2 vols, Geneva, 1977.

4. Farr's Life Tables

Since Halley's day, interest in the construction of life tables had been gathering momentum. Three quite different factors contributed to it. One was the spread of life insurance, which had been greatly stimulated by Halley's actuarial calculations. Another was the concern of doctors with mortality at different ages and its variations from district to district. And the third was the debate which generated much heat in the second half of the eighteenth century as to whether the population of England was increasing or decreasing. In each case the estimates relied on the records of births and deaths, which as Halley had pointed out were not much use unless accompained by data on the size of the population. Here and there population counts were taken by the initiative of some enlightened individual, but they were narrowly localised and almost never repeated for a long enough period. Nevertheless life tables multiplied, some constructed by insurance companies, some by doctors, some by interested amateurs, and much thought was given to the theory of the subject even though its application was inevitably faulty.

The obvious answer would have been the establishment of periodic censuses but here again opinions were sharply divided. In 1753 a bill for 'Taking and Registering an annual Account of the Total Number of People' was introduced; it was passed by the Commons but defeated by the Lords. All sorts of arguments were advanced against its advocates: it would stir up religious superstitions about 'the numbering of the people' and provoke widespread riots; it might show that the population was decreasing and thus expose our weakness to our enemies; it was an intolerable encroachment on the liberties of the subject. One particularly virulent opponent declared that he would not only refuse to answer any official who came to collect information 'regarding the number and circumstances of my family' but if the person insisted he would get his servants to throw him into the horse pond. In 1758 another, less comprehensive bill was introduced; it too was defeated.

The advocates persevered, however, one of the most active

and cogent being Arthur Young.[1] Local enumerations became more frequent and did not cause riots. Furthermore other countries were taking censuses, with demonstrably good results. The climate of opinion gradually changed and finally, in 1800, an act 'for taking an account of the Population of Great Britain, and of the Increase and Diminution thereof' was passed and the first census taken in 1801. Anyone interested in the early history of life tables and the population controversy should read Greenwood[2] and Glass.[3]

Since 1801 population censuses have been conducted in Great Britain every ten years, but it took some time for them to reach a satisfactory form. The 1801 and 1811 censuses, for example, did not include a question on age. The importance of age was demonstrated in 1815 in a practical manner by Joshua Milne's life table for Carlisle[4] based on data collected by John Heysham over the period 1779-96.[5] Besides annual figures of births and deaths for the whole period, these data included the results of two enumerations carried out in 1780 and 1787 in which the population of Carlisle was divided into five-year age groups up to age 20 and ten-year groups thereafter. With this material Milne could construct a life table that was a better approximation to reality than any of its predecessors since Halley's.

Milne's table attracted much attention and its effect was apparent in the 1821 census, which recorded age by five-year groups. However, the declaration of age was not compulsory, with the result that the returns were incomplete. The 1831 census took a backward step by only registering 'males over twenty years of age'. It was not until 1841, after the establishment of the General Register Office under Lister, that the recording of age was introduced as a standard requirement.

1. ARTHUR YOUNG, *Proposals to the Legislature for numbering the People.*

2. MAJOR GREENWOOD, *Medical Statistics from Graunt to Farr.*

3. D. V. GLASS, *Numbering the People.* D. V. GLASS (ed.), *The Population Controversy*; *The Development of Population Statistics.*

4. JOSHUA MILNE, *Treatise on the Valuation of Annuities and Assurances on Lives and Survivorships.* London, 1815.

5. JOHN HEYSHAM, *Observations on the Bills of Mortality in Carlisle for the years 1779-87.* Facsimile in *The Development of Population Statistics.*

From the 1841 census and deaths of that year Farr constructed the first life table for England and Wales;[1] his second table was based on the same census and the deaths registered during the years 1838-44[2] and his third was based on the censuses of 1841 and 1851 and the deaths during the years 1838-54.[3] The expectations of life shown in these tables for the country as a whole are very similar despite the fact that the first is based on one census and a comparatively small number of deaths and the third is based on two censuses and deaths extending over a period of seventeen years.

In order to draw attention to the importance of public health Farr also constructed life tables for cities, counties and other areas. The expectation of life at different ages provides a convenient indicator of health conditions, and he was confident that a knowledge of it in different localities would suggest possibilities of improvement, particularly in large towns where it was most needed. In table 9.1 I show side by side a number of his calculations which, without any attempt at completeness, illustrate the wide regional variations in healthiness he brought to light by this method, which is still followed today.

The columns are arranged from left to right in increasing order of life expectancy. Thus in 1841 the expectancy at birth in Manchester was 24 years, 16 years less than the average for England and 20 years less than Surrey at the same time; in London it was 31 years in the poor quarter of Whitechapel, 4 years less than the average for the whole metropolis and 6.4 less than in the rich quarter of St. George's, Hanover Square. By 1851 it had risen in the 'healthy districts' to 48.6 years. I have added to the table some later estimates, not due to Farr, for comparison. Humphrey's figures based on the deaths of 1876-80 show that the improvement in the third quarter of the century added about two years to the expectation at birth. Recent experience, in the final column, shows the strides that have been made since Farr's

1. William Farr, 'Letter to the Registrar General' including 'English Life Table' (no. 1). *Fifth Annual Report of the Registrar General*, H.M.S.O., London, 1843.

2. William Farr, 'English Life Table' (no. 2). *Twelfth Annual Report of the Registrar General*, H.M.S.O., London, 1851.

3. William Farr, *English Life Table* (no. 3). H.M.S.O., London, 1864.

Table 9.1

LIFE EXPECTANCIES IN DIFFERENT PARTS OF ENGLAND AND WALES, 1838-1983
FARR'S FIGURES COMPARED WITH LATER ESTIMATES
(males)

Age	Manchester	Liverpool	London: White-chapel	London: Metropolis	London: St. George, Hanover Sq.	England and Wales	Surrey	Healthy districts	England and Wales		
	1841*	1841*	1841*	1841*	1841*	1841*	1841*	1851§	1838-54†	1876-80★	1981-83#
0	24.2	25	31.0	35	37.4	40.2	44	48.6	39.9	41.9	71.3
1	33.1	33	..	41	..	46.7	50	..	46.7	..	..
5	..	42	..	46	..	..	51	54.4	49.7	51.5	67.3
10	40.6	41	41.6	44	47.0	47.1	49	51.3	47.1	48.2	62.4
20	33.3	33	33.5	36	39.5	39.9	42	43.4	39.5	39.9	52.7
30	26.6	27	26.7	29	32.1	33.1	35	36.5	32.8	..	43.1
40	20.6	21	21.1	22	25.2	26.6	28	29.3	26.1	..	33.5
50	15.2	16	15.9	17	18.7	20.0	21	22.0	19.5	..	24.4
60	10.3	..	10.9	..	12.2	13.6	..	15.1	13.5	..	16.5
70	6.8	..	..	..	..	8.5	..	9.4	8.5	..	10.2
80	4.6	..	..	..	..	4.9	..	5.4	4.9	..	5.8
90	3.2	..	..	..	..	2.7	..	3.0	2.8	..	..
100	1.2	..	..	..	..	1.5	..	1.7	1.7	..	..

* Source: William Farr, *Vital Statistics* (ed. Humphreys), pp. 454, 467-8, 478.
§ Source: William Farr, 'On the construction of life tables', *Philosophical Transactions of the Royal Society*, vol. 149, 1859, p. 878.
† Source: William Farr, *English Life Table* no. 3, p. cli.
★ Source: N.A. Humphreys, 'The recent decline in the English death rate', *Journal of the Statistical Society of London*, vol. XLVI, pt. II, 1883, p. 212.
Source: UK CSO, *Annual Abstract of Statistics, 1986*, p. 41.

days. One would like to know how much of the change is attributable to such possible causes as improvements in medical knowledge, greater availability of medical services, the extension of public health measures, better housing, the reduction of poverty or simply more income. And might not a higher expectation of life be a more worthy object of public policy than a higher national income?

Incidentally, Farr did not like the term, 'expectation of life', which he thought better expressed Halley's idea of the age at which 'it is an even lay' that a person of a given age will be dead, the French *vie probable*. Instead of expectation of life he would have preferred 'afterlifetime' to express the mean time which a person of a given age may expect to live after that age, the French *vie moyenne*. The two concepts are not the same since survivors do not form an arithmetical progression, but Farr's term has not been generally adopted.

5. Group-specific Mortality

Farr made innumerable uses of mortality statistics. I can do no more than give a few examples.

He was greatly interested in the mortality of different groups in the community and though his first concern was to set out the facts he always commented on his findings and tried to offer theories and conclusions about them. Table 9.2, based on the 1851 census, shows the variations in mortality associated with different occupations.[1]

The chief difficulties in drawing up this table were, first, obtaining occupational groups sufficiently large and regular to provide reliable series and, second, matching the census classifications with those used in the death registrations. Farr solved these problems by aggregation.

The rows of the table are ordered according to the mortality rates in the age group 45-54. There is a wide variation in rates over different occupations, just as we saw in table 9.1 that there

1. WILLIAM FARR, 'Mortality of males engaged in different occupations'. *Fourteenth Annual Report of the Registrar General*, H.M.S.O., London, 1853.

was a wide variation over districts. Farmers on the whole have relatively low death rates and butchers and innkeepers relatively high ones. Why, asks Farr, is the mortality of butchers so high: is it that they eat too much meat and too little fruit and vegetables; or drink too much; or are unduly exposed to heat and cold; or, most likely, that they are surrounded by decaying matter in their slaughter-house and its vicinity? He does not attempt to answer these question, but by bringing them out into the open he raised, in this case as in so many others, issues for reformers to grapple with.

Table 9.2

MORTALITY PER 1000 BY AGE AND OCCUPATION, ENGLAND, 1851

(males)

Occupation / Age	25-34	35-44	45-54	55-64	65-74	75-84
Farmer	10.2	8.6	11.1	24.9	55.3	148.0
Shoemaker	9.1	10.6	15.0	28.7	65.1	164.5
Weaver	8.0	10.6	15.4	33.0	74.6	173.1
Grocer	7.6	10.5	15.8	22.7	49.7	124.6
Blacksmith	8.1	12.4	16.5	37.2	74.4	167.1
Carpenter	9.5	10.3	16.7	29.7	65.9	142.9
Tailor	11.6	14.2	16.7	28.2	76.5	155.3
Labourer	9.8	12.5	17.3	29.2	67.9	173.9
Miner	8.5	11.4	20.2	34.5	80.5	178.7
Baker	7.6	14.8	21.2	33.0	66.8	150.7
Butcher	11.3	16.5	23.1	41.5	66.5	154.5
Innkeeper	13.8	20.5	28.3	39.0	81.5	180.8
National average for males	9.5	12.4	17.9	30.3	64.0	140.6

Source: William Farr, 'Mortality of males . . .', *14th Annual Report*, pp. xv-xxiii.

He points out that until extreme old age the death rates of labourers are not very different from the national average; and comments that the Poor Law apparently affords inadequate relief to the worn-out workman.

At an early stage in his career Farr read to the Statistical Society of London a paper on the mortality of lunatics.[1] This

1. WILLIAM FARR, 'Report upon the mortality of lunatics'. *Journal of the Statistical Society of London*, vol. IV, pt.1, 1841, pp. 17-33.

contains what must be one of the first examples of a double-decrement table. From the records of Hanwell Asylum, which opened in 1831, he was able to construct a table showing the numbers who remained in the hospital for different periods of time and the cases terminated in each of these periods either by recovery or by death. Since many patients were brought to the hospital when they were nearly dying, Farr tabulated his results at the end of the first six months and thereafter at annual intervals. In this way he was able to form table 9.3.

Table 9.3
DOUBLE-DECREMENT TABLE FOR LUNATICS ADMITTED TO HANWELL ASYLUM, 1832-38

Serial no. of period	Duration of diseases from day of admission (years)	Number of patients who:			Termination in each period:		
		remain in asylum (a)	will recover (b)	will not recover (c)	total number (d)	recoveries (e)	deaths (f)
1	0.0	1 000	380	620	217	108	109
2	0.5	783	272	511	213	112	101
3	1.5	570	160	410	61	21	40
4	2.5	509	139	370	48	12	36
5	3.5	461	127	334	43	11	32
6	4.5	418	116	302	41	11	30
7	5.5	377	105	272	35	9	26
8	6.5	342	96	246	32	8	24
9	7.5	310	88	222	..	..	..

Source: William Farr, 'Report upon the mortality of lunatics', p. 27.

The number admitted in the seven years was 1,389 but the table is reduced to 1,000 and traces the survivors in the hospital, the discharges and the deaths as far as the data allow. From a knowledge of cases terminating in each period since admission, given in column (d), column (a) of survivors in the hospital can be formed. From columns (e) and (f), in periods 3 to 8, recoveries and deaths can be seen to remain nearly in a constant proportion which if applied to the 310 entering period 9 in the hospital gives 88 recoveries and 222 deaths. If these figures are added to the figures for earlier periods in columns (e) and (f) we obtain the figures in the first row in columns (b) and (c) whence the remaining entries in these columns can be obtained by subtraction.

From this 'nosometrical table', as Farr called it, probabilities of recovering or dying within different periods can be calculated. A complete table of this kind would be useful in insuring the lives of lunatics. It would also enable us to measure the effect of treatment on the mortality and duration of diseases and to compare alternative treatments.

6. *The Fight against Cholera*

Farr's period at the General Register Office covered the dates of the last three outbreaks of cholera in 1848-9, 1853-4 and 1866. There had been an outbreak in 1832, and many years later Farr wrote: 'The cholera left medical men as it had found them – confirmed in the most opposite opinions, or in total ignorance as to its nature, its cure and the cause of its origin if endemic – or the mode of its transmission if infectious'.[1] The established view was that it was caused by airborne poisons but a newer view put forward by Dr. John Snow was that it was contagious and that it was contracted by drinking polluted water.[2]

Farr reported and monitored the epidemic which began in 1848 and caused over 53,000 deaths in 1849. In his report, which appeared in 1852,[3] he considered many factors with which cholera might be associated, including water. But he had not quite given up the airborne theory. Among the innumerable tables was one showing the relation of deaths from cholera in the various quarters of London to the elevation above the river and to a number other factors such as population density and wealth as measured by the rateable value of the houses. He showed that there was a close inverse relationship between elevation and the death rate from cholera, and on many occasions published the equation

1. William Farr, 'Report on the cholera epidemic of 1866 in England'. *Supplement to the Twenty-ninth Annual Report of the Registrar General*, H.M.S.O., London, 1868.

2. John Snow, *On the Mode of Communication of Cholera*. London, 1849; 2nd edn, 1855.

3. William Farr, *Report of the Mortality of Cholera in England 1848-49*. H.M.S.O., London, 1852.

$$c=\frac{2266}{e+13}$$

where *c* denotes the mortality per 10,000 inhabitants and *e* denotes the elevation of the district in feet above the Thames.

The incident that seems to have won him over to Snow's theory took place in 1853 in Newcastle-on-Tyne, which had a pure water supply from some distance outside the town and had been hardly affected by the 1848-49 epidemic. The outbreak in 1853 coincided with a period when the water company, in time of drought, restarted an abandoned pumping station and added Tyne water to its normal supply. Farr ticked them off thoroughly in this third *Quarterly Return* for 1853, concluding with the statement: 'no water was drawn from the Tyne after September 15, the cholera raged with less intensity and the epidemic speedily subsided'. Shortly after, in the *Weekly Return* for 19 November 1853, he commented on London's water supply and noted that the Lambeth Waterworks Company was alone among the companies supplying London to have moved their source of supply from Lambeth to Thames Ditton, above the tidal reaches of the Thames. In the following year, when cholera reached London, Farr provided Snow with death notifications and Snow discovered as many addresses as he could of cholera deaths and as far as possible the source of supply of the water where those deaths had occured. From what he could discover there were 57 deaths per 1000 houses supplied by the Southwark and Vauxhall Company compared with 11 per 1000 houses supplied by the Lambeth Company, a ratio of 5 to 1. Striking as this is, and it was published by Farr in the *Weekly Return* for 14 October 1854, Snow later suggested that these preliminary results were conservative and that the true contrast was 14 to 1.[1]

In 1866 cholera reappeared but in the meantime the London water supply had greatly improved, being all obtained from beyond the tidal waters of the city. At first, in July, only a few cases were reported but by the end of the month deaths were rising fast and in the last week 908 deaths were registered. Farr

1. John Snow, *op. cit.*, 2nd edn.

visited Poplar, one of the worst affected districts, and in his next *Weekly Report* virtually accused the East London Water Company of supplying contaminated water. The matter was taken up by *The Times* and the situation improved. An enquiry was held and Farr was supported. In his account of the 1866 epidemic[1] he also wrote on the three earlier ones; the part he played in them did much for his reputation and for the registration system of the General Register Office.

All this was done before it was known what the waterborne agent was or how it worked. This knowledge came a generation later but in the meantime Snow and Farr had found a means of stopping the spread of cholera. The outbreak of 1866 was the last in England. An excellent account of the whole saga has been given by Lewes.[2] A general appraisal of Farr's contributions to social medicine will be found in Eyler's recent book on the subject.[3]

7. The Introduction of Computing Machines

Not surprisingly, Farr was deeply interested in methods of computing and was a friend and admirer of Charles Babbage, one of the founders of the Statistical Society. Babbage spent a great deal of his time and a considerable amount of his fortune in attempts to construct and perfect calculating machines. He first had the idea of calculating numerical tables by machinery in 1812, when he was still an undergraduate at Cambridge. In 1816 he was elected a Fellow of the Royal Society. In the early 1820's he constructed a small machine based on the method of differences and in 1823, with the help of a government grant, he set out build a much larger version. A part of the machine was constructed by 1833 with facilities for printing out the results and a paper on it was contributed to the *Edinburgh Review* in 1834 by Dr. Lardner.[4]

Although Lardner went into great detail he did not describe

1. See note 1 on p. 268 above.

2. FRED LEWES, 'William Farr and cholera'; *Population Trends*, Spring 1983, pp. 8-12.

3. JOHN M. EYLER, *Victorian Social Medicine: the Ideas and Methods of William Farr.* Johns Hopkins Press, Baltimore and London, 1979.

4. D. LARDNER, Untitled article on Babbage's calculating engine. *The Edinburgh Review*, vol. LIX, no. CXX, 1834, pp. 263-327.

the mechanism, but his article led George Scheutz, a printer in Stockholm, to build with his son Edward a difference engine with a mechanism of his own design. Farr arranged for an improved version of this engine to be made for the General Register Office at the cost of £1,200 and used it to compute and print the many tables of *English Life Table* no. 3.[1] This large volume is the first computer print-out I know of.

When his work on the difference engine came to an end in the 1830's Babbage went on to design and construct an altogether more elaborate analytical engine, but the scheme was too ambitious and he died in 1871 without completing it. In all he had received from the government about £17,000 before it was decided in 1842 not to renew the grant. Thereafter he financed his research himself, sinking much of his fortune in it. Farr devoted a large part of his inaugural address as president of the Statistical Society in 1871 to his friend's life and work.[2]

8. Human Capital

Farr wrote on many other subjects but I shall mention only one more. In a paper on the equitable taxation of property,[3] he discusses taxes upon 'property in life incomes from professions, commerce, trade and manufactures', in other words human capital; a link with Petty and King. He measures this by taking the discounted expected future net earnings, that is earnings less the costs incurred in providing for the necessities of life and acquiring the skills needed to earn an income. This value can be calculated for any age, the chances of survival being taken from a life table.

He illustrates his idea with figures for agricultural labourers, whose earnings start at £12 a year at age 15, rise to £31 at age 30 and fall off at age 65. The expenses of maintenance rise from £7 a year in infancy to £15 a year at age 20, staying at that level for

1. WILLIAM FARR, *English Life Table* (no. 3), pp. cxxxix-cxliv.

2. WILLIAM FARR, 'Inaugural address'. *Journal of the Statistical Society of London*, vol. XXXIV, pt IV, 1871, pp. 409-23.

3. WILLIAM FARR, 'The income and property tax'. *Journal of the Statistical Society of London*, vol. XVI, pt I, 1853, pp. 1-44.

the rest of life. At birth such a person is not worth very much, in fact only a little more than £5, since living expenses must be met in the short run and future wages, which come much later, are reduced by discounting (at an assumed rate of 5 per cent). An individual of this type reaches his maximum value of £246 at about age 26 and has a negative value after age 70, when future living costs exceed future earnings.

In *The Money Value of a Man* Dublin and Lotka commend Farr's method, saying that it 'remains to this day [1946 in the case of my edition] the fundamental standard on which any sound estimate of the value of a man to his dependents must be based, and is the method adopted by the present writers in their computations relating to modern conditions of life'.[1]

9. Summing up

Farr reaped the harvest that had grown from the seeds sown by Graunt and Halley. He was very much the right man at the right time in the right place. He had a thorough understanding of vital statistics and knew how to squeeze the last drop of meaning out of them. He came on the scene just as civil registration and census taking, the basic sources of data, were being brought together under a single coordinating authority, the new General Register Office. And he held a key position in this office.

Furthermore his long career coincided with a period in English history when social reform was attracting increasing attention and public welfare and public service were becoming current political aims. Not that it was all plain sailing for the reformers; they met with strong resistance from the inevitable enemies of change and did not always succeed in surmounting it. But Farr, one of the most active among the innovators, had a good measure of success and contributed effectively to the successes of others.

He had an unshakable belief in the power of statistics. In his own words,

1. Louis I. Dublin and Alfred J. Lotka, *The Money Value of a Man*. Revised edn, New York, 1946, p. 12.

'Statistics underlies politics; it is, in fact, in its essence the science of politics without party colouring; it embraces all the affairs in which government, municipalities, local boards, and vestries are concerned. From this bare announcement its trascendent importance is evident. In the absence of government there is anarchy; and although a Government with little or no knowledge is better than anarchy, an ignorant Government has done – and does incalculable mischief... Government is the greatest of all arts; but is it not notorious that men without experience, without special knowledge . . . are candidates for places in the Legislature at every election where representative Government exists. I am, however, persuaded that their success will every year diminish, other things being equal; and that men well versed in politics and statistics will beat them in the end.'

Had he been an economist instead of a doctor and had there been an institution like our present Central Statistical Office, Farr would undoubtedly have picked up where Gregory King left off and would have advanced by a century the acceptance of economic statistics as a tool for public policy. As things were, he concentrated on demography and public health and made his greatest mark in those fields. I cannot conclude my summing up better than by quoting the letter Leone Levi wrote to *The Times* when Farr died:[1]

'A great luminary, who lightened the arduous and recondite paths of statistical science, has just departed from among us. Dr. Farr was a recorder of the common facts of births, deaths, and marriages, but by a wide induction he made those facts impart lessons which almost created the science of sanitation, while they enlarged and established the principles of medical science.

We shall mourn his loss at the Statistical Society . . . But a larger society will lose him – humanity itself – whose interests he so well served.'

1. *The Times*, 23 April 1883.

FOURTH LECTURE
QUANTITATIVE SOCIAL STUDIES

Frederick Morton Eden (1766-1809)
Florence Nightingale (1820-1910)
Charles Booth (1840-1916)

THE

STATE OF THE POOR:

OR,

AN HISTORY

OF THE

LABOURING CLASSES IN ENGLAND,

FROM THE CONQUEST TO THE PRESENT PERIOD;

In which are particularly confidered,

THEIR DOMESTIC ECONOMY,

WITH RESPECT TO

DIET, DRESS, FUEL, AND HABITATION;

And the various Plans which, from time to time, have been propofed, and adopted, for the RELIEF of the POOR:

TOGETHER WITH

PAROCHIAL REPORTS

Relative to the Adminiftration of Work-houfes, and Houfes of Induftry; the State of Friendly Societies; and other Public Inftitutions; in feveral Agricultural, Commercial, and Manufacturing, Diftricts.

WITH A LARGE APPENDIX;

CONTAINING

A COMPARATIVE AND CHRONOLOGICAL TABLE OF THE PRICES OF LABOUR, OF PROVISIONS, AND OF OTHER COMMODITIES; AN ACCOUNT OF THE POOR IN SCOTLAND; AND MANY ORIGINAL DOCUMENTS ON SUBJECTS OF NATIONAL IMPORTANCE.

BY SIR FREDERIC MORTON EDEN, BART.

IN THREE VOLUMES.

VOL. I.

LONDON:

PRINTED BY J. DAVIS,

For B. & J. WHITE, Fleet-ftreet; G. G. & J. ROBINSON, Paternofter-row; T. PAYNE, Mew's-gate; R. FAULDER, New Bond-ftreet; T. EGERTON, Whitehall; J. DEBRETT, Piccadilly; and D. BREMNER, Strand.

1797.

Frederick Morton Eden, *The State of the Poor.*
Title page of first edition, 1797.

CHAPTER 10

Frederick Morton Eden and the Poor of England

1. Brief Life

To a greater or lesser extent all the authors I have discussed so far were aware of the miserable condition of the poorer classes and had a desire to see them improve. Two of them, Petty and Colquhoun, actually did something about it both in word and deed. But this was only one of their interests. I shall now turn to three people for whom helping the underdog was of central importance: Frederick Eden, Florence Nightingale and Charles Booth. They were people of wide views and they saw that soup kitchens and poor relief, though better than nothing, were only palliatives, and that it was time to find out what the real state of affairs was and tell the world. Their tool of analysis, and the instrument they used to broadcast their findings, was statistics.

Frederick Morton Eden was born in 1766, the eldest son of Robert Eden, governor of Maryland, and his wife Caroline Calvert, sister to the last Lord Baltimore. Although he belonged to the kind of family that produced politicians, ambassadors and colonial governors he did not go in for a public career and not much is known of his private life. His father was created a baronet in 1776, and he inherited the title. He went up to Christ Church, Oxford, and took his first degree in 1787. In 1792 he married a Miss Anne Smith, by whom he had a number of children. He was one of the founders and later became chairman of the Globe Insurance Company. He died suddenly at the office of his company on 14 November 1809, at the early age of forty-three.

Eden had an enquiring mind and wrote on a variety of subjects. I shall mention his plan for the improvement of the port and city of London,[1] his estimates of population,[2] to which I shall return later, his pamphlet on Friendly Societies[3] and his monograph on insurance,[4] of which Colquhoun made considerable use in drawing up his estimates. But these were comparatively minor works. In 1797, at the age of thirty-one, he published his *magnum opus*, three immense volumes entitled *The State of the Poor*, on which his reputation rests. Even Marx, hard to please as he is, has a word of praise for it. In part VII of *Das Kapital* he remarks: 'Sir F.M. Eden is the only disciple of Adam Smith during the eighteenth century that produced any work of importance'.

A few more details about Eden's life and works will be found in Edgeworth,[5] Macdonell[6] and *The Gentleman's Magazine*.[7]

2. *The State of the Poor*

Eden was led to writing his great work, he tells us in the preface, by the difficulties experienced by the labouring classes as a consequence of the high prices of 1794-5, and got so interested in the subject that he thought it would be useful if he could lay before the public 'accurate details respecting the present state of the Labouring part of the community, as well as the actual Poor'. This is not as simple as it sounds; facts do not speak for themselves and to give an unbiased account of them is not easy. He visited several parishes himself to collect information but in the midst of his professional activities he could not visit enough and so called on the help of a number of clergymen. But even this was not sufficient and so he sent 'a remarkably faithful and intelligent person' to carry on the survey according to a questionnaire with which he supplied him.

1. *Porto-Bello*. London, 1798.

2. *An Estimate of the Number of Inhabitants in Great Britain and Ireland*. London, 1800.

3. *Observations on Friendly Societies for the Maintenance of the Industrious Classes*. London, 1801.

4. *On the Policy and Expediency of Granting Insurance Charters*. London, 1806.

5. F. Y. Edgeworth, 'Sir Frederick Morton Eden'. *Dictionary of Political Economy* (ed. R. H. T. Palgrave). London, 1894, vol. I, pp. 679-80.

6. G. P. Macdonnell, 'Sir Frederick Morton Eden'. *The Dictionary of National Biography*, vol. VI, pp. 356-7.

7. Anon., 'Obituary of Sir Frederick Morton Eden'. *The Gentleman's Magazine*, Dec. 1809, p. 1178.

This questionnaire was similar to that designed by Sir John Sinclair for his *Statistical Account of Scotland*[1] but adapted to cover only those aspects which Eden thought had a bearing, direct or indirect, on poverty. Thus there were questions on general matters such as population, housing, occupations, production, prices, wages, rent, taxes, religious affiliations, number of alehouses and so on, and specific questions such as how the poor were maintained, particulars of the institutions with which they were associated and of the Friendly Societies they belonged to, their usual diet, and the annual earnings and expenses of labourers, families of different compositions together with the quantities and prices of articles consumed.

Eden explains that the methods of maintaining the poor were then in a state of transition, one scheme after another having been tried without lasting success, and that they had become very expensive. He points out the need to collect a great variety of information in order to write on so complicated a subject; to discuss, for example, the size of farms or the enclosure of commons and waste lands not simply from the point of view of agricultural technology but in their impact on the public in general and the poor in particular. He describes some of the difficulties of obtaining reliable data: many people were reluctant to discuss their annual earnings with precision; some were so careless that they could not give satisfactory information; others thought that no importance could be attached to the questions and so made no attempt at accuracy; but most were afraid that the purpose of the questions was to bring about a reduction in their wages or something equally disagreeable, and so were 'unchangeably mysterious and insincere'. Anyone who has tried to collect family budget data in recent times will sympathise with him. He experienced particular resistance to his question on beer as an item of expense. He thought he would be able to get round this by approaching the excise-man and the publican; but the former said that it was not his job to answer questions on consumption and that he was not competent to do so, while the latter had an evident interest in withholding such information.

1. Creech, Edinburgh, 1791-99.

Friendly Societies, or Benefit Clubs, had made great progress in the few years before he was writing. He could not collect complete data on this subject but he was much encouraged by what he did collect. Here was an institution of great importance to the people, which had not been imposed by legislation but had been set up by the workers themselves.

Eden concludes his preface by saying that his aim is to provide information, not to draw conclusions from it. The edifice of political knowledge cannot be reared without its 'hewers of stone and drawers of water' among whom he is content to work, leaving to those who prefer it the task of 'architectural decoration'. For the same reason, while he has tried to write in a plain and simple way he has 'never wasted that time in polishing a sentence' which he 'could better employ in ascertaining a fact'.

Book I, which occupies two thirds of the first volume, contains a history of the poor from the Conquest to Eden's time. It opens with some general remarks on the pre-eminent importance of manual labour and the thin line, so easily overstepped, that separates the manual worker from destitution. At all stages of civilisation, Eden says, mankind in one respect remains the same: everyone must obtain the necessaries of life, food, raiment and habitation. Whatever may have been the case in the Garden of Eden or in a Golden Age, now

'we can neither be cloathed, lodged, nor fed, but in consequence of some previous labour. A portion, at least, of the society must be indefatigably employed . . . to supply the necessary wants of the whole. Of supernumerary-hands that are not thus destined to actual labour, a part is occupied in the various arts, to which mankind are indebted for many conveniencies and comforts . . . There are others in this great national family, who, though they "neither toil nor spin" yet command the produce of industry, but who owe their exemption from labour solely to civilisation and order: such are the owners of derivative property . . . they owe their superior advantages by no means to any superior ability of their own, but almost entirely, in a proper sense, to the industry of others. It is not the possession of land, or of money, but the command of labour . . . that distinguishes the opulent from the labouring part of the community: under the latter description I would comprehend those, whose daily subsistence absolutely depends on the daily unremitting exertion of manual labour; without meaning to stigmatize those, who are otherwise employed, as either idle, or useless members of the state. In the strict sense of the term, lawyers, physicians, and other professional men, may, perhaps, be as fairly called labourers, as miners or manufacturers . . . The rich, however, have the consolation to know that, even under any worldly misfortune, from which they or their families may suffer, it is seldom that the calamity can be aggravated by the immediate deprivation of the necessaries of life . . . With them, the use of stock previously accumulated, and the anticipation of future resources, often supply the deficiencies of the moment . . . The day labourer is sensible that, in the season "when every work of man is laid at rest" when his daily earnings are reduced to a miserable pittance, he cannot provide for his increased wants, and soften the rigours of a severe winter, by anticipating the ample wages of the following harvest: besides the interruption which he experiences from the inclemency of the seasons, another source of want is opened . . .; ready and willing to want labour, he may not be able to find employers. But the most frequent periods of difficulty and distress are those, in which the labourer is incapacitated by some of those casualties, to which human nature is perpetually liable. I need not particularize . . . Helpless infancy, and decrepit old age, are equally incapable of labour; nor are the sturdy peasant, and sedentary artificer . . . secure from casualty or sickness, which may reduce them to temporary want, or even overwhelm them with irremediable calamity.'

After this eloquent preamble Eden embarks on his historical account. This is divided into three long chapters: the first takes the story from the Conquest to the Reformation; the second, from the Reformation to the Revolution of 1688; and the third, from the Revolution to the end of the eighteenth century. The narrative is well-documented and supplemented by numerous appendices relating to acts of parliament and other records, to prices, wages and the sources for these, and to many other matters.

Eden thinks that the historian interested in the progress of society should not confine himself to the splendid scenes of national glory but should concern himself with the humbler occupations of mankind and cites Hume as perhaps the only one of our modern historians who had a proper appreciation of this point. Accordingly, he starts by describing the gradual transformation of serfs, or villeins, into free labourers, their conditions of work at different times in the Middle Ages, their standard of living, the sumptuary laws which regulated their dress, the taxes they had to pay on the few chattels they owned, the periodic attempts to fix their wages, and so on. His description is accompanied throughout by figures taken from all kind of sources, some dating as far back as the thirteenth century.

He lays great stress on the importance of figures. As he points out, time-series of wages and prices would enable us to judge what quantities of 'necessaries and conveniencies' a given amount of labour would have commanded at different times. This is the same problem as the one which Fleetwood had considered. Eden makes considerable use of Fleetwood's work but emphasises the difficulties of making price comparisons and the importance of giving the sources of price quotations. In his main table of prices Eden has separate columns for provisions, other commodities and labour, and covers the four centuries from the early thirteenth to the early seventeenth. The items are often not well-defined: thus wine is sometimes just wine, at others red wine, white wine, French wine, Anjou wine, Rochelle wine. The entries for commodities other than food and drink are rather sparse. In 1207 we find a quotation for a human being, a female villein, 4s; she does not compare favourably with a horse, which cost 5s in 1211, or with palfreys, which ranged from £1.11s.8d to £2.13s.4d in 1212. Entries such as these are historically very interesting and it must have required a great deal of research to bring them together, but they were too sporadic to make it possible to construct an index-number with them.

Obviously the lower rungs of the labouring classes led a very precarious existence even when they were employed. If they could not find employment the only resources left to them were begging and stealing. This was a serious social evil for which various remedies were tried. The charity dispensed by the monastic orders before the Reformation was far from sufficient and a number of laws were enacted during the Middle Ages to levy contributions for the relief of the poor and provide work for the unemployed, without much effect. After the dissolution of the monasteries the responsibility fell entirely on the secular authorities and on private individuals of good will. In 1603 an 'Act for the relief of the Poor' was passed in which all the existing laws were tidied up and brought together, but this did not substantially improve matters. Poverty and crime were as rampant as ever.

Much was written on the subject during the seventeenth and eighteenth centuries. Eden appends to his third volume a catalogue of publications relating to the poor which numbers 282 entries and runs from 1524 to 1797. Most of the writers he quotes think that the problem would be comparatively simple and could be handled without much expense if poverty were confined to the groups in society who could not support themselves by their own labour: the very young, the sick and disabled, and the very old. The first category relates in particular to orphans and abandoned children, though it is realised that families may have more small children than they can possibly support. But these are not the only categories: in addition there are the idle and dissolute who will not work but prefer to beg and steal: and the honest labourers who would like to work but cannot find employment.

It is debated whether the support of the poor should be left to private charity, the authorities intervening only to restrain the idle and dishonest. The objections to this solution are that it would result in the whole burden of supporting the poor falling on the generous and kind-hearted while the mean and hard-hearted would avoid their contribution; and that it is difficult to distinguish the deserving from the plausible. These considerations suggest that there is need for some official intervention to ensure that all who can contribute do so, and to sort out the deserving from the undeserving. It is generally assumed that the first class, the incapable, should be helped, that the second class, those able and willing to work, should be enabled to earn their living, and that the third class, the work-shy, should be punished or at least restrained; but individuals and families appearing as in need of assistance do not arrange themselves into these neat categories, and even if they can be classified many problems remain. For example, if the able-bodied are to be set to work what work is to be chosen? An obvious answer might be the kind of work carried on in the district with which at least some of the unemployed would be familiar. But in the absence of a rise in demand, giving this work to them would only serve to throw out of work those already engaged in it. Moreover, if the work were given to inexperienced hands the results would largely be so much spoilt raw material which could not compete with the regular product. As we have seen, Petty in discussing this problem emphasised that public works should be directed to activities that would not otherwise be carried on. But to think these out and organise them would have been beyond the capacity of most overseers of workhouses.

Despite the many difficulties there was no lack in the seventeenth and eighteenth centuries of schemes for setting the unemployed poor to work or of experiments in carrying out such schemes. Some were undertaken from humanitarian motives, such as the workshop built in Little Britain by Thomas Firmin in 1676 for the employment of the poor in linen manufacturing; he employed 1700 spinners and others besides and paid them at the current rate; but when he found that they had to work sixteen hours in order to earn 6d, he added to their earnings in various ways, such as giving free coal to good workers.

Other schemes were inspired by the high and rising cost of poor relief. Davenant's table of taxes (p. 59 above), which Eden reproduces, gives an estimate of just over £665 thousand for the poor rates in 1677, when the national income must have been around £40 million. By 1776 the rates had risen to over £1.72 million out of which about £1.53 million was actually spent on the poor, and by 1783-5 to nearly £2.17 million out of which about £2 million was spent on the poor. At that time the national income cannot have been less than £200 million: according to Colquhoun, in 1803 it was about £222 million for a much enlarged population. Thus there had been a threefold rise in the poor rates over the century. Actually, as Eden points out, this had not kept pace with the country's ability to pay them, which had increased by a factor of five. But people did not think in these terms, they only noticed the rise in the rates. And there was undoubtedly a great deal of waste in the way these were administered and of abuse by their recipients.

Since Elizabeth's Act of 1603 the Poor Laws had been repeatedly modified, always with the best intentions, but in every case an initial improvement had been followed by a deterioration in the standards of care and an increase in costs. Eden devotes his fourth chapter to a discussion of the measures in force in his own time, of the principles that should be kept in mind when framing new ones, and of possible sources of finance. Pitt had just brought out yet another bill for the reform of the Poor Laws and Eden criticizes it rather severely as being over-complicated, giving too much power to the administrators and encroaching too much on the freedom and dignity of the administered.

'What then', he asks, 'is to be done in a case which avowedly calls for the attention of the Legislature: are we to acquiesce in the unreformed continuance of a system, which is very generally admitted to be the parent of idleness and improvidence; and to be the fruitful source of endlessly accumulating expence? By no means. But before the mighty machine of reform is set in motion, I conceive, some such preliminary enquiries as these should be instituted. What are the actual evils which our Poor Laws have unquestionably created? What is their extent? What has been the effect of various local modifications of the general law in different parts of the kingdom? Are the Poor either taken better care of, or maintained at less expence, in incorporated districts, than they are in small parishes? Are their children more healthy, more orderly, or more industrious, from being educated in schools of industry? What are the comparative advantages, or disadvantages, of farming the Poor, of relieving them in a work-house, or maintaining them at their own houses; or furnishing them with the necessaries of life, or granting them pecuniary allowance, to be expended at their own discretion?

The Public have a right to ask, and therefore do ask, that such information may be laid before the House of Commons. Mr Pitt's Bill, indeed . . . proposes the appointment of proper officers to report the state of each parish. These reports . . . may so influence the course of events, as gradually to produce the much-talked-of level between wants and wages, without [further] legislative interference.'

The fifth chapter deals with the standard of living of the poor. Eden considers that the insufficiency and unwholesomeness of their diet is partly due to their ignorance of the simplest culinary principles, and proceeds to give a number of cooking recipes using ingredients within the reach of the slimmest purse. He describes their drinking habits, both alcoholic and non-alcoholic, and deplores their addiction to tea, which he is sure is bad for them unless mixed with milk and sugar. He describes how they manage to clothe themselves at the smallest possible expense and suggests ingenious methods of saving on the cost of coal for cooking and heating. He gives details of wages and prices in different counties and reproduces a table, drawn up by the magistrates of Berkshire for their own guidance, showing 'what should be the weekly income of the industrious poor' calculated on a sliding scale hitched to the price of bread. As a social document this chapter is one of the most interesting in the book.

The last chapter contains a history of the Friendly Societies set up by working men as an insurance against hard times. They were financed by voluntary subscriptions and were much encouraged by the parish authorities since their existence took some of the pressure off the poor rates. Eden describes how they had evolved from the medieval guilds and how they functioned in his time. He is much in favour of them despite some abuses to which they were subject. One in particular arouses his indignation and he goes in detail into its causes. I shall give his argument in his own words.

'Few writers on this branch of political economy [the management of the poor] have adverted to the circumstances and situation of a class of our people, who form, perhaps, the most essential link in social order and domestic happiness: I mean the *wives* of labourers . . . If the right, which every labourer possesses, of disposing of the produce of his labour, is the great incentive to industry; is it either unfair or unreasonable to presume, that the incapacity which married women labour under, of acquiring property, is one of the principal causes why they contribute so little to the fund which is to maintain a family?

In the greatest part of England, the acquisition of the necessaries of life, required by a labourer's family, rests entirely on the husband. If he falls sick, and is not a member of a Friendly Society, his wife and children must inevitably be supported by the parish . . . There are, however, various occupations, which the wife of a peasant or artificer would, it is probable, be often inclined to pursue, were she only allowed to have a voice as to the disposal of her earnings. As the Law now stands, the moment she acquires them, they become the absolute property of her husband . . . The instances are not few, where a stupid, drunken and idle man, has an intelligent and industrious wife, with perhaps both the opportunity and the ability to earn enough to feed her children; but who yet is deterred from working, from a thorough conviction that her mate would, too probably, strip her of every farthing which she had not the ingenuity to conceal.

I have been led to these reflections, by investigating the situation of some Female Benefit Clubs, which seem to be exposed to peculiar disadvantages, in consequence of the legal disability which married women labour under, of retaining the earnings of their labour in their own hands. Most of these Clubs are chiefly composed of married women: as the principal inducement to enter into them, is, to insure a decent subsistence during the lying-in month; a period, in which, of all others, a labourer's wife is in most need of extrinsic assistance. The laudable objects, however, of these excellent institutions, may be entirely frustrated by the exercise of that legal authority with which a husband is invested. As he is entitled to receive his wife's earnings, he can not only prevent her from paying her regular subscription to the Club; but if she falls sick, he is, I conceive, no less authorized by law to demand the allowance which is granted by the society, and to appropriate it to his own use.'

This plea for the liberation of women more or less concludes the historical part of *The State of the Poor*. The two books which form this volume add up to well over six hundred quarto pages. I hope the samples I have chosen give an idea of its breadth and depth.

3. Eden's Parish Reports

In the second volume and the early part of the third, Eden sets out, parish by parish, the local information he had collected. His faithful and intelligent assistant had done his best but naturally enough had not managed to obtain completely uniform data from all the places he had visited. He travelled widely, however, and we get a good picture of the expenditure and arrangements for poor relief in different parts of the country, a distinction being made between the inmates of workhouses, or poor-houses as they were sometimes called, and the people relieved in their own homes. Some parishes were able to give circumstantial accounts for several years, others could only provide sketchy information. There are usually data about baptisms, marriages and deaths, and descriptions of principal economic activities and their prosperity.

The degree of detail is at times considerable: in Epsom, Surrey, each of the fifty inmates of the workhouse is characterised by age and sex and briefly described to show why he or she has become a burden on the parish. Eden gives the list in full, commenting that it is only thus that 'an accurate knowledge can be obtained, of the kind of persons who most commonly become burthensome, as well as of the most common causes that lead to poverty.' Here are some of the entries:

'J. H. aged 43. The little work he ever did, or could do, was as a labourer, but, having always been somewhat of an idiot, he is now become quite a driveller.
D. F. aged 54; was a postillion, and employed about stables: addicted to drinking, and an idle, worthless man.
J. B. aged 28, has been a soldier: he is shockingly afflicted with bad [venereal] disorders.
J. R. aged 17. His parents having neglected . . . bringing him up to a regular course of industry, he has contracted many loose and disorderly habits . . . and he can neither be persuaded nor forced, either to go to sea, or to enlist as a soldier.
S. C. [a woman] aged 56; a lunatic.
E. K. [a woman] aged 19; of idle and profligate habits and often wretchedly diseased.
C. W. aged 18; a native of Switzerland; and now with child, it is supposed by a gentleman's butler.
W. C. aged 10; his father was enlisted in the army.
R. C. aged 10; a bastard.
T. S. aged 9; his father dead, and mother married again.
P. H. aged 10, M. H. aged 4. The father of these girls was a hairdresser; but is now at sea, on board a man of war. The mother is an idle, worthless woman.
E. G. aged 12, S. G. aged 10; daughters of a smuggler.'

The inmates, we are told, are chiefly employed in spinning. Their food is 'not only plentiful, but in general wholesome. In cases of sickness, they are regularly and carefully attended by a medical man'. There is very little information, however, on the income from the poor rate and none on its allocation except for the mention that £440 had been spent on the poor in 1776.

Epsom had three flourishing Friendly Societies, of which Eden thoroughly approved. He gives ample particulars of their membership and of the rules concerning the management of their finances. They were evidently very closely-knit and disciplined institutions, at least on paper: in one of them every member was bound to attend the funeral of a fellow-member or pay a fine of 2s. 'And the members that reside in the parish of Epsom,' the rule adds, 'shall meet at the most convenient public-house, at all funerals, and spend 2d each'.

Equally detailed is the enumeration Eden gives of the houses and inhabitants of the parish. There were 327 houses, of which 7 appear to have been unoccupied and the remaining 320 contained the number of inhabitants shown in table 10.1, equivalent to an average of 5.2 persons per house.

Table 10.1

INHABITANTS OF EPSOM, *c.* 1795

Status or occupation of head of household	Family			Servants		Total
	Males	Females	Children	Males	Females	
Gentlemen and gentlewomen	28	44	61	96	115	344
Clergy, lawyers, doctors etc.	18	22	28	12	21	101
Merchants and shopkeepers	23	23	23	7	8	84
Bakers, butchers, fishmongers (1)	11	14	41	10	6	82
Shoemakers, taylors, dressmakers	20	19	30	15	6	90
Building trades	26	20	37	3	5	91
Smiths	9	6	26	8	1	50
Other trades	18	19	33	7	3	80
Publicans and lodging houses (2)	17	19	22	2	7	67
Stable keepers and coachmen	10	9	27	3	2	51
Gardeners	20	23	45	-	-	88
Farmers	7	2	21	17	9	56
Labourers	95	93	165	1	2	356
Widows and retired tradesmen	14	26	22	3	3	68
Unspecified	20	20	17	2	4	63
Total	336	359	598	186	192	1671

Source: Frederick Eden, *The State of the Poor*, vol. III, pp.705-9.

My table is a highly compressed version of Eden's original, which specifies the status, profession or trade of almost every head of household and the number of children, servants and guests in every household, and is an example of the interesting sidelights that his survey provides.

For the parish of Birmingham the information given is different. No estimate of the population is available but Eden thought that before the war it might have numbered between 60 and 70,000 inhabitants; this was probably quite a good estimate of a rapidly growing population, given as 71,000 in 1801 and 83,000 in 1811.[1] I have tried to piece Eden's data together to give some idea of the cost of poor relief in relation to the recipients.

The governor of the workhouse made a weekly return of the number of poor in the house and the number relieved at home. If we include the patients in the infirmary with the other inmates of the house we can display his return as in table 10.2.

Table 10.2

POOR RELIEVED IN BIRMINGHAM, MID-1796

Stocks and flows in workhouse, week 30 May – 6 June							
	Entrants		Present on 30 May				Total 6 June
	Births	Admission	Men	Women	Boys	Girls	
Leavers							
Deaths			2				
Departures			2	3	2	1	
Men		8	80				88
Women		6		210			216
Boys		1			57		58
Girls	1	2				47	50
Totals 30 May			84	213	59	48	
Inmates							412
Children at nurse							290
Out-poor relieved							2 592
Out-poor given clothing							22
Total relieved							3 316

Source: Frederick Eden, *The State of the Poor*, vol. III, pp. 740.

This total may be an underestimate, as another return of the out-poor, exclusive of children at nurse and militiamen's wives, mentions 2,191 recipients in certain categories and 4,660 'per-

1. Brian Mitchell and Phillys Deane, *Abstract of Historical Statistics of Great Britain*. Cambridge University Press, 1961.

sons in receipt of relief for themselves and their families'. The size of the families is not specified and other categories are not accounted for.

The financial side of the picture can be seen from the accounts available to the overseers of the poor, as shown in table 10.3.

Table 10.3
ACCOUNT OF MONEY RECEIVED BY THE BIRMINGHAM OVERSEERS FOR THE YEAR ENDED EASTER 1796
(£)

Incomings		Outgoings	
Brought forward	1 685	Out-relief	14 892
Produce of levies	21 259	Cost of workhouse	
Reimbursements	1 048	Food, clothing, coal, medical care	4 472
Militia money	1 649	Other	3 529
Borrowing for infirmary	170	Buildings and repairs	917
		Constables	240
		Carried forward	1 761
Total	25 811	Total	25 811

Source: Frederick Eden, *The State of the Poor*, vol. III, pp. 737†.

For the period covered in table 10.3 we can construct from Eden's data only three weekly tables of the form of table 10.2. From this admittedly small sample we obtain a weekly average of 2,581 recipients of out-relief and 805 inmates (including children at nurse in the country); and if we divide these numbers into the totals for out-relief and cost of workhouse in table 10.3, we obtain £5.16s per head as the average annual payment of out-relief and £9.18s as the average cost of maintenance in the house. This gives us some idea of the order of magnitude of poor relief in Birmingham at the time, but I cannot claim any great accuracy for it as I may have misinterpreted the information available.

As I have said, Birmingham was growing fast at the end of the eighteenth century. Eden gives a table of disbursements for the poor in Birmingham from 1676 to 1792 which can be carried to 1796 from the statements I used to construct my table 10.3. The growth in the cost of poor relief can be seen from table 10.4.

Table 10.4
DISBURSEMENTS FOR THE POOR IN BIRMINGHAM, 1676-1796

Year	£
1676	329
1700	661
1722	940
1750	1 168
1775	6 510
1785	11 570
1796	24 051

Source: Frederick Eden, *The State of the Poor*, vol. III, pp. 741-3.

The book contains 181 reports on parishes and townships so that is possible to learn about the state of the poor in different parts of the country, but they are necessarily dependent on the information made available and it is not easy to aggregate or compare them. All the same we learn a lot from them. No detail is too minute to interest Eden. Whenever he can he gives the workhouse bill of fare for breakfast, dinner and supper on each day of the week. Typical diets are: for breakfast, milk porridge, gruel or broth, sometimes made from meat, sometimes from vegetables; for dinner (the midday meal), meat at least three or four times a week, alternating with bread and cheese; for supper, sometimes meat but more usually bread and cheese or a thick soup. In some cases beer is provided. Some institutions have elaborate sets of rules which Eden reproduces. In one, for instance, it is laid down that children must be washed and cleaned every day and taught to read, and that smoking is allowed only in workshops. In another, smoking in bed is strictly forbidden on pain of spending six hours in 'the dungeon'!

Many of the reports also contain accounts of the income and expenditure of poor families and more are given in appendix XII. Eden was not the first to collect household accounts from the poor. Arthur Young was interested in the matter, and in 1795, two years before Eden's work appeared, a number of budgets of agricultural labourers were published by a clergyman, David

Table 10.5

BUDGETS OF AGRICULTURAL WORKERS IN GREAT BRITAIN, 1787-1793

(after Davies)

Family income group £	Number of families	Heads per family	Income per family £	Expenditure per family £	Per cent of total expenditure: Food	Rent	Fuel	Clothes	Medical care	Other	Total
10-20	34	5.2	18	23	70.1	5.3	2.6	9.1	5.2	7.8	100
20-25	58	6.0	22	27	69.5	5.1	3.0	11.3	4.5	6.7	100
25-30	25	5.8	27	29	75.3	4.9	4.2	7.7	2.3	5.7	100
30-45	10	7.5	36	38	81.8	4.3	3.1	4.9	1.6	4.2	100
All groups	127	5.9	23	27	72.2	5.0	3.2	9.3	3.9	6.5	100

Source: George Stigler, 'The early history of empirical studies of consumer behavior', p. 97.

Table 10.6

BUDGETS OF AGRICULTURAL AND OTHER WORKERS IN GREAT BRITAIN, *c.* 1794

(after Eden)

Family income group £	Number of families	Income per family £	Expenditure per family £	Per cent of total expenditure: Food	Rent	Fuel	Clothes	Other	Total
Agricultural workers									
15-25	16	23	30	69.9	6.3	4.9	11.2	8.1	100
25-30	16	28	36	75.1	4.4	4.8	7.1	8.7	100
30-35	15	32	40	75.3	3.1	4.1	9.7	7.8	100
35-40	5	38	42	76.9	5.6	4.8	5.6	7.1	100
40+	8	45	63	76.6	4.3	3.6	9.5	6.0	100
All groups	60	. .	. .	74.5	4.6	4.4	9.0	7.6	100
Other workers									
15-25	4	22	26	68.9	8.8	7.4	6.0	8.8	100
25-35	6	28	30	73.3	5.4	7.9	4.9	8.5	100
35-40	6	36	37	78.6	5.2	6.5	1.6	8.2	100
40+	10	51	55	73.3	6.0	3.8	6.2	10.7	100
All groups	26	. .	. .	73.9	6.0	5.4	5.0	9.6	100

Source: George Stigler, 'The early history of empirical studies of consumer behavior', p. 97.

Davies, in his book *The Case of Labourers in Husbandry*.[1] Neither Davies nor Eden attempted to classify or summarise their budgets but this work has been undertaken by George Stigler.[2] With permission I reproduce his two tables as table 10.5 and 10.6.

The budgets relate to the lowest rungs of the working population and fit in fairly well with Colquhoun's figures for the poorest labourers in 1803 shown in table 6.1 on p. 187-8 above. The samples are small and there is not much sign of Engel's law in the data. In all groups average income is less than average expenditure. Davies came to the conclusion that no labourer in the South of England could cover his expenses who had more than two children not employed. The immense proportion of expenditure devoted to food exceeds what one would find nowadays in the poorest countries; and very little is spent on things other than the basic necessaries, food, rent, fuel and clothing. In years of bad harvest, or when any of the breadwinners in a family fell ill or out of work, clothing might be reduced to little more than rags, and fuel became an unattainable luxury. The accepted view was that this wretched state of affairs was due to improvidence, idleness and drunkenness. As John Burnett points out in his excellent *History of the Cost of Living*,[3] Eden and Davies were the first to put matters in their proper perspective.

4. Colquhoun's Works on Poverty and Crime

Nine years after the appearance of Eden's work, Colquhoun published his *Treatise on Indigence*. In it he gives an estimate of the number of people 'presumed to live partly or wholly on the labour of others', that is to say those who for one reason or another cannot or will not support themselves by their own labour. These numbers are brought together in table 10.7.

The 957 thousand relieved out of workhouses cost £3.061 million or about £3.2 per head; and the 83 thousand maintained in

1. Bath and London, 1795.
2. GEORGE J. STIGLER, 'The early history of empirical studies of consumer behavior'. *The Journal of Political Economy*, vol. LXII, no. 2, 1954, pp. 95-113.
3. Penguin, 1969.

workhouses cost £1.016 million or about £12.2 per head. Relating the total in the table, 1.321 million, to the population of 1801, 9.065 million, it appears that the indigent, whether relieved or not, were between 14 and 15 per cent of the population. Those relieved were over four-fifths of the total.

Table 10.7
THE INDIGENT POOR, ENGLAND AND WALES, 1803
('000)

Indigent persons relieved by parishes	
Out of work-house	
Children under 5	120
Children, 5-14	195
Adults	336
Occasionally	306
Total	957
In work-house	83
Numbers relieved	1041
Not so relieved	
Mendicants	50
Vagrants	20
Idle and immoral persons	10
Lewd and immoral women	100
Rogues and vagabonds	10
Lottery vagrants	10
Criminal offenders (highway robbers, burglars etc.)	80
Numbers not relieved	280
Total presumed to live wholly or partly on the labour of others	1321

Source: Patrick Colquhoun, *A Treatise on Indigence*, pp. 38-43.

How did this state of affairs come about? In Colquhoun's view the intentions of the Elizabethan legislators some two centuries earlier were sound: to relieve the innocent who could not support themselves and to restrain the culpable who would not except by criminal means. But for two main reasons these good intentions had not borne the fruit that might have been expected of them.

In the first place, the scheme though conceived on the national level was applied on the parochial level. This impeded the mobility of labour, led to endless transfers of families who had moved and with a change in economic conditions had become unable to support themselves in the new parish in which they were living. This parish might then seek to send them back to their original parish to avoid the cost of maintaining them and this might give rise to costly litigation between parishes. In any case, wherever they ended up the indigent had a right to relief and this would operate as a disincentive to self-help. Colquhoun thought that the amount levied for the support of the poor should be regarded as a national fund, or at least a county fund, for relieving the poor where they were. Apart from these objections, it often happened, with areas as small as parishes, that very poor parishes found themselves forced to support a large indigent population.

In the second place, there are in every community, and especially in large towns, a certain number of idle, dissolute and criminal people who are not directly restrained by courts and goals, which come into effect only after a crime has been committed. What is wanted is an adequate system of police and police intelligence which would be informed about likely criminal activities and as a result of its knowledge and watchfulness be able to prevent many crimes from being committed.

But in addition to adequate policing many things are needed to enable children to grow into good citizens and to encourage frugality in adults. The measures Colquhoun proposes are much the same as those advocated by Eden: popular education; improved arrangements for apprentices; the organisation of friendly societies on a national scale with improved regulation of their finances; and the provision of simple culinary information which he intended to publish, along with police information and articles of an improving tone, in his proposed *Police Gazette*; this was to be circulated to the fifty thousand alehouses in the country as well as to the constabulary and others concerned with criminal justice and the poor.

Colquhoun had already dealt at length with crime in *A Treatise on the Police of the Metropolis*, published in 1796. In it he gives a detailed account of the various types of people deemed to support themselves by criminal, illegal or immoral means. His list contains twenty-four categories and numbers 115 thousand persons. The book is largely concerned with how these different groups operate and what can be done about them. He is of course concerned with the reduction of crime but also with the plight of the discharged criminal, in some cases homeless, friendless, unable to gain employment; what is to become of him?

He gives a detailed estimate of depredations committed in a year in and about the metropolis. The list runs to twenty headings of which table 10.8 is a summary.

Table 10.8

DEPREDATIONS COMMITTED IN A YEAR IN THE METROPOLIS AND ITS VICINITY, *c*. 1795 (£'000)

Small thefts	710
Thefts upon rivers and quays	500
Thefts in the Thames dock-yards	300
Burglaries, highway-robberies etc.	220
Coining base money	200
Forging bills, swindling etc.	170
Total	2 100

Source: Patrick Colquhoun, *A Treatise on the Police of the Metropolis*, 3rd edn, pp. 42-44.

This enormous total he ascribes to the prosperity of London and to the immense amount of moveable property which is constantly circulating in the city and moving in and out of it in boats and wagons, which he thinks may amount to £170 million in a year. He gives a detailed description of the many types engaged in organising and carrying out these thefts and frauds, explaining the roles played by 'lumpers, scuffle-hunters, mudlarks, duffers and such like' and by the receivers and dishonest pawnbrokers who bought without asking questions and generally aided and sheltered the thieves. He knew all about the fashionable ladies who allowed their houses to be used for illegal gaming for which they received £50 a night and a share of the profits. He has two admirable stories about Monsieur de Sartine, the Minister of Police in Paris, which read like something out of Sherlock Holmes. He describes the pitifully small number of constables, customs officers and nightwatchmen available to deal with crime in London and proposes a number of remedies ranging from improvements in the law to methods of counteracting 'the mischievous devices of various kinds of fraudulent person'.

The connection between poverty and crime is obvious and had been stressed by many writers before Colquhoun, but he gave it numerical concreteness. His statistics may not be very accurate, as he himself acknowledges: 'all that is attainable is approximating facts' he says. However, his orders of magnitude cannot be very far off the mark and they drive home his arguments more effectively than words.

5. *Eden's Population Estimates*

I shall now leave poverty and crime and conclude with a brief account of Eden's estimates of the population of Great Britain and Ireland. The point of the exercise was to settle the vexed question as to whether the population had grown since the end of the seventeenth century, using the same kind of data as King and Davenant had used, namely baptisms, burials and tax returns. Eden's results were published in 1800, while the bill for the first British census was being debated in Parliament, and in his preface he looks forward to a time when the estimation of 'one of the most important (perhaps the most important) of our national resources' would no longer depend on 'ingenious guesses and plausible speculations'.

He makes separate calculations for England and Wales, Scotland, Ireland, and the maritime and military population exclusive of Indian and foreign corps.

For England and Wales he starts with a contemporary estimate of the number of assessed houses and works out several ratios which enable one to pass from assessed houses to population in various ways by appropriate multiplication. For example:

assessed houses×baptisms per assessed house=baptisms

and

baptisms×population per baptism=population

or, in figures,

$$690{,}000 \times 0.467 = 322{,}000$$

and

$$322{,}000 \times 27.75 = 8{,}935{,}500.$$

He tries different calculations using other ratios and finally reaches a population estimate of 10.71 million.

Table 10.9

POPULATION OF GREAT BRITAIN AND IRELAND, 1800-1

('000)

	Eden 1800	Official mid-1801
England and Wales	10 710	9 061
Scotland	1 500	1 625
Ireland	3 800	5 216
Total	16 010	15 902
Maritime and military	500	..
Total	16 510	..

Sources: Frederick Eden, *An Estimate of the Number of Inhabitants in Great Britain and Ireland*, p. 46. B. R. Mitchell and P. Deane, *Abstract of British Historical Statistics*, p. 8.

For Scotland he takes Sinclair's estimate of 1.526 million in 1798,[1] rounding it down to 1.5 million.

For Ireland there was a return of houses for 1791. Eden has some doubts about it but thinks he must accept it. Combined with Beaufort's estimate of 5½ persons per house[2] it gives 3.856 million, which Eden rounds down to 3.8 million.

1. John Sinclair, *The Statistical Account of Scotland*.
2. Daniel Augustus Beaufort, *Memoir of a Map of Ireland*. London, 1792.

For the maritime and military population he brings together a variety of estimates, some very hypothetical, and puts down a guess of 0.5 million.

Eden thought his figures for England and Wales approximate, his figure for Scotland too low and his figure for Ireland if anything too high. He did not get it quite right but his errors more or less compensate one another and the total for the civilian population is not misleading, as can be seen from table 10.9 in which his estimates are compared with the official mid-year estimates for 1801 given by Mitchell and Deane.

After giving his estimates Eden discusses the growth of population over the preceding century, deploring the fact that the proposal for a census in 1753 was rejected while 'all the countries now at war with us have preceded us in enumerations of the people'. He concludes with a quotation from Davenant and a comment on it:

'At the close of the last century, Davenant made the following remark on our population; taking it at 5,500,000, according to Gregory King's estimate, (which is confessedly too low), and estimating the quantity of land, in England and Wales, at 39,000,000 of acres, (which is probably near the truth), he says, "we seem now to have about 7¼ acres *per* head; but there are many reasons to think, that England is capable of nourishing double its present number of people, which, supposing them now to be 5,500,000, would be 11,000,000, and even then there will be as many acres *per* head, as they have in Holland. And, when we have this complement of men, either in the natural course of time, or sooner, by the help of good conduct, we shall be in a state of power to deal with any strength in Europe". That we have attained "this complement of men" cannot admit of much doubt: that we are "in a state of power to deal with any strength in Europe", has been proved by our exertions in the present awful contest: and I trust we shall long continue, what we now are,

"A land, that distant tyrants hate in vain".'

That a country was strong in proportion to the size of its population was then an accepted view. We may think that Eden, with his first-hand knowledge of the evils of unemployment, might have had reservations on the subject, but we should be mistaken if we did so. The Malthusian controversy had not got going and overpopulation was the last thing people worried about. Those were days of almost incessant war, in which tens of thousands of men were killed in a single battle, and of rapid industrialisation, when the new factories were absorbing many more. And all over the world there were vast territories still open to colonisation.

No, it was not overpopulation, it was indifference, ignorance and the ineptitude of governments that caused the waste of human resources and the poverty that troubled Eden and Colquhoun. The conscience of the public must be awakened. That is how they saw it and that is what their work is about.

Florence Nightingale

CHAPTER 11

Florence Nightingale and Hospital Reform

1. Brief Life

Everyone has heard of Florence Nightingale, the Lady with the Lamp, who organised the hospital at Scutari during the Crimean War and transformed the nursing service in England. Fewer people are aware of the battle she waged on the military and civil establishment after her return from the Crimea to improve the living conditions of the British soldier. Only a handful have ever seen the mass of statistical material she used as ammunition. She won her battle, although her victory was not so complete as she had wished.

Florence Nightingale was born in Florence on 12 May 1820. She was the second daughter of William and Fanny Nightingale, a rich couple unequivocally belonging to the class which Colquhoun terms 'gentlemen and ladies living on incomes'. He was a charming, intelligent, cultured, lazy dilettante, she was a fashionable society woman, fundamentally frivolous though not stupid. They both loved travelling. They had married in 1818 and gone abroad. Their first daughter had been born in Naples in 1819 and was duly christened Parthenope, the classical name for her birthplace. They returned to England with their two little daughters in 1821.

They now found that their family house in Derbyshire, Lea Hurst, was inconveniently placed for entertaining and much too small, so they kept it for summer use and bought as a principal residence a house called Embley Park near Romsey in Hampshire, which was larger and within easy reach of London. They spent the Season in London itself but did not own a house there. An indication of Florence's childhood standards can be gathered from a remark she made twenty years later at a dinner party: arguing that Lea Hurst was certainly a small house she said 'Why, it has only fifteen bedrooms'.

The two girls were educated by their father, as no governess could be found who united the intellectual equipment expected by him with the elegance and breeding demanded by their mother. This education seems to have been quite high-powered but largely classical and literary rather than mathematical and scientific. The girls were temperamentally very different, Florence sharing their father's tastes while Parthe had many characteristics of their mother. Of the two, Florence was the more beautiful, the more intelligent and the more studious. But she was an uncomfortable child, thinking herself an oddity and unlike other people; this often made her unhappy and she tended to retreat into a dream world of her own.

She was in the habit of keeping private notes of her thoughts. In one of these, dated 7 February 1837, she recorded, 'God spoke to me and called me to His service'. This experience, which occurred on three other occasions in later life, seems to have been like Joan of Arc's: she heard a voice outside herself speaking to her. God did not tell her what she was to do but she felt encouraged and confident.

When Florence was sixteen their mother began to think about the girls going out in society. This required changes at Embley: six more bedrooms, new kitchens, redecorations inside and out. William Nightingale decided to draw up the plans himself, giving the Georgian house a fashionable Gothic look. While the work was being carried out they would all travel to France and Italy and he designed an enormous carriage for the purpose. It was fitted up inside so that one could eat, rest, read and write in comfort. It had seats on the roof and was drawn by six horses mounted by postillions.

On 8 September 1837 the Nightingales left Southampton, taking with them a courier, a maid and the girls' old nurse. They travelled by leisurely stages, reaching the Riviera in December. Their stay in Italy, first in Nice then in Genoa then in Pisa and finally in Florence, was a round of gaiety, parties, balls, the opera, all of which Florence enjoyed immensely. She had the capacity to extract pleasure from everything she did. She loved the opera and, born statistician that she was, drew up a table in which she recorded and compared in detail the score, the libretto and the performance of every opera she saw; she loved dancing; she loved pictures; she loved pretty clothes, she loved serious conversation. There was much talk of Italian liberty, and she espoused the cause of the Italian patriots with fervid enthusiasm.

After nine glorious months in Italy the Nightingales proceeded to Geneva, where Florence made great friends with the historian Sismondi, whose English wife was a childhood friend of Mrs. Nightingale's. Florence constituted herself his disciple. They went for long walks together; he talked about Italian history, about politics, about economics and she listened with inexhaustible interest. Sismondi introduced his new friends to the Italian political exiles who were then in Geneva. One of them was Federico Confalonieri, who had spent fifteen years in Austrian prisons, which meant fifteen years in irons; 'he still walks as if he had chains on his legs', wrote Florence. It is easy to imagine the effect these things had on a generous young nature.

After about two months in Geneva the Nightingales went to Paris, where they spent their second winter. There again they met a large number of distinguished people to whom they were introduced by Miss Mary Clarke, an unconventional, intellectual Scotswoman of good family, a great friend of Madame Récamier, of Chateaubriand, of Fauriel and a force in the political and literary world of Paris. 'Clarkey', as they called her, took to the Nightingales, spent a great deal of time with the girls and became a family friend. Mrs. Nightingale could reflect with unalloyed pleasure on the social success of her daughters. Florence in particular had not only been much sought after as a dancing partner but had been taken seriously in intellectual circles, and her mother felt confident that a brilliant future lay ahead of her.

Back in England in April 1839, after an absence of eighteen months, the Nightingales found that the alterations to Embley would not be completed for some time and decided to spend the Season in London. The girls were presented at the Queen's birthday Drawing Room on 24 May. Again they were caught up in a whirl of gaiety.

But in Florence's case things were not what they seemed. She was bored by her idle life and asked if she could have lessons in mathematics. All sorts of objections were raised, culminating in the unanswerable argument, what use would mathematics be to her when she was married? So she worked at it in secret in her room before the others were awake and for the rest of the time played her expected role as daughter of the house, arranging the flowers, entertaining visitors, paying calls with her mother and sister, going to dinner parties and balls. And all the while, deeper down, there was something even more tormenting than boredom. Her family knew nothing of the voice that had spoken two years earlier. Florence remembered and wondered why she had heard no more. The reason, she concluded, was that she was not worthy; and so began a series of resolutions, to give up the desire to shine in society, to abandon the prospect of marriage and worldly friendship and to find out what it was that she was supposed to do. The search took another ten years, during much of which time she was intensely unhappy, irritable and on increasingly bad terms with her family, particularly her mother and sister. By 1842 she had come to realise that her life lay with the poor and suffering; by 1844 she had progressed to the point of seeing her vocation in hospitals among the sick; by 1845, having obtained some experience of nursing in the family and in the village, she realised that nursing was not just a matter of patience and sympathy but called for knowledge and skill. She must acquire them; but how?

Dr. Fowler, the head physician of the nearby Salisbury Infirmary, was an old friend and Florence thought he might support her in the idea of working in the infirmary for a few months. In December 1845 the Fowlers came to stay at Embley and Florence proposed her plan. The family were terrified and furious, the Fowlers retreated in embarrassment and Florence was left helpless and depressed. Even her father took it badly; at London dinner parties 'he would talk of nothing but spoilt and ungrateful daughters and forecast the very worse future for a race at the mercy of the modern girl'.

It must be remembered that in England in those days nursing was one of the lowest of occupations, associated with unspeakable squalor, drunkenness and loose morals. The conditions in hospitals, which were meant only for the poor, were unimaginable to us. The wards were overcrowded and filthy, the stench nauseating, the windows kept closed sometimes for months on end to keep out the cold, the patients never washed. 'It was common practice', wrote Florence some years later, 'to put a new patient into the same sheets used by the last occupant of the bed, and mattresses were generally of flock sodden and seldom if ever cleaned'. 'The nurses slept in wooden cages on the landing places outside the wards . . . where there was not light or air'. Most of them had no other home than the ward and many of them were professional prostitutes. Drunkenness was the norm. Those who did not work in hospitals were no better; Dickens' Mrs Gamp in *Martin Chuzzlewit* is not a caricature. Florence was aware of all this but she persisted in her resolution. No wonder the Nightingales were appalled.

Besides the open conflict with her family, an inner conflict, much more difficult to cope with, arose around this time: she fell in love. She had already had several offers of marriage but this time she found it very hard to refuse. The man who wanted to marry her was Richard Monckton Milnes, one of the most attractive bachelors in London society, a gifted litterateur, a rising politician, a wit, a brilliant host, famous for his breakfasts, to which he invited everyone of note. Carlyle, asked what he thought would be the first thing to happen if Christ came back to earth, said, 'Monckton Milnes would ask him to breakfast'. To these gifts he added great kindness. 'He treated all his fellow mortals as if they were his brothers and sisters', said Florence. He had a feeling for children and worked for many years, against strong opposition, to improve the treatment of young offenders. It was largely due to him that reformatories were instituted for them so that they should not be put in jails with adult criminals. He once took Florence to visit one of these reformatories and she was struck by the trust the children showed in him. 'He had the same manner for a dirty brat as for a duchess', she wrote afterwards. She dreamt of a delightful partnership with him. But then what was to become of her vocation?

A few extracts from her notebooks will give an idea of her state of mind. In 1845 she wrote: 'This morning I felt as if my soul would pass away in tears, in utter loneliness in a bitter passion of tears and agony of solitude'. 'I cannot live – forgive me, oh Lord, and let me die, this day let me die'. 'The day of personal hopes and fears is over for me, now I dread and desire no more'. 'The sorrows of Hell compass me about, pray God He will not leave my soul in Hell'. 'The plough goes over the soul'. And in 1846: 'Oh God, no more love. No more marriage, O God'.

Periodically, when the strain became more than she could bear, she fell ill. Her mother fussed over her health, her sister Parthe made hysterical scenes, her father, without making scenes, made it clear that he needed her presence. Between them, in one way or another, she was held a prisoner.

Fortunately there were a few understanding people outside the family. In October 1846, the Chevalier Christian Bunsen, Prussian Ambassador in London, sent her the *Year Book of the Institution of Deaconesses at Kaiserswerth*, a nursing institution started in 1833 from very modest beginnings by a young pastor, Theodore Fliedner, and his wife. Bunsen had mentioned Kaiserswerth to Florence in 1842 but at that time it had not rung a bell with her. Now she realised that this institution could provide the training she wanted and that its religious atmosphere raised it above suspicion. The book became her treasure.

Another helpful person was Lord Ashley, better known by his subsequent title of Lord Shaftesbury, the philanthropist and reformer. He suggested that she should study hospital returns and official publications such as the Blue Books dealing with public health and the reports of various commissions of inquiry into sanitary matters. She also obtained information on the Berlin hospitals through the Bunsens and on French hospitals through her friends in Paris. All this material was compared, indexed and tabulated by her in secret, getting up before dawn and working in her room by candlelight, wrapped in a shawl, as she had done with her mathematics.

In the autumn of 1847 she had a serious breakdown from which she was rescued by some other friends, Charles and Selina

Bracebridge. Florence had met them the year before and had formed a close friendship with Selina. Although they belonged to the generation of Florence's parents, the Bracebridges did not share their mentality. They saw that Florence was made of a different metal from her family and that the home atmosphere was stifling her. They too were capable of enthusiasm; they were passionate pro-Hellenes and Charles had taken part in a revolt against the Turks; and now all their sympathies were with the Italian patriots. They were unconventional to the point of eccentricity but it was an aristocratic, high-flown type of eccentricity which was quite acceptable to Mrs. Nightingale, and she was delighted when they suggested that Florence might accompany them to Rome, where they intended to spend the winter.

The trip was a great success. As soon as she reached Italy Florence recovered her zest for life. No one nagged, no one tried to make her change her mind. She wandered about Rome with Selina, she discovered Michelangelo, she danced, she visited hospices kept by nuns. And through the Bracebridges she met some exceptionally nice people, visitors like themselves, whom she had not met before. Among them were the future Cardinal Manning and a couple who were to play a central role in her life, Sidney and Elizabeth Herbert. Sidney Herbert had been Secretary at War in Peel's cabinet and was to return to office a few years later and become Florence's most powerful ally in her long fight for hospital and army reform. Neither of them could foresee this but they became fast friends. The Herberts had endowed a convalescent home at Charmouth and were very interested in the facts she had been collecting about public health and hospitals. When she returned to England in the spring of 1849 she stayed with them at Wilton and went to the opening of their institution.

During the autumn and winter she tried to fill the emptiness of life at home by nursing the sick cottagers on her father's estate. Her parents objected, the idea of her going into the 'black filth' of those cottages quite revolted them and they were afraid of her catching some infection. She persevered, sneaking out of the house by the back door in hopes that no one would notice, but it was all very difficult.

When the family moved to London for the Season in the spring of 1849 she wanted to take up slum visiting. Her mother effectively put a stop to it by insisting that, if so, she must be accompanied by a footman. Actually when I read this I was not surprised. As late as the 1920's a friend of mine, a girl then aged about twenty, wished to attend some university lectures in London; permission was granted provided she was accompanied by her maid. So Mrs. Nightingale's view of the proprieties was still going strong within living memory.

Frustrated on every point, Florence became again very unhappy. Her diary makes pathetic reading. Curiously, she does not seem to have borne her family a grudge for her frustration. She was convinced that it was all her fault, that God was punishing her for not being worthy. She must work on herself, she must make herself worthy. To add to her misery she was faced that summer with a very painful decision: Richard Monckton Milnes, after waiting patiently for years, insisted that she give him a definite answer. After much agonised self-questioning she finally refused him, but the strain nearly drove her out of her mind.

Once again the situation was saved by the Bracebridges, who were going on an extended tour of Egypt and took Florence with them. This time, however, the change of scene did not have the desired effect. Outwardly Florence seemed perfectly composed. She took an interest in the sights and in the social scene and wrote long and affectionate letters to her family describing everything she had seen and done; these letters were edited by Parthe and printed for private circulation in 1854 and have recently been republished.[1] But inwardly all was confusion and anguish. Her nights were sleepless; she often felt too ill to get up; three times she heard the voice of God, and she despaired because she could not follow His call.

After Egypt the party went on to Greece, but things did not improve. When they were ready to leave Greece, in the summer of 1850, Selina, who had been watching Florence with anxiety, decided to travel back via Prague and Berlin and stop at Düs-

1. FLORENCE NIGHTINGALE, *Letters from Egypt, 1849-1850*. Privately printed, 1854; new edn (ed. A. Sattin), Barrie and Jenkins, London, 1987.

seldorf so that she could visit Kaiserswerth. It was only a visit of inspection but it had a tremendous effect on Florence. She spent two weeks there and left it on 13 August 'feeling so brave as if nothing could ever vex me again'. On the last lap of the journey she wrote and sent off to the printers a pamphlet on Kaiserswerth[1] and reached home in high spirits at the end of August.

Her euphoria did not last long. The first storm broke on the day of her arrival when the family heard about the visit to Kaiserswerth. In no time at all life returned to the old pattern, but with an added complication. Parthe, still unmarried and deeply jealous of her sister, showed signs of advanced neurosis of which the outward expression, apart from fits of hysteria, was an almost insane possessiveness towards Florence. Florence must look after her, Florence must never leave her, she could not bear to be parted from Florence. And Florence promised that for six months she would devote herself exclusively to Parthe. When the six months were over, Parthe was no better and Florence was exhausted.

In the summer of 1851 she insisted that she must go back to Kaiserswerth. This time her mother gave in, but on condition that her destination be kept secret. It was agreed that they would all go to Carlsbad, ostensibly for Parthe's health, and while they were there Florence would go to Kaiserswerth and join them again in Carlsbad for the return journey. Parthe had hysterics but Florence went. She spent three months at Kaiserswerth. The regime was extremely austere but she was perfectly happy. 'This is life', she wrote to her mother. 'Now I know what it is to live and to love life'.

On her return to England she realised that if she was to get anywhere she must break loose from her family. The process was long and stormy but eventually she won. Aunts and cousins took sides, letters flew in all directions. Her father's sister, Mrs. Samuel Smith, 'dear Aunt Mai', and friends such as the Bunsens, the Bracebridges, the Herberts and Cardinal Manning

1. FLORENCE NIGHTINGALE, *The Institution of Kaiserswerth on the Rhine for the Practical Training of Deaconesses*. Printed by the inmates of the London Ragged Colonial Training School, 1851.

were all solidly behind her and put mounting pressure on her parents. Her mother was unpersuadable but her father relented and in 1853 gave her her independence by making her an allowance of £500 a year.

While the struggle was going on, Florence had made several attempts to continue her training. A plan, supported by Manning, to work with the Sisters of Mercy in Dublin fell through, but early in 1853 she managed to spend a month in Paris visiting hospitals, watching doctors examine patients, witnessing operations, and adding to her vast collection of hospital and sanitary statistics. And in April of that year a charitable committee chaired by Lady Canning offered her a post, unpaid of course, as superintendent of the Institution of the Care of Sick Gentlewomen in Distressed Circumstances, described by Florence as 'a sanatorium for sick governesses run by a committee of fine ladies'. She took up her appointment in July.

The institution had just been moved to a large house in Harley Street and Florence's first task was to alter and furnish the new premises so that they should be fit for their use. She had hot water piped to every floor, lifts installed to take the food up from the kitchen, bells that rang on every landing, gas stoves everywhere. On inspecting the stores that had been brought in from the old premises she found cupboards full of expensive jam but no brooms or brushes; household linen ragged and dirty; pillows and mattresses rotted; and so on. All this had to be straightened out as quickly and cheaply as possible, as the institution had been administered incompetently and its finances were running low. Florence went into residence at no. 1 Harley Street on 12 August 1853, while the workmen were still in the house, and the first patients began to arrive at the end of the month.

At first, needless to say, her initiatives were viewed with great suspicion. Lady Canning trusted her but the other ladies on the committee were bewildered by her innovations, the house surgeon resigned after a month, the housekeeper left, the treasurer resented her suggestions for keeping a tighter control on expenditures. With great tact she set herself to conciliate her committee, reorganised the medical side, giving the doctors full authority over the nurses, reorganised the housekeeping so as to do away with waste, and earned the devotion of her patients by her concern for their welfare both while they were in the institution and when they left it. Within six months the opposition had collapsed and things were running smoothly and efficiently.

She had long thought that what was wanted in England was a training school for nurses and now she got an opening. One of the best surgeons of the day, Dr. Bowman, who had performed an operation on one of her patients, had been much impressed by the way she ran the institution and offered her the post of superintendent of nurses at King's College Hospital, where she could carry out her training scheme. While she was considering this offer the great cholera epidemic of 1854 broke out and in August she went as a volunteer to the Middlesex Hospital to help with the nursing. And then, in the autumn, all her plans were swept away by a new, much graver emergency.

In March 1854 England and France had declared war on Russia and in April the first British troops sailed for the Crimea. Soon reports began to appear in *The Times* about the enormous number of casualties and the scandalous conditions of the British military hospitals. Sidney Herbert was again War Secretary and Florence wrote to the Herberts offering her services to the War Office. Her letter crossed with one from Sidney Herbert asking her to take a party of nurses to the Crimea. She had already collected together a small group of willing women but now she was told she must take with her a party of forty. This was not easy, but she managed to recruit thirty-eight, of whom fourteen were hospital nurses chosen from among the least disreputable that presented themselves and the rest belonged to religious institutions, including some Roman Catholic nuns. The party, completed by the Bracebridges, sailed for Turkey at the end of October and arrived at the Scutari Barrack Hospital on 5 November.

What they found there can hardly be believed: no beds, no tables, no chairs, no kitchens to provide food, no cups or buckets to bring in water; just 'long lines of men lying on the floor in blankets saturated with blood and ordure'. The stench could be smelt from outside the walls of the building. The few doctors in charge simply could not get round to all the sick and wounded and had not authority enough to commandeer adequate supplies of medicaments: there was not a single operating table in the place. The food was insufficient and disgusting and water was rationed to one pint per head per day for drinking and washing. The mortality, partly from wounds but mainly from various diseases, in particular dysentery, was horrendous. And terrible weather was advancing.

Throughout the winter and spring Florence worked with superhuman energy, often in the teeth of fierce bureaucratic opposition. When a flood of casualties came in after a battle she would be up for twenty-four hours, dressing wounds for eight hours at a stretch. With money raised in England from various sources she bought the necessary supplies in Constantinople, had the wards cleaned and whitewashed, the overflowing lavatories put in working order. She had special diets prepared in the small kitchen that had been assigned to her. The nurses quarrelled among themselves and the Catholic nuns resented her authority but she managed to keep them under control. She wrote to the widows of some of the dead men, to the families of the nurses who could not write, to the people who had sent gifts from home. She wrote long circumstantial reports to ministers in England and caused a sanitary commission to be sent out to strengthen her hand. In March 1855 she was joined by Alexis Soyer, the famous chef of the Reform Club, who was always ready to put his skill at the service of the distressed, and the patients were properly fed at last. Soyer had sound ideas about institutional cooking,[1] he even designed a camp stove for the army in the Crimea which is still in use today.

In a few months what had been a charnel house became a decent hospital and mortality dropped dramatically. The men idolised her, the commanding officers, who at first had regarded her with amused tolerance, deferred to her. The bureaucrats hated her, but however provoked Miss Nightingale did not lose her temper; if persuasion did not work she tried to get her wish-

1. ALEXIS SOYER, *Soyer's Culinary Campaign. Being Historical Reminiscences of the Late War, with the Plain Art of Cookery for Military and Civil Institutions*. London, 1857.

es sanctioned by higher authority; if this did not work either, she made the best of existing circumstances and waited for another opportunity, for she never accepted defeat. And she was untiring in her solicitude for her patients: she looked after the worst cases herself, and every night she went the round of the wards with her lamp and the men would kiss her shadow as she passed.

In May she decided she must turn her attention to the hospitals at Balaklava in the Crimea itself, about which she had received disturbing reports. She took with her four nurses and the invaluable Soyer. She was received with hostility and even insolence, which she ignored, but no sooner had she begun to sort out the worst problems than she went down with Crimean fever. For a fortnight her life hung in the balance. She was attended by Dr. John Sutherland, the head of the Sanitary Commission, who was an ally of hers and who after the war became one of her principal collaborators in her reforming campaign. She recovered, and after a few weeks' convalescence in Constantinople returned to her task.

New troubles arose both at Scutari and at Balaklava, among others the departure in July of the Bracebridges, who had been helping with the administration. They were followed by a succession of incompetent and dishonest people until their functions were taken over by Aunt Mai, who came to help in September. This was the only relief in a sea of disasters. For one thing Florence's health was giving way: she had dysentery, she had sciatica, she developed ear-ache and chronic laryngitis. For another, as the year wore on, the higher medical authorities and some of the Catholic nuns became more and more intractable, especially at Balaklava. Her directives were flouted as soon as her back was turned and were often openly resisted. When the second winter came she was near despair.

At this point public opinion came to her support. A legend had been growing round her name in England. Portraits of her, mostly imaginary, sold by the thousands, poems and songs were written about her, ships and racehorses were named after her; reports on her health were followed with anxiety, public meetings held to express 'the grateful recognition of the British people' were filled to suffocation and a Nightingale Fund was opened and quickly grew to vast proportions. All this irritated her enemies in the Crimea but made an impression on the government. One ministry had already fallen at the beginning of 1855 because of popular indignation at the conduct of the war, and the new cabinet, headed by Palmerston, realised that if the public were to get wind of how Miss Nightingale was being treated there might be another vote of censure in parliament. Something must be done.

The wheels of government grind slowly, however, and it was not until March 1856, when the war was almost at an end, that an official despatch was sent to the Crimea confirming and indeed extending Miss Nightingale's absolute authority over all matters pertaining to the female nursing staff in the military hospitals. This helped Florence up to a point. Officially her orders were to be obeyed; in fact they still met with a great deal of stonewalling. But she was determined to stay on until the last man had been shipped home and she persevered against all setbacks.

She had conceived a wider ambition than nursing the men when they were ill, she wanted to improve their conditions of service when they were well. Her recent experience had convinced her that the British soldier was not a drunken brute as the officers believed but a normal human being, with the qualities and defects common to all human beings; if anything he was better than the average because he had qualities which are not common to all human beings, courage, endurance, loyalty and a strong sense of comradeship. If he was brutal it was because he was treated brutally. If he was drunk it was because he had no place other than the drink shop to go to when he was off duty. All this must be changed and she was going to change it.

She started in May 1855, against strenuous opposition, by setting up a small reading room for the convalescent at Scutari. She had been told that she was destroying discipline; in fact the men behaved perfectly well, and eventually, with the help of one of the commanding officers sympathetic to her ideas, several recreation rooms were opened near the various hospitals and furnished with books, newspapers, writing materials, games and pictures, mostly procured from England by her. She noticed that many of the men could not read or write, so she asked for a schoolteacher to give them lessons. Again her request was refused on the grounds that 'the men would get above themselves', and again she got her way. The lessons proved so popular that in the end four schools were opened to satisfy the demand. She realised that one of the reasons why the men drank their pay away was that they had no secure deposit for their savings and no reliable channel to send money home by; even the officers mistrusted the army administrators. She started by providing these services herself and ended by obtaining from London the establishment of a regular service for postal orders. Against all prophecies, £71,000 was remitted in less than six months.

The effects of her policy were both immediate and far reaching. In the short run the incidence of drunkenness dropped as dramatically as had the incidence of death. And in the long run her initiatives sowed the seeds of a reform which amounted to a revolution in the conditions of service in the army.

When in July 1856 the time came to leave Scutari, Florence and Aunt Mai travelled home *incognito* as Mrs. and Miss Smith, Florence having declined the government's offer of a warship to bring her home in state. She arrived in England by herself, avoided the triumphal welcomes that were planned for her, took a train north and walked into the family home, Lea Hurst, unannounced.

Her mother and sister, who had been basking in her fame, had hoped that when it was all over she would relax and enjoy the fruits of it. But this was not to be. She refused all invitations, both public and private, and all requests to make public appearances or public statements. Her frame of mind can be gathered from one of her private notes written on leaving the Crimea: 'Oh my poor men: I am a bad mother to come home and leave you in your Crimean graves – 73 per cent in 8 regiments in six months from disease alone – who thinks of that now?' Her mission was to reform the War Office, to ensure that the medical and sanitary condition of the troops that she had witnessed at Scutari and the Crimea would not occur again. In her endeavour to do this she spared neither herself nor her friends; as to her enemies there was nothing she could do but fight them.

There was one invitation she did accept. In September 1856 Sir James Clark, the Queen's physician and a personal friend of the Nightingales, who had opened Florence's eyes to the reasons for her sister's mental breakdown four years earlier, invited her to stay at his house in Scotland, which was very close to Balmoral where the Queen and the Prince Consort were spending the summer. The royal couple had the highest opinion of Miss Nightingale. When she was in the Crimea they had not only given her practical help by sending useful sanitary equipment but also presented her with a personal token of their regard in the form of a diamond and enamel brooch designed by the Prince Consort himself, and now they were eager to make her acquaintance.

The meeting proved very fruitful. During her stay with the Clarks Florence was often at Balmoral and the Queen frequently drove over to have long talks with her. Both the Queen and the Prince took to her and she convinced them of the need for reform, but before action could be taken the Queen must receive the advice of her ministers. In the following week Lord Panmure, who had succeeded Sidney Herbert as War Secretary, was expected at Balmoral, and the Queen wished Miss Nightingale to remain and see him. The Queen knew what she was doing: Lord Panmure liked an easy life and was apt to get out of the way if something troublesome loomed up, and this he could not do at Balmoral. All the same, if he had not got on with Florence he could have pursued his usual delaying tactics and nothing much might have happened.

When he met her, however, Panmure was captivated, as everyone except her direct antagonists always was. With all her charge of passion she had great self-control and tact, as shown by her handling of the establishment at Scutari and Balaklava. She also had wit and charm. To top it all she was very good looking, elegant and graceful. Panmure acceded to all her requests: there was to be a Royal Sanitary Commission with instructions based on her recommendations and she was to be invited to make a confidential report, the invitation to come jointly from himself and the Prime Minister, Palmerston. Buoyed by this success, Florence went to London to prepare the ground for the Commission. Her family went with her and they all installed themselves at the Burlington Hotel, Florence to work and her mother and sister to enjoy her reflected glory. Panmure paid her an official visit there and renewed his assurances, and hopes ran high.

And then, to her disgust, silence fell. Panmure had relapsed into his customary indolence. To be more exact, the high officials at the War Office were strongly opposed to the idea of an inquiry and he hoped, characteristically, that the conflict might be resolved by his doing nothing. But he was soon disabused. Florence left him no peace and in the end she won. The royal warrants were issued on 5 May 1857, seven months after her first interview with Panmure, and a few days later the Commission Appointed to Inquire into the Regulations Affecting the Sanitary Condition of the Army began its sittings under the chairmanship of Sidney Herbert.

The work of the Commission was largely organised by Florence from her rooms in the Burlington Hotel, 'the little War Office', as it was called by the reformers. These were led by Florence herself, Sidney Herbert and Dr. John Sutherland, her friend from the Sanitary Commission in the Crimea, and helped on the statistical side by William Farr, who had already made a study of mortality in the army during the Peninsular War, as we saw in chapter 9. At the same time she was writing her confidential report for Lord Panmure. It was entitled *Notes on Matters affecting the Health, Efficiency and Hospital Administration of the British Army.*[1] A few copies were printed for private circulation but it was never published. Part of it appears in her evidence to the Commission, much of whose *Report*[2] she seems to have written herself. In the next section I shall give a few examples of the statistical tables with which she illustrated her arguments.

1. Privately printed, London, 1858.

2. U. K., Royal Commission on the Sanitary Conditions of the Army, 1857-58, *Report of the Commissioners.* H.M.S.O., London, 1858.

The next thing was to ensure that the *Report* would not be shelved, a fate not unlikely with so many anti-reformers in the War Office, not to speak of the Secretary of State's liking for a quiet life. However, Lord Panmure was persuaded to set up four sub-commissions, each to be chaired by Sidney Herbert. Their functions would be:

1. to put all barracks in sanitary order;
2. to set up a statistical department for the army;
3. to institute an army medical school;
4. to reconstruct the army medical department, revise the hospital regulations and draw up a new warrant for the promotion of medical officers.

At this point Miss Nightingale collapsed. She had returned from the Crimea exhausted; she had worked unceasingly since her return; and throughout these months she had been plagued by her mother and sister, who demanded her attention, expected her to nurse them when they were ill, gave parties in the rooms adjoining her study when they were well, commented on her exhausting herself but never offered the carriage to take her on her visits to hospitals and barracks, complained of the cold, complained of the heat, complained of the boredom of the London summer, but still would not go away. Florence had now reached a stage when she could hardly eat solid food. She was persuaded by Dr. Sutherland to go for a short break to Malvern but she would not let any of the family come with her. 'I must be alone, quite alone', she said to Parthe. 'I have not been alone for 4 years.' Her mother and sister, frightened by her condition, did not insist and she went off by herself accompanied only by a footman.

In Malvern, ill as she was, she continued to prepare the material for the four sub-commissions and early in September she summoned Dr. Sutherland to come and help. He arrived to find her apparently at death's door but still obstinately insisting on working and refusing to see her family. The only relative she would allow near her was Aunt Mai, who came to Malvern in mid-September and took her back to London at the end of the month.

Although Florence had weathered this crisis, when she returned to London she was still an invalid in danger of her life: she lay in bed or on a couch; she seldom went out; she saw people, if she saw them at all, only by appointment; and yet she continued to work indefatigably for the cause she had at heart. To further it, she drove herself and those who worked with her remorselessly. She had given up everything for it and expected others to do the same. She showed little kindness to Sidney Herbert and ignored as far as she could the kidney disease that finally killed him in 1861. She quarrelled with Aunt Mai who after years of devoted help felt it necessary to return to her family; after which Florence refused for twenty years to communicate with her. She allowed Aunt Mai's delicate son-in-law, the poet Arthur Hugh Clough, to wear himself out on her behalf, he, too, died in 1861. She treated the faithful John Sutherland with little consideration and remonstrated with him for any show of inconvenient independence. She refused to see people who had been her closest friends and fainted at any suggestion of seeing Parthe.

What was wrong with her and why did she get that way? What turned her from a just and considerate if always strong-willed woman into the pitiless virago she became after the Crimea? One can see why she was exasperated by her mother and sister but this does not explain her treatment of Aunt Mai, of whom she was very fond. In his book *Creative Malady*[1] Sir George Pickering, formerly Professor of Medicine at London and Oxford, ascribes her condition to a psychoneurosis the original purpose of which was to protect her from the interference and importunities of her mother and sister and to enable her to get on with her work undisturbed by them; and gradually her phobia extended to anyone who was not utterly and exclusively subservient to her aims. She often thought she was dying and she often wished for death. Meanwhile she could not devote herself to her mission as thoroughly as she wished, perhaps in the circumstances nobody could have, without the assistance of a 'protective' illness.

A more precise and convincing diagnosis has been advanced

1. Allen & Unwin, London, 1974.

recently by Dr. David Young, who suggests that the 'Crimean fever' which had nearly killed her in the spring of 1855 was brucellosis, a disease caused by a bacterium present in contaminated milk, which after the first acute onslaught can persist in the body for years.[1] In an interesting article on misunderstood illnesses Dr. Le Fanu gives the gist of the argument:

> 'Brucella attacks the nerves and joints, especially of the lower back, leading to severe and at times incapacitating pain. It can also cause less specific symptoms which may be misinterpreted as psychosomatic, including depression, loss of appetite, palpitations and nervous tremors.
>
> According to Dr. Young, the description of Miss Nightingale's invalidity on her return to England is consistent with the chronic form of the infection, punctuated by relapses every few years.'[2]

In Florence's case, during these relapses the spinal pain could be so severe that it could be relieved only by opium injections.

Seen in this light her extreme irritability ceases to be surprising and her perseverance in her work takes on an heroic complexion. She pursued successfully her battle with the War Office over the reforms proposed by the four sub-commissions, enlisting the help of influential journalists like Harriet Martineau. In 1859 she published her best-seller, *Notes on Nursing*, a little book intended to instruct the women of England, on whom the wellbeing of their families depended, in the elements of hygiene and health care; fifteen thousand copies were sold within a month, and it went into countless editions. In the 1860s she carried out an inquiry into the schooling of native children in the colonies and on the basis of her findings wrote a paper on the gradual disappearance of the native races when exposed to the influences of European civilisation.[3] She played a central role in steering the work of the Indian Sanitary Commission set

1. D. A. B. Young, 'Florence Nightingale's fever'. *British Medical Journal*, vol. 311, December 1995, pp. 1697-1700.

2. James Le Fanu, 'Florence Nightingale deserves our apology'. *The Times*, 18 January 1996.

3. Florence Nightingale, 'Sanitary statistics of native colonial schools'. *Transactions of the National Association for the Promotion of Social Science, 1863*, London, 1864, pp. 475-89.

up in the wake of the Indian Mutiny, as we shall see later. Her expert opinion was also sought abroad; she advised the American government on the organisation of military hospitals during the Civil War, and both the French and German governments during the Franco-Prussian war.

At the same time she continued her reform of the English hospital service. In 1860 she had founded the first training school for nurses. It was endowed by the Nightingale Fund and housed in St. Thomas' Hospital. The probationers were to be given a solid medical grounding and their character and behaviour must be above suspicion; they were to live in the hospital but their quarters must be pleasant and cheerful; their board, lodging and uniforms would be provided by the Fund and in addition they were to receive an allowance for their personal expenses. At first the scheme met with strong disapproval on the part of some members of the medical profession who did not see why nurses should be promoted from their subordinate position of housemaids, as one surgeon put it; but it did not take long for the reputation of the school to silence them. Miss Nightingale followed the progress of her girls closely, making a point of getting to know each one personally and taking a maternal interest in their welfare. She also established a school for midwives, carried out surveys of hospital conditions, advised on the organisation of district nursing, on methods of keeping hospital records, on the way new hospitals should be built; she even designed some herself, including one in Lisbon.

Her involvement in these matters did not subside until she was fairly old. With age she became less combative. Her illness burnt itself out and her affectionate nature reasserted itself. She nursed her mother in her last illness, saw more people besides her official friends, was reconciled to Aunt Mai, paid visits to the family of her sister Parthe, who had married Sir Harry Verney. She spent her last years in London where she died on 13 August 1910 aged ninety. By her wish, her tombstone at East Wellow carries the inscription: *F.N. Born 1820. Died 1910.*

Much has been written on Florence Nightingale. The best biographies are the official *Life* by Sir Edward Cook, published shortly after her death,[1] the long essay by Lytton Strachey, a classic of its kind, in *Eminent Victorians*[2] and the meticulously researched and extremely interesting full-length study by Cecil Woodham-Smith.[3] A bibliography of her works has been compiled by W. J. Bishop.[4]

2. *Some Statistics from the Crimean War*

As a statistician Florence Nightingale was not only indefatigable, she was also very competent. She was particularly concerned that people should understand statistics and use them. For this purpose she devised circular pie diagrams, her 'coxcombs' as she called them, intended to 'affect thro' the eyes what we may fail to convey to the brains of the public through their word-proof ears'. These diagrams were published as an appendix to the *Report* of the 1857 Commission and reprinted for private circulation in a pamphlet entitled *Mortality of the British Army*.[5]

To illustrate her work I have chosen two tables and three diagrams drawn up by herself and relating to conditions in the army hospitals in the Crimean War, and have brought together in a third table her data on mortality rates in selected groups of the British population.

Table 11.1 shows what happened to the troops in the eight-day passage from Balaklava to Scutari. Between September 1854 and the end of January 1855 the number of wounded or sick men who made the crossing was 13,093. Of these, 976, or 74.5 per mille, died during the passage. If this rate had continued for 365 days, the annual death rate would have been 3182 per mille. In other words, the men would have died more than three times over in their voyage across the Black Sea.

Table 11.2 shows the situation in the Scutari hospitals from 1 October 1854 to 30 June 1855. In the first two weeks of Octo-

1. MacMillan, London, 1913.
2. Chatto & Windus, London, 1918.
3. Cecil Woodham Smith, *Florence Nightingale, 1820-1910*. Constable, London, 1950.
4. W. J. Bishop, *A Bio-Bibliography of Florence Nightingale*. Dawson, London, 1962.
5. Florence Nightingale, *Mortality of the British Army, at Home and Abroad, and during the Russian War*. Harrison, London, 1858.

Table 11.1

MORTALITY ON THE JOURNEYS FROM BALAKLAVA TO SCUTARI, 1854-55

Period	Embarked at Balaklava during period	Died on voyage	Arrived at Scutari alive	Deaths per 1000 embarked
1854				
15-30 September	3 987	311	3 676	78
October	567	15	552	26.4
November	2 981	162	2 819	54.3
December	2 656	226	2 430	85
1855				
January	2 902	262	2 640	90
February	2 178	41	2 137	19
25 February-17 March	1 067	5	1 062	4.7
18 March-7 April	860	4	856	4.6

Note: on board about 8½ days

Source: U.K. Royal Sanitary Commission 1857-58, *Report of the Commissioners*, p. 363.

Table 11.2

MORTALITY IN THE SCUTARI HOSPITALS, 1854-55

Period	Days	Sick population	Cases treated	Deaths	Annual % death rate in sick population	Death as % of cases treated
1854						
October 1-14	14	1 993	590	113	148	19.2
Oct. 15-Nov. 11	28	2 229	2 043	173	101	8.5
Nov. 12-Dec. 9	28	3 258	1 944	301	121	15.5
Dec. 10-Jan. 6	28	3 701	3 194	572	202	17.9
1855						
Jan. 7-31	25	4 520	3 072	986	319	32.1
Feb. 1-28	28	4 178	3 112	1 329	415	42.1
Feb. 25-March 17	21	3 779	1 621	510	235	31.5
March 18-April 7	21	3 306	1 650	237	125	14.4
April 8-29	21	2 803	1 190	127	79	10.7
April 30-May 19	21	2 018	1 350	70	60	5.2
May 20-June 9	21	1 504	996	48	56	4.8
June 10-30	21	1 442	1 266	28	34	2.2

Source: U.K., Royal Sanitary Commission 1857-58, *Report of the Commissioners*, pp. 364-5.

ber 113 men, or about 6 per cent of the sick and wounded, died; this is equivalent to an average death rate of about 3 per cent per week or 148 per cent per year. In the four weeks of the following February 1329 died, or 32 per cent of the total, which is equivalent to a weekly average of 8 per cent and an annual average of 415 per cent. In the last three weeks of June 28 men died, which is equivalent to 0.65 per cent per week and 34 per cent per year. Even allowing for the change of season, the difference is staggering.

It is made even more staggering by the coloured diagrams in the pocket of the back cover. The large diagram on the right compares the number of deaths from wounds (red), deaths from infectious diseases (blue) and deaths from other causes (black) in all the hospitals of the war zone between April 1854, when the first troops landed, and March 1855; and the story is picked up (by the dotted line with arrows) in the small diagram on the upper left, which goes from April 1855 to March 1856, when the war was almost over. The features that immediately strike one in these diagrams are the contrast between the red and blue areas and the rapidity with which the shaded areas shrink after Florence's intervention had begun to take effect. The third (monochrome) diagram, in the lower left-hand corner, illustrates the figures given in the fifth column of table 11.2 above; it relates only to the Scutari hospital between 1 October 1854 and 30 June 1855 and shows week by week the deaths in the sick population expressed as annual percentage rates.

It will be noticed that the large 'pie' on the right and the small one on the bottom left look incomplete in that their circumferences are not drawn and only the shaded areas are shown. This is an ingenious way of saving space. As it is, the original fold-out sheet in the *Report* measures 42.5×43.5 centimetres. If the missing circumferences were drawn in, the diameter of the larger circle would be about 53 centimetres and that of the smaller one about 21 centimetres, the shaded areas would be as shown and the remainder of the enclosed spaces would be empty. Thus the size of the sheet would be roughly quadrupled without any addition to the information it conveyed.

Other tables given by Florence compare the death rates in the Crimea with the death rates in the troops at home and in the civilian male population in England and Wales. I have summarised this information in table 11.3.

Table 11.3
COMPARATIVE MORTALITY
CRIMEA *v*. ENGLAND AND WALES, ARMY *v*. CIVILIAN MALES
Mid-19th century

Crimea		England and Wales		
Period	Deaths per thousand per annum	Category in the population		Deaths per thousand per annum
January 1855	1 173.5	Effective men of the army at home		
January 1856	21.5	All regiments		17.5
		Guards		20.4
May 1855	203	Line regiments		18.7
May 1856	8			
1 Jan.-31 May 1855	628	Civilians of army age		
1 Jan.-31 May 1856	11.5	Whole country		9.2
		Rural population		7.7
		Manchester, 'one of the unhealthiest cities'		12.4
		Age groups		
		20-25	Soldiers	17.0
			Civilians	8.4
		25-30	Soldiers	18.3
			Civilians	9.2
		30-35	Soldiers	18.4
			Civilians	10.2
		35-40	Soldiers	19.2
			Civilians	11.6

Source: U.K., Royal Sanitary Commission 1857-58, *Report of the Commissioners*, pp. 368-9.

In this table the most telling comparison is that between the three top figures in each category: deaths per thousand in the civilian population, 9.2 per year; deaths per thousand in the army at home, 17.5 per year; deaths per thousand in the Crimea as recorded during January 1855, 1173.5. This is a terrible story. No wonder she wrote 'our soldiers enlist to death in the barracks'.

Doubtless this situation was due to incompetence, inertia and callousness on the part of the people in charge, but it was also largely due to ignorance. Miss Nightingale's figures were a revelation. They were also an indictment of the incompetent and lazy, who resented it bitterly, just as they had in the Crimea. Changing the mentality of an institution like the British military establishment and the practices of a bureaucratic leviathan like the War Office was a task that few people would have contemplated; Florence Nightingale not only contemplated it, she achieved it. Slowly, slowly, with the officials fighting every inch of the way, a great transformation took place.

The first offensive was led by Sidney Herbert. As chairman of Panmure's four sub-commissions he put in train a number of fundamental reforms, and when in 1859 he was again offered by Palmerston the War Office he accepted it in order to carry them out. In spite of failing health he worked with great resolution. Under his administration the living conditions of the men in barracks and hospitals both at home and abroad were materially improved, an Army Medical School was founded and a start was made on the reorganisation of the Army Medical Department in the War Office to include among other innovations a Statistical Branch. Had he not died in 1861 much more would have been done, but even so what he achieved in those few years is impressive. The first Medical Report on the Health of the Army was issued in 1861, and in her account of Herbert's public services Florence was able to give figures showing that in the three years of his ministry the mortality among the new recruits stationed in England had been halved.[1]

1. FLORENCE NIGHTINGALE, *Army Sanitary Administration and its Reform under the late Lord Herbert*. London, 1862.

His disappearance was a near disaster. His last words had been 'Poor Florence... poor Florence, our joint work unfinished', and sure enough after his death several attempts were made, some of them successfully, to reverse his policies. Florence was in despair but she did not give up the fight and found other allies. In 1863 Lord Stanley wrote to her: 'Do not fear that Lord Herbert's work will be left unfinished: sanitary ideas have taken root in the public mind, and they cannot be treated as visionary... The ground that has been gained cannot be lost.' Indeed, first through Palmerston and then through Gladstone she managed to get the right people appointed to key positions and her involvement in army affairs remained unabated. 'I have done nothing else for seven years but write Regulations', she wrote to a friend in 1864, and she continued to do so for several years more, usually with positive results.

Although with time her influence at the War Office declined, hardly a year went by without her advice being sought on some point or other. At the end of her life what a friend had written to her in 1858 was proved right: 'To you more than to any man or woman alive will henceforth be due the welfare and efficiency of the British Army'.

3. Sanitary Conditions in India

Perhaps Florence Nightingale's most remarkable undertaking in the 1860's was her inquiry into the health of the army and general sanitary conditions in India. When the Indian Mutiny broke out in 1857 Florence had proposed to go out to India as she had to Scutari but Sidney Herbert had dissuaded her, saying he needed her help with the four sub-commissions. She complied with his wish but immediately pressed for another Royal Commission to be set up. This was done in 1859, with Dr. Sutherland and Dr. Farr among the members and Sidney Herbert in the chair. A few weeks later, however, he became War Secretary, upon which he resigned the chairmanship of the Indian Commission. He was by now a sick man, greatly overworked, and could not face adding that to his other commitments.

The Royal Commission on the Health of the Army in India, to give it its full title, was now chaired by Lord Stanley, a cool, level-headed man who proved a useful ally though he lacked Sidney Herbert's dedication and irritated Florence by his slowness and his refusal to by-pass official channels. The Commission did not go to India; it sat in London and it should have started taking evidence late in 1859 but the assembling of the necessary data proved a complicated business and the sittings did not begin until the autumn of 1861.

Following the Mutiny, the government of India had formally passed from the East India Company to the Crown but the transfer took a long time to complete. When in May 1859 Florence started collecting data for her inquiry she found that there were no satisfactory records either at the head office of the Company with respect to its troops or at the War Office with respect to the Queen's troops, so she decided to collect information at first hand. In consultation with Sir John McNeill, an old friend from the Crimean days, and Sir Charles Trevelyan, then Governor of Madras, she drafted a *Circular of Enquiry* which was sent to every military station in India. She also wrote to the two hundred largest stations asking for copies of regulations dealing with sanitary affairs and to high-ranking military and medical officers whose cooperation was essential. The *Circular* was designed to produce statistical information for the past ten years, and it did: when the Indian Sanitary Commission's *Report*[1] came to be published the station returns occupied a folio volume of one thousand pages of small print.

As these returns reached England they were sent to Florence who analysed them with the help of Sutherland and Farr. By August 1862 the analysis was finished. Florence, who for some reason that I cannot explain did not qualify as a witness, was asked for her comments and the resulting *Observations by Miss Nightingale*[2] were incorporated in the *Report.*

1. U. K. Royal Commission on the Sanitary State of the Army in India, 1861-62, *Report of the Commissioners*. H.M.S.O., London, 1863.

2. Florence Nightingale, *Observations on the Evidence Contained in the Stational Reports Submitted to the Royal Commission on the Sanitary State of the Army in India*. Privately Printed, London, 1863.

The *Observations* told another terrible story and Miss Nightingale did not pull her punches. She dealt with all aspects of a soldier's life in India: the sanitary defects of the military stations, the men's diet, their intemperance, their want of occupation and exercise, the running of military hospitals, the design of barracks, hill towns, native troops, native lines, even the position of soldiers' wives. Many of her details were quite revolting, and to drive her points home she illustrated her remarks with woodcuts executed by her cousin Hilary Bonham-Carter after sketches sent from India, for this innovation the Treasury made her pay not only for the blocks but also for the extra printing costs involved.

The annual death rate of the British army in India was 69 per thousand, due not so much to fighting or to tropical diseases as to the kind of conditions that had produced such a high rate of mortality at Scutari and were much aggravated in India by the climate. The prevalent killer diseases fell into two groups: cholera, diarrhoea and dysentery, caused by bad water, lack of drainage, and overcrowding; and liver diseases, caused by over drinking, over-eating and lack of exercise. In some places native bazaars were allowed within the cantonments, which made matters worse. It was clear that the health of the army was part of the wider issue of Indian sanitary conditions generally.

This state of affairs must not be allowed to continue. Before the Commission's *Report* appeared Florence had a number of copies of the *Observations* privately printed and sent them to the Queen and other important people. When the *Report* was published in 1863 a discreditable confusion arose: the government withheld its distribution and issued in its stead an abridged version, much watered down and prepared without Florence's knowledge. Florence riposted by putting the *Observations* on sale to the general public. She also published the gist of the *Report* in a paper entitled 'How people may live and not die in India'[1] which she presented to the Edinburgh meeting of the National Association for the Promotion of Social Science.

By now Miss Nightingale was recognised as the authority on

1. *Transactions of the National Association for the Promotion of Social Science, 1863*, London, 1864, pp. 501-10.

sanitary conditions in India; viceroys and high officials visited her, by appointment always, to be instructed in these matters; and she had the support of the press. So she could not be ignored. She was asked to draft a set of guidelines for the War Office and her *Suggestions in regard to Sanitary Works required for the Improvement of Indian Stations*[1] were adopted by the government and put into effect. In 1873 she was able to present to the same Association another paper, 'How some people have lived and not died in India',[2] in which it was shown that in the intervening ten years the death rate in the Indian Army had dropped from 69 per thousand to 18 per thousand.

The other object of her campaign, the introduction of public health measures for the civilian population, was also achieved. In 1867 the government at last gave in to her arguments and established in the India Office a Sanitary Department responsible for the whole country. The immediate results were disappointing because the new department did not have enough bite to take effective action, but eventually both its authority and its finance were strengthened and the long-awaited improvements were brought about.

4. Hospital Statistics

In the late fifties and early sixties, Florence devoted a considerable amount of time to hospital design and management in which statistics had an important part to play.

In 1858 she contributed to the Liverpool meeting of the Association for the Promotion of Social Science a paper in two parts on the sanitary conditions of hospitals and the defects in the construction of hospital wards.[3] In the first part she emphasised the importance of not crowding large numbers of sick under one roof and the bad effects that resulted from a

1. Issued by the Barrack and Hospital Improvement Commission, H.M.S.O., London, 1864.

2. *Transactions of the National Association for the Promotion of Social Science, 1873*, London, 1874, pp. 463-74.

3. *Transactions of the National Association for the Promotion of Social Science, 1858*, London, 1859, pp. 462-82.

deficiency of space, ventilation and light; and in the second part she commented on the problems of hospital design and illustrated her remarks with French and British plans of civil and military hospitals, much to the advantage of the French. She gave the ground plan of one wing of the recently built Royal Victoria Hospital at Netley, to the design of which she had been whole-heartedly but unavailingly opposed, and compared it with the ground plan of the Vincennes military hospital. These papers were expanded into a book, *Notes on Hospitals*,[1] which came out in 1859. It ran into three editions and led to Miss Nightingale constantly being asked for advice on hospital construction.

In 1860 the International Statistical Congress was held in London. Miss Nightingale, who had been elected in 1858 a Fellow of the Statistical Society of London (later the Royal Statistical Society), took part in planning the sessions on sanitary statistics. Much interest was expressed in her scheme for uniform hospital statistics, a topic which she also discussed in a paper presented in 1861 to the Dublin meeting of the Association for the Promotion of Social Science.[2] Here she set out her ideas on the information that a hospital should be able to provide for analytical and comparative purposes. Her suggestions were unanimously adopted by the London hospital authorities. In the *Statistical Journal* for 1861 the Superintendent of Guy's Hospital provided statistics for the seven years ending in 1860, drawn up on principles similar to those of Miss Nightingale,[3] and in the volume for 1862 tables were given for the fourteen general hospitals of London in 1861.[4]

Two examples will illustrate the contribution Miss Nightingale made to medical administration. She devised a cost-accounting system for the army medical services which was put

1. 1st edn, Parker, London, 1859; 3rd edn, rewritten, Longmans, 1863.

2. FLORENCE NIGHTINGALE, 'Hospital statistics and hospital plans'. *Transactions of the National Association for the Promotion of Social Science, 1861*, London, 1862, pp. 554-60.

3. J. C. STEELE, 'Numerical analisis of the patients treated in Guy's Hospital for the last seven years, from 1854 to 1861'. *Journal of the Statistical Society of London*, vol. XXIV, Sept. 1861, pp. 374-401.

4. [FLORENCE NIGHTINGALE], 'Statistics of the general hospitals of London'. *Journal of the Statistical Society of London*, vol. XXV, Sept. 1862, pp. 384-8.

into operation in the early 1860's and was still in operation after the second world war, when it was favourably reported on by the Select Committee on Estimates; for all I know it is still in operation today. In 1859 she was consulted by St. Thomas' Hospital because a railway company wanted to build a line through their site. The medical superintendent thought the hospital should be moved and the site sold. After going into the matter Miss Nightingale agreed with him and at his request wrote to the Prince Consort, who was one of the governors. At the last moment the point was raised whether it would be right to move the hospital away from the local community that depended on it. With the help of Farr, Miss Nightingale showed that the hospital drew its patients from a wide area and there should be no objection to moving it. Finally, she persuaded the hospital authorities not to demand so large a sum that it would almost certainly be reduced on arbitration. A price was agreed upon and the hospital moved to Lambeth.

In the late 1860's she embarked on a statistical inquiry into the treatment of maternity cases in hospital. Outbreaks of puerperal fever were very frequent, especially in workhouse infirmaries. She collected a large amount of information from doctors and hospitals both in England and abroad and came to the conclusion that the main causes of deaths in childbirth were overcrowding and proximity to medical and surgical cases. An abstract of her findings, *Introductory Notes on Lying-in Institutions*, came out in 1871. Among other examples of the danger of overcrowding she gives that of an institution where in one maternity ward with eight beds the mortality had been 8 per thousand; when the number of beds was halved the mortality dropped to 3.4 per thousand. Further, she had found that the death rate among women delivered at home was much lower than that prevailing in hospitals. Clearly the answer was not only separate maternity wards but separate rooms. The same conclusion was reached, independently, by the great gynaecologist Sir James Simpson, with whom she corresponded.

5. *Florence Nightingale as Statistician: a Perspective View*

Although there is much more that could be said about Florence Nightingale's work in her later years, I shall content myself with one example: her campaign to get what Quetelet called social physics and what she called applied statistics more widely used as a policy tool and accepted as a university subject.

Adolphe Quetelet, who laid the foundations of statistics as a science, was also the foremost exponent of its application to the study of man in society. In 1835 he had published *Sur l'homme et le développement de ses facultés, ou Essai de physique sociale,*[1] and in 1842 it had been translated into English. This work and others by him had had a profound influence on Florence's formation. In 1860 he attended the Statistical Congress in London to which, as we have seen, she contributed a paper on hospital statistics. Though an invalid and unable to attend the sessions, she placed her suite at the Burlington at Farr's disposal in connection with the congress, and many distinguished statisticians, among them Quetelet, came to visit her. She had long wanted to meet him and from this date a friendship sprang up. In 1872 he sent her copies of *Physique sociale* and *Anthropométrie.*[2] Florence annotated her copy of *Physique sociale* extensively; her notes have recently been published by Diamond and Stone together with a memoir of Quetelet which she began to write after his death but never finished.[3]

Florence had what can properly be termed a passion for statistics. She found them 'more enlivening than a novel'. She came to attach an almost mystical significance to them as the gateway to an understanding of what she called 'the character of God.' Poring over columns of figures was her idea of bliss. In our day her achievements as a hospital reformer have over-

1. Bachelier, Paris, 1835; Engl. transl, *A Treatise on Man and the Development of his Faculties,* Chambers, Edinburgh, 1842. Expanded version, entitled *Physique sociale: ou Essai sur le développement des facultés de l'homme,* Murquardt, Brussels, 1869.

2. Adolphe Quetelet, *Anthropométrie, ou Mesure des différentes facultés de l'homme,* Murquardt, Brussels, 1870.

3. Marion Diamond and Mervyn Stone, 'Nightingale on Quetelet'. *Journal of the Royal Statistical Society,* ser. A, vol. 144: pt 1, pp. 66-79; pt 2, pp. 176-213; pt 3, pp. 332-51.

shadowed the statistical groundwork which underlies them, but in her lifetime her reputation as a statistician stood high. She was, as I have said, a Fellow of the Royal Statistical Society, and among other marks of international recognition she was made in 1877 an honorary member of the American Statistical Association.

In her endeavour to promote the study of statistics at universities she first sought the help of Benjamin Jowett, the Master of Balliol, who was an intimate friend of hers. Her arguments were the same as those we have seen urged by Farr:

> 'The Cabinet Ministers, the army of their subordinates . . . have for the most part received a university education, but no education in statistical method. We legislate without knowing what we are doing. The War Office has some of the finest statistics in the world. What comes of them? Little or nothing. Why? Because the Heads do not know how to make anything of them . . . What we want is not so much . . . an accumulation of facts, as to teach men who are to govern the country the use of statistical facts.'

She wrote to Jowett letter upon letter on the subject and to lend weight to her arguments sent him a copy of *Physique sociale*.

Nothing came of this attempt, but twenty years later she had another try. In 1891 she wrote to Francis Galton who was a cousin of another friend of hers, Douglas Galton, the army's leading expert on barrack construction. Again she drew attention to the importance of an understanding of statistical facts to those who were to govern the country and illustrated her point with examples drawn from education, crime, pauperism and the condition of India. Politicians, she said, did not use the statistics they had in legislating and administering, they used them only 'to "deal damnation" across the floor of the H[ouse] of C[ommons] at the Opposition and *vice versa*'. She asked Galton to consider the curriculum necessary to teach the subject and the possibility of establishing a statistical professorship or readership at Oxford.

Galton thought about the matter and expressed his approval of Miss Nightingale's intentions. But he saw difficulties. Anyone appointed to a post at Oxford would be somewhat isolated and would not attract much of an audience unless his subject had a place in the examinations. He suggested a post at the Royal Institution in London with the requirement of six lectures and an essay a year. He consulted others and the final proposal was to start by offering a small prize for an essay on selected topics in social statistics. Miss Nightingale agreed to the suggestion, without, I imagine, much enthusiasm. The long vacation was coming on and Galton felt it was useless to proceed for the time being. The idea faded away.

This story is told in detail by Karl Pearson in his magnificent *Life of Francis Galton.*[1] As might be expected, he is extremely sympathetic to Miss Nightingale's proposal and says

> 'were I a man of wealth I would see that Florence Nightingale was commemorated, not only by the activities symbolised by the "Lady of the Lamp" but by the activities of the "Passionate Statistician". I would found a Nightingale Chair of Applied Statistics.'

In his paper on Florence Nightingale in the *Journal of the American Statistical Association*[2] Edwin Kopf describes the characteristics that make for a good applied statistician and concludes, 'In all these respects Miss Nightingale exhibited the prime qualities of one thoroughly versed in the art of preparing and reflectively analysing social data'. He goes further: 'Florence Nightingale', he says, 'may well be assigned a position in the history of social statistics next to those occupied by Quetelet and Farr.'

It is high time this were more generally recognised.

1. *The Life, Letters and Labours of Francis Galton*. Cambridge University Press, vol. II (1924), pp. 414-24.

2. EDWIN W. KOPF, 'Florence Nightingale as statistician'. *Journal of the American Statistical Association*, vol. 15, no. 116, 1916, pp. 388-404.

Charles Booth

CHAPTER 12

Charles Booth and the London Working Classes

1. Brief Life

The wealthy philanthropist, like the maecenas, is a figure that has always existed. In some periods one or other of these two forms of beneficence has been a sort of collective phenomenon has taken what might be called epidemic proportions. In the field of art patronage the Italian Renaissance is the supreme example. In the field of philanthropy the English nineteenth century is undoubtedly one of the outstanding ones. The list of British industrial magnates who devoted large sums to the furtherance of philanthropic schemes is a long one, but in general these worthies were content with giving directions about what they wanted done with their money. Charles Booth has the distinction of having descended into the arena in person.

Charles Booth is often confused with his namesake William Booth, the founder of the Salvation Army. In fact the two men were not related, and oddly enough they never even met. Although they both worked for and among the poor, their aims and their methods were very different. William Booth was a passionate, simple-minded missionary, a 'religious emotionalist', as one of his biographers has aptly termed him. He had had personal experience of poverty as a child in Nottingham and his fiery spirit had revolted at the state of moral as well as material degradation in which so many of his fellow-beings lived. Their sufferings must be relieved and above all their souls must be saved. Beginning as a penniless revivalist preacher, he soon attracted enough support to feed, clothe and shelter thousands of destitutes, but the burden of his message never varied: salvation is to be sought not in this world but in the next. Charles Booth, on the other hand, was a clear-minded man of business, who without ever having experienced poverty had great sympathy for its victims and wanted not simply to alleviate it but as far as possible help to remove its causes. The struggling poor should be made self-reliant and capable of commanding a decent living wage; in other words, salvation could and should be sought in this world, and he would do his best to further it.

Charles James Booth was born in Liverpool on 30 March 1840, the third son of a prosperous and charitably-minded corn merchant and his wife Emily Fletcher. It was a united and affectionate family and Charles had a carefree childhood with his two brothers and two sisters and a host of cousins and friends, all from the upper rungs of the Liverpool business community. He was a bright boy, interested in everybody and everything, but not academically inclined. Unlike his brilliant brother Tom, a future Cambridge wrangler, he did not do particularly well at school. The only subject he was really good at was arithmetic, and on the strength of that his father decided, wisely as it turned out, that the best career for him would be in business. Accordingly, he left school at sixteen and went to be trained in business practices in the shipping firm of Lampert and Holt, who were family connections.

After working there for a few years he joined the import-export agency his eldest brother Alfred had set up in New York in partnership with an American, who had subsequently left. The Booth brothers were thus the sole proprietors of the business, and Charles soon became its leading spirit although he was the junior partner. He had all the qualities that mark the successful entrepreneur: imagination, readiness to take risks, inexhaustible energy, attention to detail, exceptional organising ability and a flair for promising opportunities. Unlike his brother, to whom business was merely a means of making enough money to set himself up as a country gentleman, he enjoyed the 'risks, pleasures and excitements' of it quite independently of the profits it brought. To these characteristics he added a belief in fair dealing, considerateness for the feelings of others, be they his associates, his employees or his clients, and a frank and open manner which attracted people, though he had inherited from his father a certain reserve which made it difficult for him to get on terms of familiarity with any but his most intimate friends and relations.

He remained in New York long enough to get the hang of the business and then came back to Liverpool to look after the English end of it. The once numerous Booth household was now reduced to two, himself and his unmarried sister Emily. Both his father and his mother had died prematurely and so had his brother Tom, to whom he had been very close, his sister Anna was married and Alfred was in New York. But Emily was a good companion, keeping house for him and sharing in all his interests.

What the Booth brothers dealt in was skins, and Charles set himself to learn the technicalities of the trade. He visited the tanneries that supplied the skins for export, getting to know both masters and men. 'To learn to talk to people is an excellent thing . . . I am determined to break down this stupid "Booth reserve" in myself and others so far as I can', he wrote to Alfred. He went down to the port to meet the ships that brought in skins from America and personally inspected the cargoes to judge of their quality. He developed the practice of drawing up statistical tables of the information he collected and worried his easy-going unmethodical brother with requests for data: 'My "statements" strike you as childish . . . but I think they are worth doing. We must put an end to this sloppy brotherly way of doing business or we shall pay dearly for it.'

As a result of these efforts the business, which had been ailing, was put on a solid footing and Charles was able to pursue a much more ambitious project he had been nursing for some time, that of starting a shipping line and opening up direct trading with South America. His letters to Alfred are full of it: 'I think this is the large scheme to which we ought to work towards, and I would let everything else suffer first. The real plan of succeeding in business is to choose such a course that the tide of affairs is with you.' He asked Alfred to send him a list of all the ships that put into New York harbour from the West Indies and Central America. Alfred demurred but Charles insisted: 'I still think I should like to have the Shipping List here and so if it is not very costly please send it. I want to look up the trade with the Windward Islands and Rio de Janeiro. I made a lot of statistics about this trade which are very satisfactory. It is a rattling big one.'

His enthusiasm was catching. He persuaded Alfred and Emily

to join in the enterprise and the three of them invested most of the capital they had inherited from their father in two steamships to be built by a local shipbuilder. In February 1865 Charles reported to Alfred that 'The boats are contracted for by Hart and Sinnott at . . . a lump sum of £16,000 each', and a year later the first ship of the Booth shipping line steamed out of port bound for Para in Brazil with Charles on board.

During the next five or six years he worked unremittingly to build up the business and his efforts were rewarded, but he had driven himself so hard as seriously to impair his health. And there were other factors that added to the strain. Charles had a strong conviction, rooted in the nonconformist traditions of his family, that the rich and successful had a duty to do what they could to relieve suffering and poverty, but he had as strong a belief that the way to do this was not just to give money but to free the working classes from their dependence on charity. Everybody round him, rich and poor alike, seemed to take it for granted that the rich should be rich and the poor poor, and that people must be content with doing their duty in the station in life in which God had been pleased to put them. This was nice for the rich, who could go to church with a clear conscience, but unacceptable to Charles. The spectacle of the rich doling out alms and the poor accepting them passively sickened him, and he began to question the religious principles on which this attitude was based and to look for some other philosophical system that would fit his convictions better. Positivism seemed to be the answer, and he embraced Comte's ideas wholeheartedly, seeing in them the right conceptual framework for a new social order.

He discussed these matters endlessly with a group of like-minded friends and with them considered ways of breaking the established pattern. They began by pinning their hopes on the Liberal party and three times canvassed the slums of Liverpool in the Liberal interest, and each time the slum dwellers, to whom an election merely meant free drinks all round, returned the Conservative candidates they were used to. Charles instituted in his own business 'a sort of risk fund' for his employees, which was partly a profit-sharing scheme and partly an insurance against sickness, but his example was not followed by other employers. He took an active interest in the trade union movement, in which his cousin Henry Crompton played a leading part. With Crompton and others he sponsored a project for a Trades Hall designed to provide a meeting place which would 'emancipate the members of trades' societies from the thraldom of the public house where they generally met to the exclusion of the more intelligent and responsible members', but the project was not sufficiently backed by the rank and file and dwindled to a modest reading-cum-lecture room. Clearly what was wanted was to educate the poor. There was no State education and Charles and his friends calculated – the calculation was almost certainly made by Charles – that there were in the city at least 25,000 children who were neither at work nor at school. They approached the various denominational institutions with an offer to contribute 5 shillings (£0.25) for each child that would be admitted, but this raised a hornets' nest of sectarian protests: everyone agreed that educating the poor was a good thing, but no one would countenance the possibility that the subscription of a Nonconformist supporter might be spent on the education of an Anglican or, even worse, a Roman Catholic child, and *vice versa*. So this plan too had to be abandoned. Frustrated at every point, most of the would-be reformers gave up the fight, but to Charles the disappointment was bitter.

It was during this period of nervous stress coupled with intensive business activity that he met his future wife, Mary Macaulay, niece of the famous historian, an attractive, lively and high-minded girl who also came of philanthropic stock: her grandfather, Zachary Macaulay, had devoted his life to the campaign for the abolition of slavery and had been the first governor of Sierra Leone, the colony of liberated slaves founded by Wilberforce. Mary, who lived in London, had come to Liverpool in 1868 to be bridesmaid at the wedding of a cousin with one of Charles' friends and on that occasion had met Emily Booth, who had introduced her to the group. They immediately adopted her and while she was staying with her cousin she became one of its liveliest members, taking part in their discussions and contributing to a little family magazine of which

Charles was the editor. Thus the two young people got to know each other fairly well. Charles was strongly attracted, Mary less so. Brought up in London in a milieu of men of letters and politicians such as her uncle the historian and high-ranking civil servants such as her father, she was scornful of Liverpool society, which she found narrow and provincial: the only pursuit the men took seriously was business, and their wives' charitable committees were nothing but gossiping sessions, she said. These opinions, which she expressed freely, did not endear her to Charles' friends but they did not put Charles off. For a long time his 'Booth reserve' prevented him from showing his feelings, and the fact that he and Mary lived in different cities did not make things easier. Finally in the spring of 1871 he took the plunge and proposed. Mary, totally unprepared, was taken aback. Her first reaction was to ask her father to reject the proposal. Charles, however, would not take no for an answer and insisted on being allowed then and there to plead his cause in person. A few weeks later they were married.

Life together at first was not easy. Mary had discovered that there was much more to Charles than met the eye, and she had learnt to love him, but they were both strong characters and the process of adaptation to each other's beliefs and habits of thought was painful. And she could not overcome her dislike of Liverpool society. For their part Charles' friends had not forgotten her outspoken comments when she had first met them, and they resented her as much as she resented them. Matters were made worse by the fact that Charles' health was breaking down. He was deeply depressed, had lost all confidence in his powers, could not work and could not eat. Finally it was agreed that he must take a rest, and at the end of 1873 the Booths left for Switzerland with their newborn baby Antonia.

The recovery was extremely slow and was still far from complete when they returned to England in the spring of 1875. They did not go back to Liverpool but took a house in London. Mary introduced her husband to her large circle of friends and gradually his spirits began to revive, though his anorexia persisted. Mary's cousin Beatrice Potter, the future Mrs. Sidney Webb, has left us a pen-portrait of him at this time:

'Nearing forty years of age, tall, abnormally thin, garments hanging as if on pegs, the complexion of a consumptive girl, and the slight stoop of the sedentary worker, a prominent aquiline nose, with moustache and pointed beard barely hiding a noticeable Adam's apple, the whole countenance dominated by a finely-moulded brow and large, observant grey eyes, Charles Booth was an attractive but distinctly queer figure of a man . . . Observed by a stranger, he might have passed for a self-educated idealistic compositor or engineering draughtsman; or as the wayward member of an aristocratic family . . . or as a university professor; or, clean shaven, and with the appropriate collar, as an ascetic priest, Roman or Anglican; with another change of attire, he would have "made up" as an artist in the Quartier Latin. The one vocation which seemed ruled out, alike by his appearance and by his idealistic temperament, was that of a great captain of industry pushing his way by sheer will-power and methodical industry . . . into new countries, new processes and new business connexions.'

During his absence the activities of the firm had languished and profits were alarmingly low. Charles' intervention was urgently needed. He was not well enough to undertake regular office work but he could travel, and so he went with Mary for a business trip to Brazil in one of the company's ships. He came back a new man. The resumption of his favourite activity, coupled with the long restful spells at sea – the voyage took three months each way – had almost completely restored his energies. He opened an office in London and resumed the direction of affairs, dividing his time between London, Liverpool and New York. It took him two or three years to repair the damage caused by his partners' incompetence but eventually things took a turn for the better, and when in 1880 Alfred surrendered the chairmanship to him the firm was on an even keel again.

This does not mean that he relaxed. He continued to control every transaction personally, travelling all over the place both in England and abroad, widening his circuit as his business contacts grew. We are told that for years he never slept in the same bed for more than three consecutive nights except when he was on an ocean crossing. His tastes were frugal, he always travelled second class and usually stayed in modest lodgings, where he got the feel of the place better than he would have in an expensive hotel. For all his reserve he was very interested in people and seems to have been good at making friends with them, no matter what their class, occupation or country might be. The better to understand what made them tick he would attend the meetings of local political groups and workmen's associations and the services of all religious denominations. In fact, had he not been such a superlative businessman one might say he had missed his vocation; he would have made a very good anthropologist.

To complete my sketch of this eccentric tycoon I shall quote from two letters he wrote to his partners around this time:

'Tom's idea, and the practice also, adopted in America and perhaps always hitherto in our business, seems based on the idea that it is our object to get the better of the men we sell to. To let them in for buying what if they knew what we know they would not buy. I doubt if it succeeds even then; but it injures our business to act on this idea, whether it succeeds or not. It is not our interest to get the better of either the men we buy from or those we sell to – but to do the best we can for each, subject to a moderate remuneration for ourselves.'

'Our place is, and our object should be – to pay *as much* as we can and to sell *as cheap* as we can – not the reverse as it might seem and to hold the balance as fairly and steadily as may be between the sellers here and the buyers in America. It is also essential . . . that we should be perfectly open at this side with those who sell to us as to the prices we get for their goods, which if we aim to get nothing but a commission is quite practicable. If we attempt secrecy, they suspect we are making a lot of money and seek outside for other buyers to set against us. If they don't look for other buyers they expect us to fix the prices fairly without bargaining, and this is what we have to do oftener than not.'

This policy paid. There is no doubt that the firm's reputation for commercial integrity was one of the factors of its success.

His marriage also turned out a success. When he was away from home he wrote to Mary every day, sometimes twice a day, long circumstantial letters full of details and reflexions about his work, his experiences, the people he had met and the political and social scene, and Mary wrote back in the same vein. With six children to bring up – a seventh had died in infancy – two households to manage, one in London and one in the country, a number of philanthropic commitments, a host of friends and an insatiable appetite for reading, her life was as full as his but she too found the time for a daily letter. From this dense correspondence there emerges a clear picture of their relationship. They had their differences, but these were overridden by great affection and confidence, mutual respect, and a close community of interests.

Pressure of business had not made Booth lose sight of his other dominant concern, poverty. England was suffering from a prolonged recession, there had been a steady decline in agriculture and a consequent influx from the country into the cities, unemployment was running high and conditions in the overcrowded slums were getting worse and worse and led to repeated riots. Parliament was wrangling about Home Rule for Ireland and paid little attention to anything else, and it was left to private individuals of good will to deal with the mounting social evil.

The more energetic and dedicated among them worked in the slums to bring about immediate practical improvements in the standard of living of those in greatest need. The outstanding examples in London are Octavia Hill, who instituted the housing associations whereby hundreds of families living in unspeakable tenements were decently re-housed; and the Reverend (later Canon) Samuel Barnett and his wife, who in their parish of St. Jude's, Whitechapel, 'the worst in the diocese, inhabited mainly by a criminal population', successfully pioneered adult education, founding among other things Toynbee Hall, the first 'university settlement' for the working classes.

Others made it their task to stir up public opinion by holding meetings, leading protest marches and writing books and pamphlets. One of these, *The Bitter Cry of Outcast London* by Andrew Mearns, which came out in 1883 and described what the author had seen with his own eyes, created such a sensation that commissions of inquiry were set up in every large city to report on conditions in the local slums. On the political side the Radicals and Socialists were naturally very vocal, and in 1884 their influence was strengthened by the appearance on the scene of two new groups, the Labour Representation Committee – the future Labour Party – and its intellectual wing the Fabian Society.

Booth followed these developments closely. He knew most of the people concerned, attended meetings of groups as diverse as the Social Democratic Federation, founded by the radical journalist Henry Hyndman, and the Political Economy Club, talked with Beatrice Potter, the Barnetts and other field workers and listened to anybody who had anything to say on the subject. For instance we are told by his wife that

'Among his friends at this time were several working men of Socialist opinions, and two of these were invited to spend three evenings at his house for a sort of symposium; they expounding the advantages of their system, while Booth himself and his friend and cousin, Alfred Cripps, suggested difficulties. These talks were prolonged for many hours on each occasion, and were of the most friendly character throughout.'

The more Booth listened the more convinced he became that people were talking with insufficient knowledge of the matter, and that what was needed as a basis for policy was a thorough study of the facts, showing who the poor were, how they lived and what factors, personal and social, were responsible for their condition. He was opposed to Socialism as an ideology and believed the black picture painted by socialist writers to be grossly exaggerated. In 1885 Hyndman published the results of a partial inquiry undertaken among London wage-earners by the Social Democratic Federation, according to which 'there were not fewer than twenty-five per cent who existed below the line of reasonable subsistence'. Booth contended that this statement, based on a selected number of districts, 'could not possibly be substantiated over the whole area', but he could offer no solid counterproofs. A first attempt he had made the preceding year to clarify the position by using census data on occupations had got him nowhere. In 1885 he had become a Fellow of the Royal Statistical Society, and in 1886 he reported on his findings to the Society in a paper in which he strongly criticized the lacunae and inconsistencies in the data, which made it impossible to draw any useful, coherent conclusions from them.[1] So he decided to carry out his own investigation, beginning with the East End and extending gradually to the whole city.

1. CHARLES BOOTH, 'Occupations of the people of the United Kingdom'. *Journal of the Royal Statistical Society*, vol. XLIX, pt II, 1886, pp. 314-444.

He directed the survey himself and spent seventeen years and over £33,000 on it. He collected his information partly by direct enquiries, partly from the records of the District School Board visitors and partly from a number of charitable bodies. He also made use of census data and the records of workhouses. He was helped by his wife and numerous assistants, including Beatrice Webb, who was one of his most valued advisers. The work began in the autumn of 1886 and the preliminary results were presented to the Royal Statistical Society in May 1887[1] and were followed by a second paper read to the Society a year later.[2] The first full report on the East End, *Life and Labour of the People*, was published in two volumes in 1889 and 1891;[3] a second edition, in nine volumes and covering the whole city, came out in 1892-97;[4] and the third and final, in seventeen volumes, appeared in 1902-3.[5]

The way the survey was carried out is characteristic of Booth's mode of operating. Each member of the team was allotted a specific task, their reports were collated and edited by Booth; and his drafts were submitted to his wife, who wrote them up in final form, corrected the proofs and saw the books through the press. Although she did not want her contribution to be known, it was in fact an essential time-saving element in the assembly line, for Booth had not relinquished either the running of his business or his incessant travelling; the only difference was that now, wherever he was, in a train, in lodgings, on a ship, he worked on the material for the survey. Sleep and food were reduced to a minimum: his office lunch would often consist of a fruit eaten standing at his high desk. When he was in London he went for long exploratory walks and even spent periods as a lodger in some of the poorer districts, choosing his lodgings at random as he saw a room advertised in a window and living with the family as one of them. Weekends as far as possible were spent with Mary and the chil-

1. CHARLES BOOTH, 'The inhabitants of Tower Hamlets, their condition and occupations'. *Journal of the Royal Statistical Society*, vol. L, pt II, 1887, pp. 326-401.

2. CHARLES BOOTH, 'Condition and occupations of the people of East London and Hackney, 1887'. *Journal of the Royal Statistical Society*, vol. LI, pt II, 1888, pp. 276-339.

3. Williams & Norgate, London.

4. Macmillan, London.

5. Macmillan, London.

dren at their country house in Leicestershire, Gracedieu Manor, where they entertained their friends, often including members of his team. And when he was totally exhausted he would go off on his own for a few weeks' break in some quiet sunny place abroad where he could walk and sketch, his favourite way of relaxing.

The publication of the results gave the public a shock, for the picture they revealed was darker than any that had been published before, darker even than that painted by Hyndman; and the quality of the research they implied was impressive. It earned Booth a high regard among statisticians: in 1892-93 he was President of the Royal Statistical Society and in 1899 he was elected a Fellow of the Royal Society, the most flattering recognition of all. It is indeed a monumental achievement and in the sections that follow I shall try to give an idea of its contents.

On Booth himself the effect of his findings was to convert him to the belief that a measure of State intervention – what he called 'limited socialism' – was necessary, though he hesitated to give prescriptions for particular reforms. He made an exception in favour of old-age pensions, about which he had strong feelings. Under the existing Poor Laws the only refuge for the penniless old to end their life in was the workhouse, where people were herded in squalid and humiliating conditions and husbands and wives were separated. This to Booth seemed monstrous and he became convinced that the humane and dignified solution to the problem lay in State pensions. He began his campaign in 1891, as usual with a paper read to the Statistical Society.[1] The immediate response ranged from incredulous surprise to downright disapproval, but he persevered. In 1892 he published an enlarged version of his paper[2] and followed it up with a book in 1894.[3] The stir which these publications created led to two Royal Commissions, both of which turned Booth's proposal down; but the meetings had been stormy and the matter was far from closed. In 1899 Booth published another book, entitled *Old Age Pensions and the Aged Poor*,[4] which carried his argu-

1. CHARLES BOOTH, 'Enumeration and classification of paupers, and State pensions for the aged'. *Journal of the Royal Statistical Society*, vol. LIV, pt IV, 1891, pp. 600-43.

2. CHARLES BOOTH, *Pauperism, a Picture, and the Endowment of Old Age, an Argument*. London, 1892.

3. CHARLES BOOTH, *The Aged Poor in England and Wales: Condition*. London, 1894.

4. CHARLES BOOTH, *Old Age Pensions and the Aged Poor: a Proposal*. London, 1899.

ments further and contained the startling statement that the measure might involve a 'socialist transfer' of as much as £20 million. Everything worth having costs money, he added. His campaign succeeded, though it took another ten years and a change of government for success to materialise: the Old Age Pensions Act was passed in 1908 under a Liberal administration.

Another proposal he advanced to relieve the density of housing in the poor quarters was for a coordinated network of public transport connecting the inner city to the suburbs, thus enabling the working population to live in healthier surroundings, but nothing came of it. His last major piece of public service was his appointment in 1905 to the Royal Commission on the reform of the Poor Laws, from which he resigned in 1908 on account of ill health, and his last published work was a little book on industrial unrest, which came out in 1913.[1] Though slowed down by age and illness he continued to take part in public debate until the end of his life. He died at Gracedieu on 23 November 1916. His pen had fallen from his hand a week before as he was writing a paper on the industrial reconstruction needed after the war.

Further details of his life and work will be found in the *Memoir* by his wife,[2] the *D.N.B.* entry by F.W. Ogilvie,[3] the full-length biography by T.S. and M.B. Simey, which also contains an evaluation of his standing as a social scientist,[4] and the family chronicle by his granddaughter Belinda Norman-Butler.[5] A history of the shipping firm has been written by A.H. John.[6]

2. *London Poverty*

Writing about his survey of the London poor, Booth describes his aim in the following words: 'My object has been to show the

1. Charles Booth, *Indusrial Unrest and Trade Union Policy*. London, 1913.
2. [Mary Booth], *Charles Booth: a Memoir*. London, 1918.
3. F. W. Ogilvie, 'Charles Booth'. *The Dictionary of National Biography 1912-1921*, pp. 48-50.
4. T. S. and M. B. Simey, *Charles Booth, Social Scientist*. Oxford University Press, 1960.
5. Belinda Norman-Butler, *Victorian Aspirations: the Life and Labour of Charles and Mary Booth*. London, 1972.
6. A. H. John, *A Liverpool Merchant House*. London, 1959.

Table 12.1

CLASS DISTRIBUTION OF THE POPULATION OF EAST LONDON AND HACKNEY, 1887

(percentages)

Class / District	Shore-ditch	Bethnal Green	White-Chapel	St George's	Stepney	Mile End	Poplar	Hackney	All districts
In poverty									
A. Loafers, street vendors, criminals, homeless	1.0	1.2	3.3	1.5	1.5	0.8	1.1	0.9	1.2
B. Shiftless casual workers	9.4	16.0	8.9	15.1	15.8	6.8	12.9	8.6	11.2
C. Helpless intermittent earners	10.6	12.6	10.7	12.5	6.1	6.0	6.2	5.8	8.3
D. Regular small earners	19.2	14.9	16.3	19.7	14.7	12.6	16.3	8.4	14.5
Total	40.2	44.7	39.2	48.8	38.1	26.2	36.5	23.7	35.2
In comfort									
E. Standard regular labour	45.4	39.8	43.3	38.1	41.5	52.0	45.2	34.3	42.3
F. Artisans, foremen, etc.	11.1	11.3	11.3	10.5	13.7	14.9	13.4	17.8	13.6
G. Shopkeepers, clerks etc. (l. middle class)	2.1	3.0	4.4	2.3	4.5	4.5	3.1	6.0	3.9
H. Professional men etc. (u. middle class)	1.2	1.2	1.8	0.3	2.2	2.4	1.8	18.2	5.0
Total	59.8	55.3	60.8	51.2	61.9	73.8	63.5	76.3	64.8
All classes	100.0	100.0	100.0	100.0	100.0	100.0	100.0	100.0	100.0

Source: Charles Booth, *Life and Labour*, 2nd edn, vol. 1, p. 36.

Table 12.2

CLASS DISTRIBUTION OF THE POPULATION OF LONDON, 1887-88

Registration District	Population	Percentage in poverty				Percentage in comfort			All Classes
		A	B	C and D	Total	E and F	G and H	Total	
lborn	150 177	1.6	15.7	31.6	48.9	45.8	5.3	51.1	100.0
George's-in-the-East	47 578	1.5	15.1	32.3	48.9	48.7	2.4	51.1	100.0
hnal Green	127 641	1.2	15.9	27.5	44.6	51.2	4.2	55.4	100.0
Saviour's (entire parish)	196 880	2.8	9.2	31.4	43.4	50.2	6.4	56.6	100.0
Olave's	138 199	0.6	12.9	28.7	42.2	53.7	4.1	57.8	100.0
oreditch	121 161	1.0	9.4	29.8	40.2	56.5	3.3	59.8	100.0
iitechapel	73 518	3.3	8.9	27.0	39.2	55.4	5.4	60.8	100.0
pney	62 063	1.4	15.8	20.8	38.0	55.2	6.8	62.0	100.0
eenwich	166 992	0.5	10.7	25.6	36.8	47.2	16.0	63.2	100.0
plar	166 393	1.1	12.9	22.5	36.5	58.6	4.9	63.5	100.0
stminster	38 893	0.0	17.1	17.9	35.0	54.9	10.1	65.0	100.0
y	42 561	1.3	6.3	23.9	31.5	53.9	14.6	68.5	100.0
ngton	296 968	1.0	7.5	22.7	31.2	47.9	20.9	68.8	100.0
Pancras	235 323	0.9	6.9	22.6	30.4	54.4	15.2	69.6	100.0
mberwell	245 287	0.5	5.4	22.7	28.6	49.2	22.2	71.4	100.0
ndsworth	295 097	0.2	4.2	23.0	27.4	53.3	19.3	72.6	100.0
rylebone	152 280	0.9	6.5	20.0	27.4	49.0	23.6	72.6	100.0
Giles	39 230	3.5	12.9	10.3	26.7	50.4	22.9	73.3	100.0
le End Old Town	110 321	0.7	6.8	18.6	26.1	66.9	7.0	73.9	100.0
mbeth	291 577	0.2	5.1	20.8	26.1	52.7	21.2	73.9	100.0
olwich	111 210	0.0	3.2	21.5	24.7	59.4	15.9	75.3	100.0
ham	164 988	0.9	4.7	19.1	24.7	39.0	36.3	75.3	100.0
nsington	174 429	1.2	4.0	19.5	24.7	42.1	33.2	75.3	100.0
elsea	88 315	0.5	3.4	20.6	24.5	57.1	18.4	75.5	100.0
and	28 688	0.9	11.2	11.8	23.9	47.2	28.9	76.1	100.0
ckney (including Stoke Newington)	207 047	0.8	8.0	14.3	23.1	52.7	24.2	76.9	100.0
ddington	120 614	0.2	0.9	20.6	21.7	51.8	26.5	78.3	100.0
George's, Hanover Square	139 600	0.7	4.4	16.5	21.6	57.4	21.0	78.4	100.0
wisham and Penge	109 247	0.2	3.1	14.8	18.1	44.5	37.4	81.9	100.0
mpstead	66 893	0.0	1.1	12.4	13.5	52.5	34.0	86.5	100.0
districts	4 209 170	0.9	7.5	22.3	30.7	51.5	17.8	69.3	100.0
nates of institutions	99 830								
London	4 309 000								

rce: Charles Booth, *Life and Labour*, 2nd edn, vol. II, end of volume (pages not numbered)

numerical relation which poverty, misery and depravity bear to regular earnings and comparative comfort, and to describe the general conditions under which each class lives.' The basic method he used to do this is set out in his initial paper of 1887.[1] For each district he drew up a matrix with what he terms 'sections' in the rows and 'classes' in the columns. The sections are classified according to the occupation of the head of the family, male and female heads being distinguished separately. The classes are defined by reference to subjective assessments of the standard of living of the family and not simply on measured income. There are 39 sections, beginning with the humblest types of occupation, and 8 classes arranged in ascending order of status, from 'A, lowest class' to 'H, upper middle'. Those in classes A and B are below the poverty line, those in C and D are on it, and those in E through H are above it.

How did Booth set about constructing his matrices? In his first paper he dealt with the five Tower Hamlets. His figures related to 1886-7. He obtained control totals of a number of demographic magnitudes by updating the 1881 census, and he obtained the number of heads of families with children of school age, and the number of these children, from the district school board visitors; the visitors also gave him the occupation of the family head. He then had to estimate the number of heads of families without schoolchildren, the number of wives, of unmarried adults of both sexes, of young people aged 15-20 and of children above and below school age. He made these estimates by apportionment, basing himself on the known distribution of family heads and schoolchildren, subject to the controlling totals derived from the census. He then distributed the population in each occupational group over the eight classes. In 1888 he extended his coverage to three more districts, calling the whole area East London and Hackney. Table 12.1 shows in percentages his allocation of the population of the eight districts over the eight classes.

In all, the eight districts contained rather more than 900,000 inhabitants, or nearly one quarter of the population of London.

1. Charles Booth, 'The Inhabitants of Tower Hamlets'.

As can be seen from table 12.1, the proportion of very poor and poor, classes A through D, varies considerably from district to district: from 23.7 per cent in Hackney to 48.8 per cent in St. George's-in-the-East, the mean for the whole area being 35.2 per cent. Hyndman's estimate, it will be remembered, was 25 per cent, though he did not specify districts.

By 1889 the survey had been extended to the rest of London, and similar tables, relating to the period 1887-89 and classified by School Board blocks and divisions, were constructed for the whole city. These data, tabulated by registration districts as was table 12.1 and arranged in descending order of poverty, are shown in table 12.2.

Thus at the time there was less poverty in London as a whole than in the East End but the difference is perhaps less than might be expected. This is largely due to the high figures for Holborn, Southwark and East Lambeth (St. Saviour's and St. Olave's), Greenwich and Westminster. Of course if we make the district small enough we can obtain almost any figure between 0 and 100 percent.

3. The Causes of Poverty

Booth tried to quantify the relative importance of the factors which caused poverty. He did this by asking a number of School Board visitors who were particularly conversant with the poorest families to fill in a questionnaire for a sample of 4,000 families. Sure of the *bona fides* of his informants, he trusted that any individual bias would largely disappear in the aggregation. The results are set out in table 12.3, again in the form of percentages.

These figures support the modern belief that while personal habits such as loafing and drinking are the primary causes of a certain amount of poverty, they are, contrary to a widespread opinion in Booth's time, relatively unimportant compared with low and irregular earnings, large families and ill health.

Table 12.3
AN ANALISYS OF THE CAUSES OF POVERTY IN EAST LONDON, 1889
(percentages)

Cause of poverty / Class	Very Poor A and B	Poor C and D
Loafers	4	0
Questions of employment		
Casual work	43	0
Irregular work, low pay	9	0
Regular earnings, low pay	0	20
Irregular earnings	0	43
Small profits	3	5
Total	55	68
Questions of habit		
Drink (husband or both)	9	7
Drunken or thriftless wife	5	6
Total	14	13
Questions of circumstance		
Illness or infirmity	10	5
Large family	8	9
Illness or large family and irregular work	9	5
Total	27	19
All categories	100	100

Source: Charles Booth: *Life and Labour*, 2nd edn, vol. 1, p. 147

4. A Few Family Budgets

Although Booth did not base his qualifications by class on measured income or expenditure, he did collect a limited number of family budgets, 6 from class B, 10 from classes C and D, 10 from class E and 4 from class F, or 30 in all for a period of five weeks, and he gave a commentary on the families that lived on them. While insufficient for statistical analysis, these budgets have some interesting features and illustrate well the levels of poverty he was talking about even though they probably give an unduly favourable picture, since it would only be the more steady and reliable families that would or could give the detailed information asked for. Table 12.4 gives a condensed summary of Booth's data, with shillings and pence converted to £ decimals.

Booth made an adjustment to equivalent adults by counting a man aged 20 or above as 20, a woman aged 15 or above as 15, and children according to their age, adding up the resulting numbers and dividing by 20. The apparent average size of the families is attributable to the small samples and is not representative, however. As to the budgets, Booth found that in many cases expenditure exceeded apparent income, though in my summary this only occurs on average in the poorest class. Total expenditure per head rises a little over 2.4-fold from class B to class F. Food expenditure per head is around 60 per cent of the total in all classes and rent is about equal to other non-food expenditure. Clothes and medicines are excluded because they are occasional expenses and too irregular to record.

Table 12.4

FAMILY INCOME AND EXPENDITURE IN LONDON, *c.* 1890

(averages)

Family size and budget \ Class	B	C and D	E	F
Adult male equivalents per family	3.44	3.12	2.50	2.00
	£	£	£	£
Supposed weekly income	0.25	0.38	0.50	0.77
Declared expenditure				
Food (incl. drink)	0.18	0.21	0.27	0.43
Rent	0.06	0.08	0.09	0.14
Other (excl. clothes and medicines)	0.05	0.06	0.09	0.14
Total	0.29	0.35	0.45	0.71

Source: Charles Booth, *Life and Labour*, 2nd edn, vol. 1, p. 138.

5. *Elementary Education in London*

In the third volume of the second edition of *Life and Labour* Booth turned his attention to education and particularly to elementary education, the form of schooling that came the way of the class he was primarily interested in. Things had changed since he had first tried to organise some schooling for the Liverpool children. An

Act of 1870 had made elementary education compulsory up to age 12 inclusive, and state schools had sprung up in every town. The schools were administered by School Boards under the control of local authorities and financed partly by fees and partly by government grants. The teaching requirements were specified in a Code laid down by the Department of Education.

Booth has nothing but praise for the London Board schools: 'in every quarter . . . they stand, closest to where the need is greatest . . . uniformly handsome, commodious, and for the most part substantial and well arranged'. Each school had three divisions, infants, boys and girl. A child could be sent to school at the age of three, an important consideration for the hard-pressed working mother, attendance was compulsory at five, and at seven an examination was taken to pass into the boys or girls division. A final examination at thirteen concluded this stage. For those who wanted to move on to secondary education, which was optional, provision was made in other institutions.

In 1890 there were 441,609 children on the books of the 388 elementary Board school and a further 207,942 children in 591 voluntary elementary schools, either protestant or catholic, or nearly 650,000 in all. The Board schools, were classified into six grades based on weekly fees charged, which depended on the income level of the population living in their catchment area, and a similar classification was made for voluntary schools. Corresponding to the six Board school grades, the fees were: free, 1d or 2d, 3d, 4d, 6d, not more than 9d, the maximum permitted by law. Considering that the old penny was equivalent to approximately 2/5 of a decimal penny, these fees seem very small indeed; yet, small as they seem, they were in many cases remitted. Booth makes an interesting remark:

> 'In schools under the London Board there is nothing, beyond the aspect and condition of the children who fill them, to distinguish those with different rates of fees one from another. The buildings, the staff, the educational appliances, the requirements of the Code, are the same for every class. It is the children alone who vary. Voluntary schools, to a great extent, except as regards the requirements of the Code, differ according to the fees, endowements, or other means of support, and also with the management.'

By blowing up his sample of voluntary schools to cover all the children attending such schools and classifying all the children into his classes, Booth was able to cross-classify the school populations by social class, grade of school and type of institution, Board, protestant voluntary and catholic voluntary. An aggregated version of the tabulation is given in table 12.5. The classes very poor, poor and comfortable correspond to Booth's A and B, C and D, E and above; the school grades 1, 2 and 3 correspond to the Board's categories I and II, III and IV, V and VI; and the institutional division is simply between Board and voluntary.

Although in table 12.5 the social classes are assigned on the A,B,C, . . . scale as in the earlier tables dealing with the whole population, the two measures are not strictly comparable, the measure for children showing much higher figures for poverty: 13.4 per cent and 38 per cent respectively for the A-B and C-D classes as opposed to the 8.4 and 22.3 per cent shown in table 12.2. There are several reasons for this. The original calculation was based on detailed information from School Board visitors, who knew most of the families in their area, followed by house visits by members of the survey team in the case of East London and street by street assesment in the rest of the city. The classification of the children, on the other hand, was based on teachers' approximate estimates of the proportions of the various classes to be found among their pupils, and Booth believed that this method, even if the standards were in principle the same, lent itself to exaggeration and would lead to higher figures than would have been obtained if it had been possible to rate the children individually. He also thought that in many cases children did not receive their fair share of the family income and so would tend to appear poorer than their families. Finally, he considered that children in the 'comfortable' class should be compared with families in classes E and F only, omitting classes G and H since most of the G and H children received their education elsewhere. When all allowances were made, the one certain thing that emerged from this alternative calculation was that his original assesment did not overstate the extent of poverty.

Table 12.5

ELEMENTARY SCHOOL ATTENDANCE IN LONDON, 1889-90

School grade and type of school \ Class		Very poor A and B	Poor C and D	Comfortable E and above	All Classes
		Number of pupils			
1. I and II:	Board	47 556	101 874	31 908	181 338
	voluntary	11 194	17 708	13 121	42 023
	Total	58 750	119 582	45 029	223 361
2. III and IV:	Board	18 515	83 330	92 160	194 005
	voluntary	7 821	30 434	84 584	122 839
	Total	26 336	113 764	176 744	316 844
3. V and VI:	Board	1 865	12 089	52 312	66 266
	voluntary	86	1 117	41 877	43 080
	Total	1 951	13 206	94 189	109 346
All grades:	Board	67 936	197 293	176 380	441 609
	voluntary	19 101	49 259	139 582	207 942
	Total	87 037	246 552	315 962	649 551
		Percentage of school population			
1. I and II:	Board	7.3	15.7	4.9	27.9
	voluntary	1.7	2.7	2.0	6.4
	Total	9.0	18.4	6.9	34.3
2. III and IV:	Board	2.9	12.8	14.2	29.9
	voluntary	1.2	4.7	13.0	18.9
	Total	4.1	17.5	27.2	48.8
3. V and VI:	Board	0.3	1.9	8.1	10.2
	voluntary	0.0	0.2	6.4	6.6
	Total	0.3	2.0	14.5	16.8
All grades:	Board	10.5	30.4	27.2	68.0
	voluntary	2.8	7.6	21.4	32.0
	Total	13.4	38.0	48.6	100.0

Note: Components do not always add up to totals because of rounding-off errors.

Source: Charles Booth, *Life and labour*, 2nd edn, vol. III, pp. 197-8.

Booth's statistical tables are followed by an account of how the system worked, its good points and its bad points. The Board's buildings were fine, the facilities adequate, the majority of the teachers dedicated and understanding. The defects, which were most apparent in the lower grade schools, were to be traced partly to poverty, partly to the irresponsibility of many of the parents and partly to the requirements of the Code to which the teaching had to conform.

The law required parents to ensure that their children received a certain minimum of education but not a certain minimum of food. The description of how children of the lowest classes lived leaves one wondering that so many survived. The author's style is sober and straightforward, with no frills, and all the more telling for that:

'We find our school usually on the skirts, or standing in the midst of a crowded, low, insanitary neighbourhood . . . foul-smelling and littered with garbage of every kind . . . The houses are old, damp and dilapidated . . . Few families in the neighbourhood occupy more than a couple of rooms. Fully a third live in a single one, often so small and unwholesome that sickness is a constant tenant too. Here, in a space that would hardly suffice for the graves of a household, father, mother and children, sometimes a lodger too, work out the problem of domestic life.

Not that the children are much in the home. Their working hours are divided between school and the streets. Bedtime is when the public-houses close. The hours before that are the liveliest of all the twenty four, and they swarm about undisturbed till then. They have no regular meal times. When they are hungry the mother puts into their hands a "butty", *i.e.* a slice of bread with a scrape of dripping, lard, or the current substitute for butter, and sends them off to consume it on the doorstep or in the street. The youngest of the brood she supplies with a "sugar butty", *i.e.* a "butty" with as much sugar as will stick upon the scrape. A draught of stale tea usually goes with it. When funds are low, or where drink forestalls the children's bread, the scrape and cold tea vanish, the sugar butty is a thing of the past, the slice from the loaf becomes an intermittent supply, neighbours help out with the children's meals, and free meals at school keep starvation from the door.'

Booth, however, was not altogether happy about existing

arrangements for a free meal every school day, since while it would help the children it would be taken advantage of by shiftless and indifferent parents, and by reducing the minimum cost of bringing up a family, would ultimately reduce the minimum wage. Of course if parents could or would not feed their children this would have to be done by charity or by the State but it should be done under controlled conditions which would discourage parental irresponsibility and reduce the burden it was storing up for the future.

Irregularity of attendance at school was largely attributable to parental neglect, the number of wilful truants being, in Booth's opinion, comparatively small. Under the Education Act of 1876 provision had been made for day industrial schools for neglected children. These were not of a reformatory character and children could be sent to one for a period of three years on a magistrate's order. The parents were required to pay up to 2 shillings a week towards the cost. The child went home each night and attendance officers were empowered to enter the house and take it back to the school. If after six months or so the child had attended regularly, it could be let out 'on licence' and return at any time within the three-years period. Unfortunately the London School Board, exemplary in other respects, did not adopt these provisions; but they were adopted by other large school boards throughout the country to the great advantage of the children affected.

The required teaching was mainly directed to the cultivation of brain power and memory and gave little encouragement to physical, practical and, for girls, domestic education. The three to five-year-olds got kindergarden treatment, but at five things became more serious and at seven the children had to be ready for an examination in Standard I which included 'reading from books containing words of more than one syllable, spelling, writing, addition, subtraction, half the multiplication table, singing by note as well as by ear, needlework for girls, and either drawing or needlework for boys'. Six standards were set by the Code. The fifth and sixth were optional, but before leaving school at thirteen every child was expected to have passed Standard IV. Booth gives a synopsis of its requirements, which would surprise a modern schoolteacher:

'Reading with fluency and expression from any book chosen by the Inspector.

Writing any passage of prose or poetry from dictation, with spelling. More than three mistakes "fail" a child.

Arithmetic, compound rules with principles, reduction, tables of weight, length, area, capacity etc.

Needlework for girls, drawing for boys. Singing.

Recitation of eighty lines of poetry, the meaning and allusions being properly understood.

Class subjects, grammar, geography, elementary science, history. Two of these are usually taken.'

These requirements were within the reach of children from the better-class families; some of the brighter ones even reached Standards V and VI. But to the street urchins of classes A and B they literally made no sense. Booth describes the scene during a grammar lesson:

'The boys . . . were evidently trying to attend; but they looked dazed and beaten, their faces worried and vacant . . . yet the same boys, when questioned presently on things that came home to them . . . showed no lack of shrewdness and common-sense. Their faces changed. The slum look fell off. Their individuality came out. All looked eager, bright, responsive . . . A lesson in the fact that "cram" and education are not the same.'

Such was the state of affairs when Booth published his findings in the first edition of *Life and Labour*. The teachers deplored it as much as he did but were powerless to change it, as the Code regulations were strict and the State grant depended on examination results; so they were forced to 'cram' or the school would lose part of its grant. In his concluding remarks to this section Booth pointed out the defects of the Department's policy and suggested a number of reforms, adding:

'Another not less pressing need with children of the lowest or the poorest class, who have not encouragement at home, is to have school work made attractive to them, so that they neither hate it while it lasts, nor fling it aside the moment release from attendance comes. The Department in the past has taken little account or none of this, or of other distinctively class requirements. Things useless and distasteful to children of this type have been rigorously exacted, while the crowded time-table found no space for those that are needed most.'

Shortly after, however, things improved. In a note added in his second edition Booth was able to say:

'The inquiry of which the results are given in this chapter occupied the seven months ending April, 1890. It was concluded, therefore, before that turn in the educational tide which set in with the issue of the New Code towards the end of the same year. Various reforms of the nature indicated in the text have been commenced or carried out since then. The pernicious system of "payment by results" has been abandoned . . . A freer hand has been given to managers and teachers, the rigidity of the Code has been to some extent relaxed . . . the necessity for manual and domestic training has been more fully recognised . . . and direct encouragement given to the development of right habits and character, in place of the sole inexorable "cram" which former Codes demanded. The *Education Act* of 1891 has also been passed, transferring the payment of school fees from the parent to the public.'

It is probable that much of the credit for these changes should go to Booth.

6. An Alternative Measure: Crowding

Booth trusted that in apportioning the population among his eight classes he had got the orders of magnitudes about right. Still, he wanted a check. At his suggestion, the population census of 1891 contained a question about crowded housing conditions, which had not formed part of his original definition of the standard of living. This he thought might provide an alternative approach to the measurement of poverty. In 1893 he reported the results to the Statistical Society.[1]

When the totals of the two calculations were compared, the census figures seemed to confirm his earlier estimates: the proportion of the population living two or more in one room was very similar to the proportion of very poor and poor obtained by the original method, as shown in table 12.6.

On further analysis, however, this similarity appeared to be fortuitous: the two methods did not give alternative measures

1. Charles Booth, 'Life and labour of the people in London: first results of an inquiry based on the 1891 census'. *Journal of the Royal Statistical Society*, vol. LVI, pt IV, 1893, pp. 557-93.

Table 12.6

DISTRIBUTION OF THE POPULATION OF LONDON BY CLASS AND DEGREE OF CROWDING, 1889 and 1891

Class			Degree of crowding (excluding institutional population)		
	Number of persons	% of population		Number of persons	% of population
Very poor and poor			Crowded		
A and B	354 444	8.4	4 or more more per room	187 921	4.6
C and D	938 293	22.3	3 to 4 per room	304 449	7.4
Total	1 292 737	30.7	2 to 3 per room	801 702	19.5
			Total	1 294 072	31.5
			Not crowded	2 821 034	68.5
Comfortable					
E and F	2 166 503	51.5			
G and H	749 930	17.8			
Total	2 916 433	69.3			
All classes	4 209 170	100.0	All categories	4 115 106	100.0
Inmates of institutions	99 830	–	Inmates of institutions		
			Barracks and merchant ships	17 312	–
			Hospitals, workhouses etc.	79 325	–
			Total	96 637	–
Total population	4 309 000*		Total population	4 211 743§	

* Booth's estimate for 1889.

§ 1891 census.

Source: Charles Booth, 'Inquiry based on the 1891 census', *JRSS*, vol. LVI, pp. 565-6.

for all the districts, some of which showed considerable discrepancies between crowding and poverty, as can be seen from table 12.7.

Table 12.7
CROWDING *VERSUS* POVERTY: THE TWO MEASURES COMPARED OVER DISTRICTS. LONDON *c.* 1890

Registration District	Crowding	Poverty	Difference
			Excess of crowding over poverty
St. Giles	47.0	27.0	20.0
Whitechapel	55.5	39.0	16.5
Strand	38.0	24.0	14.0
Marylebone	41.5	27.5	14.0
St. Pancras	42.5	30.0	12.5
Shoreditch	50.5	40.0	10.5
St. George's in the East	59.5	49.0	10.5
Mile End Old Town	35.0	26.0	9.0
St. George's, Hanover Sq.	29.5	21.5	8.0
Holborn	56.5	49.0	7.5
Chelsea	32.0	24.5	7.5
Paddington	27.5	21.5	6.0
Westminster	40.0	35.0	5.0
Bethnal Green	49.5	45.0	4.5
Stepney	41.0	38.0	3.0
Hampstead	16.5	13.5	3.0
Kensington	26.5	25.0	1.5
Islington	32.0	31.0	1.0
Lambeth	27.0	26.0	1.0
Fulham	25.5	25.0	0.5
St. Saviour's	44.0	43.5	0.5
			Excess of poverty over crowding
City	30.0	31.0	1.0
Hackney	19.0	23.0	4.0
Woolwich	20.5	25.0	4.5
St. Olave's	36.5	42.0	5.5
Poplar	30.5	37.0	6.5
Wandsworth	17.5	27.0	9.5
Camberwell	18.5	29.0	10.5
Lewisham	7.0	18.0	11.0
Greenwich	19.5	36.0	16.5

Source: Charles Booth, 'Inquiry based on the 1891 census', *JRSS*, vol. LVI, p. 567.

In this table the districts are the same as those in table 12.2 facing p. 354 above but rearranged in order of discrepancy. Thus in St. Giles there is far more crowding than poverty, in Fulham the two measures are almost the same, and in Greenwich there is far more poverty than crowding.

There were many reasons for these differences. The historical location of many London trades and the need to live near your place of work: in central districts such as St. Giles and the Strand there was no lack of good jobs, and many of the people living in crowded conditions were not poor. The heterogeneity of the city's population, composed partly of born Londoners, partly of immigrants from the country and partly of immigrants from Ireland and the Continent, especially Italy and Poland: these different groups set different values on space and fresh air compared with other objects of expenditure. The different levels of rent for comparable accommodation in different parts of the city and especially between the inner and outer ring: in Greenwich there was much poverty but there was also plenty of space and the rents were low. The changing character of the housing available in different areas: everywhere rows of modest but quite decent workmen's houses were being demolished to make room for expensive residences and the poorer inhabitants had to squeeze in somewhere else as best they could. And so on.

If one looked at the districts in greater detail, however, one found, even in the more affluent ones, blocks or whole streets of run-down tenements in which poverty and crowding went hand in hand. After a thorough overhaul of each district Booth came to the conclusion that in spite of the anomalies described above 'the two investigations confirm each other, and rather gather strength from close comparison'.

He returned to this point two years later in the introduction to the industry inquiry. Referring to the figures in table 12.6 he says:

'A man and his wife and one child, or a widow with two children, may occupy only one room; or a family of six or seven may have only two rooms; and yet not be "very poor" in the sense of suffering "chronic want". But when four or more persons live in one room or eight or more in two rooms, there must be great discomfort, and want of sufficient food, clothing, and firing must be a frequent incident. I have, therefore, drawn a line at this point, and find 188,000 people who are undoubtedly very poor. Further, of the 300,000 people who live three or from three to four in a room, it may be that half would correctly be placed in the same category. If so, we have about 340,000 in all of "very poor" amongst the crowded, a number which compares closely with the 350,000 of the old classification.'

In looking at table 12.6 it must be remembered that one room meant just that: one room. There was no question of separate kitchen or washplace, though in some tenements there may have been communal facilities. It will come as a surprise to many people that a hundred years ago over 30 per cent of Londoners lived under such conditions. It certainly came as a surprise to Booth's readers.

7. The Industry Inquiry

The industry inquiry, which occupies volumes V to IX of *Life and Labour*, came out between 1895 and 1897. It was based on the census of 1891 and so, in attempting a social classification of families engaged in different trades, Booth adopted his crowding measure, supplemented in the case of the better-off by a measure based on the number of servants in the household. The poverty measure was now somewhat out of date and it would have been impracticable to apply it. As to servants, he considered that 'although the number of servants kept is no certain test of wealth, it is at any rate a very fair test of expenditure, and an almost absolute test of the style of life'.

The industry volumes are organised around a classification of the population by occupations or trades grouped into industries as far as this was possible from the census returns. Two enumerations are used, one by type of activity and the other by families. Eighty-eight occupational categories are distinguished for the active population and to these is added a large, heterogeneous category which Booth terms 'the unoccupied classes' but which I shall call 'the inactive' to avoid confusion with the term 'unoccupied' which he also uses to describe housewives, young children and other family members who do not have a job. Just as there are unoccupied members of active families so there are occupied members of inactive families. The inactive families are largely to be found among the wealthy and the very poor.

The industrial enumeration gives the total number of individuals engaged in each type of activity, divided into employers, employees and own-account workers, irrespective of family connection. Males and females are distinguished and some information is given on their age and on their distribution over London districts. The unoccupied population is lumped together in one undifferentiated group, the only distinctions being sex and age (10+ and under 10).

In the family enumeration family members are divided into 'heads', 'others occupied' and 'unoccupied', the families being grouped according to the activity of the head. We do not know the activities in which the 'others occupied' are engaged but we are not likely to go very wrong if, following Booth, we assume that most of them would be working in the same trade as that of the head of their family and only the surplus would be working in other trades. On this assumption, the difference between the total number engaged in a given activity and the number of occupied family members shows whether, on balance, these families supply labour to other activities or are supplemented by labour from others. The family picture is completed by Booth's social indicators based on number of servants and crowding. People without a household of their own, namely inmates of institutions and caretakers of empty houses, are entered separately.

Table 12.8 is a compressed version of Booth's double tabulation. Reading along the rows, the sum of the two first entries shows the total number of people engaged in a given activity. The third entry, if positive, shows the excess of occupied family members over the total number working in that activity; if negative, it shows the number of workers coming into it from other family groups. Thus the sum of these three entries gives the number of occupied family members irrespective of trade. Taking row 1, for instance, we find 3,680+2,258=5,938 people engaged in architecture and civil engineering and 806 engaged in other

Table 12.8

DISTRIBUTION OF THE POPULATION OF LONDON OVER ACTIVITIES AND OVER HOUSEHOLDS, 1891

Occupational category of family head	Heads of families	Others in same activity (irrespective of family)	Occupied outside own family	Unoccupied	All family members (including lodgers)	Servants	All household members	Percentage crowded
	1	2	3	4	5	6	7	8
Building trades								
1 Architects, civil engineers etc.	3 680	2 258	806	9 041	15 785	3 461	19 246	4.0
2 Builders and builders' labourers	6 871	1 995	5 826	19 611	34 303	1 510	35 813	19.0
3 Masons, slaters and tilers	4 750	1 742	2 896	13 502	22 890	106	22 996	46.0
4 Bricklayers	14 330	5 097	7 927	40 257	67 611	85	67 696	54.0
5 Carpenters and joiners	24 805	9 689	13 450	67 009	114 953	568	115 521	31.0
6 Plasterers and paperhangers	5 111	1 780	3 203	14 848	24 942	46	24 988	51.0
7 Painters and glaziers	22 982	9 684	10 927	61 924	105 517	439	105 956	49.0
8 Plumbers	5 141	4 205	-84	14 794	24 056	142	24 198	36.0
9 Locksmiths, gasfitters etc.	3 492	1 820	1 394	9 672	16 378	113	16 491	40.0
Totals	91 162	38 270	46 345	250 658	426 435	6 470	432 905	–
Woodworkers								
10 Cabinet makers, upholsterers etc.	29 617	22 995	7 134	77 527	137 273	1 420	138 693	45.0
11 Carriage builders	6 276	3 332	2 637	16 600	28 845	257	29 102	37.0
12 Coopers etc.	2 571	1 024	1 883	6 913	12 391	54	12 445	36.0
13 Shipwrights, barge and boat builders	1 704	556	1 359	4 616	8 235	62	8 297	22.0
Totals	40 168	27 907	13 013	105 656	186 744	1 793	188 537	–

Table 12.8 continued

Occupational category of family head	Heads of families	Others in same activity (irrespective of family)	Occupied outside own family	Unoccupied	All family members (including lodgers)	Servants	All household members	Percentage crowded
	1	2	3	4	5	6	7	8
Metal workers								
14 Engineering, iron shipbuilding etc.	15 484	9 510	4 152	42 373	71 519	882	72 401	27.0
15 Blacksmiths, gunsmiths etc.	8 189	4 078	3 611	22 820	38 698	130	38 828	42.0
16 Other workers in iron and steel	6 561	4 133	1 926	18 228	30 848	444	31 292	38.0
17 Workers in other metals	9 524	7 736	780	26 458	44 498	552	45 050	43.0
Totals	39 758	25 457	10 469	109 879	185 563	2 008	187 571	–
Precious metals, watches and instruments								
18 Jewellers, gold and silver smiths etc.	4 588	4 055	579	11 400	20 622	1 101	21 723	22.0
19 Watches and clocks	2 693	1 588	1 296	6 197	11 774	381	12 155	21.0
20 Scientific and electrical instruments	4 150	4 108	-791	10 455	17 922	593	18 515	26.0
21 Musical instruments, toys etc.	5 459	4 948	380	13 899	24 686	469	25 155	32.0
Totals	16 890	14 699	1 464	41 951	75 004	2 544	77 548	–
Sundry manufacturers								
22 Glass, china and earthenware	2 498	2 473	-327	6 842	11 486	179	11 665	47.0
23 Chemicals etc.	2 285	3 551	-1 441	5 927	10 322	570	10 892	29.0
24 Soap, candles, glue etc.	1 056	1 139	-102	2 646	4 739	207	4 946	29.0
25 Leather dressing, tanning etc.	8 076	7 663	567	21 188	37 494	862	38 356	29.0
26 Saddlery, harness etc.	2 342	1 535	746	5 827	10 450	128	10 578	34.0
27 Brush making	2 470	3 071	-273	5 817	11 085	130	11 215	40.0
Totals	18 727	19 432	-830	48 247	85 576	2 076	87 652	–

Table 12.8 continued

Occupational category of family head	Heads of families	Others in same activity (irrespective of family)	Occupied outside own family	Unoccupied	All family members (including lodgers)	Servants	All household members	Percentage crowded
	1	2	3	4	5	6	7	8
Printing and paper								
28 Printers	18 048	22 001	-5 941	47 257	81 365	854	82 219	34.0
29 Bookbinders	4 289	11 563	-7 262	9 527	18 117	124	18 241	41.0
30 Paper manufacturers	3 008	11 711	-8 653	6 241	12 307	251	12 558	49.0
31 Stationers	3 423	5 460	-1 904	7 920	14 899	857	15 756	17.0
32 Booksellers and newsagents	4 386	3 394	767	10 099	18 646	1 436	20 082	15.0
Totals	33 154	54 129	-22 993	81 044	145 334	3 522	148 856	–
Textiles								
33 Silk and fancy textiles	1 764	3 047	-915	2 807	6 703	331	7 034	27.0
34 Woollens, carpets etc.	1 076	1 624	-481	2 358	4 577	147	4 724	45.0
35 Dyers and cleaners	896	1 050	-27	2 095	4 014	112	4 126	28.0
36 Hemp, jute and fibre	1 424	1 917	-282	3 235	6 294	97	6 391	47.0
37 Indiarubber, floor cloths etc.	1 386	1 688	-357	3 607	6 324	216	6 540	33.0
Totals	6 546	9 326	-2 062	14 102	27 912	903	28 815	–

Table 12.8 continued

Occupational category of family head	Heads of families	Others in same activity (irrespective of family)	Occupied outside own family	Unoccupied	All family members (including lodgers)	Servants	All household members	Percentage crowded
	1	2	3	4	5	6	7	8
Clothing and footwear								
38 Tailors	21 403	30 943	-7 589	45 389	90 146	1 730	91 876	40.0
39 Boot and shoe makers	21 151	17 838	4 636	52 083	95 708	906	96 614	45.0
40 Hatters	2 253	3 228	-859	4 971	9 593	234	9 827	30.0
41 Dressmakers and milliners	15 840	67 608	-51 996	10 763	42 215	1 489	43 704	24.0
42 Seamstresses, shirtmakers etc.	7 249	11 238	-5 845	4 527	17 169	157	17 326	36.0
43 Machinists	1 939	8 724	-7 107	3 135	6 691	24	6 715	43.0
44 Trimming, umbrellas etc.	5 571	14 107	-8 016	10 219	21 881	686	22 567	36.0
45 Drapers, hosiers, silk mercers etc.	7 241	23 685	-14 929	15 288	31 285	3 092	34 377	10.0
Totals	82 647	177 371	-91 705	146 375	314 688	8 318	323 006	–
Food, drink and tobacco								
46 Millers, sugar refiners etc.	1 231	1 089	15	3 251	5 586	228	5 814	34.0
47 Brewers, mineral-water makers etc.	2 803	1 593	865	7 600	12 861	505	13 366	37.5
48 Tobacco manufacturers and tobacconists	4 143	5 485	-1 148	10 286	18 766	678	19 444	33.0
49 Bakers and confectioners	11 090	14 668	-1 670	27 449	51 537	1 490	53 027	26.0
50 Milk sellers	5 407	4 762	385	14 271	24 825	713	25 538	22.0
51 Butchers and fishmongers	16 248	12 389	3 449	44 589	76 675	3 735	80 410	23.5
52 Grocers, oil and colour-men	15 870	15 661	853	39 345	71 729	3 299	75 028	15.5
53 Publicans	11 050	3 941	14 141	26 066	55 198	6 011	61 209	10.0
54 Lodging and coffee house keepers etc.	8 107	2 897	13 527	12 720	37 251	5 610	42 861	5.0
Totals	75 949	62 485	30 417	185 577	354 428	22 269	376 697	–

Table 12.8 continued

Occupational category of family head	Heads of families 1	Others in same activity (irrespective of family) 2	Occupied outside own family 3	Unoccupied 4	All family members (including lodgers) 5	Servants 6	All household members 7	Percentage crowded 8
General dealers and businessmen								
55 Ironmongers, glass and china dealers	4 724	4 440	750	11 307	21 221	1 726	22 947	15.0
56 Corn, wood and coal dealers	4 360	2 204	2 217	11 603	20 384	1 604	21 988	18.5
57 General shopkeepers	7 137	7 104	482	16 521	31 244	503	31 747	40.0
58 Costermongers	5 825	7 035	-1 218	12 053	23 695	65	23 760	65.0
59 Bankers, merchants, brokers etc.	13 278	6 714	5 308	32 912	58 212	13 722	71 934	6.0
60 Commercial clerks	40 737	67 686	-35 416	96 772	169 779	11 810	181 589	10.0
Totals	76 061	95 183	-27 877	181 168	324 535	29 430	353 965	–
Transport, gardeners etc.								
61 Cabmen, coachmen, omnibus drivers etc.	32 588	15 617	10 300	85 147	143 652	585	144 237	46.0
62 Carriers	25 248	18 553	2 260	70 968	117 029	230	117 259	56.0
63 Railway service	15 357	9 397	3 764	41 976	70 494	518	71 012	28.0
64 Railway labour	2 567	930	1 456	6 810	11 763	53	11 816	42.0
65 Gardeners etc.	7 615	4 478	2 503	17 951	32 547	491	33 038	23.5
66 Country labour	2 270	1 504	664	5 988	10 426	307	10 733	39.0
67 Seamen and fishermen	3 592	8 482	-5 478	8 648	15 244	589	15 833	30.5
68 Watermen and lightermen	4 079	1 972	1 684	11 703	19 438	128	19 566	35.0
Totals	93 316	60 933	17 153	249 191	420 593	2 901	423 494	–

Table 12.8 continued

Occupational category of family head	Heads of families	Others in same activity (irrespective of family)	Occupied outside own family	Unoccupied	All family members (including lodgers)	Servants	All household members	Percentage crowded
	1	2	3	4	5	6	7	8
Labourers								
69 Dock and wharf service	1 620	476	1 095	4 702	7 893	249	8 142	25.0
70 Dock labourers	9 602	4 960	3 432	25 383	43 377	20	43 397	62.5
71 Coal porters	3 243	1 594	996	9 652	15 485	14	15 499	64.0
72 Gaswork service	4 358	1 511	2 067	13 155	21 091	72	21 163	44.0
73 Warehousemen	17 715	45 841	-29 910	42 153	75 799	473	76 272	45.0
74 General labourers	44 551	35 196	2 495	117 430	199 672	103	199 775	58.5
75 Factory labourers	3 544	5 087	-2 111	9 160	15 680	10	15 690	41.5
76 Artisans and engine-men n.e.s.	9 700	8 332	557	26 520	45 109	281	45 390	37.0
Totals	94 333	102 997	-21 379	248 155	424 106	1 222	425 328	–
Public service and professional								
77 Civil and municipal service	13 518	13 707	-2 557	34 026	58 694	4 979	63 673	14.0
78 Waterworks and municipal labour	3 669	1 240	2 246	9 374	16 529	64	16 593	53.0
79 Police and prisons	8 577	3 690	1 589	25 374	39 230	179	39 409	26.0
80 Army and navy (officers and men)	3 867	11 979	-9 827	8 299	14 318	5 653	19 971	10.5
81 Law: barristers, solicitors and clerks	7 755	6 816	-962	17 787	31 396	8 030	39 426	5.0
82 Medicine: doctors, nurses, chemists etc.	11 028	15 480	-5 653	16 916	37 771	7 759	45 530	12.5
83 Art and amusement	9 968	14 275	-5 745	18 555	37 053	3 069	40 122	19.0
84 Literature and science	2 636	1 861	126	5 436	10 059	1 610	11 669	7.0
85 Education	6 540	21 021	-14 024	11 152	24 689	2 648	27 337	5.0
86 Religion	4 728	3 869	1 159	9 479	19 235	3 830	23 065	6.0
Totals	72 286	93 938	-33 648	156 398	288 974	37 821	326 795	–

Table 12.8 concluded

Occupational category of family head	Heads of families	Others in same activity (irrespective of family)	Occupied outside own family	Unoccupied	All family members (including lodgers)	Servants	All household members	Percentage crowded
	1	2	3	4	5	6	7	8
Domestic service								
87 Domestic servants	19 224*	286 938	-271 445	34 709	69 426*	1 027	70 453	38.5
88 Extra services	39 668	53 348	-10 857	45 085	127 244	886	128 130	40.5
Totals	58 892	340 286	-282 302	79 794	196 670	1 913	198 583	–
Inactive								
89 Own means, pensioners, students, gypsies etc.	126 877	1 206 796	-1 104 587	162 466	391 552	63 511	455 063	14.0
All occupations in census	926 766	2 329 209	-1 468 522	2 060 661	3 848 114	186 701	4 034 815	–
Inmates of institutions etc.								
Hotels and lodging houses	–	–	–	–	–	–	45 813	–
Shops (employees living on premises)	–	–	–	–	–	–	15 321	–
Barracks and merchant ships	–	–	–	–	–	–	17 312	–
Hospitals, workhouses, prisons etc.	–	–	–	–	–	–	79 325	–
Institutional servants	–	–	–	–	–	–	9 633	–
Total	–	–	–	–	–	–	167 404	–
Servants in charge of empty houses	–	–	–	–	–	–	9 524	–
Total population	–	–	–	–	–	–	4 211 743	–

* Includes only those who have homes of their own. The others are enumerated with the families they serve.

Source: Charles Booth, *Life and Labour*, 2nd edn, vols. V–VIII, *passim*.

activities, which gives 5,938+806=6,744 occupied persons in that group of families. By adding the 9,041 unoccupied we obtain the total of family members, 15,785; and by adding the 3,461 servants we obtain the total of household members. In this group of families, which contains the upper rungs of the building trade, the proportion of servants is high and the proportion living in crowded conditions, 4 per cent, is low. By contrast, if we look at row 8 we find 5,141+4,205=9,346 plumbers, of whom 84 come from other family groups, so the total number occupied in plumbers' families is 9,346−84=9,262. Adding the unoccupied and the servants we obtain 9,262+14,794+146=24,198 household members. In this case the number of servants not surprisingly, is very small and the crowding index, 36 per cent, very high.

Although the family groups are not at all homogeneous as regards living standards, being composed of people working in different trades and at different levels within trades, it is clear that crowding varied immensely over trades. Table 12.9 shows its extent in the twenty most crowded occupational groups.

As we saw in table 12.6, the mean of this distribution is 31.5 per cent, much lower than the most common percentage which is around 45. Booth would have liked a quantitative explanation of this phenomenon but, apart from the fact that multiple regression analysis was only in its infancy, the real difficulty lay in assembling the necessary data. He collected what information he could on representative earnings and working time in different trades but there were many allowances to be made: the cost of tools supplied by the workmen, the cost of the journey to work, the level of rents in different neighbourhoods. Then there were the character of the parents and the possibility of supplementing the income of the chief earners to be considered. All these complications did not prevent him from giving a good qualitative account of the phenomena he was studying but made a rigorous quantitative analysis virtually impossible.

Table 12.9

THE TWENTY MOST CROWDED OCCUPATIONAL GROUPS, LONDON 1891

Booth's section number	Occupational category of family head	All household members	Percentage living in inner ring	Percentage of crowding		
				Inner ring	Outer ring	All London
58	Costermongers	23 760	63.5	71.0	55.0	65.2
71	Coal porters	15 499	34.4	74.0	59.0	63.9
70	Dock labourers	43 397	64.5	63.0	61.0	62.4
74	General labourers	199 775	37.2	70.0	51.5	58.5
62	Carriers	117 259	49.8	62.0	50.0	56.6
4	Bricklayers	67 696	30.6	66.0	48.0	53.7
78	Waterworks and municipal labour	16 593	36.6	64.0	47.0	53.1
6	Plasterers and paper-hangers	24 988	22.3	62.0	48.0	50.8
30	Paper manufacturers	12 558	60.5	61.0	30.0	49.0
7	Painters and glaziers	105 956	30.7	59.0	44.0	48.8
36	Hemp, jute and fibre workers	6 391	61.9	55.0	34.0	46.8
61	Cabmen, coachmen etc.	144 237	34.5	54.5	41.0	45.7
3	Masons, slaters and tilers	22 996	33.0	60.0	39.0	45.7
10	Cabinet makers, upholsterers etc.	138 693	56.2	55.0	33.0	45.3
73	Warehousemen and messengers	76 272	57.4	53.0	34.0	45.2
34	Workers in woollens, carpets etc.	4 724	58.7	55.0	30.0	44.9
39	Boot and shoe makers	96 614	54.9	56.0	31.0	44.8
72	Gasworks service	21 163	24.4	54.5	40.0	43.8
22	Glass and earthenware workers	11 665	52.2	57.0	28.0	43.2
17	Workers in other [non-ferrous] metals	45 050	49.0	52.0	34.0	42.7

Source: Charles Booth, *Life and Labour*, 2nd edn, vols v-viii, *passim*.

8. The Work as a Whole

In my account of Booth's great work I have concentrated on its statistical side, trying to bring out its essential points. Even so, what I have shown is only the tip of the iceberg. Every aspect of the survey is illustrated by table after table of extremely detailed data; and accompanying them there is an immense amount of descriptive and anecdotal material of which I can give only the briefest indication.

The poverty series occupies four volumes, and the subtitle of the first two, 'London street by street', speaks for itself. In his introductory chapter Booth says, referring to the East End: 'The 46 books of our notes contain no less than 3,400 streets or places, and every house and every family with school children is noted, with such information as the [School-Board] visitors could give about them'. The same source was used for the rest of London. For information on the households that were outside the purview of the visitors there were the parish clergy, the police, a number of independent social workers such as Octavia Hill, Booth's team of assistants and of course Booth himself, indefatigably tramping the streets. He visited a good many houses when he was working on the East End but when the inquiry spread to the whole of London, rather more than four million people, he had to content himself with a more impressionistic treatment. In his own words,

> 'In dealing with East London (and afterwards with Central London and Battersea) the unit taken was the family. In extending over the larger area the street has been substituted as a working basis. Instead of noting the number of children going to school from each household with the employment and social position of its head, we have contented ourselves with stating the number of the children street by street, dividing them as to class according to what is known of the parents, but giving only general particulars of the occupations.'

In the end every street in London was recorded with its salient characteristics, and Booth complemented his verbal and numerical descriptions with a set of street maps coloured according to the social condition of the residents. Like Florence Nightingale, he believed in the efficacy of the visual impact. The colours go from black for the destitute (class A) to yellow for the well-to-do (classes G and H), passing through dark blue (B), light blue (C), mauve (D), pink (E) and red (F). In streets of a mixed character the colours are laid in stripes.

Booth was shaken by his findings. In commenting on them he says:

'My own ideas on this subject have taken shape gradually in the course of my work. In beginning my inquiry I had no preconceived ideas, no theory to work up to, no pet scheme into agreement with which the facts collected were to be twisted or to which they would have to be squared. At the same time the consideration and the hope of remedies have never been out of my mind.

The state of things which I describe in these pages, though not so appalling as sensational writers would have us believe, is still bad enough to make us feel that we ought not to tolerate it in our midst if we can think of any feasible remedy . . . The difficulties, which are certainly great, do not lie in the cost. As it is these unfortunate people cost the community one way or another considerably more than they contribute. I do not refer solely to the fact that they cost the State more than they pay directly or indirectly in taxes. I mean that altogether, ill-paid and half-starved as they are, they consume or waste or have expended on them more wealth than they create.

What I have to propose may be considered as an extension of the Poor Law. What is the Poor Law system? It is a limited form of Socialism – a Socialistic community . . . living in the midst of an Individualist nation . . . My idea is to make the dual system, Socialism in the arms of Individualism, under which we already live, more efficient by extending somewhat the sphere of the former and making the division of function more distinct. Our Individualism fails because our Socialism is incomplete.'

What he advocates is not the dole but a system of State training and employment which would do away with one of the principal causes of indigence and demoralisation, irregular earnings. Given security of employment, the lowest classes would gradually 'be pushed upwards into self-supporting habits', with beneficial repercussions all up the scale, since 'improved *morale* of labour would go hand in hand with better organisation of industry'. *Mutatis mutandis*, we might be listening to Petty.

Volume III, to which six of Booth's assistants contributed besides himself, is devoted to what Booth calls special subjects. The first chapter deals with housing blocks, grouped under four headings: (i) belonging to philanthropic associations, (ii) belonging to large property owners, mainly commercial, (iii) belonging to private (often anonymous) landlords, and (iv) erected by employers for their workpeople. Each group is assessed in terms of light and air, sanitation, and class of residents; the group that gets the lowest mark for sanitation is group (iii).

The next three chapters deal with immigration, including an interesting account of the East End Jews, who 'in the midst of the chaotic elements of East London' constituted a closely knit community with a distinct religious and social life of its own; there were between 60 and 70,000 of them, and about half were recent immigrants from Russia and Poland. The volume ends with three chapters on education, of which I have given a sample in section 5 above.

Volume IV, again by a variety of authors, is a sort of prelude to the industry inquiry, focusing specifically on the trades of East London. The reasons for this selective treatment are given by Booth in an introductory note:

'In dealing with East London we have found some of the local employments to be so characteristic of the life of that part of London, and a knowledge of their conditions so necessary to the consideration of the evils called "sweating", that we have devoted separate articles to them . . . No such case exists for dividing other districts of London industrially from the Metropolis.'

The trades in question are dock labour, tailoring, bootmaking, the furniture trade, tobacco manufacturing and silk weaving. The authors describe minutely the nature of the work and the skills required in each occupation, the way in which the various trades were organised, the growth of trade unions, and the information they were able to obtain on earnings and hours. The volume ends with a chapter on women's work and a final chapter on sweating. We are told by Booth that these descriptions relate to the period immediately preceding the strikes of 1889-90, which brought about some changes for the better. By the time he embarked on the much wider industry inquiry things had improved, as is clear from comparing the chapters in this volume with the corresponding chapters in the later ones.

The industry series comprises five volumes. In volumes V to VIII each of the eighty-nine occupational groups distinguished in table 12.8 above gets a chapter to itself; every chapter opens with a set of statistics, which is followed by a description of working conditions, methods of production, character of the labour force etc. in each of the trades of which that group is composed. Volume IX is in three parts. The first summarises the statistics of the eighty-nine groups in a series of comparative tables. The second consists of an abstract of the contents of all the preceding volumes. And in the third Booth surveys the London industrial scene as a whole. Among other topics there is an interesting analysis of the trade unions, a comparison of large and small enterprises, and a chapter on 'industrial remedies'. The measures he would like to see implemented are: improved education, 'the basis of industrial reform'; raising the age of legal employment; restriction of the casual employment of the young; discontinuing the employment of young mothers, 'on the example given by poor Jewesses'; and the registration and inspection of workshops. He is also strongly in favour of co-operation and copartnership. As agents of remedial action he lists employers and wage earners, Parliament, central and local government, consumers, and public opinion, in that order.

A third series of seven volumes discusses religious and moral influences, to which Booth, 'a respectful agnostic' as he described himself, attached great importance. They are essentially studies of institutions and attitudes, leading to the conclusion that religion played only a small part in the lives of the majority of the people.

There is a final volume, the seventeenth, which is really a collection of odds and ends, some of them quite interesting: the spread of London and the problems it gave rise to, pubs and drinking habits, prostitution, crime and the police, public administration, philanthropic organisations, and so on. As Booth says, it would have taken him at least another three years and another three volumes to develop these subjects properly, which would have taxed the patience of the public to say nothing of his own. In his concluding section he looks at the improvements that had taken place since the inception of his survey, improvements which he attributes to the growing number of individuals and institutions actively interested in reform. Much remained to be done, but the book ends on a hopeful note.

Booth was aware that his work provided a static picture: he was concerned with things as they are. 'I have not undertaken', he wrote, 'to investigate how they came to be so, nor, except incidentally, to indicate whither they are tending'. Fortunately, at the end of the 1920's the London School of Economics instituted a *New Survey of London Life and Labour*[1] directed by Hubert Llewellyn-Smith, a nephew of Booth's who had assisted him in the original inquiry. Among the people who helped Llewellyn-Smith was Arthur Bowley, who had done so much to advance the theory and practice of sample surveys.

Stylistically the seventeen volumes of the Booth inquiry, though the work of many people, are remarkably uniform. One senses a firm editorial hand holding the reins. Booth disliked sensationalism: however grim the subject matter, it is presented in a straightforward, factual way and is all the more convincing for it. A passage from volume I is a good indication of his attitude:

> 'East London lay hidden from view behind a curtain on which were painted terrible pictures: – Starving children, suffering women, overworked men; horrors of drunkenness and vice; monsters and demons of inhumanity; giants of disease and despair. Did these pictures truly represent what lay behind, or did they bear to the facts a relation similar to that which the pictures outside a booth at some country fair bear to the performance or show within? This curtain we have tried to lift.'

He did lift it, and there can be little doubt that many of the reforms of the last hundred years were inspired by the state of affairs he so painstakingly delineated.

Booth did not allow himself to be sidetracked into trying to answer the question of whether 'the hen of theorising preceded or followed the egg of fact-finding'. He contented himself with the reflection, 'I think Political Economy needs badly to step

1. 9 vols., P. S. King London, 1930-35.

back just now – we have too many hasty deductions and too much cutting out of complicating considerations – which are never cut in nature'. At the end of the day the object of studying society is to understand it better and so 'make it more possible than it is now to avoid the wrong and choose the right path onward'.

William Petty and the others I have been talking about would have agreed with this sentiment.

COMMENTS

PHYLLIS DEANE*

Let me begin by confessing that I have a very personal reason for feeling happy as well as privileged to be assigned the role of a discussant at Sir Richard Stone's lectures in this series. For he – who is now the leading English political arithmetician, arguably the most distinguished of those who have followed the tradition started by Sir William Petty – was one of the research advisers who first set me to work in that area four and a half decades ago. It was then that I began to apply to underdeveloped countries the system of social accounting which Richard Stone and James Meade had devised for the United Kingdom economy under the inspiration of J. M. Keynes. After the war when I joined the Cambridge Department of Applied Economics, of which Richard Stone was the first Director, he was again my mentor and the most fertile source of stimulating research ideas. It will surprise no one who has had the good fortune to collaborate with Dick Stone that the work on Gregory King's national income estimates to which he has referred in his first lecture as 'Professor Deane's work' is as much due to him as to me. Nor will it surprise any of his colleagues that he has now, on coming back to this subject in 1986, 'stuck his neck out' and further developed the social accounts based on King's estimates. It is worth noting that Richard Stone has never had any inclination to 'privatise' his own contributions to the advancement of knowledge. In this he has more in common with the seventeenth- and eighteenth-century political arithmeticians than with many of their twentieth-century descendants, who seem often to be more concerned to copyright their academic achievements than to share them with the rest of the world.

My own contribution to the debate today will take the form of some brief observations inspired by Richard Stone's lectures, focusing on three general aspects of the creation and evolution of the tradition of political arithmetic: first the Baconian heritage, second the connection between political arithmetic and political economy, and third the contribution of early political arithmeticians to modern economic history.

* Emeritus Professor of Economic History, University of Cambridge.

1. *The Baconian Heritage*

During the scientific revolution of the seventeenth century, those who were concerned with the social and economic problems faced by governments of expanding mercantile economies were inspired by the intellectual vision of scholar-statesmen such as Francis Bacon, and brilliant natural scientists such as Galileo, to attempt a disciplined advancement of basic economic knowledge. Richard Stone has emphasised Petty's Baconian attitude to understanding the world we live in and indeed all the early political arithmeticians were deeply committed to the Baconian scientific method, though Petty was perhaps the most explicit in his acknowledgments to Bacon.

What fired the imagination of English Restoration scientists about Bacon's approach to scientific method were essentially three things. *First* there was his rejection of dogmatism and ritualism and his rousing calls for a new start: e.g. 'We must begin anew from the very foundations, unless we revolve for ever in a circle with mean and contemptible progress.' *Second* there was his vision of a broad collaborative research programme in which the various seekers after truth – among whom he distinguished the ant-like collectors of facts, the spider-like theorists and the bee-like analysts (late nineteenth-century economists such as Alfred Marshall liked to think of themselves as the bees) – would each make their vital contribution to the cumulative advancement of knowledge about the universe. *Third* there was his clear moral vision of the goals of the research enterprise, his confidence that the knowledge thus amassed would serve not only God (by decoding the divine book of nature) but also man (by revealing ways of bettering his material conditions of life). In effect, those who were concerned with questions of what was later called political economy felt themselves to be part of the same collective research project as the natural scientists.

The late seventeenth century was an age in which the educated elite – natural scientists, philosophers, bankers, merchants, theologians and public officials – called increasingly for empirical evidence on economic problems (particularly statistical data) and habitually sought advice on such questions from a broad spectrum of scientists, philosophers and other informed observers. In this climate of opinion it was not surprising that the rational, calculating, empirical techniques of analysis that were yielding such exciting new research results in the natural sciences came to be applied to the study of society – especially since it was practising natural scientists such as Petty who were among the first to undertake systematic research on socio-economic policy issues. Petty indeed was a forerunner of the modern breed of economic adviser. His essays were addressed to contemporary policy-makers, claimed to be politically neutral, and justified their prescriptions in terms of the *national* interest rather than in terms of the interests of particular social groups. His pamphlet, containing the first-ever estimates of the national income of England and Wales, was written during the 1665-67 war with Holland and focused on the practical problems of financing the nation's war effort. I find myself irresistibly reminded of the famous official British White Paper, *An Analysis of the Sources of War Finance and an Estimate of the National Income and Expenditure in 1938, 1940 and 1941* Cmd. 6347, April 1942, which contained the first estimates of United Kingdom social accounts; for this was the first in an annual series of papers produced by Richard Stone and his team at the U. K. Central Statistical Office, in order to inform Parliament and the whole nation of the calculations on which the British Chancellor's war budgets were based.

2. *Political Arithmetic and Political Economy*

Most of Petty's pamphlets on economic matters were circulated privately in manuscript and published posthumously; for the second half of the seventeenth century was an era in which giving politico-economic advice to governments was a hazardous occupation and was best done discreetly. Their common message, however, concerning the importance of basing economic policies on empirical evidence and on reasoned quantitative assessments of the nation's human and material resources was wholly in tune with the spirit of the age. It was Petty's friend

John Graunt, for example, the London draper, who took the first steps towards the modern science of demography by applying a logical technique of coordination and deduction to the few vital statistics that had been collected over the preceding century. His aim was to produce the first reasoned estimates of total population not only for the metropolis but for the country as a whole. So impressed were the Fellows of the newly created Royal Society by his pamphlet that they welcomed him to their select fellowhip in 1662, within a month of publication of the first edition. In so doing they earned the hearty approval of their royal patron Charles II who (according to Sprat, their first secretary and historian) 'gave his particular charge to His Society, that if they found any more such tradesmen, they should be sure to admit them all without more ado.' In the event, it was Graunt rather than Petty who inspired Gregory King's demographic estimates in the 1690s, for Petty's way with statistics was impressionistic and sometimes careless. Graunt and King, on the other hand, were methodical as well as ingenious in compiling and testing their estimates against alternative sources of evidence and were undoubtedly better statisticians than Petty. To modern economic historians, wishing to make use of seventeenth-century estimates of national income and wealth, Gregory King's results seem more carefully justified, more internally consistent and hence more convincing as indicators of the economic dimensions of England and its rivals in war or in commerce than Petty's figures.

Nevertheless it was Petty's imaginative and ambitious deployment of his estimates as bases for economic analysis and policy prescription that earned him his enduring reputation as the leading political arithmetician. By the same token, it is doubtful whether Gregory King's national income estimates would have had a more than ephemeral currency had they not been dramatically and analytically deployed by the Tory pamphleteer Charles Davenant. More significant, however, than the explicit or implicit degree of political bias displayed by the early political arithmeticians was that they – particularly Graunt, Petty, King and Davenant – effectively constituted an informal team engaged in the first research programme in applied economics.

Accordingly, the problem of whether Petty or Graunt was the author of *Observations on the Bills of Mortality* (usually attributed to the latter), or whether Davenant or King discovered 'Gregory King's Law' is as elusive as the question whether the table of social accounts for England and Wales in 1688 which appeared in the Department of Applied Economics monograph *British Economic Growth 1688-1959* (Cambridge, 1962), should be attributed to Deane or Stone. The point is that the outputs of a research programme are the joint products of a collective intellectual enterprise and are not readily or usefully attributable to individual contributors.

To late twentieth-century economists the golden age of political arithmetic which characterised the half-century following the Restoration seems so close in spirit and style to the applied economics of our own generation that its failure to develop further from such a promising starting-point is surprising. During the middle decades of the eighteenth century, Petty's (or less commonly, King's) estimates of national income were often cited by mercantilist pamphleteers without any attempt to update them. It is notable, moreover, that Political Arithmetic had acquired a distinctive identity in the educated community well before Political Economy. For example, the third (1797-1801) edition of the *Encyclopaedia Britannica* contained a long entry for Political Arithmetic, largely devoted to repeating miscellaneous figures from Petty and Davenant, but no entry for Political Economy. Not until the 4th edition (1810) did an entry for Political Economy, based largely on Adam Smith's *Wealth of Nations*, appear and it began with a reprint of the entry for Political Arithmetic from the 3rd edition. Occasionally, we find an eighteenth century pamphleteer concerned to justify a specific policy prescription, or to defend the interests of a particular group, by drawing on the politico-arithmetical tradition. Joseph Massie, for example, updated King's 1688 table of family incomes and expenditures in order to put into national perspective his own estimates of tax incidence in a polemic robustly entitled: *A Computation of Money that hath been exorbitantly Raised upon the People of Great Britain by the Sugar Planters in one Year from 1759 to January 1760: shewing how much Money a Family of each Rank Degree or Class hath lost by that rapacious Monopoly*. Similarly, Arthur Young, who took upon himself the role of spokesman for the agricultural sector, made some relatively well-informed estimates of national agricultural output in reporting on his *Tours* of the northern and eastern counties of England, and associated these estimates with some rash guesses of value added in manufacturing, commerce and various other industries. Young, who had a deservedly high reputation as an agricultural economist, but lacked distinction as an exponent of political economy, was probably the last of the political arithmeticians in the original sense of the term. Certainly he was the last economist to write under that banner, which by the 1930s had been exclusively appropriated by the demographers.

Actually, by the time Adam Smith wrote *The Wealth of Nations* (1776) the English tradition of political arithmetic was in the doldrums: though in France the physiocratic *tableau économique* had temporarily revived the 'art of reasoning by figures upon matters relating to government'. No doubt Adam Smith himself helped to put it out of fashion in Britain, by announcing that he had 'no great faith in political arithmetick' – while shamelessly cribbing the political arithmeticians' figures to buttress some of his own arguments. Fortunately the tradition of quantifying total national income or wealth was not lost; and as the stock of published annual official statistics – first on international trade, much later on population and public finance – expanded, the bases for such calculations became less speculative or anecdotal. In setting their economic analyses and prescriptions within a framework of national income aggregates, on whose structural relationships and relative magnitudes the nation's productive strength and taxable capacity evidently hinged, the political arithmeticians had made a major contribution to the science of political economy. A long, if sporadic, stream of national income estimates was accordingly produced by diligent researchers following in Petty's or King's footsteps – usually in relation to issues of war finance or taxable capacity or comparative economic strength. At the turn of the century, for example, Pitt's plans to raise an income tax to finance the war with France stimulated a flurry of national income estimates. At about the same time, George Chalmers reprinted King's *Natural and Political Observations and Conclusions upon the State and Condition of England* in an appendix to the fourth (1802) and later editions of his best-seller, *Estimate of the Comparative Strength of Great Britain and of the Losses of her Trade*, which had first appeared in 1782. That was what inspired Patrick Colquhoun, then researching the poverty problem, to update King's famous table of incomes by families for his *Treatise on Indigence* (1806). Less than a decade later, Colquhoun using substantial new population and other records, developed his statistical enterprise to the ambitious scale described by Sir Richard Stone. This set the stage for the subsequent stream of nineteenth century estimates of national income, which included Pablo Pebrer's *Taxation, Expenditure, Power, Statistics and Debt of the Whole British Empire* (1833) and ended with Michael Mulhall's *Dictionary of Statistics* (4th edition 1898). To an increasing extent, however, these were primarily exercises in descriptive statistics rather than economic analysis thus falling short of the political arithmeticians' ideal. It could be said that the analytical approach to the study of national income was effectively ignored by leading classical and neoclassical economists until the middle decades of the twentieth century when Keynes' macroeconomic theorising revolutionised their discipline.

3. Political Arithmetic and Economic History

If the research programme initiated in the golden age of political arithmetic had lost its progressive momentum by the early eighteenth century it had nevertheless bequeathed two significant data sources to later generations of applied economists, particularly those with an interest in economic history: (1) a miscellany of empirical estimates bearing on the state of the English economy in the seventeenth century; and (2) the first annually compiled, detailed, published series of official statistics relevant to macroeconomic analysis, viz the overseas trade returns. Davenant, for example, was appointed the second Inspector-General of Imports and Exports. Writers on economic affairs who were concerned to quantify their evidence were thus able to draw on this legacy to keep alive the scientific tradition of political arithmetic. Gradually during the nineteenth century the national inheritance of systematically compiled and published official statistics was expanded, developed and strengthened. By the twentieth century, when the world economy was plunged into interwar depression, and professional economists were recovering their interest in macroeconomic analysis, the annual outflow of quantitative data – the raw material of political arithmetic – had become a swelling flood. It was then that a new, sophisticated sub-discipline – econometrics – issued from the marriage of quantitative economics and mathematical economic theory, and began to fill the academic journals with articles incomprehensible to the non-specialist majority of economists. However, the older, more commonsensical, pragmatic tradition of political arithmetic was not altogether submerged by the mathematicisation of economic and statistical theory: it enjoyed a revival during and after World War II under the joint stimulus of Keynesian national income analysis and the postwar preoccupation with policies for economic growth and development. In this context of ideas the estimates of the early political arithmeticians were brought into currency again as part of the raw material mined by economic historians concerned to explain the transition from pre-industrial to modern rates of economic growth.

It soon became evident, however, that using historical national income estimates to answer today's questions concerning the long-term growth process is a highly ambiguous and often subjective exercise. For there are two features of an industrial revolution which create special problems in any attempt to measure the course of economic change by means of national income statistics. The first is the relatively obvious one of severe data deficiencies characteristic of a pre-industrial economy. The second is that the transition to an industrialised economy involves profound and relatively rapid shifts in the organisation of production, structure of output and disposition of resources. In other words, it defines a period in which the components of national income, output and expenditure undergo radical changes in character and relative importance. The second group of problems is the more intractable. For although it may be possible to improve the quality of some of the data available to the original political arithmeticians, by applying modern research techniques and exploiting new sources of data – as the historical demographers have done so successfully for the population estimates – the problems of change in output and expenditure structures, and above all in relative valuations, raise index number problems which are not susceptible to single or simple solutions.

This is not the sort of problem over which seventeenth-century political arithmeticians needed to agonise. To my mind, for example the most striking feature of the table of price comparisons which Sir Richard Stone drew out of Bishop Fleetwood's price data is that the ratio of change as between say primary products and manufactures differed so little – in spite of the fact that the period taken into account stretched over almost two and a half centuries and covered the so-called price revolution. It is thus not surprising that when Davenant took over the responsibility for reporting the English international trade returns, he fell into the convenient habit of applying more or less constant prices to each item of merchandise; though by the second half of the eighteenth century this shortcut method of valuation made the returns unsuitable as indicators either of the annual balance of trade or of the real rate of growth in aggregate imports and exports. By then of course the mercantilist concern with the balance of payments had been supplanted by the classical economists' focus on economic growth. But the change *both* in relative prices, *and* in patterns of output and expenditure, associated with the industrial revolution were so radical that attempts to measure the nation's growth rate depended crucially on the weights used to calculate the index of change in the overall aggregates.

PETER LASLETT*

The first of Sir Richard Stone's British empiricists, John Graunt, was made a founder member of the Royal Society by express direction of the King, Charles II. The monarch was anxious that his new intellectual and scientific association should be on the look-out for persons like Graunt, a tradesman, not a member of the elite, a social scientist and a demographer. Charles wrote as if he feared that the Royal Society might fail to do this.[1]

From the very beginning, then, the men and women who interest us were in a somewhat dubious position as to status, as was the activity which they pursued, mostly part-time. A mixed bunch, if ever there was one: a number of commercial figures like Graunt himself, with a thick streak of the self-made man in them; a marginal civil servant, Gregory King; a gardener's son, William Farr; and the pampered daughter of a rich upper-class family, Florence Nightingale. Typical English amateurs is how Stone described them, a somewhat complacent classification perhaps, appropriate rather to the days of British success than to a time when unprofessional English persons are being blamed for British failure. At the risk of being sententious I shall go a little further into the status of empirical social enquiry and the reasons why it has taken so long to establish itself as an activity in itself, something which one can indeed *profess*.

If we reflect on the history of social statistics of which Sir Richard himself is so eminent a representative in our day, we shall not find conventional accounts as to how and why such studies evolve to be very satisfactory.

Although the twelve practitioners he has chosen are not intended as representative, their dates, situations and interconnections suffice to show that progressive enlightenment hardly

* Co-founder and Advisory Director of the Cambridge Group for the History of Population and Social Structure.

1. The subsequent history of that body seems to justify him; of the 12 figures dealt with only Young, Farr and Booth became Fellows of the Royal Society after Petty, Graunt and Halley. In the 1990s, of the total membership of the Royal Society and the British Academy, which has taken over its responsibilities to the humanities and the social sciences, at most 5% or 6% are social scientists in the sense that Graunt can be called such.

describes the story of empirical social enquiry, let alone unilinear intellectual progress. A beginning was made at the expected time and place, during the flowering of natural philosophy in England in the second half of the 17th century with a parallel send-off in France, but the movement was then interrupted before ever it got properly established.

Confining attention to English speakers is a distortion of course, and disposes us to overlook Vauban, Struyck or Süssmilch and early Italian names like Botero which had preceded them by a century. But if we compare empirical social enquiry with empirical physical enquiry in Britain as it proceeded in the century succeeding Newton and Boyle, the difference is startling. Social structural information and awareness were not increased for a century after flying starts was made, and much was forgotten, to be rediscovered in a somewhat desultory way during the nineteenth century. Some of it had to wait in fact for our own lifetime.[1]

This did not prevent the progressive elaboration of economic, social and political *theory*, as opposed to social investigation, as Rousseau succeeded Hume, Condorcet succeeded Adam Smith and finally Ricardo succeeded Malthus.

By the time of Malthus, to be sure, the literature of empirical social enquiry had resumed its career, though it could not be said to be flourishing in Britain. Young, Eden and Colquhoun were among those responsible. But as important in my view was the rather different body of persons who persuaded governments, in Europe and the U.S.A., with Britain lagging a little, to institute official censuses and to record births, marriages and deaths. To me it is an astonishing fact that Malthus did nothing to help in the long and arduous campaign to bring in a British census, although his, the most influential theory in the history of demog-

1. Knowledge about the size and structure of the household, for example, was not added to as far as I can see between the 1700s and the 1960s, and so much of what had been known to Petty or King was lost sight of that an entire theory was built up about family history on ignorance, ignorance of a kind which could not have been possible if the attitude to such investigations shown by the original pioneers had been maintained. See Peter Laslett, 'Gregory King, Thomas Malthus and the origins of English social realism', *Population Studies*, 39, 1985 (Laslett, 1985). I have borrowed extensively from this study in what follows.

raphy, decidedly required accurate, up to date demographic statistics.[1] An exquisite example, it might be said, of the tension between the empirical and the theoretical in science, natural science or social science.

Whilst political economy rose in status and became institutionalized – Malthus was, it must be remembered, the first holder of a chair in economics in the English-speaking world – empirical social enquiry remained unprogressive, marginal, miscellaneous, pursued by unrelated individuals scattered about the intellectual fabric. This may be one of the reasons why the personalities whom Stone has sought out to comment upon prove to be so fascinating.

If the progress and consolidation of rational enquiry is scarcely effective in explaining the staccato history of empirical social enquiry in England, the alternative explanatory tradition variously described as ideological, class motivated or economic-reductionist does little better. It is true that each of Stone's selected authors could be described in a general way as bourgeois in outlook and interest. But it is simply untrue that social information grew in the 18th and 19th centuries in consonance with the growth in the numbers and influence of agricultural improvers, commercial and industrial entrepreneurs and plain capitalists. Moreover a realistically bourgeois outlook is difficult to reconcile with an anxious pre-occupation with the situation of the poor and the poorest, which Stone finds to be common to all his subjects, and which entirely dominated two of them, Eden and Booth. To claim that their motivation was to discover exactly how much it would take in the way of transfer of resources to ensure that the dispossessed made no move to disrupt the class-dominated social structure would be to push economic reductionism to absurd, unacceptable lengths. It is the deep ignorance about the social facts which strikes the historian as he contemplates the great Victorian and the Edwardian middle

1. Laslett, 1985. The census movement succeeded in the interlude between the first, 1798, edition of Malthus' *Essay*, and the much longer, second, or empirical edition of 1803, almost an independent work, and the first British census was taken in 1801. Malthus certainly took its findings into account and certainly engaged in empirical research of his own but cannot be said to have shown any great insight into the social or family structure of the population about which he generalized.

class, rather than their knowledge, an ignorance which gave Charles Dickens, George Eliot and Jack London their literary opportunities.

There were those in England by the year 1800 who had begun to search out statistics so as to condemn a social order which was making the rich richer and the poor poorer. Not only were humanitarians like Eden, and his predecessor by a year or two, David Davies, working out the heartrending household budgets of labourers in poverty, but revolutionaries, Anglo-Saxon style, like Tom Paine had begun to reckon income distribution so as to introduce redistribution through the system of taxation, or even something like expropriation (see Paine's *Rights of Man*, Part II, 1792). The British Left has always based its knowledge of the social arrangements which it set out to attack on an indigenous tradition of enquiry which was independent of Marx and of Continental socialism in general. Tracing the ultimate origins of the statistical preoccupations of the Fabians and the Webbs back to the earliest work of Graunt, Petty and King stands as a challenge to intellectual historians. It would have to be pursued largely beneath the surface for much of its length, with vagaries and discontinuities conspicuous at every stage.

I have insisted elsewhere on the resistance to empirical social evidence, on social opacity as it was called, though that phrase has many other suggestive meanings, as the explanation of why the Gregorian attitude took so long to establish itself. Gregorian was an adjective drawn from the name of Gregory King, and one of the objects of the exercise was to suggest reasons why King published nothing on social statistics and never had the intellectual effect which should be expected from a genius like his. Social opacity can be invoked in order to suggest why it should be that the subsequent history of empirical social enquiry should have been so miscellaneous and unsystematic, until the 20th century. I am obliged to repeat here, however, that the Gregorian outlook is not of itself sufficient for a social scientist. He has to have the Malthusian attitude as well, that of theoretical enquiry (Laslett, 1985). Gregorians, however, are much rarer than Malthusians.

There are two further observations to be made, the first on the occasions when the intermittent Gregorian attitude will tend to manifest itself. Political arithmetic began its career in England when government found itself in need of social information which had always been lacking and when enough of those in power themselves were in close association with a body of intellectuals able and willing to provide that information. Petty, as Stone makes clear, was an indispensable figure in the administration of the English and Scottish plantations in Ireland. He moved in and out of the Royal Court and legislative circles with that disengaged familiarity we associate in Britain with John Maynard Keynes. But Petty was decidedly not alone in this respect in his country at the time. John Locke, the greatest of the English philosophers, and a very prominent figure in the 1690s, amongst administrators and politicians as well as intellectuals, was consulted about the posthumous publication of Petty's *Political Arithmetick* in 1691. So close were the connections between the literati, the natural scientists and the men in power that when a decision had to be made about the recoinage in the middle of that decade, reports were requested from John Locke, Isaac Newton, Christopher Wren and Gregory King. There is evidence that Gregory King was given unprecedented, and perhaps unrepeated access to taxation returns in 1695 and 1696, at the climax of the war with Louis XIV, so that he could write advice to the government on '*How to pay for the war*' very much in the spirit of the famous tract of that name published in 1940 by Keynes himself.

When this constellation of personalities sank below the horizon and the situation changed, such enquiries were no longer possible and opacity returned.

King's *Natural and Political Observations* lay neglected in manuscript versions, one of them located, I believe, amongst the papers of the Treasury. Something like the same situation as that of the 1690s recurred when the Napoleonic war was bearing so hard upon British resources a century or so later, and when King's *Observations* did get into print. I shall not try to manipulate this thesis so as to take account of the activities of the other writers on the list, but proceed to my final observation. This is on the character and use of the work which they did and the writings which they left behind them.

A frequent response of a contemporary scholar to these documents is to judge them almost entirely on the extent to which they are reflections, one to one, feature for feature reproductions, of the social arrangements depicted, photography in fact. Important as it is that the facts and figures should be correctly apprehended by historians, it is surely incorrect for them to make their judgements in this way. No observer, in the present but especially in the past, the uncounting, unmethodical, 'unscientific' past, could ever see all that the social scientist would want to see, and with complete fidelity to fact. If the historical sociologist is after information of that description, he must use the Pettys, the Kings, the Colquhouns and the Farrs for their insights, their guidance round the social structure and the sources. But he must do his own work for himself, on his own materials, not expect them to have done it for him. The proper description of works of political arithmetic is literature, and literature is not photography, nor must we treat it as such.

GIUSEPPE PARENTI*

I was particularly interested and delighted to read the full versions of the biographical notes and the to listen to Stone's lively presentation of them in his introduction to the 'portraits'. I also appreciated the numerous cross-references between the works of different authors which, together with the biographical notes and the re-evaluations of their estimates, helps one evaluate their contributions as self-made economists or demographers. These evaluations are not always easy to make because of the many overlaps and remaining doubts as to their true authorship. One has the impression that in Great Britain, perhaps more than any other country at that time, i.e. between the middles of the seventeenth and eighteenth centuries, the circulation of ideas – manuscripts, learned letters, publications and anonymous pamphlets – was far more intense than in our times, perhaps also due to the part played by active societies and scientific circles.

Furthermore, the seventeenth century is pictured in Stone's lively monographs as one of exceptional energy and intense perturbations in all fields: political, institutional, religious, philosophical, scientific and, in a more general way, cultural. Perturbations which lay open to question even the charisma of power and authority in all its forms, even in the scientific field (with Bacon), opening the way to the search for new beliefs; these could only find foundations in observation of *nature and facts*. Petty's skilful entry into the 'invisible club' group and, subsequently, into the Royal Society – where I believe he was welcomed more as an inventor and naturalist than as an economist – gave scientific support to the rough estimates of the first political arithmeticians. This drew them to the attention of the new emergent political directives (first founded on authority of the Prince) and on the country's social and economic problems. The real 'innovation' consisted in the collection, comparison and elaboration of administrative data – at first used as a check of the Administration's current activities in sanitation, fiscal matters, customs and others – from which to generate regulations, indications or verifications even of strategic

* Late Emeritus Professor of Statistics, Università degli Studi, Firenze; Member of the Accademia dei Lincei.

value. At first it was more a formal innovation than a fundamental one. In fact one often started out from numerical data which had been presented simply as 'plausible' – but neither verified nor verifiable, often consisting of pure 'assumptions' – to demonstrate the plausibility of a proposal for which one did not want to provide support through abstract reasoning.[1]

When I began teaching statistics, some fifty years ago, it was almost an obligation – at least in Italy – to get the course going with some lessons on the history of statistics, in which one never omitted to mention political arithmeticians and Anglo-Saxon authors who had been the first to make use of certain elementary statistical techniques.

I will keep to this topic during the few comments I shall make on Stone's lectures. I would like to dedicate my first notes to Fleetwood, an author I had to deal with many years ago (in 1940) during a study on the history of price index numbers.[2] After the war, Kendall also made a study of the same subject; he did not forgo the opportunity of commenting on my results as well, which were in no great conflict with his. Fleetwood, as Stone reminds us, had not managed to determine the overall price variations of goods; nevertheless he elaborated and defined in an exemplary manner – and in my mind in a way which is still up-to-date – the concept of a cost of living index. His referral in his *Cronicon Preciosum*[3] – as Stone reminds us – to a problem that was supposed to have been set him by an Oxford University student (the case of conscience of the student, wanting to benefit from a scholarship founded two and a half centuries before, when prices had been much lower, having to swear to having an income of less than five pounds, a sum which by then was totally insufficient to live on), I think in fact it was more of a 'rhetorical' question, that is to say formulated to give substance, following

1. For an in-depth analysis of relations between changes in English society and the development of empirical research in the field of economics and society, compare also J. and M. Dupâquier, *Histoire de la demographie*, Paris, 1985, pp. 145-210; W. Letwin, *The origins of scientific Economics*, Methuen, London, 1963; A. M. Dell'Oro, *History of Statistics*, Giuffrè, Milano, 1965, pt viii (*From political to stochastic arithmetic*).

2. Giuseppe Parenti, La tecnica e il significato dei primi numeri indice dei prezzi, *Economia*, vol. xxvi, no. 5/6, 1940, pp. 1-31.

3. My citations refer to the 1707 edition, published anonymously in London, with the sub-title: *An account of English money, the price of corn and other commodities from the last 600 years*.

the custom of political arithmeticians, to a conceptual elaboration which had slowly been maturing in his mind.[1] In fact. already in 1694, more than ten years before the publication of *Cronicon Preciosum*, in a public sermon directed against coin clippers – the moment having already passed for theological disputes on economic matters – Fleetwood, then Chaplain to William III, expatiated in his demonstration as to how the clipper was damaging the whole community with his fraud, bringing about or helping to bring about a depreciation of the currency and therefore an increase in exchange rates.[2] And in his *Cronicon* – at first published anonymously as a 'letter to an Oxford student' – he says of 'having thought a great deal on the problem before it had been put to him'; he extends his reasoning to more general problems, such as to the lack of adjustment of the income limits which gave one access to the active electorate, fixed many years previously in monetary terms (40 pounds a year) and by then no longer capable of making a selection on the basis of status; according to the author's judgement, the latter was and would have been necessary to guarantee the good functioning of Parliament.[3]

In any case, I still maintain, as I did then, that in setting himself the task of establishing the equivalence of a fixed sum of money through time as a problem of conscience, Fleetwood could not but end up defining in extremely clear terms the fundamental logic not only for cost of living indexes based on fixed consumption but also for those relating to 'equal well being' tied to variable consumption. He states in fact that if the founder of the stock exchange had fixed an income limit – which at that time Fleetwood equated to a clergyman's prebend[4] – sufficient therefore to ensure a modest but decent standard of living (simple and virtuous), he certainly also had in mind the retention of such guidelines for the future. Not only would future price variations be allowed for, but changes in the way of living would also be taken into consideration. The income limit would however exclude, says Fleetwood, those expenses which are

1. This is the third of the three problems (referred to by Stone during his lesson) outlined in chapter 1 of *Cronicon Preciosum* ('The Case'), pp. 1-19.

2. See also W. Fleetwood, *A sermon against clipping* [1694], Kriss, 1843, referred to in W. Letwin, *op. cit.*, pp. 80-1.

3. *Cronicon Preciosum*, pp. 170 and 172-4.

4. *Cronicon Preciosum*, p. 138.

now deemed necessary by the corrupt ways of the young and which are not compatible with a simple and virtuous life.[1]

I believe that this kind of approach, so specific in nature, is still valid today in explaining how and why the indexes proposed for the measurement of 'equal well being' in both general and abstract terms are still difficult to interptret, even today, and so little used; because logic requires an explanation for both the criteria and the limits of 'acceptability' of the structural changes in consumer trends in *specific* and *concrete* terms.

I had the opportunity of talking to Kendall (at the time when this article in the history of the price indexes came out) of my interpretation, which may have been rather overdone, of the concepts which had evolved in Fleetwood's mind and conscience. In spite of not being in total agreement with me, Kendall replied in his usual sarcastic way, as was his wont, that in any case my interpretation was no worse founded than that presented by those who attribute Young with the elaboration of the concept of weighting of economic indexes, as well as with the critique on the use of non weighted price indexes.

And since I've made reference to Young – the author whose *Tours* were so amusingly recalled by Stone, quoting passages from the original texts – I would like to add that I really find some of his tales rather hard to believe (as for example his solitary tour of France in 1788, when he would have had to travel 1,500 miles in two and a half months, and on a blind horse at that!) and consequently can hardly consider the very rich sets of data he collected – probably not very critically – during his tours, which he subsequently published, to be very reliable. And yet this whimsical and amusing character is also the author of works of different tones, as Stone recalled, including some of a popular, financial or methodological nature. Amongst the latter I would like to mention the proposal presented to Parliament (in 1771) for the institution of five-yearly censuses of the population; in its ample introduction he underlines in an effective way the advantages which could be drawn from having analytical demographic and manageable data for all the national territory and

1. 'Your founder did certainly intend *his scholars* should live like *other scholars* . . . the way of living being now much changed from what it was long ago, you must be at liberty to live in the same manner . . .', *Cronicon Preciosum*, pp. 170-1.

individual countries at one's disposal. In effect these data would have permitted not only the revision of the gross estimates attempted to date, but could have combined with administrative data – equally distributed, analytical and manageable – in providing sound evidence for the decisions then taken on the basis of opinions, often of a selfish nature at that![1]

In the conclusions of his proposal he spars an objection which might have been put to him by someone fearful that the diffusion of analytical information on the population might be of use to the enemy. He demonstrates that the latter could have drawn little advantage from the knowledge of census data, whereas their internal diffusion would have permitted the learned and other people interested in these kinds of problems to draw deductions and indications useful to the politicians; these have neither the inclination nor the time to undertake such detailed analyses. Even the participation of citizens to the public cause would have been facilitated.[2]

Young's proposal did not attract a following, nor perhaps could it have had one since the difficulties which would have been incurred in carrying out such surveys would have been completely disproportionate to the logistical capacities of the administrative structures of those days. Nevertheless Young's text does fine work in reasoning the thesis on the usefulness of quantitative analyses *for decision making purposes*; besides, it is a thesis which is more or less explicitly shared by all political arithmeticians.

At that time data was almost always handled through simple analyses of a comparative nature, in which temporal references consisted of 'communibus annis' or 'at medium' or 'year after year', referring to intervals of several years, the length of which varied from case to case. I don't believe any of these were arithmetical means –

1. A. Young, *Proposals to the Legislature for Numbering the People* (p. 45), in: D. V. Glass (ed.), *The Development of Population Statistics*, Gregg, Farnborough, 1973.

2. 'Many facts might appear, from which very important deductions might be made if attentively considered by studious private men, whose leisure and inclinations lead them to such sort of studies; observations might be made which would point out methods of advancing industry and population or preventing their decline. But who can suppose that people high in office (whatever their abilities) can have leisure necessary for attending to such affairs? Hence therefore the open liberal policy of making known to a free people their real state and situation, should be pursued, that every man may know the fact and reason on its causes and consequences' (*ibid.*, pp. 34-40).

at least not often – (in which case he could have used the term 'average' which, as far as I know, was already in use at that time), but rather estimates of 'normal' values meant to suppress bothersome variations which would have distorted the comparisons one wished to make. This, however, is an hypothesis which needs verifying.

Let us now turn to Graunt and Petty, two authors whose long standing friendship and reciprocal cultural exchanges, their personality contrasts and diversities in attitudes and experiences notwithstanding, are well portrayed by Stone. The former is a patient and scrupulous researcher, a curious but critical observer of facts, a man of modest academic and civil ambitions. In contrast, if one is to believe the writings of Young and Davenant, Petty is described as having an eclectic brain, of being extremely active, driven by excessive ambitions in every field: scientific, administrative, political; a public relations man capable of penetrating the most diverse circles, a skilful salesman of his scientific wares in those moments and places which would most benefit his business and career. These critiques despite the fact that Young and Davenant were Petty's admirers.

We don't know when Graunt started working on his 'bills of mortality'. One cannot exclude that Petty edged him on in that direction, having met (and helped) him some ten years before the publication of his *Observations*, Petty may have also provided stimuli and assistance to continue and broaden his research and to publish his results in his first and only book, in 1662. Nevertheless, in the *Treatise of Taxes* published by Petty that same year – his first and, in Stone's and my opinion, possibly best contribution to economics – one sees a completely different approach from that of Graunt's *Observations*, in spite of doubts of attribution which have come all the way down to us.

Amongst other points, there is a passage in the conclusions of *Observations* (which some see as being influenced by Petty) which is completely unparalleled in the *Treatise of Taxes*. When speaking of the value of land, Graunt distinguishes an 'intrinsic value', defined by the quantity and quality of products it yields 'communibus annis', and an 'extrinsic' or accidental value due to all those reasons which make it possible for a land situated close to a large market to be worth twice as much as another situated elsewhere, even though having the same intrinsic value. Here then was the cause which gave rise to differences in coefficients (years purchase) on the basis of which lands in different locations were evaluated.[1] Petty, on the other hand, even if only in a marginal note of his *Treatise* (in which he nevertheless makes reference to the *Observations*), seems first to want to evaluate the cash value (usus fructus per annum) of the 'communibus annis' production (using an analogical contrivance on which I will not dwell), then to capitalise the earnings with the coefficient 21, equivalent to the average interval between three generations . . . 'few men having reason to take care of more remote posterity'. Only subsequently does he go on to explain why the market coefficients (years purchase) might be higher or lower than the ones he indicated as being 'natural': either due to the different guarantees of safety given the property by its location, or for the different possibilities of exploitation, or for the different interval between generations found in different situations.[2]

In his preface to the *Treatise of Taxes*, Petty states he wrote the work to 'liberate' his mind of the many ideas which had accumulated therein in his daily contact with the country's problems; he had not intended to apply them to specific places or circumstances. He considers nevertheless that his arguments may proove of some use to the Duke of Ormond, who was about to set up a government in Ireland. Letwin even thinks that the work might have been written by Petty for the specific purpose of supporting his candidature to an important position:[3] such is his bad 'careerism', rightly or wrongly attributed to him. Certainly, though, similar suspicions rise up spontaneously when reading *Verbum Sapienti*;[4] this book was clearly written to illustrate the poor distribution of fiscal burdens in England, but also to 'give a hand' to the king, involved in a costly war with Holland and in difficulties with Parliament, which was turning down his requests to increase the already heavy ordinary and extraordinary taxes. Using

1. JOHN GRAUNT, *Natural and Political Observations upon Bills of Mortality*, 1676.
2. *A Treatise of Taxes and Contributions*, reprinted in C. H. Hull (ed.) *The Economic Writings of Sir W. Petty*, vol. 1, pp. 44-6.
3. W. LETWIN, *op. cit.*, p. 141.
4. In C. H. Hull (ed.), *op. cit.*, vol. 1, pp. 102-20.

conjectural estimates and calculations, Petty first builds up a rough Balance of the National Economy, which Stone showed us in tabular form; he then goes on to demonstrate that there are still margins left on which to broaden the taxable assessment. He gets to these results using bold estimates and intricate reasoning which make it difficult to follow trends and to evaluate the degree of reliability of some of his considerations. It seems to me, for example, that the route which Petty took to calculate the 'value of the people' had not been that of capitalising on the (estimated) expenses of tenants using an appropriate coefficient (years purchase), which would have been difficult for him to justify, but rather that of taking for granted and obvious the fact that the nation's total wealth was imputable to landowners and tenants alike, in the same proportion in which overall costs are allocated to the two categories. Obviously this is equivalent to capitalising the income of tenants with the same coefficient as used for other incomes, that from the earth in particular, 'being in its nature as perpetual' (as Stone maintains); but it does follow a different logic. In fact, Petty thinks it right that both tangible and personal capital be taxed proportionally to the same extent, both being the fruit of labour.[1]

In a subsequent paragraph Petty also explains how the capacity of workers' contributions could easily be raised to 10% of their salary by making them miss a meal a week and reducing by one quarter the two-hour meal and rest period during the day's work.

King and Davenant also form a pair in whose scientific production one notes a certain confluence of mutual contributions. Under certain aspects King resembles Graunt in the systematic nature and critical sense with which he collects data, which he does both as an amateur and on official business and not specifically for the purpose of supporting specific theses of directions. Davenant resembles Petty, not in temperament, but because he tends to expound on both his and King's research and to exploit the contributions of political arithmetics. He does however deepen its logical foundations, its

1. 'It seems reasonable that what we call the wealth or provision of the Nation, being the effect of the former or past labour, should not be conceived to differ from efficiencies in being, but should the rated alike and contribute alike to the common necessities'. *Ibid.*, para. 8, chapter II.

methodological aspects and in particular the need to base estimates on solid data, always verified critically by facts (this in contrast with Petty whose estimates, based on generally fragile evidence, make one suspect, as Davenant affirms, that they were directed more to pleasing the powerful than to expressing his real beliefs).

At this point I would like to make a brief mention of the famous 'King's law', attributed to Davenant by many authors or thought to be the fruit of some exchange of ideas between the two friends. I call it 'famous' because it has caught the attention of many economists even up to very recent times. The same also occurred in Italy, where some fifty years ago there was a rekindling of interest in this topic following a historical-statistical study of mine on the price of grain: I had examined the relationships between prices and crops for the Siena region, in the seventeenth century, arriving at conclusions quite contrary to those which appear in 'King's table', as reported by Stone.[1]

Investigating both wheat and other grain, I found in fact that price variations in the Siena region were on the average always *less* than inversely proportional to crop variations; I observed that the 'table's' contrasting behaviour could not be explained simply by differences of location and institution, but presumably was attributable to some distortion of the data used.

The reference to King's law in my early work had been nothing but a juvenile display of scholarship, and I certainly would not have brought it up here had not Einaudi, in reviewing my volume, given any weight to those observations. Referring to the testimony of several authors, he confirmed the hypothesis that the formulation of the 'table' had been based on the judgements of experts in some way personally interested in its application, and that Davenant had formalized and spread its use to persuade those in power into having him replace the Dutch – whose arbitrations were mentioned by Stone – who purchased cereals from England during successful crop years (assisted by export incentives which were almost continually paid out after 1688), only to sell them back to those same English in

1. G. Parenti, *Prezzi e mercato del grano a Siena, 1546-1765* (Prices and market for wheat in Siena, 1546-1765), C. Cya, Florence, 1942, reprinted in *Studies of the history of prices*, Maison des Sciences de l'Homme, Paris, 1981.

lean years, at very high prices.[1] In a subsequent note entitled 'The paternity of the so-called King's law',[2] Einaudi, with his usual diligence, made a thorough survey of all works which had appeared on the subject, confirming his thesis that the law, first conceived by King, had almost certainly been redrawn in its known form by Davenant. According to Einaudi, Davenant must have been aware both of a writing by Sir Walter Ralegh who had placed a value of two million pounds on the earnings of the Dutch with their arbitrations during a single year and a half of shortage, and of a note of King's who affirmed that such a profit was possible if the price of grain had increased fourfold and the shortage had been equivalent to one quarter of the average crop.

I wanted to mention this point of Einaudi's at the end of my talk because it confirms *with facts* that the works of arithmeticians were often instrumental in nature. One can therefore understand why they might have manipulated some of the scant and uncertain information available, but it does impose extreme caution to whoever might want to use their data today.

1. Luigi Einaudi, La scoperta dell'America e il rialzo dei prezzi in Italia (The discovery of America and price increases in Italy), in *Rivista di Storia Economica*, year VIII, 1943, pp. 21-33.

2. In 'Rivista di Storia Economica', year VIII, 1943, pp. 33-8.

MASSIMO LIVI BACCI*

The Banca Commerciale's kind invitation to participate in Sir Richard Stone's 'Mattioli Lectures' was for me both an honour and a happy occasion with a double intellectual pleasure: to listen to the masterly lectures of one of the great political arithmeticians of our time – Professor Stone in person – and to read once more the original text of some of the founders of the disciplines of statistics and demography. I will restrict my presentation to those authors which are most congenial to me: Graunt, King and Halley. I could also have included Petty, the most famous of political arithmeticians but his great fame is greater than the rigours with which he dealt with the issues of demography. Davenant did not judge him very flatteringly, as professor Stone mentioned, and before him, I believe, Gregory King observed: 'Sir William Petty was lookt upon as the best Computer of his times, But in all his Computations of the Numbers of People in England and London, it is Evident he designed to Represent both the one and the other much greater than they truly were; And tho' Writing to the Publick might make it Excusable so to do, Yet least those Publick Accounts of His should be too much Relyed on by those who seat at the Helm, to whom a true account of the Kingdom is more necessary than to others I shall endeavour to give such an Account thereof as Will bear the Touchstone of Truth'.[1]

I will only make a brief mention of Halley. Halley is the perfect demographer and statistician; in fact, the life table he produced for the city of Breslau (Wroclaw) is technically perfect, given the hypotheses implied.[2] As is common knowledge to demographers, the life table is constructed on the basis of the age distribution of a concrete population whose rate of growth is assumed to be zero. This is the only case for which it is admissible to consider, as does Halley, the root of the table as being the sum

* Professor of Statistics, Università di Firenze.

1. D. V. GLASS, Two papers on Gregory King, in D. V. GLASS and D. E. C. EVERSLEY (eds.), *Population in History*. Arnold, London, 1965, p. 160.

2. E. HALLEY, 'An estimate of the degrees of mortality of mankind', (eds.) v. n. 1, p. 241.

of births and equal to the sum of deaths, and to obtain the survivors for each age bracket by subtracting from the root the deaths which occurred between the moment of birth and the given age. The attempts made in the first place by Graunt, and repeated subsequently by Petty on the Bills of Mortality for London and Dublin – says Halley – did not give satisfactory results not only because the age distribution of deaths was missing, but because in the two cities deaths exceeded births, 'by reason of the great and Casual Accession of Strangers who die therein' (in other words the population was not stationary). But in the case of Breslau, a stationary condition was almost observed, because the 6,193 births for the five-year period 1687-91 only slightly exceeded the 5,869 deaths. The city was far removed from migratory currents ('Confluence of Strangers'), being well away from the sea ('as much a Mediterranean Place as can be desired'). Furthermore – Halley points out – there is only a slight difference between numbers of births and deaths, which 'may perhaps be balanced by the Levies for the Emperor's Service in his Wars'. In principle that may be correct, even if only in the unlikely event that the conscripts had the same age distribution as that of the population whence they were being taken. As far as Breslau is concerned, therefore, a zero population growth seems on the whole guaranteed; Halley, perfectly aware that such an assumption is necessary, proceeds with his calculations.

But the accuracy of calculations notwithstanding – only with the availability of census type data for Sweden would Wargentin be able, a century later, to calculate a life table based on an approximation of the probability of death – Halley has a modern and almost perfect grasp of the multiple uses a life table can be put to, which he describes in an almost definitive manner.

For diametrically opposed reason, therefore (one for his perfection and the other for his coerciveness), neither Halley nor Petty managed to reawaken my curiosity. Instead, I was attracted to John Graunt, the real founder of demography as a science, who is the most precise, able and intuitive of political arithmeticians. He does not falter when faced with a scarcity of data; rather, he extracts a maximum of information from what is available to him, always using logical, conjectural but never imaginary procedures. I draw some excerpts from his work *Observations on the Bills of Mortality*[1] which, still representative today of viable research problems to population historians, underline his originality of thought and freshness of observation.

Graunt distinguishes between epidemic and chronic illnesses;[2] the former, 'acute and epidemical disease', are related to the 'healthfulness of the air', or as we would say today, with the healthiness of environmental conditions; epidemic illnesses can be severe and frequent but, nervetheless, those who come out of them unscathed can go on to enjoy a long life. Longevity is instead precluded under conditions favourable to chronic illnesses, such as the 'wholesomeness of food'; in fact 'where the proportion of chronical distemper is great . . . man being long sick and always sickly, cannot live to any great age, as we see in several sorts of Metal-men who, although they are less subject to Acute diseases then others, yet seldom live to be old . . .'. Today we still wonder about the difference between an infective and a chronic disease and the relationship of both with nutrition and environment; Graunt was already aware of the problem.

In another context, Graunt observes that 'few are starved' since only 51 out of 230,000 deaths registered over a period of twenty years appeared to have been due to this cause.[3] He comments, furthermore, that the numerous 'Beggars, swarming up and down this City . . . seem to be most of them healthy and strong'. And yet we are accustomed to attributing the high mortality rates of past centuries to poor nourishment: but there remains an unsolved problem. Were the masses really suffering from malnutrition during years of severe shortages? And was their death rate really the result of nourishment rather than of the worst possible hygienic conditions and with other risks arising from the transmission of infective diseases?

Why, in London, 'few are Murthered . . . whereas in Paris few nights escape without their Tragedy'?[4] Are these differences due

1. Graunt's text, and references to it which follow, are contained in C. H. HULL (ed.), *The Economic Writings of Sir William Petty*, vol. 2. New York, 1963.

2. *Ibid.*, p. 350.

3. *Ibid.*, pp. 352-3.

4. *Ibid.*, p. 354.

to institutional factors (citizens being under the protection of order in London, 'no man settling into a Trade for that employment') or perhaps to cultural factors, such as the 'natural abhorrence of that inhuman Crime, and all Bloodshed, by most English men'? The history of violence has yet to be written, and differences between populations appear very reluctant to change with time, retaining different levels of contrast between the English and the Irish, America and Europe, the North and the South . . . What are the factors which maintain these behavioural differences – are they institutional or economic, cultural or environmental?

When pondering on the history of medicine, Graunt poses the problem of the first appearance of rickets; in fact 'of the rickets we find no mention among the casualties until the year 1634 . . . Now the question is, Whether the Disease appear about that time: or whether a disease, which had been long before, did then first receive its name?'[1] Whistler and Glisson were the first to describe rickets in 1645 and 1650. The origins of this illness, in some way connected with malnutrition and the absence of some essential nutrients, are still unclear today. Perhaps it really was a new disease, brought about by a worsening of urban life in a rapidly expanding London. Besides, when competent observers describe a disease for the first time and suspect it to be something new, they are almost always right; so it had been the century before with Fracastoro and typhoid, and in the following century with Gaspar Casal and pellagra. We may also ask ourselves what other disease might have been the cause of a rapid spread of deaths through London at that time: the 'rising of the lights' or 'lungs' or 'bellows of the body'. Perhaps an asthmatic-type disease associated with the diffusion of coal as fuel; a tubercular disease or, in any case, a disease connected with the worsening of urban living conditions?

In another context, Graunt measures the high percentage of women died in childbirth . . . 'not one Woman of a hundred (I may say of two hundred) dies in her Labour. If this be true in these Countries, where Women hinder the facility of their Child-

1. *Ibid.*, p. 357.

bearing by affected straitening of their Bodies: then certainly in America, where the same is not practiced, Nature is little more to be taxed as to Woman, than in Brutes, among whom not one in some thousands do dye of their Deliveries: what I have heard of the Irish women confirms me herein'.[1] These are important observations, still valid today: we still know very little of past maternity death rates and of the influence of different childbirth practices on the mortality of mothers and their children.

Graunt's curiosity is also attracted by other phenomena which are still in large part unexplained today; for example, why, during the years of pestilence, and in other 'sickly years' as well, is there a net decline in the birth rate compared to normal years?[2] 'The question is whether teeming women died, or fled or miscarried.' He exercised his acumen on some specific cases in an attempt to separate one cause from another. Today we would add a reduction in sexual relations and birth control during catastrophic times to the three aforementioned causes. But, like Graunt, we are unable to distinguish one cause from another.

Population losses during years of plague are very high; that of 1625, for example, killed 54,000 Londoners, about a seventh of the total population.[3] And yet the population fills the voids and returns to preceding levels by the second year after the plague, a certain sign that immigrants were pouring in from the countryside and nearby villages to take the place of the deceased. Graunt is further interested in the interaction between city and country when he notices that even when there is a chronic excess of deaths over births the city's population increases. But why are there more deaths than births? With the acumen of an able contemporary demographer, Graunt singles out three causes: the low percentage of the population of child-bearing age; the unhealthiness of the urban environment; the sterility of couples. The low percentage of breeders is justified by the particular social make-up of the population of London, where occasional visitors, apprentices, sailors and sick people abound: all of whom are unmarried or separated from their spouses, even if

1. *Ibid.*, p. 361.
2. *Ibid.*, pp. 366-7.
3. *Ibid.*, pp. 367-8, 372-4.

temporarily, but still add to the percentage of those who do not contribute to reproduction. As far as unhealthiness is concerned 'it may well be supposed, that although seasoned Bodies may, and do live near as long in London as elsewhere, yet new-comers and children do not: for the Smoaks, Stinks, and close Air, are less healthful that of the Country; otherwise, why do sickly Persons remove into the Country air?' Finally, examining the causes of increased sterility, one finds excesses of every kind, 'Adulteries and Fornications . . . Add to this, that the minds of men in London are more thoughtful, and full of business, than in the Country, where their work is corporal Labour and Exercises; All which promote Breeding, whereas Anxieties of the mind hinder it'. Today, one would call this 'anxiety' 'stress', an identical and equally indefinable concept. Returning to the subject of the higher death rate in the city, the embryonic survival table proposed by Graunt, based largely on conjectural data, would give a life expectancy at birth of only 18 years; at that time in England it was more like 30 to 35 years: but it would hardly have been surprising, had it been true: in Geneva, at that time, it was around 20 years, and in Manchester, according to Farr's calculations, it was approximately 24 years at the beginning of the last century.

Like Graunt, Gregory King is a fine statistician, untiring in his search for more efficient ways to make his data speak and describe exciting demographic and economic events. Professor Stone clearly documented, as had done David Glass previously, the skill with which King had been able to reconstruct, on the basis of limited and uncertain data, the size of the population of England and Wales, arriving at results which have since been convalidated by modern research. Glass had stressed King's accuracy, which could also be inferred from the replies given to Robert Harley's queries on some points of the manuscript King had sent him. Glass credits King with having associated, in the wake of Graunt's observations, pollution with mortality. According to King, coal fumes are responsible for both women's reduced fertility and for the higher infant mortality rate of London . . . 'I am clearly of opinions it suffocates & destroys a Multitude of Infants, Tho' perhaps in New Castle it may not have the same operation, where the Air is sharper, the Town not above a 50th part of London, nor nothing near so closely built'.[1]

But in addition to this short reference to urban death rate and its relationship to pollution, I became interested in three other topics relevant to the study of the history of nutrition and mortality. The first deals with a sort of first formulation of Engel's law, again following what Glass, whit his sharpness, had conceived. King argues against Petty's estimates of family consumptions, which he finds too low; in the more modest families, whose total annual expenses were three pounds per capita, approximately two of these went for their 'Dyet'. In middle-income families with seven pounds' expenses per capita four pounds went for food; the 'better sort' families, with fifty pounds annual expenses, 'spend less than a Third in Dyet'.[2]

Professor Stone spoke praisingly of King's well known law in his presentation, and Giuseppe Parenti – the only scholar to have attempted its empirical verification for past times – added his very subtle comments. I will recall that Schumpeter had observed that in spite of the notoriety of King's law, it had never crossed economists' minds to perfect and extend it, not until 1914, when H. L. Moore gave the go-ahead, after over two hundred years' delay, to an avalanche of statistical demand curves.[3] King had postulated a constant demand for wheat with variations of prices more than proportional to annual production variations. Parenti found just the opposite for Siena. We know that a number of factors can influence the relationship between production and prices, but one cannot refrain from correlating these presumed relationships with the covariance between price trends and deaths. During the sixteenth and seventeenth centuries, years when cereal prices skyrocketed, there are often marked increases in the death rate; however, this relationship appears to be much stronger on the Continent – in France and Italy, for example – than in England. Increasing numbers of deaths during times of shortage is certainly related to reduced cereal consump-

1. D. V. GLASS, *op. cit.*, p. 164.

2. *Ibid.*

3. J. SCHUMPETER, *History of Economic Analysis*, New York, Oxford University Press, 1954.

tions and starvation of the population: but it could be that the reduced correlation between prices and deaths in England with respect to the Continent was due to differences in demand curves or to the fact that the English population was, overall, better fed and therefore less vulnerable. These questions are still unresolved and at the centre of an interesting debate.

The last point I would like to dwell on is that of estimates on the consumption of meat by the English population. Abel and Braudel have confirmed the hypothesis that the consumption of foodstuff by the masses, so rich in the late Middle Ages after the plague, became poorer in subsequent centuries, finally improving slowly during the last century. In particular, there was an exceptional consumption of meat in the late Middle Ages (Abel guesses 100 kilograms a year per capita in Germany); but the demographic increase in subsequent centuries made fields and pastures less and less convenient. They were replaced by cereal cultivations, and meat consumption decreased until it reached its nadir in the first part of the last century. This trend was perhaps less dramatic in England, Holland and Eastern Europe. King investigates the subject of meat consumption: 1.6 million English 'eat flesh constantly', meaning daily; 0.7 million consume it 5 days a week; 1.8 million twice a week; 1.2 million only once and 0.2 million never. On the average, 32.33 kilograms a year per person; far less than in medieval Germany, but roughly twice as much as was consumed in France at the end of the *ancien régime*, or in Germany at the beginning of the nineteenth century, or in Italy following National Unity.

We have talked at length and well on the historical and philosophical roots of political arithmeticians during these lectures; their ways of observing facts, of measuring them, connecting and interpreting them were certainly new. If some former echo comes to mind, perhaps it reminds us of another great merchant civilisation – fourteenth and fifteenth century Florence – already accustomed to counting and measuring, to the chronicles of Giovanni Villani with his evaluations of the population density of his city, to the writings and memoirs of merchants and civil servants. This seed, however, did not germinate.

E. A. WRIGLEY*

I wish to comment on two aspects of Sir Richard Stone's discussion of 'Some British empiricists in the social sciences', one general and one more particular.

Stone drew attention to the Baconian epistemology reflected in the writings of the early political arithmeticians. In their hands this was ultimately deeply subversive of a long-established intellectual and moral order. Men such as Graunt, Petty and King may have appeared to immerse themselves chiefly in limited and particular issues, yet the effect of their work tended to liberate the study of society from an older framework of thought in a manner reminiscent of the contemporary changes in the natural sciences. It is perhaps symbolically appropriate that Petty should have been a founder Fellow of the Royal Society. If pattern and meaning can be found by the consideration of *number*, *weight* and *measure*,[1] as the political arithmeticians succeeded in doing, a belief in the immanent dependence of human action and the social order upon divine agency becomes superfluous, just as the same is true in relation to the motion of the planets or the flight of an arrow.

Though the political arithmeticians may have been unconscious of the implications of their new methods, the effect was ultimately revolutionary. The tools used became more powerful as time went on – arithmetic was supplemented by algebra; the study of variance was added to the use of means; eventually sampling theory helped to overcome some of the problems associated with the use of large data sets – but the fundamental break with the past is visible even in their earliest writings. For it was not so much number, weight and measure *in se* which mattered, but the opportunity which quantitative data offered to test consistency, to make inferences about missing information, to note the existence of relationships or correlations, in short to find structure, which slowly transformed what was meant by saying that a particular issue was intelligible.

* Professor of Economic History, University of Cambridge.

1. Above, ch. 1, p. 37.

Graunt, for example, was already displaying this habit of mind when he suspected under-registration of baptisms in London in the later 1650s. Implicitly he argued that the risk of dying in childbed was broadly constant per thousand confinements. If therefore the number of deaths in childbed increased substantially from 1631 to 1659 but the number of baptisms recorded did not increase, it was reasonable to use the rise in the former as a measure of the defectiveness of the latter.[1] He may or may not have been justified in his assumption. It is conceivable, if improbable, that the maternal mortality rate rose sharply in this period, but the accuracy of this assumption is unimportant compared with the innovatory way in which he tried to find a solution to the problem of deciding about the reliability of his data. A much greater emphasis upon a particular mode of reasoning was to lead to a slow transformation in the conventional way of understanding the functioning of society and economy and of accounting for observed phenomena. Or take Petty's struggle to reconcile disparate information about population size, capital stocks, income to the several factors of production, and average earnings, and to articulate his data into a coherent set of rational accounts. At one level this was an ingenious but limited exercise in arithmetic and logic, but at another level a deadly challenge to the received wisdom about understanding the genesis and distribution of wealth in society, conducted on a different plane from that of, say, the medieval canonists or the Calvinists of the preceding century. To the degree that the new approach endowed old topics with new order and meaning, it was capable of showing the way to a new conception of social function and social action. Adam Smith stood waiting in the wings.

My second comment relates to a theme which was a frequent preoccupation of most of the writers whose work Stone has surveyed. It might be said, with only mild oversimplication, that the subject matter of the writers discussed by Stone is represented by the four Ps – production, population, poverty and power. The third of these, poverty, was a principal concern of several of Stone's list of empiricists – Colquhoun, Eden and Booth – and a

1. Above, ch. 7, p. 212.

major concern for the others. Poverty was not, of course, a problem peculiar to England: indeed it was a more grievous problem in other countries handicapped by less productive economies. But nowhere else perhaps did poverty figure so prominently in social theorising and economic analysis. It became a distinctive feature of the writings of the social empiricists.

Poverty was a universal problem for which there could be no final solution in a traditional economy because of the limited productive potential which was one of the defining characteristics of pre-industrial societies generally. There was biblical authority for treating poverty as an ineluctable problem. When a jar of precious ointment was poured over his head as a mark of respect in the house of Simon the Leper, Jesus had defended himself from the criticism of his disciples that it was a squandering of wealth that might have been expended with greater benefit on the poor by saying in effect that poverty was beyond control by human agency: 'Ye have the poor always with you', he said.[1] Nevertheless the perception of the problem in England changed somewhat in Tudor England, a change which was reflected in national legislation. The Elizabethan Poor Law provided a new institutional framework for the treatment of poverty. It was no longer to be a matter solely for the family, for the church, or for private charity, but was to become the responsibility of the principal local unit of political organisation, the parish.

The new Poor Law combined with the new types of investigation pursued by the social empiricists began to result in a less passive attitude towards poverty. Petty, as Stone has reminded us, defined six principal heads of public expenditure. Of these two were the 'care of the poor' and 'measures to alleviate unemployment', and these were the only two heads on which Petty considered that *more* should be spent.[2]

The extent of poverty and man's capacity to act effectively to limit it were both much affected by two of the other Ps that concerned the British social empiricists; production and population. It was the ratio between the two which largely determined real incomes per head, and this in turn measured the scale of poverty

1. The words are those to be found in the King James version.

2. Above, ch. 1, pp. 18 and 20.

and governed the degree to which resources could be released to assist the poor without serious detriment to other members of society. Some of the most interesting and original work of Petty and King consisted in their attempts to establish the order of magnitude of national income, of population size, and therefore of average income, while at the same time investigating the distribution of income levels between different groups in society. Much of this was done with the problems associated with the existence and prevalence of poverty prominently in mind. The very well-known table of national social structure constructed by Gregory King, with its division of the population into those increasing and those decreasing the wealth of the kingdom, is a vivid tribute to the centrality of this issue and to the sophistication with which it was approached.

The problem of poverty was a constant reminder that in developing a new calculus of wealth and power the old order of moral issues could never be neglected. The fact that this was so provides a link between the two issues on which I have chosen to concentrate in my comment. Measuring the wealth, population and power of the English state, or making comparisons between England and the states with which she was in rivalry, Holland and France, was the focus of much work by the political arithmeticians, and in pursuing these objects they laid some of the foundations of the disciplines of economics and demography, but it was uncongenial to their habit of mind to attempt those tasks in a purely 'Machiavellian' fashion. Moral considerations, and perhaps a sense of political realities, made it necessary to pay attention to the question of transfer payments between the fortunate and the unfortunate. It was a major, not a marginal issue in relation to public finance in England in the late seventeenth century (and indeed over a much larger span of time). Stone's remodelling of Gregory King's national accounts for 1688 shows that poor relief accounted for almost a quarter of the total sum raised in local and national taxes,[1] strong testimony both to the scale of the problem and to its intractability.

Discussions of poverty always involved the issue of sheep and

1. Above, ch. 3, p. 98, table 3.7.

goats. Which members of society should have a claim as of right on communal resources? The elderly, the sick, the orphaned and the widowed were usually regarded as sheep, but what about those out of work? Which groups should be actively excluded from gaining access to communal resources whatever their ingenuity and persistence? Unquestionably the able-bodied but lazy, the criminals, the scroungers, but no doubt others as well. Too many claimants might cause social or economic breakdown. And again, how could those who were able to work, and might indeed he anxious to work, be placed in employment without the unwelcome knock-on effect of displacing those already in work because of the effect of subsidised competition (a major concern of Eden)? The problem of unemployment, of what the Elizabethans called the sturdy beggars, proved intractable, essentially because, although it was true that with each new mouth there came a pair of hands, experience showed that mouths needed constant feeding, but hands often lacked the opportunity for useful work.

The social empiricists varied greatly in their views about what was desirable. Some early writings would not have carried conviction to later generations. For example, Halley's wish to secure a larger population by encouraging early marriage would have horrified those nineteenth-century writers influenced by Malthusian ideas.[1] But there was also an early appreciation of the intricacy of the problems involved in balancing desiderata in the context of an analysis of population, production, poverty and power. The desire to rival France suggested the importance of increasing the number of 'fencible' men, but the example of Holland, with a much smaller population but high income per head, showed that economic power could be as important as numbers in determining national strength. The Dutch example showed that a high taxable capacity might offset mere numbers. Humane considerations in relation to poverty and the calculus of power might both point to the advantage of a relatively small population enjoying a relatively high standard of living.

There is a calculus of population, production and power which is, in a sense, value-free. Difficult as it may be to carry out,

1. Above, ch. 8, p. 251.

the operation is not, so to speak, intrinsically loaded with moral imperatives. With poverty it was otherwise and the prominence of poverty in the writings of most of the social empiricists coloured their discussions not only of poverty but of many aspects of the economy and the polity, retaining within the new school of thought elements which obliged them to continue to pay attention to those traditional moral considerations which had once been the ground of all social theorising.

The claims which the unfortunate could properly make upon the more favoured, the reciprocal ties between the individual and the collectivity, the limits to the absoluteness of rights of possession and property, were certain to obtrude into economic and social analysis as long as poverty figured prominently in all serious discussions of the economic and demographic constitution of society. The state had placed poverty in the political arena, had by implication denied that it should be regarded as something to be accepted as an act of God, and in so doing had thrust the problem of social redistribution and prescribed transfer payments into the centre of the political stage, where indeed it still remains. The content of the writings of the social empiricists reflects this.

Poverty in England, its definition, and the social experiments embarked upon in attempts to deal with it, have recently been the subject a massive study by Himmelfarb. In it she suggests that from the sixteenth to the nineteenth century England was universally regarded as peculiarly concerned with the problem of poverty and especially assiduous in debating it and in collecting quantitative data about it through Royal Commissions, Parliamentary inquiries, the efforts of statistical societies, and private investigation.[1] The result was a plethora of schemes to alleviate the problem. The history of British social empiricists set out by Stone illustrates its long ancestry. Denominating them as empiricists might appear to suggest that they were chiefly engaged in description. The near-universal presence of poverty on their agenda, however, ensured that prescription also found a place in their work and endowed it with a distinctive flavour.

1. G. Himmelfarb, *The Idea of Poverty. England in the Early Industrial Age*. London, 1984, pp. 4-5.

RICHARD STONE
AN AUTOBIOGRAPHICAL SKETCH

I was born in London on 30 August 1913, the only child of Gilbert and Elsie Stone. My school days were spent first at Clivedden Place Preparatory School and then at Westminster School, which I attended from 1926 to 1930. At Westminster I was on the classical side: my father, who was a barrister, destined me for the law, and for this a classical education was deemed indispensable. As a result I learnt little mathematics beyond elementary arithmetic, algebra and geometry and was rather bored. I expect I could have had a more interesting education if I had shown more interest in what I was taught, but as a boy my passion was model-building; not mathematical models but models of trains and boats, an activity in which my father was a skilled and enthusiastic collaborator.

In 1930 my father was appointed a High Court judge in Madras. When he was about to leave for India he consulted the school about what was to be done with me. I think it would be a very good thing if he were to accompany you, said the headmaster, he doesn't seem to be doing much good here. So I had a year's break in India between school and university.

From 1931 to 1935 I was an undergraduate at Cambridge in my father's old college, Gonville and Caius, which was particularly strong in medicine and the law. However, after two years of law I switched to economics, much to my father's disappointment. At that time the world was in the depth of the great depression and my motive for wanting to change subject was the belief, bred of youthful ignorance and optimism, that if only economics were better understood the world would be a better place.

My college did not have an economist among its Fellows and so for my weekly supervisions I was sent to Richard Kahn at King's College. This was a piece of great good fortune, as Kahn was not only a brilliant theorist but also a stimulating and encouraging supervisor. Another of my teachers to whom I owe much was Colin Clark, who was lecturer in statistics and who became a close friend. Finally there was Keynes, who was in the habit of giving a short course of lectures on whatever book he happened to be writing; at that time the book on the stocks was *The General Theory*. I was invited to become a member of his

Political Economy Club, which met in his rooms at King's. He was kind to me as he was to all young people, but it was only later that I got to know him well.

Unlike my school performance, my undergraduate career had been uniformly successful, and after I had taken my degree in 1935 my college offered me a research studentship. But while I was much tempted by this opportunity, I had done only two years of economics and was not quite sure that I was ready for research. Furthermore, my father was anxious to see me settled in a job and so I did not take up my studentship but joined the staff of a firm of Lloyds brokers in the City. I was never cut out for a business career but I did learn a good deal about life from my brief encounter with the insurance world.

My job was not so heavy that I could not carry on with the kind of work that interested me. In 1936 I married Winifred Mary Jenkins, who had also read economics at Cambridge, and we spent much of our spare time writing on economic subjects. In particular, we were responsible for a little monthly called *Trends*, which appeared as a supplement to the periodical *Industry Illustrated*. Colin Clark had been running it and bequeathed the task to me when he went to Australia in 1937. Following in his footsteps, we filled it every month with indicators of British economic conditions: employment, output, consumption, retail trade, investment, foreign trade, prices and so on. From time to time we would add a special article on regional employment, say, or the economic recovery of Germany, or the American stock market; in short on any subject that seemed to us topical.

Trends was small and modest, nevertheless it must have attracted some attention as in 1939 I was asked whether I would be prepared to join the staff of the Ministry of Economic Warfare which was to be set up in the event of war. I accepted, and when on 2 September war did break out I reported for duty.

I remained in the Ministry about nine months, in the section responsible for shipping and oil statistics. Then in the summer of 1940 I was transferred to the Central Economic Information Service of the Offices of the War Cabinet, where James Meade was preparing the groundwork for a survey of the country's economic and financial situation and wanted somebody to help with the statistical side. By December 1940 Meade and I had completed a set of estimates which we showed to Keynes, who was then a member of the Chancellor's Consultative Council at the Treasury, and through his advocacy they were published as the second part of a White Paper entitled *An Analysis of the Sources of War Finance and an Estimate of the National Income and Expenditure in 1938 and 1940*, which accompanied the budget of 1941. Our estimates consisted of three tables relating to the national income and expenditure, personal income, expenditure and saving, and the net amount of funds required by and available from private sources for government purposes. They hardly amounted to a set of national accounts but they were a beginning. In constructing the accounts we made use of residual estimation. The balancing of the accounts, therefore, threw little light on the accuracy of the entries. But the sources for the first two tables were largely independent of those for the third, and the fact that for 1940 the sum of the first two residuals was not very different from the third encouraged us to think that the results were not grossly inaccurate.

The Chancellor in his budget speech emphasised that the publication of official estimates of national income and expenditure should not be regarded as setting a precedent. In fact they established themselves as an annual feature and have appeared in increasingly elaborate form ever since. At the instigation of Keynes, whose assistant I had become, I continued to be responsible for them until I left the government service at the end of the war.

The United States and Canada had also for some time been making estimates of national income and national expenditure, more detailed than ours though not cast in the form of balancing accounts, and while the three countries used similar concepts and definitions it was clear that some adjustments would be needed to obtain reasonably comparable tables. So in 1944 I was sent over to see how far agreement could be reached. I met my Canadian opposite number, George Luxton, in Ottawa and we travelled down to Washington for discussions with Milton Gilbert and his team at the Department of Commerce. The meetings were very friendly and the results extremely satisfactory, so that my first taste of international cooperation could not have been more encouraging.

In 1940 my marriage had been dissolved, and in 1941 I had married Feodora Leontinoff. From a background in philosophy, she had become in 1939 the Secretary of the National Institute of Economic and Social Research, which had been founded the year before. At the outbreak of war the director and his staff had been absorbed into the Ministry of Economic Warfare, and Feodora's initial function was simply that of caretaker. The survival of the Institute looked very uncertain, but thanks to the drive of Henry Clay and Geoffrey Crowther and to Feodora's energy and talent for administration it came to life again.

In 1945 the war ended and I was chosen to be the first director of the newly established Department of Applied Economics in Cambridge. Between leaving the government service and taking up my new post I had a break of about three months, which I spent at the Institute of Advanced Study in Princeton. I intended to use my time there writing up my ideas on a social accounting system for the measurement of economic flows, a thing I had wanted to do for years but had not had time for during the war. What happened was that in Princeton I met Alexander Loveday, the Director of Intelligence at the League of Nations, who wanted a paper on the problems of defining and measuring the national income and related totals for consideration by the League's Committee of Statistical Experts. He asked me if I would undertake the work and naturally I accepted. I soon had a memorandum ready and it was discussed in Princeton while I was still there by a subcommittee convened by Loveday. Their report was eventually published by the United Nations in Geneva in 1947 under the title *Measurement of National Income and the Construction of Social Accounts*, with my memorandum as an appendix.

In Europe, interest in social accounting had been growing and I had around that time many fruitful exchanges with my European colleagues. The catalyst, again, was an international body. In the late 1940's the Organisation for European Economic Cooperation was established in Paris with the initial aim of administering American aid under the Marshall Plan. It was decided, at the instigation I think of Richard Ruggles, that the national accounts would provide a useful framework for reviewing the progress of the member countries, and with this in mind a National Accounts Research Unit was set up in Cambridge under my direction. The brief my European colleagues and I were given was, first, to produce a standard system of accounts; second, to prepare studies of the national accounts of individual countries; and, third, to train other statisticians from member countries in the appropriate techniques. It was a lively group, which included visitors from Austria, Denmark, France, Greece, the Netherlands, Norway, Sweden and Switzerland. Several reports resulted from our activity, among them *A Simplified System of National Accounts* and *A Standardised System of National Accounts*, published by the OEEC in 1950 and 1952 respectively. The research lasted from 1949 to 1951, when its work was taken over by the economics and statistics section of the Organisation in Paris, then directed by Milton Gilbert.

Concurrently with this work, my main research interest at the Department of Applied Economics was the analysis of consumers' behaviour. I had made a start on this during the war at the National Institute of Economic and Social Research as part of a large project I had in mind for estimating the British national accounts for the interwar period, so that we should have series going back over the 1920's and 1930's comparable as far as possible with the official estimates that had been started in 1941. My first paper on the subject, 'The analysis of market demand', was read to the Royal Statistical Society and published in its journal in 1945. After moving to Cambridge I had continued my work with the help of Deryck Rowe of the National Institute, and eventually two large volumes appeared, the first in 1954 and the second in 1967, under the title *The Measurement of Consumers' Expenditure and Behaviour in the United Kingdom, 1920-1938*. At the time of the publication of the first volume I wrote a paper, applying to British data a system of demand equations which I termed the linear expenditure system, in which the price of each commodity appeared along with income in each of the equations. The model had been devised by Lawrence Klein and Herman Rubin as a basis for constructing a constant-utility index of the cost of living. It is now superseded, but it had a good innings and has been used all over the world.

During the early 1950's I made a number of trips abroad in connection with the national accounts. In 1950 I visited India with Simon Kuznets and J. B. D. Derksen to advise the National Income Committee on methods of estimation and in 1952 I spent some time in Athens on a similar mission to the Ministry of Coordination.

In July of that same year I was called to New York by the UN Statistical Office, who wished to establish a standard system of national accounts and was convening a committee of experts for the purpose. I was chosen as chairman and work began. The weather was so hot that we decided to sleep by day and work by night. This proved very effective: our report was formulated, discussed and written in one month and was published by the UN with very little delay as *A System of National Accounts and Supporting Tables* (SNA).

In 1952 not many statisticians were familiar with national accounting and so there was no need for elaborate discussions outside the committee. The position was very different twelve years later, when the major revision of the SNA began. By that time most statistical offices were contructing national accounts and it was desirable to have a series of regional consultations if the new system was to prove acceptable. The consultative period lasted from 1964 to 1968 and the main task of explaining the revised version to committee after committee devolved on my friend Abraham Aidenoff of the UN Statistical Office. The new system appeared in 1968 as a *System of National Accounts*. I was responsible for writing the first four chapters and the remainder was the work of Aidenoff.

In 1955 I gave up the directorship of the Department of Applied Economics on being appointed P. D. Leake Professor of Finance and Accounting in the University. My duties in this capacity were to advance knowledge in my subject and live within five miles of the University Church, two commitments which suited me very well.

Towards the end of the 1950's, stimulated by Alan Brown who had been working with me at the Department since 1952, I thought it would be a good idea to bring together various studies that were in progress at the Department and build an econometric model of the British economy. This was the start of the Cambridge Growth Project. In 1962 Alan and I published our ideas in *A Computable Model of Economic Growth*, the opening volume in our series *A Programme for Growth*. The beginnings were comparatively modest, though the principal characteristics of the model were present from the outset; it was a disaggregated model in which several branches of production, types of commodity, consumers' goods and services and government purposes were distinguished, and it was based on a social accounting matrix. At first it was a static model which provided projections for a period about five years ahead without considering the path that would be followed in reaching the projected situation. Now it is one of the largest existing models of a national economy, and under the influence of T. S. Barker, who succeeded me as director of the Project, it has assumed a dynamic form: given an initial state of the economy and future values of the exogenous variable such as tax rates and the level of world trade, which we do not try to model, we can solve the several thousand equations of the system iteratively year by year so as to trace the course of each of the endogenous variable into the future. The model can also be used for purposes other than forecasting. Just for the record I should add that the team engaged on the Project, though changing in composition through the years, has never numbered more than ten people.

In 1956 my wife Feodora had died after a long illness. In 1960 I married Giovanna Croft-Murray (*née* Saffi) who, though not formally trained as an economist, has been for the last twenty-five years my partner in all my work. We wrote two books together, *Social Accounting and Economic Models* (1959) and *National Income and Expenditure* (1961). The latter was an expanded fifth edition of a little book Meade and I had written in 1944; it went into five more editions, the last one appearing in 1977. Giovanna played a large part in editing the twelve volumes of *A Programme for Growth* which described the Cambridge Growth Model up to 1974, and threw herself with particular enthusiasm into the work on social demography and demographic accounting which I began in 1965.

I started this work with the idea of introducing education and training into the Growth Model. This never came to anything but I continued to work on education and eventually was asked by the Organization for Economic Cooperation and Development to prepare a report on the subject for their Committee for Scientific and Technical Personnel. In this I explained what demographic accounting is, what kind of information is needed to carry it out and how it can be used as a basis for model-building. The report was illustrated by examples drawn from the British educational system and was published by the OECD in 1971 under the title *Demographic Accounting and Model-Building*. In 1970 the UN Statistical Office became interested in developing an integrated system of social and demographic statistics and called me in as a consultant. After preparing several drafts for the usual round of discussion, I finally wrote the report which was published by the UN in 1975 under the title *Towards a System of Social and Demographic Statistics* (SSDS).

As with the revised SNA, the interpreter of the SSDS throughout the world during the period of gestation was Aidenoff. My long collaboration with him, like my collaboration with Milton Gilbert at the OEEC and with Alan Brown on the Cambridge Growth Project, was one of the many happy working relationships of my life.

In the last ten years my interest has focused on three subjects. I have continued my work on social demography. I have tried out on the British national accounts the adjustment method on which I had written a paper in 1942 with David Champernowne and James Meade entitled 'The precision of national income estimates'. And I have given some thought to mathematical simulation models of economic growth and fluctuation, their stability and their control.

In 1980 I retired from my University post. My retirement, however, has not severed my links with the two colleges with which I had been associated throughout my life in Cambridge: King's College, where I have held a Fellowship since 1945, and Gonville and Caius College, where I spent my undergraduate days and where I have been an Honorary Fellow since 1976. Nor has it altered my habits much except in so far as it has enabled me to work full time where I have always preferred to work, at home. Recently a period of ill health has slowed me down, but now things are improving and I have started to pick up the threads again. I look forward to a productive 1985.

POSTSCRIPT

This brief autobiography was written by Richard Stone to accompany his Nobel Lecture published in *Les Prix Nobel 1984* and is reproduced here by kind permission of the Nobel Foundation. The optimistic note on which it ends was justified: his health did improve and he was able to resume working, though not in the directions suggested in his penultimate paragraph. His interest turned increasingly towards the history of his subject. The principal product of this phase was the Mattioli Lectures of 1986 and their expansion into the present volume. He also wrote two papers applying econometric analysis to seventeenth-century data, one on consumers' behaviour and the other on war finance; four on the more recent developments in national accounting; and one on the present state of games theory. His last work was a paper on Adam Smith's views on the functions of the State in the economy. After that his health took another turn for the worse and although his mental capacity was not impaired his physical energy was exhausted. He died on 6 December 1991 in the seventy-ninth year of his life.

BIBLIOGRAPHY OF RICHARD STONE'S WORKS 1936-1990

1936

1. A study of costs (with W. A. TWEDDLE). *Econometrica*, vol. 4, no. 3, 1936, pp. 226-41.

1937

2. 'Trends' (with W. M. STONE). Monthly articles in *Industry Illustrated*, June-December 1937.

1938

3. The marginal propensity to consume and the multiplier (with W. M. STONE). *The Review of Economic Studies*, vol. VI, no. 1, 1938, pp. 1-24.
4. 'Trends' (with W. M. STONE). Monthly articles in *Industry Illustrated*, January-December 1938.

1939

5. Indices of industrial output (with W. M. STONE). *The Economic Journal*, vol. XLIX, no. 195, 1939, pp. 477-85.
6. Pitfalls in assessing the state of trade (with W. M. STONE). In *British Management Yearbook 1939* (ed. R. PUGH), Pitman, London, 1939, pp. 21-78.
7. 'Trends' (with W. M. STONE). Monthly articles in *Industry Illustrated*, January-May 1939.

1941

8. The construction of tables of national income, expenditure, savings and investment (with J. E. MEADE). *The Economic Journal*, vol. LI, nos. 202-3, 1941, pp. 216-31; reprinted in *Readings in the Concepts and Measurement of Income* (eds. R. H. PARKER and G. C. HARCOURT), Cambridge University Press, 1969.

1942

9. The national income, output and expenditure of the United States of America, 1929-41. *The Economic Journal*, vol. LII, nos. 206-7, 1942, pp. 154-75. Comment by Milton GILBERT in vol. LIII, no. 209, 1943, pp. 82-3.

10. The precision of national income estimates (with D. G. CHAMPERNOWNE and J. E. MEADE). *The Review of Economic Studies*, vol. IX, no. 2, 1942, pp. 111-25.

1943

11. National income in the United Kingdom and the United States of America. *The Review of Economic Studies*, vol. X, no. 1, 1943, pp. 1-27.

12. The fortune teller. *Economica*, New Series, vol. X, no. 37, 1943, pp. 24-33.

13. Two studies on income and expenditure in the United States. *The Economic Journal*, vol. LIII, no. 209, 1943, pp. 60-75.

1944

14. Employment in U.S. manufacturing. *The Economic Journal*, vol. LIV, no. 214, 1944, pp. 246-52.

15. *National Income and Expenditure* (with J. E. MEADE). Oxford University Press, 1944; 2nd and 3rd editions, Bowes and Bowes, Cambridge, 1948 and 1952; 4th edition, Bowes and Bowes, London, 1957. See also no. 79 below.

1945

16. The analysis of market demand. *Journal of the Royal Statistical Society*, vol. 108, pts. 3 and 4, 1945, pp. 1-98.

1946

17. John Maynard Keynes (obituary). *Economisch-Statistische Berichten* (Amsterdam), 17 July 1946.

18. Lord Keynes: the new theory of money. *Nature*, vol. 158, 9 November, 1946, p. 652.

19. The national income: a statistical account of the British economy. *The Times*, 27 May 1946.

20. National income and expenditure: the local authority sector. *Local Government Finance*, July 1946, pp. 1-3.

21. Economic models with special reference to Mr. Kaldor's system (with E. F. JACKSON). *The Economic Journal*, vol. LVI, no. 224, 1946, pp. 556-67.

22. Social accounting in Holland. *Accountancy*, October 1946.

1947

23. Definition and measurement of the national income and related totals. Appendix to *Measurement of National Income and Construction of Social Accounts*, UN, Geneva, 1947.

24. Social accounting: I. National income before and since the war; II. Consumption and the course of prices. *The Times*, 29 and 30 August 1947.

25. On the interdependence of blocks of transactions. *Supplement to the Journal of the Royal Statistical Society*, vol. IX, nos. 1-2, 1947, pp. 1-45.

26. Prediction from autoregressive schemes and linear stochastic difference systems. Paper presented at the ISC, Washington, 1947. In *Proceedings of the International Statistical Conferences*, 1947, vol. V (*Econometric Society*), 1951, pp. 29-38.

27. The measurement of national income and expenditure: a review of the official estimates of five countries. *The Economic Journal*, vol. LVII, no. 227, 1947, pp. 272-98.

1948

28. National accounting and national budgeting for economic policy. *Nationalekonomiska Föreningens Förhandligar, 1947* (Stockholm), pt. 3, 1948, pp. 63-72.

29. Social accounting, aggregation and invariance. *Cahiers du Congrès International de Comptabilité*, 1948. French translation in *Economie Appliquée*, vol. II, no. 1, 1949, pp. 26-54.

30. The analysis of market demand: an outline of methods and results. *Review of the International Statistical Institute*, vol. 16, no. 1/4, 1948, pp. 23-35.

31. *The Role of Measurement in Economics*. The Newmarch Lectures, 1948-49. Cambridge University Press, 1951; facsimile edn, Gregg Revivals, Aldershot, 1994.

32. The theory of games. *The Economic Journal*, vol. LVIII, no. 230, 1948, pp. 185-201.

33. The presentation of the central government accounts (with F. Sewell BRAY). *Accounting Research*, vol. 1, no. 1, 1948, pp. 1-12.

34. British output in 1946-47 (with C. F. CARTER and W. B. REDDAWAY). *The Times*, 18 February 1948.

35. National income: shift of purchasing power from rich to poor. *The Times*, 3 June 1948.

36. *The Measurement of Production Movements* (with C. F. CARTER and W. B. REDDAWAY). Cambridge University Press, 1948; reprinted, 1965.

37. A new index of industrial production (with C. F. CARTER, W. B. REDDAWAY and F. WINTER). *Bulletin of the London and Cambridge Economic Service*, vol. XXVI, 1948.

38. *The Distribution of Income and Saving*. W. F. L. 359, The National Savings Committee. H.M.S.O, London, 1949.

1949

39. Functions and criteria of a system of social accounting. Paper presented at the IARIW conference, Cambridge, 1949. In *Income and Wealth*, Ser. 1, Bowes and Bowes, Cambridge, 1951.

40. The use of sampling methods in national income statistics and social accounting (with J. E. G. UTTING and J. DURBIN). Paper presented at the ISI conference, Berne, 1949. *Review of the International Statistical Institute*, vol. 18, no. 1/2, 1950, pp. 21-44; reprinted in *Accounting Research*, vol. 1, no. 4, 1950, pp. 333-56.

1950

41. The relationship between input-output analysis and national accounting (with J. E. G. UTTING). Paper presented at the first International Conference on Input-Output Techniques, Driebergen, 1950. In *Input-Output Relations*, H. E. Stenfert Kroese, Leiden, 1953.

1951

42. Simple transaction models, information and computing. Paper presented at a conference on Automatic Control, Cranfield, 1951. *The Review of Economic Studies*, vol. XIX (2), no. 49, 1951-52, pp. 67-84.

43. The demand for food in the United Kingdom before the war. *Metroeconomica*, vol. III, no. 1, 1951, pp. 8-27.

44. The use and development of national income and expenditure estimates. In *Lessons of the British War Economy* (ed. D. N. CHESTER), Cambridge University Press, 1951.

45. Inter-country comparisons of the national accounts and the work of the national accounts research unit of the OEEC (with Kurt

HANSEN). Paper presented at the IARIW conference, Royaumont, 1951. In *Income and Wealth*, Ser. III, Bowes and Bowes, Cambridge, 1953.

1952

46. Systems of aggregative index numbers and their compatibility (with S. J. PRAIS). *The Economic Journal*, vol. LXII, no. 247, 1952, pp. 565-83.

1953

47. Model-building and the social accounts: a survey. Paper presented at the IARIW conference, Castelgandolfo, 1953. In *Income and Wealth*, Ser. IV, Bowes and Bowes, London, 1955.

48. Recent developments in national income and social accounting (with Milton GILBERT). Paper presented at the ISI conference, Rome, 1953. *Bulletin de l'Institut International de Statistique*, vol. XXXIV, no. 2, 1954, pp. 367-97; reprinted in *Accounting Research*, vol. 5, no. 1, 1954, pp. 1-31.

49. Forecasting from econometric equations: a further note on derationing (with S. J. PRAIS). *The Economic Journal*, vol. LXIII, no. 249, 1953, pp. 189-95.

50. Report of the evaluative committee for *Econometrica* (with P. A. SAMUELSON and T. C. KOOPMANS). *Econometrica*, vol. 22, no. 2, 1954, pp. 141-6.

1954

51. Input-output and the social accounts. Paper presented at the second International Conference on Input-Output Techniques, Varenna, 1954. In *The Structural Interdependence of the Economy* (ed. T. BARNA), Wiley, New York; Giuffrè, Milan, 1955.

52. Linear expenditure systems and demand analysis: an application to the pattern of British demand. Paper presented at the second International Conference on Input-Output Techniques, Varenna, 1954. *The Economic Journal*, vol. LXIV, no. 255, 1954, pp. 511-27; also in *The Structural Interdependence of the Economy* (ed. T. BARNA), Wiley, New York; Giuffrè, Milan, 1955.

53. Misery and bliss. Paper presented at the World Population Conference, Rome, 1954. *Proceedings of the World Population Conference, 1954*,

vol. v, pp. 779-98, UN, New York, 1955; also in *Economia Internazionale*, vol. VIII, no. 1, 1955, pp. 72-93. Included in no. 118 below.

54. The way the money went. *The Times*, 25 and 26 February 1954.

55. *The Measurement of Consumers' Expenditure and Behaviour in the United Kingdom, 1920-1938*, vol. I (with D. A. Rowe and others). Cambridge University Press, 1954.

1955

56. National income and national accounts: their construction and use in economic policy (in Greek). *Review of Economic and Political Sciences* (Athens), vol. x, no. 1-2, 1955, pp. 1-33.

57. Transaction models with an example based on the British national accounts (in Spanish). *Boletin del Banco Central de Venezuela*, vol. XV, nos. 119-21, 1955, pp. 12-29; English original, *Accounting Research*, vol. VI, no. 3, 1955, pp. 202-26.

58. Some estimation problems in demand analysis (with J. Aitchison and Alan Brown). *The Incorporated Statistician*, vol. 5, no. 4, 1955, pp. 165-77.

59. Aggregate consumption and investment functions for the household sector considered in the light of British experience (with D. A. Rowe). Paper presented at the IARIW conference, Hindsgavl, 1955. *Nationaløkonomisk Tidsskrift* (Copenhagen), vol. 94, pts. 1 and 2, 1956, pp. 1-32.

1956

60. *Quantity and Price Indexes in National Accounts*. OEEC, Paris, 1956.

61. *Social Accounting and Economic Models* (in Turkish). Ajans-Türk Matbaasi, Ankara, 1956.

1957

62. The market demand for durable goods (with D. A. Rowe). *Econometrica*, vol. 25, no. 3, 1957, pp. 423-43; reprinted in *Consumer Behaviour* (eds. A. S. C. Ehrenberg and F. G. Pyatt), Penguin Books, Harmondsworth, 1971.

1958

63. Can economists help business? *The Accountant*, 22 March 1958, pp. 337-40.

64. Dynamic demand functions: some econometric results (with D. A. ROWE). *The Economic Journal*, vol. LXVIII, no. 270, 1958, pp. 256-70.

65. Questions and answers. December 1958. Unpublished.

1959

66. Market forecasting and the family income. *The Times Review of Industry*, vol. 13, no. 153 (new series), 1959, pp. 6 and 9.

67. *Social Accounting and Economic Models* (with Giovanna CROFT-MURRAY). Bowes and Bowes, London, 1959; Japanese translation (with additions), Tōyō Keisai Shinposha (New Publishing Co. of the Eastern Economist), 1964; Spanish Translation (with no. 79 below), Ediciones Oikos-tau, Barcelona, 1965.

1960

68. A comparison of the economic structure of regions based on the concept of distance. *Journal of Regional Science*, vol. 2, no. 2, 1960, pp. 1-20. Included in no. 118 below.

69. A dynamic model of demand (in Polish). *Przeglad Statystyczny* (Warsaw), vol. VII, no. 3, 1960, pp. 255-70. English original in no. 118 below.

70. Social accounts at the regional level: a survey. Paper presented at the OEEC conference on Regional Economic Planning, Bellagio, 1960. In *Regional Economic Planning: Techniques of Analysis*, OEEC, Paris, 1961. Included in no. 118 below.

71. Three models of economic growth. Paper presented at the International Congress for Logic, Methodology and Philosophy of Science, Stanford, 1960. In *Logic, Methodology and Philosophy of Science* (eds. E. NAGEL, P. SUPPES and A. TARSKI), Stanford University Press, 1962. Included in no. 118 below.

72. The durability of consumers' durable goods (with D. A. ROWE). *Econometrica*, vol. 28, no. 2, 1960, pp. 407-16; reprinted in *Readings in Economic Statistics and Econometrics* (ed. A. ZELLNER), Little, Brown and Co., Boston, 1968.

1961

73. An econometric model of growth: the British economy in ten years' time. *Discovery*, vol. XXII, no. 5, 1961, pp. 216-19.

74. Consumers' wants and expenditures: a survey of British studies since 1945. In *L'évaluation et le rôle des besoins de biens de consommation dans les divers régimes économiques*, Centre National de la Recherche Scientifique, Paris, 1963. Included in no. 138 below.

75. How fast can Britain grow? *The Director*, vol. 13, no. 11, 1961, pp. 268-8.

76. *Input-Output and National Accounts*. OEEC, Paris, 1961. Russian translation, Statistica Publishing House, Moscow, 1964.

77. Multiple classifications in social accounting. Paper presented at the ISI conference, Paris, 1961. *Bulletin de l'Institut International de Statistique*, vol. XXXIX, no. 3, 1962, pp. 215-33. Included in no. 118 below.

78. Population mathematics, demand analysis and investment planning (in Polish). *Przeglad Statystyczny* (Warsaw), vol. VIII, no. 2, 1961, pp. 127-36. English original in no. 118 below.

79. *National Income and Expenditure* (with Giovanna STONE). 5th edition, rewritten, of no. 15 above, 1961; 6th edition, 1962; 7th edition, 1964; 8th edition, 1966; 9th edition, 1972; 10th edition, 1977; all Bowes and Bowes, London. Spanish translation (with no. 67 above), Ediciones Oikos-tau, Barcelona, 1965; Japanese translation, 1969.

80. A long-term growth model for the British economy (with Alan BROWN). Paper presented at the IARIW conference, Tutzing, 1961. In *Europe's Future in Figures* (ed. R.C. GEARY), North-Holland Publishing Co., Amsterdam, 1962.

1962

81. A demonstration model of economic growth. *The Manchester School of Economic and Social Studies*, vol. XXX, no. 1, 1962, pp. 1-14. Included in no. 118 below.

82. Some aggregation problems in input-output analysis (in Polish). *Przeglad Statystyczny* (Warsaw), vol. IX, no. 1, 1962, pp. 25-8.

83. Models for seasonal adjustment (in Polish). *Przeglad Statystyczny* (Warsaw), vol. IX, no. 2, 1962, pp. 119-34. English original in no. 138 below.

84. The housekeeper and the steersman. *L'industria*, no. 4, 1962, pp. 417-26. Included in no. 118 below.

85. *A Computable Model of Economic Growth* (with Alan BROWN). No. 1 in *A Programme for Growth*, Chapman and Hall, London, 1962; Czech

translation, The Economico-Mathematical Laboratory of the Czechoslovakian Academy of Sciences, Prague, 1965.

86. *A Social Accounting Matrix for 1960* (with Alan BROWN and others). No. 2 in *A Programme for Growth*, Chapman and Hall, London, 1962.

87. Behavioural and technical change in economic models (with Alan BROWN). Paper presented at the IEA conference, Vienna, 1962. In *Problems in Economic Development* (ed. E. A. G. ROBINSON), Macmillan, London, 1965.

88. Output and investment for exponential growth in consumption (with Alan BROWN). *The Review of Economic Studies*, vol. XXIX, no. 80, 1962, pp. 241-5.

89. A post-war expenditure function (with D. A. ROWE). *The Manchester School of Economic and Social Studies*, vol. XXX, no. 2, 1962, pp. 187-201.

90. A generalisation of the theorem of Frisch and Waugh (in Polish). *Przeglad Statystyczny* (Warsaw), vol. IX, no. 4, 1962, pp. 401-3. English original in no. 138 below.

1963

91. Computational analogue of economic growth (in Ukrainian). *Avtomatika* (Kiev), no. 5, 1963, pp. 39-45.

92. Consistent projections in multi-sector models. Paper presented at the IEA conference, Cambridge, 1963. In *Activity Analysis in the Theory of Growth and Planning* (eds. E. MALINVAUD and M. O. L. BACHARACH), Macmillan, London, 1967. Included in no. 138 below.

93. Models of the national economy for planning purposes. *Operational Research Quarterly*, vol. 14, no. 1, 1963, pp. 51-9. Included in no. 118 below.

94. Possible worlds. *The Investment Analyst*, no. 6, 1963, pp. 10-14.

95. Social accounting and standardised national accounts (in Spanish). *Informacion Comercial Española* (Madrid), no. 356, 1963, pp. 31-9. English original in no. 138 below.

96. The *a priori* and the empirical in economics. *L'industria*, no. 4, 1963, pp. 467-86. Included in no. 118 below.

97. The analysis of economic systems. Paper presented at the seventh study week of the Pontifical Academy of Sciences, Rome, 1963. In

Pontificiae Academiae Scientiarum Scripta Varia, no. 28 (2 vols), 1965; also in *The Econometric Approach to Development Planning*, North-Holland Publishing Co., Amsterdam, 1965.

98. A programme for economic growth (with Alan Brown). *Data Processing*, vol. 5, no. 2, 1963, pp. 70-7.

99. *Economic Growth and Manpower* (with Alan Brown, Graham Pyatt and Colin Leicester). Report of the BACIE spring conference, 1963. British Association for Commercial and Industrial Education, London, 1963.

1964

100. A framework for economic decisions. *Moorgate and Wall Street*, Spring 1964, pp. 5-24; reprinted in *Models for Decision* (ed. C. M. Berners-Lee), English Universities Press, London, 1965.

101. British economic balances in 1970: a trial run on Rocket. Paper presented at the sixteenth symposium of the Colston Research Society, Bristol, 1964. In *Econometric Analysis for National Economic Planning* (eds. E. Hart, G. Mills and J. K. Whitaker), Butterworths, London, 1964. Included in no. 118 below.

102. Computer models of the economy. *New Scientist*, vol. 21, no. 381, 1964, pp. 604-5; reprinted in *The World of 1984*, vol. 2 (ed. N. Calder), Penguin, Harmondsworth, 1965.

103. Mathematics in the social sciences. *Scientific American*, vol. 211, no. 3, 1964, pp. 168-82 (edited version); reprinted in *Mathematics in the Modern World*, Freeman, San Francisco and London, 1968. Polish translation, *Matematyka w Swiecie Wsopolczesnym*, Polish Scientific Publishers (PWN), Warsaw, 1966. Title essay of no. 118 below (original version).

104. Private saving in Britain, past, present and future. *The Manchester School of Economic and Social Studies*, vol. XXXII, no. 2, 1964, pp. 79-112. Included in no. 118 below.

105. The changing pattern of consumption. In *Problems of Economic Dynamics and Planning* (essays in honour of Michal Kalecki), Polish Scientific Publishers (PWN), Warsaw, 1964. Included in no. 118 below.

106. *The Model in its Environment* (expanded version of no. 97 above). No. 5 in *A Programme for Growth*, Chapman and Hall, London, 1964; reproduced in part in *Automatica*, vol. 4, no. 2, 1966, pp. 55-71.

107. Transitional planning. In *On Political Economy and Econometrics* (essays in honour of Oskar Lange), Polish Scientific Publishers (PWN), Warsaw, 1964. Italian translation, *L'industria*, no. 3, 1966, pp. 327-46. Included in no. 118 below.

108. Demand analysis and projections for Britain: 1900-1970: a study in method (with Alan BROWN and D. A. ROWE). In *Europe's Future Consumption* (ed. J. SANDEE), North-Holland Publishing Co., Amsterdam, 1964; reprinted in shortened form in *Consumer Behaviour* (eds. A. S. C. EHRENBERG and F. G. PYATT), Penguin, Harmondsworth, 1971.

109. The methodology of planning models (with Colin LEICESTER). Paper presented at the NBER conference, Princeton, 1964. In *National Economic Planning* (ed. M. F. MILLIKAN), National Bureau of Economic Research, New York, 1967. Italian translation, *L'industria*, no. 4, 1968, pp. 409-31.

110. Models for demand projections. In *Essays on Econometrics and Planning* (in honour of P. C. Mahalanobis, eds. C. R. RAO and others); Pergamon Press, Oxford; Statistical Publishing Society, Calcutta, 1964. Included in no. 138 below.

1965

111. A model of the educational system. *Minerva*, vol. III, no. 2, 1965, pp. 172-86. Included in no. 118 below.

112. Modelling economic systems (in Russian). *Economics and Mathematical Methods* (Moscow), vol. I, pt. 3, pp. 363-90, and pt. 4, pp. 502-14, 1965.

113. The Cambridge Growth Project. *Cambridge Research*, October 1965, pp. 9-15.

114. The social accounts from a consumer's point of view. Paper presented at the IARIW conference, Lom, 1965. *The Review of Income and Wealth*, Ser. 12, no. 1, 1966, pp. 1-33. Abridged version, entitled 'Simple financial models based on the new SNA', included in no. 138 below.

1966

115. Input-output and demographic accounting: a tool for educational planning. *Minerva*, vol. IV, no. 3, 1966, pp. 365-80. Russian translation, *Economics and Mathematical Methods*, vol. III, no. 3, 1967, pp. 355-69. Included in no. 138 below.

116. Mathematical models in educational planning: a view of the conference. Introduction to the proceedings of a meeting held by the OECD, Paris, 1966. In *Mathematical Models in Educational Planning*, OECD, Paris, 1967. Included in no. 138 below.

117. Mathematical models of the economy. *Bulletin of the Institute of Mathematics and its Applications*, vol. 2, no. 3, 1966, pp. 77-87. Title essay of no. 138 below.

118. *Mathematics in the Social Sciences and Other Essays* (containing nos. 53, 68, 69, 70, 71, 77, 78, 81, 84, 93, 96, 101, 103, 104, 105, 107 and 111 above). Chapman and Hall, London, 1966. Polish translation, *Matematyka w Naukach Spolecznych*, Polish Economic Publishers (PWE), Warsaw, 1970. Chinese translation, Publishing House of Beijing Economic College (PHBEC), Beijing, 1944.

119. National income. In *Chambers' Encyclopaedia*, fourth edition, 1966.

120. Official statistics: a golden treasury or a working tool? Memorandum submitted to the Sub-Committee on Economic Affairs. In *Fourth Report from the Estimates Committee*, H.M.S.O., London, 1966.

121. National and sector balance sheets: uses, concepts and statistical problems. Report for the UN Statistical Office, April 1966. Unpublished.

122. Our unstable economy: can planning succeed? Sixth annual lecture of the U. K. Automation Council, December 1966. Reproduced in *Electronics and Power*, vol. 13, 1967, pp. 40 *et seq.*, and in *Control*, vol. II, no. 104, 1967, pp. 64-6. Italian translation, *L'industria*, no. 3, 1967, pp. 350-61. Included in no. 138 below.

123. Spending and saving in relation to income and wealth. *L'industria*, no. 4, 1966, pp. 471-99. Included in no. 138 below.

124. *The Measurement of Consumers' Expenditure and Behaviour in the United Kingdom, 1920-1938*, vol. II (with D. A. ROWE). Cambridge University Press, 1966.

1967

125. Economic and social modelling. Paper presented at a CEIR conference, London, 1967. In *Mathematical Model Building in Economics and Industry*, Griffin, London, 1968.

126. The generation, distribution and use of income. Paper presented at the ISI conference, Sydney, 1967. *Review of the International*

Statistical Institute, vol. 36, no. 2, 1968, pp. 148-57. Included in no. 138 below.

127. The use of social accounting matrices in building planning models. Paper presented at the IARIW conference, Maynooth, 1967. Included in no. 138 below.

128. An example of demographic accounting: the school ages (with Giovanna STONE and Jane GUNTON). Paper presented at the IARIW conference, Maynooth, 1967. *Minerva*, vol. VI, no. 2, 1968, pp. 185-212. Included in no. 138 below.

1968

129. Demographic input-output: an extension of social accounting. Paper presented at the fourth International Conference on Input-Output Techniques, Geneva, 1968. In *Contributions to Input-Output Analysis*, vol. I (ed. A. P. CARTER and A. BRÓDY), North-Holland, Amsterdam, 1970.

130. A comparison of the SNA and the MPS. Paper presented at the Symposium on National Accounts and Balances, Warsaw, 1968. Polish translation in *Bilanse Gospodarki Narodowej*, Warsaw, 1968. English original in no. 138 below.

131. The revision of the SNA: an outline of the new structure. Paper presented at the symposium on National Accounts and Balances, Warsaw, 1968. Polish translation in *Bilanse Gospodarki Norodowej*, Warsaw, 1968. English original in no. 138 below.

132. Input-output projections: consistent price and quantity structures. *L'industria*, no. 2, 1968, pp. 212-24. Included in no. 138 below.

133. Control of an economic system. In *Encyclopaedia of Linguistics, Information and Control*, Pergamon Press, Oxford, 1969.

1969

134. Foreign trade and full employment: an input-output analysis. *L'industria*, no. 4, 1969, pp. 431-43. Included in no. 138 below.

135. *Demographic Accounting and Model Building*. OECD, Paris, 1971.

136. Economic and demographic accounts and the distribution of income. Paper presented at the Symposium on National Economic Modelling, Novosibirsk, 1970. Russian translation, *Economics and*

Mathematical Methods, vol. VII, no. 5, 1971, pp. 658-66; English original, *Acta Oeconomica*, Vol. 11, no. 2/3, 1973, pp. 165-76.

1970

137. An integrated system of demographic, manpower and social statistics and its links with the system of national economic accounts. Report discussed by an expert group convened by the Statistical Office of the UN, Geneva, 1970. *Sankhyā*, Ser. B, vol. 33, pts. 1 and 2, 1971, pp. 1-184.

138. *Mathematical Models of the Economy and Other Essays* (containing nos. 74, 83, 90, 92, 95, 110, 114 (part), 115, 116, 117, 122, 123, 126, 127, 128, 130, 131, 132, and 134 above). Chapman and Hall, London, 1970.

139. Process, capacity and control in an input-output system. *L'industria*, no. 1/2, 1973, pp. 3-17.

140. The fundamental matrix of the active sequence. Paper presented at the Fifth International Conference on Input-Output Techniques, Geneva, 1971. In *Input-Output Techniques* (eds. A. Bródy and A. P. Carter), North-Holland, Amsterdam, 1972. French translation, *Cahiers du Séminaire d'Econométrie*, no. 14, 1972, pp. 9-23.

1971

141. A system of social matrices. Paper presented at the IARIW Conference, Ronneby, 1971. *The Review of Income and Wealth*, Ser. 19, no. 2, 1973, pp. 143-66. Spanish translation, *Desarrollo Económico* (Buenos Aires), vol. 13, no. 49, 1973, pp. 169-97.

142. The evaluation of pollution: balancing gains and losses. *Minerva*, vol. X, no. 3, 1972, pp. 412-25.

1972

143. A Markovian education model and other examples linking social behaviour to the economy. *Journal of the Royal Statistical Society*, Ser. A, vol. 135, pt. 4, 1972, pp. 511-43.

144. Transition and admission models in social demography. Paper presented at a Conference on Quantitative Social Theory and the Study of Formal Organizations, Virginia, 1972. *Social Science Research*, vol. 2, no. 2, 1973, pp. 185-230; also in *Social Indicator Mod-*

els (eds. K. C. LAND and S. SPILERMAN), Russell Sage Foundation, New York, 1975.

145. Demographic growth and the cost of education. In vol. 1 of *Population Growth and Economic Development in the Third World* (ed. L. TABAH), 2 vols, International Union for the Scientific Study of Population, Ordina Editions, 1976.

1973

146. Personal spending and saving in postwar Britain. In *Economic Structure and Development* (essays in honour of Jan Tinbergen, eds. H. C. BOS, H. LINNEMANN and P. de WOLFF), North-Holland, Amsterdam, 1973.

147. Statistics (in Italian). In *Enciclopedia del Novecento*, Istituto della Enciclopedia Italiana, 1984.

148. Demographic variables in the economics of education. Paper presented at the IEA Conference, Valescure, 1973. In *Economic Factors in Population Growth* (ed. A. J. COALE), Macmillan, London, 1976. Hungarian translation of a preliminary version, *Demográfia*, vol. XVII, no. 1, 1974, pp. 11-41.

1974

149. Random walks through the social sciences. Paper presented at the Sixth International Conference on Input-Output Techniques, Vienna, 1974. Unpublished.

150. What is wrong with the national accounts? Paper prepared for the Statistical Office of the United Nations for submission to the Statistical Commission. May 1974. Unpublished.

151. Towards a model of inflation: a survey of some recent findings on the determinants of changes in wages and prices. October 1974. Unpublished.

1975

152. Social statistics and social policy. Paper presented at the 40th Session of the ISI, Warsaw, 1975. *Bulletin de l'Institut International de Statistique*, vol. XLVI, no. 1, 1975, pp. 498-510. Reproduced in *Statistical Policy in Less Developed Countries*, IDS Communications no. 114, University of Sussex, 1975. French version, *Economie et Statistique*, no. 75, 1976, pp. 21-6. Hungarian translation, *Demográfia*, vol. XVIII, no. 4, 1975, pp. 467-78.

153. The expanding frontiers of input-output analysis. Paper presented at the 40th Session of the ISI, Warsaw, 1975. *Bulletin de l'Institut International de Statistique*, vol. XLVI, no. 1, 1975, pp. 306-21.

154. Modelling the educational system. Paper presented at a Research Planning Conference on the Demography of Educational Organizations, Cambridge, Mass., 1975. Unpublished.

155. Introduction to *Social Accounting Methods for Development Planning: a Case Study of Sri Lanka* by Graham PYATT, Alan R. ROE and associates. Cambridge University Press, 1977.

156. Direct and indirect constraints in the adjustment of observations. In *Nasjonalregnskap, Modeller og Analyse* (essays in honour of Odd Aukrust), Statistisk Sentralbyrå, Oslo, 1975.

1976

157. Major accounting problems for a world model. Paper presented at a working seminar on Global Opportunities and Constraints for Regional Development, Harvard University, Cambridge, Mass., 1976. In *Problems of World Modeling* (eds. K. W. DEUTSCH and others), Ballinger, Cambridge, Mass., 1977. Hungarian translation, *Demográfia*, vol. XX, no. 1, 1977, pp. 23-55.

158. Michael James Farrell (obituary). *Annual Report of the Council of King's College, Cambridge*, 1976, pp. 34-6.

159. Abraham Aidenoff, 1913-1975 (obituary). *International Statistical Review*, vol. 44, no. 3, 1976, pp. 383-4.

1977

160. The evolution of the Cambridge Growth Project. Lecture given at the Institut für Siedlungs- und Wohnungswesen der Westfälischen Wilhelms-Universität, Münster. In *Beiträge zur Strukturpolitik*, Materialien zum Siedlungs- und Wohnungswesen und zur Raumplanung, no. 18, Münster, 1977. Hungarian translation, *Statistikai Szemle*, vol. 56, no. 3, 1978, pp. 236-49.

161. Introduction to *Inland Revenue Report on National Income, 1929*. Department of Applied Economics, University of Cambridge, 1977.

162. Introduction to *Econometric Contributions to Public Policy* (proceedings of the IEA conference, Urbino, 1976, eds. R. STONE and W. PETERSON), Macmillan, London, 1978.

163. Harry Gordon Johnson (obituary). *Annual Report of the Council of King's College, Cambridge*, 1977, pp. 24-6.

164. Discussion of Professor Abramovitz's paper on 'Rapid growth potential and its realisation: the experience of capitalist economies in the postwar period', presented at the Fifth World Congress of the IEA, Tokyo, 1977. In *Economic Growth and Resources*, vol. 1, *The Major Issues* (ed. E. MALINVAUD), Macmillan, London, 1979, pp. 34-44.

165. Is America's intrinsic capacity for economic growth greater than Britain's? 1977. Unpublished.

1978

166. Introduction to *Towards a Methodology for Projecting Rates of Literacy and Educational Attainment*. UNESCO, Paris, 1978.

167. The disaggregation of the household sector in the national accounts. Paper presented to the World Bank SAM Conference, Cambridge, England, 1978. In *Social Accounting Matrices: a Basis for Planning* (eds. G. PYATT and J. I. ROUND), The World Bank, Washington, D. C., 1985.

168. Multipliers for Quesnay's *Tableau*. In *Social Accounting Matrices: a Basis for Planning* (eds. G. PYATT and J. I. ROUND), The World Bank, Washington, D. C., 1985.

169. Keynes, political arithmetic and econometrics. The Keynes Lecture in Economics, 1978. In *Proceedings of the British Academy*, vol. LXIII, 1980.

170. Input-output analysis and economic planning: a survey. Paper presented at the International Symposium on Mathematical Programming and its Economic Applications, Venice, 1978. In *Mathematical Programming and its Economic Applications* (eds. G. CASTELLANI and P. MAZZOLENI), Angeli, Milan, 1981.

171. Jacob Marschak, 1898-1977 (obituary). *Journal of the Royal Statistical Society*, Ser. A, vol. 142, pt. 1, 1979, pp. 80-1.

172. Tribute to Luigi Solari. Address presented to the European Meeting of the Econometric Society, Geneva, 1978. In *Qualitative and Quantitative Mathematical Economics* (ed. J. H. P. PAELINCK), Nijhoff, The Hague, 1982.

173. Can matrix multipliers be decomposed in the general case? December 1978. Unpublished.

174. A review of UNIDO's World Industry Cooperation Model in the light of developments in economic model building. December 1978. Unpublished.

1979

175. Where are we now? A short account of the development of input-output studies and their present trends. Paper presented at the Seventh International Conference on Input-Output Techniques, Innsbruck, 1979. In *Proceedings of the Seventh International Conference on Input-Output Techniques*, UN, New York, 1984. Russian translation, *Economics and Mathematical Methods*, vol. xv, no. 6, 1979, pp. 1094-109; Hungarian translation, *Statisztikai Szemle*, vol. 63, no. 6, 1985, pp. 555-70.

176. Sigmoids. Opening address to the Royal Statistical Society Conference, Oxford, 1979. *Bulletin in Applied Statistics (B.I.A.S.)*, vol. 7, no. 1, 1980, pp. 59-119.

177. *Aspects of Economic and Social Modelling*. Lectures delivered at the University of Geneva, 1979. Droz, Geneva, 1981.

1980

178. A simple growth process tending to stationarity. *The Economic Journal*, vol. 90, no. 359, 1980, pp. 593-7.

179. The relationship of demographic accounts to national income and product accounts. Paper presented at the SSRC Workshop on Social Accounting Systems, Washington, D.C., 1980. In *Social Accounting Systems: Essays on the State of the Art* (eds. F. T. JUSTER and K. C. LAND), Academic Press, New York, 1981.

180. The adjustment of observations. March 1980. Unpublished.

181. Whittling away at the residual: some thoughts on Denison's growth accounting. *Journal of Economic Literature*, vol. XVIII, no. 4, 1980, pp. 1539-43.

182. Political economy, economics and beyond. Royal Economic Society, Presidential Address, 1980. *The Economic Journal*, vol. 90, no. 360, 1980, pp. 719-36.

183. A marital status transition matrix: England and Wales, 1972, males. July 1980. Unpublished.

184. Model design and simulation. *Economic Modelling*, vol. 1, no. 1, 1984, pp. 3-23. Retitled 'A model of cyclical growth' in *Nonlinear*

and Multisectoral Macrodynamics (essays in honour of Richard Goodwin, ed. K. VELUPILLAI), Macmillan, London, 1990.

185. Random shocks in a simple growth model. *Economic Modelling*, vol. 1, no. 3, 1984, pp. 277-80.

1981

186. Balancing the national accounts: the adjustment of initial estimates – a neglected stage in measurement. In *Demand, Equilibrium and Trade* (eds. A. INGHAM and A. M. ULPH), Macmillan, London, 1984.

187. The international harmonisation of national income accounts. *Accounting and Business Research*, vol. 12, no. 45, 1981, pp. 67-79.

188. Life profiles and transition matrices in organizing sociodemographic data (appendix to 'Active life profiles for different social groups' by Dudley SEERS). In *Economic Structure and Performance* (essays in honour of Hollis B. Chenery, eds. M. SYRQUIN, L. TAYLOR and L. E. WESTPHAL), Academic Press, San Diego, 1984.

189. Working with what we have: how can existing data be used in the construction and analysis of socio-demographic matrices? Paper presented at the IARIW conference, Gouvieux, 1981. *The Review of Income and Wealth*, Ser. 28, no. 3, 1982, pp. 291-303.

1982

190. How accurate are the British national accounts? In *Specification Analysis in the Linear Model* (essays in honour of Donald Cochrane, eds. M. L. KING and D. E. A. GILES), Routledge and Kegan Paul, London, 1987.

1983

191. Accounting matrices in economics and demography. In *Mathematical Methods in Economics* (ed. F. van der PLOEG), Wiley, New York, 1984.

1984

192. Two populations and their economies (with M. WEALE). Paper presented at the Annual Conference of the Regional Science Association, Canterbury, 1984. In *Integrated Analysis of Regional Systems* (eds. P. W. J. BATEY and M. MADDEN), London Papers in Regional Science no. 15, Pion, London, 1986.

193. Robert Malthus. Address to the Conference of the British Society for Population Studies, Cambridge, 1984. In *The State of Population Theory* (eds. D. COLEMAN and R. SCHOFIELD), Blackwell, Oxford, 1986.

194. The accounts of society. Nobel Memorial Prize Lecture, 1984. In *Les Prix Nobel 1984*, Almquist and Wicksell International, Stockholm, 1985.

195. Richard Stone (an autobiographical sketch). In *Les Prix Nobel 1984*, Almquist and Wicksell International, Stockholm, 1985.

1985

196. Foreword to *Materials for a Balance of the Soviet National Economy, 1928-1930* (eds. S. G. WHEATCROFT and R. W. DAVIES). Cambridge University Press, 1985.

197. James Alan Calvert Brown: an appreciation. *Oxford Bulletin of Economics and Statistics*, vol. 47, no. 3, 1985, pp. 191-7.

198. Entries on: the Matrix multiplier; R. G. D. ALLEN; A. L. BOWLEY; R. C. GEARY; M. G. KENDALL; E. ROTHBARTH; and J. C. STAMP. In *The New Palgrave*, Macmillan, London, 1987.

1986

199. Social accounting: the state of play. *The Scandinavian Journal of Economics*, vol. 88, no. 3, 1986, pp. 453-72.

200. Progress in balancing the national accounts. In *National Income and Economic Progress* (essays in honour of Colin Clark, eds. D. IRONMONGER, J. PERKINS and TRAN VAN HOA), Macmillan, London, 1988.

201. Some British empiricists in the social sciences. Mattioli Lectures. Original version (typescript).

1987

202. When will the war end? *Cambridge Journal of Economics*, vol. 12, 1988, pp. 193-201.

203. Some seventeenth century econometrics: consumers' expenditure. Solari Lecture, Geneva, 1987. *Revue européenne des sciences sociales*, vol. XXVI, no. 81, 1988, pp. 19-41.

1988

204. Some seventeenth century econometrics: public finance. Lecture for the Ninth Centenary Celebrations of the Università degli Studi di Bologna. *Revue européenne des sciences sociales*, vol. XXVII, no. 83, 1989, pp. 5-32.

205. Adjusting the national accounts. Lecture presented at the Central Institute of Statistics, Rome, September 1988. In *Nuova Contabilità Nazionale, Annali di Statistica*, Ser. IX, vol. 9, ISTAT, Rome, 1990.

206. The national accounts today and tomorrow (in Italian). *Rivista di Politica Economica*, vol. LXXIX, Ser. III, no. 2, 1989, pp. 3-38.

207. A leaf from Plutarch. In *Celebrating R. M. Goodwin's 75th Birthday, Quaderni del Dipartimento di Economia Politica*, no. 100, Università degli Studi di Siena, May 1990.

1989

208. The theory of games revisited. In *A Century of Economics* (eds. J. D. HEY and D. WINCH), Blackwell, Oxford, 1990.

209. Professor Sir John Hicks (obituary). *The Caian: The Annual Record of Gonville and Caius College, Cambridge*, November 1989, pp. 100-5.

210. The ET Interview (interviewer M. H. PESARAN). *Econometric Theory*, vol. 7, 1991, pp. 85-123.

1990

211. Public economic policy: Adam Smith on what the State and other public institutions should and should not do. Paper presented at a conference for the bicentenary of Adam Smith's death, Edinburgh, July 1990. In *Adam Smith's Legacy*, Routledge, London and New York, 1992.

REFERENCES

ANON., Obituary of Sir Frederick Morton Eden. *The Gentleman's Magazine*, Dec. 1809, p. 1178.

ARMITAGE Angus, *Edmond Halley*. Nelson, London, 1966.

AUBREY John, *Brief Lives* [*c.* 1667-92] (ed. Oliver LAWSON DICK), Penguin, Harmondsworth, 1972.

BARNETT George E. (ed.), *Two Tracts by Gregory King*. Johns Hopkins Press, Baltimore, 1936.

BEAUFORT Daniel Augustus, *Memoir of a Map of Ireland . . . Containing a short account of its present state civil and ecclesiastical*. W. Faden, London, 1792.

BETTANY George Thomas, William Farr. *The Dictionary of National Biography*, Oxford University Press, vol. VI, pp. 1090-1.

BISHOP William John, *A Bio-Bibliography of Florence Nightingale*. Dawson, London, 1962.

BÖCKH R., Halley als Statistiker. *Bulletin of the International Statistical Institute*, vol. VII, no. 1, 1893, pp. 1-24.

BOOTH Charles, Occupations of the people of the United Kingdom, being a re-statement of the figures given in the Census returns arranged to facilitate comparison. *Journal of the Royal Statistical Society*, vol. XLIX, pt. II, 1886, pp. 314-444.

BOOTH Charles, The inhabitants of Tower Hamlets (School Board division), their condition and occupations. *Journal of the Royal Statistical Society*, vol. L, pt. II, 1887, pp. 326-401.

BOOTH Charles, Condition and occupations of the people of East London and Hackney, 1887. *Journal of the Royal Statistical Society*, vol. LI, pt. II, 1888, pp. 276-339.

BOOTH Charles, Enumeration and classification of paupers, and State pensions for the aged. *Journal of the Royal Statistical Society*, vol. LIV, pt. IV, 1891, pp. 600-43.

BOOTH Charles, *Pauperism, a Picture, and the Endowment of Old Age, an Argument*. Macmillan, London, 1892.

BOOTH Charles, Life and labour of the people in London: first results of an inquiry based on the 1891 census. *Journal of the Royal Statistical Society*, vol. LVI, pt. IV, 1893, pp. 557-93.

BOOTH Charles, *The Aged Poor in England and Wales: Condition*. Macmillan, London, 1894.

BOOTH Charles, *Old Age Pensions and the Aged Poor: a Proposal.* Macmillan, London, 1899.

BOOTH Charles, *Industrial Unrest and Trade Union Policy.* Macmillan, London, 1913.

BOOTH Charles and others, *Life and Labour of the People.* 2 vols, Williams & Norgate, London 1889 and 1891.

BOOTH Charles and others, *Life and Labour of the People in London.* 9 vols, Macmillan, London, 1892-7.

BOOTH Charles and others. *Life and Labour of the People in London.* 17 vols, Macmillan, London, 1902-3.

[BOOTH Mary], *Charles Booth: a Memoir.* Macmillan, London, 1918; republished by Gregg Press, Farnborough, 1968.

BURNETT John, *A History of the Cost of Living.* Penguin Books, Harmondsworth, 1969.

CARLI Gian Rinaldo, *Delle monete e della istituzione delle zecche d'Italia.* Vol. I, The Hague (Venice), 1751, reprinted with additions, Mantova, 1754; vol. II, Giovanelli, Pisa, 1757; vol. III, Giunti, Lucca, pt. 1, 1759, pt. 2, 1760. Abridged reprint in *Scrittori classici italiani di economia politica* (ed. P. Custodi), Parte moderna, vol. XIII, Destefanis, Milan, 1804, pp. 13-227.

CARR-SAUNDERS A. M., *World Population: Past Growth and Present Trends.* Clarendon Press, Oxford, 1936.

CHALMERS George, *An Estimate of the Comparative Strength of Great Britain*, 4th edn (*A New Edition, . . . to which is now annexed Gregory King's Celebrated State of England*). Stockdale, London, 1802.

CHANDLER Tertius, and Gerald Fox. *3000 Years of Urban Growth.* Academic Press, New York, 1974.

CLARK Colin G., *National Income and Outlay.* Macmillan, London, 1937.

CLERKE Agnes Mary, Edmond Halley. *The Dictionary of National Biography*, Oxford University Press, vol. VIII, pp. 988-93.

COKE Roger, *A Treatise Wherein is Demonstrated that the Church and State of England are in Equal Danger with the Trade of it.* London, 1671.

COLQUHOUN Patrick, *A Treatise on the Police of the Metropolis.* C. Dilly, London, 1796; 7th edn, with additions, 1806.

COLQUHOUN Patrick, *A Treatise on Indigence.* J. Hatchard, London, 1806.

COLQUHOUN Patrick, *A Treatise on the Wealth, Power and Resources of the British Empire in Every Quarter of the World.* Joseph Mawman, London, 1814; 2nd edn, with additions and corrections, 1815.

COOK Edward, *The Life of Florence Nightingale.* 2 vols, Macmillan, London, 1913.

COOMBS D., Dr. Davenant and the debate on Franco-Dutch trade. *The Economic History Review*, vol. II, no. 10, 1957, pp. 94-103.

COOPER Thompson, John Graunt. *The Dictionary of National Biography*, Oxford University Press, vol. VIII, pp. 427-8.

COOPER Thompson, Gregory King. *The Dictionary of National Biography*, Oxford University Press, vol. XI, pp. 131-3.

CREEDY John, On the King-Davenant "law" of demand. *Scottish Journal of Political Economy*, vol. 33, no. 3, 1986, pp. 193-212.

CULLEN William, *Synopsis Nosologiæ Methodicæ.* Edinburgh, 1769.

DAVENANT Charles, *An Essay upon Ways and Means of Supplying the War.* Jacob Tonson, London, 1695; reprinted in *The Political and Commercial Works of Charles Davenant* (ed. C. WHITWORTH), London, 1771.

DAVENANT Charles, A Memorial concerning the Coyn of England [1695]. First published in *Two Manuscripts by Charles Davenant* (ed. A. P. USHER), Johns Hopkins Press, Baltimore, 1942.

DAVENANT Charles, A Memorial concerning Creditt [1696]. First published in *Two Manuscripts by Charles Davenant* (ed. A. P. USHER), Johns Hopkins Press, Baltimore, 1942.

DAVENANT Charles, *An Essay on the East India Trade.* Knapton, London, 1696; reissued as an addendum to vol. II of *Discourses on the Publick Revenues*, 1698; reprinted in *The Political and Commercial Works of Charles Davenant* (ed. C. WHITWORTH), London, 1771.

DAVENANT Charles, *Discourses on the Publick Revenues, and on the Trade of England.* 2 vols., Knapton, London, 1698; reprinted in *The Political and Commercial Works of Charles Davenant* (ed. C. WHITWORTH), London, 1771.

DAVENANT Charles, *An Essay upon the Probable Methods of Making a People Gainers in the Ballance of Trade.* Knapton, London, 1699; reprinted in *The Political and Commercial Works of Charles Davenant* (ed. C. WHITWORTH), London, 1771.

DAVIES David, *The Case of Labourers in Husbandry.* G. G. & J. Robinson, Bath and London, 1795.

DEANE Phyllis, The implications of early national income estimates for the measurement of long-term growth in the United Kingdom. *Economic Development and Cultural Change*, vol. IV, no. 1, 1955, pp. 3-38.

DEANE Phyllis and W. A. COLE, *British Economic Growth 1688-1959*. Cambridge University Press, 1962; 2nd edn, 1967.

DIAMOND Marion and Mervyn STONE, Nightingale on Quetelet. *Journal of the Royal Statistical Society*, ser. A, vol. 144, 1981: pt. 1, pp. 66-79; pt. 2, pp. 176-213; pt. 3, pp. 332-51.

DUBLIN Louis I. and Alfred J. LOTKA, *The Money Value of a Man*. Ronald Press, New York, 1936; revised edn, 1946.

DUTOT Charles de FERRARE, *Réflexions politiques sur les finances et le commerce*. 2 vols, Prévost, The Hague, 1738; reprinted (ed. HARSIN), Droz, Paris, 1935.

EDEN Frederick Morton, *The State of the Poor*. 3 vols, Davis, London, 1797; facsimile edn, Cass, London, 1966.

EDEN Frederick Morton, *Porto-Bello: or a Plan for the Improvement of the Port and City of London*. B. White, London, 1798.

EDEN Frederick Morton, *An Estimate of the Number of Inhabitants in Great Britain and Ireland*. Wright, London, 1800.

EDEN Frederick Morton, *Observations on Friendly Societies for the Maintenance of the Industrious Classes during Sickness, Infirmity, Old Age and Other Exigencies*. J. White, London, 1801.

EDEN Frederick Morton, *On the Policy and Expediency of Granting Insurance Charters*. Burton, London, 1806.

EDGEWORTH Francis Ysidro, Sir Frederick Morton Eden. *Dictionary of Political Economy* (ed. R. H. T. PALGRAVE), Macmillan, London, 1894, vol. I, pp. 679-80.

ESPINASSE Francis, Patrick Colquhoun. *The Dictionary of National Biography*, Oxford University Press, vol. IV, pp. 859-61.

EVANS G. Heberton, Jr., The law of demand – the roles of Gregory King and Charles Davenant. *Quarterly Journal of Economics*, vol. 81, no. 3, 1967, pp. 483-92.

EVELYN John, *Diary* [1641-1706] (ed. H. B. WHEATLEY). 4 vols, Bickers, London, 1906.

EYLER John M., *Victorian Social Medicine: The Ideas and Methods of William Farr*. Johns Hopkins Press, Baltimore and London, 1979.

FARR William, Vital statistics. Ch. VII in J. R. MCCULLOCH, *Statistical Account of the British Empire*, Knight, London, 1837; 2nd edn, 1839.

FARR William, Statistical nosology. *First Annual Report of the Registrar General*, H.M.S.O., London, 1839.

FARR William, Report upon the mortality of lunatics. *Journal of the Statistical Society of London*, vol. IV, pt. I, 1841, pp. 17-33.

FARR William, Letter to the Registrar General including English Life Table [no. 1]. *Fifth Annual Report of the Registrar General*, H.M.S.O., London, 1843.

FARR William, English Life Table [no. 2]. *Twelfth Annual Report of the Registrar General*, H.M.S.O, London, 1851.

FARR William, *Report of the Mortality of Cholera in England 1848-49*. H.M.S.O., London, 1852.

FARR William, The income and property tax. *Journal of the Statistical Society of London*, vol. XVI, pt. I, 1853, pp. 1-44.

FARR William, Mortality of males engaged in different occupations. *Fourteenth Annual Report of the Registrar General*, H.M.S.O., London, 1853.

FARR William, On the construction of life-tables, illustrated by a new life-table of the healthy districts of England. *Philosophical Transactions of the Royal Society*, vol. 149, 1859, pp. 837-78.

FARR William, *English Life Table* [no. 3]. H.M.S.O., London, 1864.

FARR William, Report on the cholera epidemic of 1866 in England. *Supplement to the Twenty-ninth Annual Report of the Registrar General*, H.M.S.O., London, 1868.

FARR William, Inaugural address. *Journal of the Statistical Society of London*, vol. XXXIV, pt. IV, 1871, pp. 409-23.

FARR William, *Vital Statistics* (ed. N.A. HUMPHREYS). Stanford, London, 1885.

FITZMAURICE Lord Edmond, *The Life of Sir William Petty*. John Murray, London, 1895.

FITZMAURICE Lord Edmond, Sir William Petty. *The Dictionary of National Biography*, Oxford University Press, vol. XV, pp. 999-1005.

FLEETWOOD William, *Chronicon Preciosum: or An Account of English Money, the Price of Corn and Other Commodities, for the last 600 Years*. 1st edn (anon.) Harper, London, 1707; reprinted in *A Complete Collection of the Sermons, Tracts and Pieces of all Kinds . . . by Dr. William Fleetwood* (ed. W. Powell), Midwinter and Butterworth, London, 1737; reissued with the author's name and an 'Appendix Containing an Historical Account of Coins from William the Conqueror to the Restoration', Osborne, London, 1745.

Fortrey Samuel, *England's Interest and Improvement, Consisting in the Increase of the Store and Trade of this Kingdom.* Cambridge, 1663.

Gazley John G., *The Life of Arthur Young.* American Philosophical Society, Philadelphia, 1973.

Glass David V., Graunt's life table. *Journal of the Institute of Actuaries,* vol. 76, 1950, pp. 60-4.

Glass David V., John Graunt and his *Natural and Political Observations. Proceedings of the Royal Society,* ser. B, vol. 159, 1963, pp. 2-37.

Glass David V., Two papers on Gregory King. In *Population in History* (eds. D. V. Glass and D.E.C. Eversley), Arnold, London, 1965.

Glass David V., *Numbering the People.* D.C. Heath, Farnborough, 1973.

Glass David V. (ed.), *The Population Controversy.* Gregg International, Farnborough, 1973.

Glass David V. (ed.), *The Development of Population Statistics.* Gregg International, Farnborough, 1973.

Goldsmith Raymond W., *Comparative National Balance Sheets.* University of Chicago Press, 1985.

Gompertz Benjamin, On the nature of the function expressive of the law of human mortality, and on a new method of determining the value of life contingencies. *Philosophical Transactions of the Royal Society,* vol. xxxvi, 1825, pp. 513-85.

Graetzer J., *Edmund Halley und Caspar Neumann: ein Beitrag zur Geschichte der Bevölkerungs-Statistik.* S. Schottlaender, Breslau, 1883.

Graunt John, *Natural and Political Observations Mentioned in a following Index, and made upon the Bills of Mortality.* 1st edn, Martyn, Allestry and others, London, 1662; reprinted (ed. F. W. Willcox), Johns Hopkins Press, Baltimore, 1939; facsimile in *The Earliest Classics – John Graunt – Gregory King* (ed. P. Laslett), Gregg International, Farnborough, 1973. 2nd edn, London, 1662. 3rd edn (much enlarged), London, 1665. 4th edn, Oxford, 1665. 5th edn (with additions by Petty?), London, 1676; reprinted in *The Economic Writings of Sir William Petty* (ed. C. H. Hull), Cambridge University Press, 1899; Kelly, New York, 1964. See also Willcox.

GREENWOOD Major, Graunt and Petty. *Journal of the Royal Statistical Society*, vol. XCI, pt. I, 1928, pp. 79-83.

GREENWOOD Major, *The Medical Dictator and Other Biographical Studies.* Williams & Norgate, London, 1936.

GREENWOOD Major, *Medical Statistics from Graunt to Farr.* Cambridge University Press, 1948.

HALLEY Edmond, Letter to John Houghton concerning the number of acres in England and Wales, together with estimates of the acreage of each county. Written *c.* 1682-3 and published in *A Collection of Letters for the Improvement of Husbandry and Trade* (ed. J. HOUGHTON), no. XXIV, 20 Jan. 1693, pp. 68-70, and no. XXV, 27 Jan. 1693, pp. 71-3.

HALLEY Edmond, An estimate of the degrees of mortality of mankind drawn from curious tables of the births and funerals at the city of Breslaw; with an attempt to ascertain the price of annuities upon lives. *Philosophical Transactions of the Royal Society of London*, vol. XVII, no. 196, 1693, pp. 596-610; reprinted in *Degrees of Mortality of Mankind by Edmund Halley* (ed. L. J. REED), Johns Hopkins Press, Baltimore, 1942.

HALLEY Edmond, Some further considerations on the Breslaw bills of mortality. *Philosophical Transactions of the Royal Society of London*, vol. XVII, no. 198, 1693, pp. 654-6; reprinted in *Degrees of Mortality of Mankind by Edmund Halley* (ed. L.J. REED), Johns Hopkins Press, Baltimore, 1942.

HARE F. A. C., *William Farr, F.S.S., M.D, F.R.S., C.B., &c, &c.* London, 1884.

HEYSHAM John, *Observations on the Bills of Mortality in Carlisle for the years 1779-87.* Carlisle City Library; National Library of Medicine, Bethesda, U.S.A.; facsimile in *The Development of Population Statistics* (ed. D.V. GLASS), Gregg International, Farnborough, 1973.

HIGGS Henry, Arthur Young. *The Dictionary of National Biography*, Oxford University Press, vol. XXI, pp. 1272-8.

HOLMES G. S., Gregory King and the social structure of preindustrial England. *Transactions of the Royal Historical Society*, 5th series, vol. 27, 1977, pp. 41-68.

HULL Charles Henry (ed.), *The Economic Writings of Sir William Petty.* 2 vols, Cambridge University Press, 1899; Kelly, New York, 1964.

HUME Leonard J., Charles Davenant on financial administration. *History of Political Economy*, winter 1974, vol. IV, no. 4), pp. 463-77.

HUMPHREYS Noel A., The recent decline in the English death rate, and its effect upon the duration of life. *Journal of the Statistical Society of London*, vol. XLVI, pt. II, 1883, pp. 189-224.

HUMPHREYS Noel A., Biographical sketch of William Farr. In William FARR, *Vital Statistics* (ed. N. A. HUMPHREYS), Stanford, London, 1885.

JEVONS W. Stanley, *The Theory of Political Economy*. Macmillan, London, 1871.

JEVONS W. Stanley, *Money and the Mechanism of Exchange*. P. S. King, London, 1875.

JOHN A. H., *A Liverpool Merchant House*. Allen & Unwin, London, 1959.

KENDALL Maurice G., The early history of index numbers. *Review of the International Statistical Institute*, vol. 37, no. 1, 1969, pp. 1-12; reprinted in *Studies in the History of Statistics and Probability*, vol. II (eds. M. G. KENDALL and R. L. PLACKETT), Griffin, London, 1977.

KEYNES John Maynard, Newton, the Man. First published in *The Collected Works of John Maynard Keynes*, Macmillan, London, 1972, vol. X, *Essays in Biography*, pp. 363-74.

KEYNES John Maynard, *The General Theory of Employment, Interest and Money*. Macmillan, London, 1936; in *The Collected Writings of John Maynard Keynes*, vol. VII, Macmillan, London, 1973.

KING Gregory, *Vitae Gregorij King Fecialis Armorum primo Rouge Dragon titulo deinde Lancastriensis occursus praecipui* (an autobiography). MS copy, Bodleian Library, Rawlinson C. 514; printed in J. DALLAWAY, *Inquiries into the Origin and Progress of the Science of Heraldry*, Gloucester, 1793.

KING Gregory, *A scheme of the Rates and Duties Granted to His Majesty upon Marriages, Births and Burials, and upon Batchelors and Widowers, for the Term of Five Years, from May 1. 1695*. Bill and Newcomb, Printers to the King, London, 1695. British Library, 816.m.6(80).

KING Gregory, *Notebook* ('The Burns Journal'). MS *c.* 1695, Greater London Record Office; facsimile in *The Earliest Classics – John Graunt – Gregory King* (ed. P. LASLETT), Gregg International, Farnborough, 1973.

KING Gregory, *Natural and Politicall Observations and Conclusions upon the State and Condition of England*. MS copy dated 1696, British Library, Harley MSS 1898; first printed in full as Appendix I in George

CHALMERS, *An Estimate of the Comparative Strength of Great Britain*, Stockdale, London, 1804; reprinted in *Two Tracts by Gregory King* (ed. G. E. BARNETT), Johns Hopkins Press, Baltimore, 1936; facsimile of Chalmers edition in *The Earliest Classics – John Graunt – Gregory King* (ed. P. LASLETT), Gregg International, Farnborough, 1973.

KING Gregory, *Observations & Conclusions Natural and Political upon the State and Condition of England* ('the Kashnoor MS'). MS copy dated 1696, with comments by Robert HARLEY and answers by KING dated 1697, National Library of Australia.

KING Gregory, *A Scheme of the Inhabitants of the city of Gloucester* [1696]. First published as Appendix II in George CHALMERS, *An Estimate of the Comparative Strength of Great Britain*, Stockdale, London, 1804.

KING Gregory, 'The Stafford Diary': miscellaneous notes in *ΕΦΗΜΕΡΙΣ, or a Diary Astronomical Astrological Meteorological for 1696* (inscribed on fly-leaf 'Grigorius King Arm. Fecialis Lancastriensis. Natus 13 Dec. 1648'). Stafford Record Office.

KING Gregory, *A Computation of the Endowed Hospitals and Almhouses in England* [1697]. First published as Appendix III in George CHALMERS, *An Estimate of the Comparative Strength of Great Britain*, Stockdale, London, 1804.

KING Gregory, *Of the Naval Trade of England a° 1688 and the National Profit then arising thereby*. MS copy (undated), Bodleian Library, Rawlinson MSS, D919. First printed in *Two Tracts by Gregory King* (ed. G. E. BARNETT), Johns Hopkins Press, Baltimore, 1936.

KOPF, E. W., Florence Nightingale as statistician. *Journal of the American Statistical Association*, vol. 15, no. 116, 1916, pp. 388-404; reprinted in *Studies in the History of Statistics and Probability*, vol. II (eds. M. G. KENDALL and R. L. PLACKETT), Griffin, London, 1977.

LANSDOWNE Henry Charles Keith PETTY-FITZMAURICE, fifth Marquis of (ed.), *The Petty Papers*. 2 vols, Constable, London, and Houghton Mifflin, Boston and New York, 1927.

LARDNER DR., Untitled article on Babbage's calculating engine. *The Edinburgh Review*, vol. LIX, no. CXX, 1834, pp. 263-327; reprinted in *The Works of Charles Babbage* (ed. M. CAMPBELL-KELLY), Pickering, London, 1989, vol. 2, p. 118-86.

LASLETT Peter (ed.), *The Earliest Classics – John Graunt – Gregory King*. Gregg International, Farnborough, 1973.

LAUDERDALE James MAITLAND, eighth Earl of, *An Inquiry into the Na-*

ture and Origins of Public Wealth, and into the Means and Causes of its Increase. Edinburgh, 1804; Italian transl., *Biblioteca dell'Economista*, vol. v, 1st ser., 1854, pp. 1-139.

LE FANU James, Florence Nightingale deserves our apology. *The Times*, 18 January 1996.

LEVI Leone, Dr. Farr. Letter to *The Times*, 23 April 1883.

LEWES Fred, William Farr and cholera. *Population Trends*, no. 31, spring 1983, pp. 8-12.

LINDERT Peter H. and Jeffrey G. WILLIAMSON, Revising England's social tables 1688-1812. *Explorations in Economic History*, vol. 19, 1982, pp. 385-408.

LINDERT Peter H. and Jeffrey G. WILLIAMSON, Reinterpreting Britain's social tables, 1688-1913. *Explorations in Economic History*, vol. 20, 1983, pp. 94-109.

LINNÆUS Carl, *Genera Morborum*. Uppsala, 1759.

LLEWELLYN-SMITH Herbert and others, *New Survey of London Life and Labour*. 9 vols, P. S. King, London, 1930-35.

LOWE Joseph, *On the Present state of England in Regard to Agriculture, Trade and Finance*. Longman and others, London, 1822; 2nd edn, 1823.

McCULLOCH John Ramsey, *A Statistical Account of the British Empire*. 1st edn, 1 vol., Knight, London, 1837; 2nd edn, 2 vols, 1839.

MACDONELL George Paul, Sir Frederick Morton Eden. *The Dictionary of National Biography*, Oxford University Press, vol. VI, pp. 356-7.

MAUNDER W. F., *Bibliography of Index Numbers*. International Statistical Institute, Athlone Press, London, 1970.

MEARNS Andrew, *The Bitter Cry of Outcast London*. Jones, Clark & Co., London, 1883.

MILNE Joshua, *Treatise on the Valuation of Annuities and Assurances on Lives and Survivorships; on the Construction of Tables of Mortality; and on the Probabilities and Expectations of Life*. 2 vols, Longman & others, London, 1815.

MITCHELL Brian and Phyllis DEANE, *Abstract of Historical Statistics of Great Britain*. Cambridge University Press, 1961.

NIGHTINGALE Florence, *Letters from Egypt, 1849-1850*. Privately printed, 1854; new edition (ed. A. SATTIN), Barrie & Jenkins, London, 1987.

NIGHTINGALE Florence, *The Institution of Kaiserswerth on the Rhine for the*

Pratical Training of Deaconesses. Printed by the inmates of the London Ragged Colonial Training School, 1851.

NIGHTINGALE Florence, *Notes on Matters Affecting the Health, Efficiency and Hospital Administration of the British Army . . . Presented by Request to the Secretary of State for War.* Privately printed, Harrison, London, 1858.

NIGHTINGALE Florence, *Mortality of the British Army, at Home and Abroad, and during the Russian War.* Reprinted from the *Report* of the 1857 Royal Sanitary Commission. Harrison, London, 1858.

NIGHTINGALE Florence, Notes on the sanitary conditions of hospitals, and on defects in the construction of hospital wards. *Transactions of the National Association for the Promotion of Social Science, 1858*, J. Parker, London, 1859, pp. 462-82.

NIGHTINGALE Florence, *Notes on Nursing.* Harrison, London, 1859.

NIGHTINGALE Florence, *Notes on Hospitals.* Parker, London, 1859; 3rd edn, rewritten, Longmans, Green & Co., London, 1863.

NIGHTINGALE Florence, Hospital statistics and hospital plans. *Transactions of the National Association for the Promotion of Social Science, 1861*, Parker & Bourne, London, 1862, pp. 554-60.

NIGHTINGALE Florence, *Army Sanitary Administration, and its Reform under the late Lord Herbert.* McCorquodale, London, 1862.

[NIGHTINGALE Florence], Statistics of the general hospitals of London, 1861. *Journal of the Statistical Society of London*, vol. XXV, Sept. 1862, pp. 384-8.

NIGHTINGALE Florence, *Observations on the Evidence Contained in the Stational Reports Submitted to the Royal Commission on the Sanitary State of the Army in India.* Privately printed, Stanford, London, 1863.

NIGHTINGALE Florence, Sanitary statistics of native colonial schools and hospitals. *Transactions of the National Association for the Promotion of Social Science, 1863*, Longmans, Green & Co., London, 1864, pp. 475-89.

NIGHTINGALE Florence, How people may live and not die in India. *Transactions of the National Association for the Promotion of Social Science, 1863*, Longmans, Green & Co., London, 1864, pp. 501-10.

[NIGHTINGALE Florence], *Suggestions in regard to Sanitary Works required for the Improvement of Indian Stations.* Issued by the Barrack and Hospital Improvement Commission, H.M.S.O., London, 1864.

NIGHTINGALE Florence, *Introductory Notes on Lying-in Institutions.* Longmans, Green & Co., 1871.

NIGHTINGALE Florence, How some people have lived, and not died, in India. *Transactions of the National Association for the Promotion of Social Science, 1873*, Longmans, Green & Co., London, 1874, pp. 463-74.

NORMAN-BUTLER Belinda, *Victorian Aspirations: the Life and Labour of Charles and Mary Booth*. Allen & Unwin, London, 1972.

OGILVIE Frederick Wolfe, Charles Booth. *The Dictionary of National Biography, 1912-1921*, Oxford University Press, 1927, pp. 48-50.

PARENTI Giuseppe, La tecnica ed il significato dei primi numeri indice dei prezzi. *Economia*, new series, vol. XXV, no. 6, 1940, pp. 1-31.

PARETO Vilfredo, La legge della domanda. *Giornale degli Economisti*, 2nd ser., vol. X, 1895, pp. 59-68.

PEARSON Karl, *The Life, Letters and Labours of Francis Galton*. 4 vols, Cambridge University Press, 1914 (vol. I), 1924 (vol. II), 1930 (vols. IIIA and IIIB).

PEARSON Karl, *The History of Statistics in the 17th and 18th Centuries*. Lectures delivered between 1921 and 1933 (ed. E. S. PEARSON). Griffin, London, 1978.

PEPYS Samuel, *Diary* [1660-69] (ed. H. B. WHEATLEY). 10 vols, Bell, London, 1893.

PETTY William, *History of the Cromwellian Survey of Ireland, called 'The Down Survey' 1655-6* (ed. T. A. LARCOM). Irish Archaeological and Celtic Society Publications, vol. 15, Dublin University Press, 1851.

PETTY William, *A Treatise of Taxes and Contributions*. 1st edn, Brooke, London, 1662; reprinted in *The Economic Writings of Sir William Petty* (ed. C. H. HULL).

PETTY William, *Verbum Sapienti* [1665]. First published with *The Political Anatomy of Ireland*, Browne and Rogers, London, 1691; reprinted in C. H. HULL (ed.), *op. cit.*

PETTY William, *The Political Anatomy of Ireland* [1672]. First published with *Verbum Sapienti*, Browne and Rogers, London, 1691; reprinted in C. H. HULL (ed.), *op. cit.*

PETTY William, *Political Arithmetick* [*c.* 1671-76]. 1st edn, Clavel and Mortlock, London, 1691; reprinted in C. H. HULL (ed.), *op. cit.*

PETTY William, *Quantulumcumque concerning Money* [*c.* 1682]. 1st extant edn, London, 1695; reprinted in C. H. HULL (ed.), *op. cit.*

PETTY William, *Another Essay in Political Arithmetick Concerning the Growth of the City of London, 1682*. 1st edn, Pardoe, London, 1683; 2nd edn, in *Several Essays in Political Arithmetick*, Clavel and Mortlock, London, 1699; reprinted in C. H. HULL (ed.), *op. cit.*

PETTY William, *Observation upon the Dublin Bills of Mortality, 1681*. 1st edn, Pardoe, London, 1683; 2nd edn, incorporating *Further Observation upon the Dublin Bills* [1682], Pardoe, London, 1686; both reprinted in C. H. HULL (ed.), *op. cit.*

PETTY William, *Five Essays in Political Arithmetick*. 1st edn (in French and English), Mortlock, London, 1687; reprinted in C. H. HULL (ed.), *op. cit.*

PETTY William, *A Treatise of Ireland* [1687]. First published in C. H. HULL (ed.), *op. cit.*

PHELPS BROWN E. H. and Sheila V. HOPKINS, Seven centuries of the prices of consumables, compared with builders' wage-rates. *Economica*, vol. XXIII, no. 92, 1956, pp. 296-314; reprinted in *Essays in Economic History*, vol. II (ed. E. M. CARUS-WILSON), Arnold, London, 1962.

PICKERING George, *Creative Malady*. Allen & Unwin, London, 1974.

POWELL W., Preface to *A Complete Collection of the Sermons, Tracts and Pieces of all kinds that were written by . . . Dr. William Fleetwood* (ed. W. POWELL), Midwinter & Butterworth, London, 1737.

PTOUKHA Michel, John Graunt, fondateur de la démographie (1620-1674). *Congrès International de la Démographie*, vol. 2, section on Démographie Historique, Paris, 1937, pp. 61-74.

QUETELET Lambert Adolphe Jacques, *Sur l'homme et le développement de ses facultés: ou, Essai de physique sociale*. Bachelier, Paris, 1835. English transl., *A Treatise on Man and the Development of his Faculties*, Chambers, Edinburgh, 1842. Expanded version, entitled *Physique sociale: ou, Essai sur le développement des facultés de l'homme*, Murquardt, Brussels, 1869; reprinted by Scholars Facsimiles and Reprints, Gainsville, Florida, 1969.

QUETELET Lambert Adolphe Jacques, *Anthropométrie, ou mesure des différentes facultés de l'homme*. Murquardt, Brussels, 1870.

RAYNAL Guillaume Thomas François, *Histoire philosophique et politique des établissements et du commerce des Européens dans les deux Indes*. Geneva, 4 vols, 1770, 10 vols, 1781.

REED Lowell J., Introduction to *Degrees of Mortality of Mankind by Edmund Halley* (ed. L. J. REED). Johns Hopkins Press, Baltimore, 1942.

RONCAGLIA Alessandro, *Petty: la nascita dell'economia politica*. Etas Libri, Milan, 1977. Engl. transl. by M. E. SHARPE, Armonk, New York, 1985; also University College Cardiff Press, 1985 (English title, *Petty: the Origins of Political Economy*).

SAUVAGES Pierre Augustin BOISSIER de la CROIX de, *Nosologia Methodica Sistens Morborum Classes, Genera et Species*. Amsterdam, 1763; 2nd edn, Amsterdam, 1768.

SHUCKBURGH-EVELYN George, An account of some endeavours to ascertain a standard of weight and measure. *Philosophical Transactions of the Royal Society of London*, vol CXIII, pt. 1, 1798, pp. 132-76.

SIMEY T. S. and M. B. SIMEY, *Charles Booth, Social Scientist*. Oxford University Press, 1960.

SINCLAIR John, *The Statistical Account of Scotland*. 21 vols, W. Creech, Edinburgh, 1791-99.

SMITH Adam, *An Inquiry into the Nature and Causes of the Wealth of Nations*. 1st edn, Strahan, Cadell, London, 1776; Glasgow edn (eds. R. H. CAMPBELL and A. S. SKINNER), Clarendon Press, Oxford, 1976.

SNOW John, *On the Mode of Communication of Cholera*. Churchill, London, 1849; 2nd edn, 1855.

SOYER Alexis, *Soyer's Culinary Campaign. Being Historical Reminiscences of the Late War, with the Plain Art of Cookery for Military and Civil Institutions*. Routledge, London, 1857.

SPRAT Thomas, *The History of the Royal Society of London, for the Improving of Natural Knowledge*. Martyn & Allestry, London, 1667.

STEELE John Charles, Numerical analysis of the patients treated in Guy's Hospital for the last seven years, from 1854 to 1861. *Journal of the Statistical Society of London*, vol. XXIV, September 1861, pp. 374-401.

STIGLER George J., The early history of empirical studies of consumer behavior. *The Journal of Political Economy*, vol. LXII, no. 2, 1954, pp. 95-113.

STRACHEY Lytton, Florence Nightingale. In *Eminent Victorians*, Chatto & Windus, London, 1918.

STUDENSKI Paul, *The Income of Nations*. New York University Press, 1958.

SUTHERLAND Ian, John Graunt: a tercentenary tribute. *Journal of the Royal Statistical Society*, Ser. A, vol. 126, pt. 4, 1963, pp. 537-56.

The Times. Atlas of the World. The Times Newspapers Ltd., London, 1967.

U. K. Central Statistical Office. *Annual Abstract of Statistics 1986.* H.M.S.O., London, 1986.

U. K. Royal Commission on the Sanitary Conditions of the Army, 1857-58. *Report of the Commissioners.* H.M.S.O., London, 1858.

U. K. Royal Commission on the Sanitary State of the Army in India, 1861-62. *Report of the Commissioners.* H.M.S.O., London, 1863.

U. N. Statistical Office. *Demographic Yearbook 1984.* U. N., New York, 1986.

Usher A. P. (ed.), *Two Manuscripts by Charles Davenant.* Johns Hopkins Press, Baltimore, 1942.

Venables Edmund, William Fleetwood. *The Dictionary of National Biography,* Oxford University Press, vol. vii, pp. 269-71.

Waddell D. A. G., The writings of Charles Davenant. *The Library,* 5th ser., no. 11, 1956, pp. 206-12.

Waddell D. A. G., Charles Davenant and the East India Company. *Economica,* new ser., no. 23, 1956, pp. 261-4.

Waddell D. A. G., Charles Davenant (1656-1714) – a biographical sketch. *The Economic History Review,* 2nd ser. vol. xi, no. 2, 1958, pp. 279-88.

Waddel D. A. G., Charles Davenant. *International Encyclopedia of the Social Sciences,* Macmillan and Free Press, 1968, vol. 4, pp. 14-16.

Watt Francis, Charles Davenant. *The Dictionary of National Biography,* Oxford University Press, vol. v, pp. 549-50.

Whewell William, Mathematical exposition of some doctrines of political economy. Second memoir [Apr. 1850]. *Transactions of the Cambridge Philosophical Society,* vol. 9, pt. 1, 1850, pp. 128-56.

Whitworth Charles (ed.), *The Political and Commercial Works of Charles Davenant, collected and revised by Sir C. W.* 5 vols, Horsfield and others, London, 1771.

Wicksteed Philip Henry, On certain passages in Jevon's *Theory of Political Economy. The Quarterly Journal of Economics,* vol. iii, April 1889, pp. 293-314; reprinted in the *The Common Sense of Political Economy* (ed. Lionel Robbins), Routledge, London, 1933, vol. ii, pp. 734-54.

WILLCOX Walter F., Introduction to *Natural and Political Observations made upon the Bills of Mortality by John Graunt* (a reprint of the first edition, ed. W. F. WILLCOX). Johns Hopkins Press, Baltimore, 1939.

WOOD Anthony, *Athenae Oxonienses.* Bennet, London, 1691 (vol. I) and 1692 (vol. II); 2nd edn, revised, Knaplock, Midwinter and Tonson, London, 1721.

WOODHAM-SMITH Cecil, *Florence Nightingale, 1820-1910.* Constable, London, 1950.

WORLD HEALTH ORGANISATION, *Manual of the International Statistical Classification of Diseases, Injuries and Causes of Death.* 2 vols, W.H.O., Geneva, 1977.

WRIGLEY E. A. and R. S. SCHOFIELD, *The Population History of England, 1541-1871.* Arnold, London, 1981.

YEATS Dr. (ʿΙΑΤΡΟΣ), Memoir of Patrick Colquhoun, Esq., L.L.D. *The European Magazine and London Review*, 1818, pp. 187-92, 305-10, 409-13 and 497-503.

YOUNG Arthur, *A Six Weeks' Tour through the Southern Counties of England and Wales.* Nicoll, London, 1768.

YOUNG Arthur, *A Six Months' Tour through the North of England*, 4 vols, Strahan and Nicoll, London, 1770.

YOUNG Arthur, *The Farmer's Tour through the East of England.* 4 vols, Strahan, London, 1771.

YOUNG Arthur, *Proposals to the Legislature for numbering the People.* Nicoll, London, 1771; facsimile in *The Development of Population Statistics* (ed. D. V. GLASS), Gregg International, Farnborough, 1973.

YOUNG Arthur, *Political Arithmetic.* Pt. I, Nicoll, London, 1774; pt. II, Cadell, London, 1779.

YOUNG Arthur, *A Tour in Ireland.* Cadell and Dodsley, London, 1780.

YOUNG Arthur, Memoirs of the last thirty years of the *Editor's* farming life. *Annals of Agriculture*, vol. XV, 1791, pp. 152-97.

YOUNG Arthur, *Travels during the years 1787, 1788 and 1789.* 2 vols, W. Richardson, Bury St. Edmunds, 1792; 2nd edn, W. Richardson, London, 1794; Irish edn, Cross, Wogan *et al.*, Dublin, 1793.

YOUNG Arthur, An Inquiry into the Progressive Value of Money in England. *Annals of Agriculture*, vol. 46, pt. 2., Macmillan, London, 1812.

YOUNG Arthur, *Autobiography* (ed. M. BETHAM-EDWARDS). Smith, Elder & Co., London, 1898.

YOUNG Arthur (ed.), *Annals of Agriculture, and Other Useful Arts*. Monthly from 1784 to 1809; pt. 2 of vol. 46 appeared in 1812, pt. 3 in 1818.

YOUNG David A. B., Florence Nightingale's fever. *British Medical Journal*, vol. 311, Dec. 1995, pp. 1697-1700.

YULE G. Udny, Crop production and price: a note on Gregory King's law. *Journal of the Royal Statistical Society*, vol. LXXVIII, pt. II, 1915, pp. 296-8.

INDEX

INDEX

THIS EDITION WAS DESIGNED IN COLLABORATION WITH GIOVANNA STONE. THE TEXT IN BASKERVILLE (VAL VERSION) THE REPRODUCTIONS AND THE PRINTING ARE WORK OF STAMPERIA VALDONEGA, ARBIZZANO, VERONA.

OCTOBER MCMXCVII